T0319631

THE TRIUMPH OF BROKEN PROMISES

THE **TRIUMPH**
OF **BROKEN PROMISES**

THE END OF THE COLD WAR

AND THE **RISE OF NEOLIBERALISM**

FRITZ BARTEL

HARVARD UNIVERSITY PRESS   CAMBRIDGE, MASSACHUSETTS & LONDON, ENGLAND   2022

Library of Congress Cataloging-in-Publication Data

Names: Bartel, Fritz, author.
Title: The triumph of broken promises : the end of the Cold War and the
   rise of neoliberalism / Fritz Bartel.
Description: Cambridge, Massachusetts : Harvard University Press, 2022. |
   Includes bibliographical references and index.
Identifiers: LCCN 2021045328 | ISBN 9780674976788 (cloth)
Subjects: LCSH: Neoliberalism. | Cold War. | Recessions—History—20th
   century. | Financial crises—History—20th century. |
   Capitalism—History—20th century. | Communist countries—Economic
   conditions—20th century.
Classification: LCC HB95 .B367 2022 | DDC 330.12/2—dc23/eng/20220104
LC record available at https://lccn.loc.gov/2021045328

To Mom, Dad, Mitch
and Amanda

CONTENTS

THE TRIUMPH OF BROKEN PROMISES

Introduction

Making and Breaking Promises

AS CHRISTMAS CAME to Europe in 1989, those who had long lived under the yoke of communism had many reasons to celebrate. In quick and unexpected succession, the authoritarian governments that had ruled over the eastern half of the continent since shortly after the Second World War had peacefully collapsed. Citizens who had long resisted communism's countless injustices had begun to take their place in the governing chambers of Warsaw, Budapest, and Prague. On the night of November 9, the Berlin Wall had fallen, vanquishing the most oppressive symbol of Europe's division and Eastern Europe's captivity. East German citizens, separated for four decades from their freer and richer countrymen in West Germany, had begun to use a new slogan of unity—"Wir sind ein Volk" (We are one people)—and German reunification looked to be a real possibility for the first time since the early postwar years. In Moscow, Soviet general secretary Mikhail Gorbachev's launch of glasnost and perestroika had transformed Soviet society, set Eastern Europe free to choose its own fate, and allowed all Europeans to imagine a future in which they lived in one "common European home" rather than two antagonistic blocs. In Washington, former US president Ronald Reagan had worked with Gorbachev to strive for a world free of nuclear weapons, and his successor, George H. W. Bush, would soon speak of a "new world order" that might yet deliver permanent peace and prosperity to a weary but hopeful world. Taken together, the evidence of political progress was so swift and overwhelming that observers had begun to speak of 1989 as an annus mirabilis, a year of miracles. After decades of stolid oppression, winds of hope and renewal were in the air.

But László Kézdi did not care. The end of the Cold War may have been a momentous development in the grand scheme of history, but it was little solace for Kézdi, a Hungarian pensioner living in Budapest, as he watched his economic security evaporate before his eyes. The Hungarian government was making life across the country worse with each passing day, and Kézdi could feel it. Government officials had announced that pensioners would be receiving a Christmas bonus to ease their economic woes, but the temporary cash infusion paled in comparison to the rising cost of everything in Hungarian society. By mid-December, Kézdi was fed up, and he took to the pages of one of the country's leading newspapers to express his displeasure in an open letter to the nation's chief financial official. "Minister of Finance László Békesi!" he began. "I am turning to you with the following respectful request: With the Christmas bonus . . . please also send me an appropriately long and sturdy rope as an extra gift. I do not think I need to detail what purpose this rope will serve."[1]

Kézdi explained that he had earned his current state pension through forty-two years of hard work. Under the communist government, that pension had provided Kézdi with a comfortable, if unglamorous, life. But now the times were changing. Recently, the government had begun to raise prices on everything. Gas, electricity, mortgages, food, public transportation, and even medicine were all becoming more expensive. These price increases left Kézdi in a desperate bind, he wrote, unable to afford "a decent human life." The grim prospects left him "no choice" but to contemplate the end of his days and make his special request. "Respected Mr. Békesi!" he concluded, "to lighten the burden on the state budget, I repeat my request: Please issue the extra bonus, a strong rope, to me. Thank you in advance, László Kézdi."[2]

It was no accident that Kézdi's biting missive appeared at a time of profound political change. Economic discipline—broadly defined as government policies that intentionally cause domestic economic hardship—was the cause of Kézdi's sarcastic anger, and it was a potent political force in the last two decades of the Cold War.[3] Nine years earlier, in the most powerful country on earth, the chairman of the United States Federal Reserve, Paul Volcker, had felt the brunt of a similar backlash. As his restrictive monetary policy put millions of Americans out of work and forced the country into the deepest recession of the postwar period, construction workers had expressed their anger by mailing the Fed chairman unused two-by-fours from houses they could no longer build. Car salesmen sent coffins to the Federal Reserve full of keys to unsold cars, and farmers blocked the Fed's front entrance with their tractors to protest the rising costs of doing business.[4] The stiff resistance to his policies led Volcker to conclude that policy makers always try to avoid causing economic downturns because "that is when the political flak ordinarily hits."[5]

Despite their efforts at avoidance, leaders on both sides of the Iron Curtain were hit with the political flak of economic discipline many times in the 1970s and 1980s. This book is a history of why those moments of discipline arrived and how they produced two of the defining global transformations of the twentieth century: the peaceful end of the Cold War and the rise of neoliberal capitalism. Scholars have produced insightful work on both of these transformations, but they have not yet understood them as interconnected products of a shared history—specifically, the history of the world economy in the late twentieth century. Historians of neoliberalism—which I will define as a political ideology that uses markets to increase the free flow of goods and capital across state borders, increase inequality within nation-states, and limit the state's role in the provision of economic and social security for its citizens—have long traced its intellectual history, but they have paid less attention to how its rise intersected with the Cold War.[6] Scholars of the end of the Cold War have produced three decades of insightful scholarship, but they have generally given short shrift to the role of the global economy in causing the Cold War's demise.[7]

This book aims to recover that role by focusing on three of the forces that dominated global political economy in the late twentieth century: energy, finance, and economic discipline.[8] All three forces rose to prominence in the wake of the oil crisis of 1973, which is where our story will begin, and their intertwined histories over the following two decades significantly contributed to the end of the Cold War and the rise of neoliberal capitalism.

The histories of energy, finance, and economic discipline provide powerful analytical tools for examining these transformations because their widespread emergence in the 1970s and 1980s profoundly shifted the political, economic, and ideological terrain on which the Cold War was fought. When the conflict began in the 1940s, democratic capitalist and state socialist governments had raced to expand the social contracts that prevailed in their societies in order to win the hearts and minds of their populations. They had raced, in other words, to promise their people a better life and deliver on that promise. After the economic horrors of the Great Depression gave rise to fascism and world war, it was a fundamental premise of political life in both East and West after 1945 that a government's chief domestic responsibility was to harness the forces of industrial modernity to improve the economic security and well-being of its people. Democratic capitalism and state socialism stridently disagreed about what mix of security and prosperity was best—unable to match the West's prosperity, communist governments promised their citizens greater economic security—but their difference was one of degree, not of kind. Whether communist or capitalist, governments in the first two and a half decades in the Cold War raced to expand their social contracts.

I call this shared political terrain of the first half of the Cold War "the politics of making promises." Capitalist and communist states competed with each other by offering their people two different versions of industrial modernity, two different sets of government promises. To be sure, governments did not make promises to all their citizens equally; the politics of making promises most often reinforced the racial, ethnic, and gender hierarchies that prevailed within countries. Nevertheless, welfare states emerged across the West in the middle of the century to redistribute the economic gains of the market, and governments empowered labor unions to allow the working class to share equitably in the benefits of industrial capitalism.[9] In the East, Soviet leader Nikita Khrushchev used the Soviet Union's decade of stellar economic growth and scientific advancement in the 1950s to declare that the country would reach communism—the final stage of economic advancement and social organization in Marxism-Leninism—by 1980. Along the way, the Communist Party would modernize the country through government-directed industrialization and provide its citizens with job security, housing, social mobility, plentiful food, quality education and health care, longer vacations, and shorter work hours.[10] These conveniences were the fodder of postwar political legitimacy, and the two sides in the Cold War based their claim to superiority on their governments' ability to provide a bountiful and equitable distribution of industrial modernity's good life.

The economic crises of the 1970s upended the material basis of this competition and made the politics of making promises untenable. The emergence of energy and finance as potent forces in the global economy transformed the Cold War from a competition to expand social contracts into a competition to discipline them. Energy and financial markets placed immense pressure on governments on both sides of the Iron Curtain to adjust their domestic economies to meet the demands of the global marketplace. These adjustments came in many guises: deindustrialization, the drive to increase energy efficiency, competition with the newly industrialized nations of East Asia, and the broad shift from what economists call extensive economic growth (the production of more output by increasing inputs of capital, labor, and land) to intensive economic growth (the production of more output through a more efficient use of those inputs). Despite their varied forms, all these adjustments pointed in a single direction: policies of economic discipline.

This made capitalist and communist governments' cardinal challenge in the 1970s and 1980s diametrically different from the one that had prevailed since 1945. Rather than racing to increase the well-being of their people, governments in both East and West were forced at times to decrease the economic prosperity and security in their societies. Rather than making promises, governments were forced to break them. Like the economic pressures to which they responded, these broken promises came in many forms: cutting subsidies to powerful interest groups, shutting down unprofitable companies, laying off redundant workers, imposing monetary and fiscal austerity, and liberalizing trade and capital flows. Despite these varied forms, breaking promises was always and everywhere an extremely difficult political act. No government, whether capitalist or communist, could take pleasure or pride in seeing it through. After 1973, however, this new "politics of breaking promises" became the terrain on which democratic capitalism and state socialism waged their contest, and the stakes of this new struggle were nothing short of existential. Governments that could successfully impose economic discipline without inviting a destabilizing social backlash would survive; those that could not would collapse.

Thus, this book argues the Cold War began as a race to *make* promises, but it ended as a race to *break* promises. Democratic capitalism prevailed in the Cold War because it proved capable of breaking promises and imposing economic discipline. Communism collapsed because it could not. Neoliberalism rose as the Cold War waned because its promarket, anti-statist rhetoric provided governments with an ideological framework for breaking promises. Electoral democracy and neoliberal ideology gave Western states the political and ideological tools to meet the challenge of breaking promises. Lacking these tools, the communist states of the Eastern Bloc democratized their political systems and reformed their ideology in the 1980s as a means of imposing economic discipline. The end of the Cold War, then, was a triumph of broken promises because it was the challenge of imposing economic discipline that ultimately brought the conflict to its end and gave rise to the neoliberal global economy of the late twentieth century.

◆ ◆ ◆

Before proceeding, it is perhaps best to define what I mean by the end of the Cold War. What was it, and what is required to explain it?[11] I have come to believe that the end of the Cold War involved four distinct processes that unfolded at the end of the 1980s:[12] the end of the nuclear and conventional arms races between the Soviet Union and the United States,[13] the end of the global ideological competition between democratic capitalism and state socialism,[14] the peaceful collapse of communist states in Eastern Europe (with the brief exception of Romania) and the Soviet Union,[15] and the reunification of Germany.[16]

Two things immediately stand out about these processes. First, they occurred both *within* and *between* nation-states. Second, they involved change in material and ideational structures—or, put more simply, *power* and *identity*. Each of the processes that comprised the end of the Cold War took place on a continuum of these four traits. The end of the nuclear arms race serves as an illustrative example. It clearly depended on both diplomacy between the superpowers and domestic politics within each state. But it also depended on significant changes in the relative standing of superpowers in the international system and changes in how the Soviet leadership understood its place in the world. The revolutions of 1989 were a different mix of changes in power and identity both within and between nation-states. A perquisite for the revolutions' occurrence was the Soviet Union's decision to refrain from intervening to stop them—a change between states—but they were also crucially determined by developments within Eastern European countries. The revolutions resulted from changes in material power—energy and capital markets, I will argue—but also from changes in how state socialist governments understood the socialist identity they had long espoused.

Thus, the first challenge in writing the history of the end of the Cold War is that it requires an explanation that integrates change across these dimensions—domestic politics and international relations, as well as power and identity. In the specific context of the end of the Cold War, this challenge means that explaining the end of the Cold War *as a geopolitical conflict* requires an explanation of the collapse of communism *as a system of governance*. The fact that so much of the end of the Cold War was determined by processes of domestic change means any history of it that only considers developments in international relations will be incomplete. The same holds true for material and ideational structures. Any explanation that considers only one or the other will be inherently limited. Therefore, the history of the end of the Cold War must include explanations across all four dimensions: change both within and between nation-states and change in both power and identity.

The second challenge of explaining the end of the Cold War is that it stands out in history for one profound reason: at every step of the way, those in possession of imperial and authoritarian power *willingly* and *peacefully* gave it up. This exceptional development occurred both within and between nation-states. The Soviet Union retreated from its pursuit of global confrontation with the United States as well as its empire in Eastern Europe, and at the same time, political leaders throughout the Eastern Bloc gave up power peacefully within their own societies (with Nicolae Ceauşescu in Romania again serving as a brief exception). This unique and fundamental characteristic of the end of the Cold War is what made it so difficult to predict before it occurred and continues to make it so difficult to explain in retrospect. Therefore, explanations of the end of the Cold War that lack a compelling reason for why those in possession of imperial and authoritarian power consistently gave it up in the late 1980s will remain incomplete.

A third challenge of the history of the end of the Cold War is timing. The Cold War persisted for four decades, long enough for one of its most perceptive observers to title it a period of "long peace" between the Great Powers.[17] Then suddenly, in the late 1980s, it disappeared. The question of timing is therefore of predominant importance. Any compelling explanation of the end of the Cold War must attend not only to the question of why but also to the question of why *then*.

The last challenge of the history of the end of the Cold War is to explain the character of its principal outcome: the emergence, with varying degrees of success, longevity, and legitimacy, of electoral democracies and neoliberal market economies in the nation-states that formerly comprised the Eastern Bloc. In retrospect, it is easy to take these outcomes for granted, but as the end of the Cold War unfolded, few believed them to be foregone conclusions. Since neoliberal market economies and electoral democracies were not the only possible outcomes, why did they emerge? Answering this question is the final challenge of writing the history of the Cold War's end.

This book meets these challenges on the basis of two foundations: the use of new and illuminating evidence from archives on both sides of the former Iron Curtain and the formulation of a new framework for connecting economic and political change in the late Cold War. This new framework begins from the conviction that the oil crisis of 1973 dramatically increased the importance of energy resources and financial markets in international politics. This increase was so decisive that it spurred a fundamental change in the global competition between democratic capitalism and state socialism: it privatized the Cold War.

◆ ◆ ◆

For the first two and a half decades of the Cold War, energy and financial markets played relatively small roles in the politics of making promises in both East and West. Until its collapse in 1971, the Bretton Woods system pegged Western currencies to each other at fixed values and controlled the flow of short-term capital across national borders in the Western world. The global financial markets that would come to play such a large role in the 1970s and 1980s—known as the Euromarkets—did not exist in the 1940s, hardly existed by the end of the 1950s, and remained relatively small throughout most of the 1960s. The Eastern Bloc did not participate in the Bretton Woods system, but its member states maintained even firmer control over trade and finance than their Western counterparts. Eastern Bloc currencies were not convertible into each other or Western currencies, which meant they too were completely under governmental control. And other than a few banking outposts in the West that were used to conduct international trade, the bloc as a whole remained isolated from the nascent development of the Euromarkets.

As for energy, it was cheap and plentiful in the capitalist world and cheap and scarce in the communist world until the early 1970s. This simultaneous ubiquity in the West and scarcity in the East ironically made it less important in both blocs than it would become after 1973. In the West, oil's low price and uninterrupted flow allowed governments to build mass-consumption industrial societies after the Second World War that showed little regard for oil's use or country of origin. Only after 1973 would Western societies awaken to the implications of their fervent consumption of a commodity whose price and production levels they did not control.[18] In the East, the Soviet government spent the 1950s searching its vast hinterland for oil deposits, and in the 1960s, it struck black gold in western Siberia, where it found some of the largest oil fields in the world. Developing these fields took time, so it was only in the early 1970s, right before the oil crisis struck, that the Soviet Union and, by extension, the entire Eastern Bloc enjoyed "for the first time the luxury of cheap and efficient energy."[19] After the oil shock, this luxury would fill the Kremlin's coffers through oil and natural gas exports to the world market, and energy would become the material basis of Soviet power. This was squarely a post-1973 development, however. For the first two and a half decades of the Cold War, neither energy nor finance played a significant role in the race to make promises in both East and West.

Instead of energy or finance, both Eastern and Western states based their power and legitimacy before 1970 on something else: industrialized economic growth. As shown in Figure I.1, the global economy experienced a historically unique period of high growth in the three decades following the Second World War. Nothing like it had come before, and nothing like it has come since.[20]

Because of this growth, people around the world, but particularly within the Eastern and Western Blocs, experienced sustained increases in their standard of living on a scale never before seen in human history. In the capitalist world, this period would be remembered under a number of names that signal its uniqueness: the West Germans called it the *Wirtschaftswunder* (the economic miracle), the French called it *les trente glorieuses* ("the glorious thirty" years), and historians now simply refer to it as "the golden age" of capitalism.[21] Not to be outdone, the Eastern Bloc matched the growth of the capitalist West during this period. Over the entire period 1950–1973, per capita GDP grew at an average annual rate of 4.1 percent in Western Europe, 2.5 percent in the United States, 3.8 percent in Eastern Europe, and 3.4 percent in the Soviet Union.[22] The two blocs, of course, were not economic equals. The West began the postwar period as a vastly richer territory and remained vastly richer in the early 1970s. Moreover, mass consumption became a reality in the West while it remained only a far-off aspiration in the East. But for the first two decades

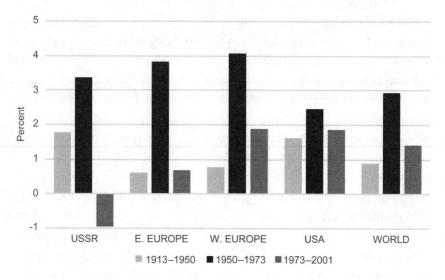

Figure i.1 **Average annual per capita economic growth in three periods.**
Data source: Angus Maddison, *The World Economy: Vol II, Historical Statistics* (Paris: OECD, 2006), 640, table 8b.

of the Cold War, Eastern Bloc governments could credibly claim to be matching or exceeding the growth of the West.

Perhaps the most famous moment in this early race to make promises came in 1959, when Soviet first secretary Nikita Khrushchev and US vice president Richard Nixon met in Moscow for their famous impromptu "Kitchen Debate." As they toured an American exhibition hall meant to show off the many material benefits of the capitalist way of life, the two leaders began debating the merits of their respective systems. In front of a global TV audience, Nixon sang the praises of his system, which could provide "any steel worker" with an affordable home complete with a dishwasher and color television. Khrushchev boasted that under communism, workers were "entitled to housing" and stated that in another seven years the Soviet Union would be "at the level of America, and after that we'll go farther. As we pass you by, we'll wave 'hi' to you, and then if you want, we'll stop and say, 'please come along behind us.'"[23] For its first twenty-five years, then, the Cold War was a competition between two systems of government promises underwritten by unprecedented economic growth.

Then, around 1970, something unexpected happened. Contrary to the confident predictions of both democratic capitalism and state socialism, economic growth in *both* systems severely stagnated. The causes of this stagnation were manifold. The rapid economic gains accompanying postwar reconstruction were exhausted; extensive growth had run its course; workers' incomes bulged in the late 1960s while their employers' profits cratered; and most importantly, productivity began a long-term decline from which it has yet to recover.[24] Normally, international historians only focus on the rigid economic stagnation of the Eastern Bloc during the 1970s and 1980s. But "The Great Slowdown" and "The Descent of Growth" are subtitles in the leading histories of capitalism, not communism, for the period after 1970.[25] Only in the 1980s, after growth had recovered slightly and inflation had significantly receded in capitalist countries, did Western confidence in the natural superiority of capitalism over communism return. Throughout the 1970s, the West's economic problems appeared equally intractable to any of those bedeviling the East.[26]

It was in this context of slower growth that the oil crisis of 1973 burst onto the scene and changed the world economy and the Cold War forever. The fourfold increase in the price of the world's most important commodity (Figure I.2) gave birth to both the pressure to break promises *and* the means of avoiding that pressure. On the one hand, the price shock made the energy-intensive industrialized economies of both East and West obsolete and ignited the long-term transition to a deindustrialized developed world. Countless bankruptcies, job losses, and moments of austerity over the next three decades flowed from this fundamental change in the global economy. On the other hand, that same fourfold increase accelerated the development of two vast pools of wealth—global capital markets and energy resources—that nation-states could use to *avoid* making the difficult transition to a world of high energy prices.

The meteoric rise of financial and energy wealth in the 1970s gave rise to the defining feature of the privatized Cold War: nation-states' guns and butter became dependent on finance and oil. As long as states had access to either global capital markets or energy wealth, they could continue to fund their foreign and domestic policies and delay adjusting to the shocks of the oil crisis. They could, in other words, continue to fight the Cold War abroad and make promises at home.

If, however, states lost access to one or both of these pools of wealth, then they would have to implement the politics of breaking promises to regain the favor of capital markets or outlast a downturn in world energy prices. Breaking promises could force governments to alter both their domestic and foreign policies through cutbacks on commitments to

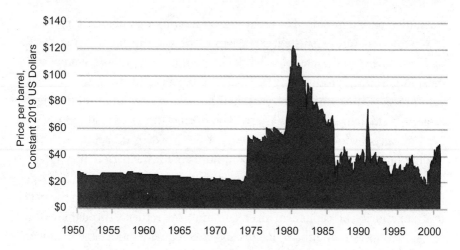

Figure i.2 **The world price of oil in the second half of the twentieth century.**
Extracted and reformatted from "Crude Oil Prices—70 Year Historical Chart," MacroTrends, accessed Jun5, 2021,
https://www.macrotrends.net/1369/crude-oil-price-history-chart.

domestic constituencies, international allies, or national defense. In the chapters that follow, we will observe instances of all three.

This meant that at the heart of the privatized Cold War was a social question: how to discipline the postwar social contracts that had developed in both the East and the West after the Second World War. States' ability to break promises would prove to be the key difference between those states that survived and those that went extinct. Placing this social question at the center of the privatized Cold War means that ideology and domestic politics are essential components of its history. National leaders needed to justify revisions to the social contract in ideological terms to domestic constituencies. To meet this challenge, political leaders transformed their state's governing ideologies and domestic political structures during the privatized Cold War. As we will see, the success or failure of these transformations proved decisive.

Therefore, on the fundamental question of the relationship between economic and political change, this book adopts a very particular point of view, and it is here that the history of the Cold War intersects with the history of neoliberalism. In the privatized Cold War, the economic challenge of breaking promises drove governments to adopt political and ideological "new thinking" in both East and West. Cold War historians normally identify "new thinking" as the particular idealistic movement that arose among the reformers around Mikhail Gorbachev in the Soviet Union. But when one pulls back from the particular context of Soviet history, it is clear that many governments on both sides of the Iron Curtain adopted new thinking of various types during the 1970s and 1980s. These new forms of thinking emanated from diverse ideological traditions, but they shared one commonality—they were all approaches to implementing economic discipline. They were all, in other words, neoliberal approaches to governance.

This is not to say that change in the global economy completely determined the *creation* of new thinking, but rather to argue that it drove the *adoption* of new thinking within governments and societies. Whether it was Thatcherism in Great Britain, monetarism and deregulation in the United States, perestroika and glasnost in the Soviet Union, or roundtable democratization in Poland and Hungary, governments in power adopted these forms of new thinking because they appeared to provide the ideological and political means required to achieve the end of breaking promises.

Margaret Thatcher and Mikhail Gorbachev are often held up as paragons of opposing types of "new thinking" in the 1980s: Thatcherism and perestroika, respectively. But Gorbachev's and Thatcher's own thinking on the relationship between perestroika and Thatcherism suggests more similarities than first meet the eye. In 1987, the general secretary recounted to his comrades in the Soviet Politburo his recent interactions with Western European leaders, Thatcher most prominent among them. "They too are carrying out a perestroika," he told his comrades. They "act harshly . . . the capitalist way," he continued, and the Soviets had "a different situation and different ideas." But, he said, "we too cannot flinch."[27] Two years later, Thatcher also saw a parallel. In a 1989 meeting with Gorbachev, she told the general secretary that she empathized with the immensity of his challenges because she had launched "an analogous perestroika" in her country.[28] Energy and finance thrust the challenge of breaking promises onto nation-states after 1973, and domestic political orders and ideologies adjusted to meet the challenge.

They converged, in fact, toward neoliberalism. By the late 1980s, governments on *both* sides of the Iron Curtain were trying to increase the free flow of goods and capital across their borders, governments on *both* sides were trying to limit the state's role in the provision of economic and social security for their citizens, and governments on *both* sides were trying to increase inequality within their states. Thatcher's and Gorbachev's comparisons to each other were not mere word play; they were instead mutual recognitions of a shared challenge and even a shared goal—carrying out painful domestic economic reforms in the hope of relaunching economic growth in their countries.

Though the domestic challenge of breaking promises ultimately determined nation-states' fate in the privatized Cold War, developments at the international level were of vital importance as well. Indeed, through energy and financial markets, developments in the international system were what forced governments to address the challenge of breaking promises domestically. Although these changes occurred at the international level that did not mean they were necessarily products of interstate relations. The privatized Cold War was a world in which state and nonstate actors vied for influence and control. Many changes in energy and financial markets were outside the control of any particular nation-state. In the privatized Cold War, nonstate economic and financial actors were often as important as, and many times even more important than, governments. This was the period when the nebulous but all-important opinion of "the market" began to decide the fate of nations.

Governments could not fully control energy or financial markets, but they could wield power in the privatized Cold War by altering other states' access to energy or finance. Statecraft in this new international system consisted of granting or denying other states' access to energy and financial resources, and late Cold War diplomacy reflected this reality. In the 1970s, the Soviet Union and its Western adversaries fought a quiet battle for control of Eastern Europe through energy and capital markets—the Soviets by granting its bloc allies growing and subsidized deliveries of oil and natural gas, and the West by granting Eastern Bloc states growing and subsidized access to global capital markets. In the 1980s, the process reversed. The Soviet influence over the bloc waned as the growth and subsidy of its energy deliveries tapered off, and the West's influence increased as it sought to attach conditions to the Eastern Bloc's access to credit.

Therefore, statecraft mattered in the privatized Cold War. But the power of diplomacy was always limited by the fact that nation-states, even very powerful ones like the United States and the Soviet Union, could never completely control other states' access to finance and energy. The opinions of global market actors always existed alongside Cold War statecraft, and together they were the two key international determinants of any state's access to energy and finance in the privatized Cold War.

◆　◆　◆

It will not surprise the reader that this privatized Cold War framework closely maps onto the dimensions of change identified at the beginning of this introduction. The privatized Cold War produced changes within and between states, as well as changes in power and identity. This close alignment means that the framework I have outlined can potentially explain the collapse of communism as a system of governance and, in so doing, can explain the end of the Cold War as a geopolitical conflict.

Providing such an explanation will be the central task of the chapters that follow. The book is divided into two parts. Part 1 is devoted to explaining the emergence of capital markets and energy resources as decisive forces in international politics and the shift from making to breaking promises in East and West after the oil crisis of 1973. Its overriding message is a straightforward one: between 1973 and 1985, democratic capitalist states successfully met the challenge of breaking promises and communist states did not. This disparity left Western governments in a strong domestic position by the mid-1980s and gave them leverage in the form of sovereign debt over many of the socialist states of Eastern Europe. This debt would prove decisive to the Cold War's end. In Part 2 I take up the four processes identified earlier as central to the end of the Cold War: the end of the nuclear and conventional arms race, the end of the global ideological competition, the collapse of state socialist governments, and the reunification of Germany. Here we will see how the intertwined histories of energy, finance, and economic discipline produced the dramatic events we now call the collapse of communism and the end of the Cold War.

Though I discuss many countries throughout the Eastern and Western Blocs, I have focused this history on Poland, Hungary, East Germany, and the Soviet Union in the East and Great Britain, the United States, and to a lesser extent West Germany in the West. The focus on events in Washington, Moscow, Bonn, and London hopefully begs no questions. But the choice of Poland, Hungary, and East Germany out of the states in Eastern Europe requires further explanation. I focus attention on these three countries because they initiated the seismic changes of 1989. Other countries in the region had their own unique histories of debt, energy, and economic discipline—Romania, for example, infamously paid back its debt at a severe cost to its own people, while Czechoslovakia escaped severe Western financial dependence—but they were not the countries leading the push for change in 1989. In order to explain the stunning developments of that year, one needs to explain the particular course of events in Warsaw, Budapest, and East Berlin.

There is one other country whose absence from the book deserves explanation. Since the late 1970s, the People's Republic of China has accomplished its remarkable rise to global power by doing many of the things the communists in this book failed to do: introducing market reforms, jettisoning the content of its ruling ideology, and, most tragically, violently repressing its citizens' calls for change in 1989. In this way, it would appear to present a significant challenge to the argument presented here. But it is important to recall that China began its reforms from a very different starting point than the Soviet Union, the countries of Eastern Europe, or, for that matter, the developed nations of the West. Rather than being an industrialized country where manufacturing and heavy industry formed the backbone of the economy, China in the 1970s was an overwhelmingly rural and agrarian society where over 80 percent of the population still lived in the countryside.[29] Instead of having a politically sclerotic government where entrenched bureaucratic and economic interests resisted reform, China in the 1970s had just emerged from the Cultural Revolution, in which the state's governing hierarchies, ideology, and daily life had been thrown into disarray. And because chaos and destitution were such widely shared experiences across China in the 1970s, large sections of the population (beginning, most importantly, with the country's farmers) clamored to be set free from the state's economic control.[30] These differences did not rigidly predestine the course of reform in Beijing, but they did make the Chinese transformation altogether different from the countries under consideration here. The politics of breaking promises were not absent in China, but overall, the reform experience was one of managing industrialization and economic growth, not deindustrialization and economic discipline.[31]

Through the countries this book does focus on, it aims to provide a new interpretive framework for understanding the end of the Cold War and the rise of neoliberalism as interrelated products of global economic change in the late twentieth century. To do that, it will finally have to answer the three questions identified at the outset: Why did the holders of imperial and authoritarian power in the Eastern Bloc willingly give it up? Why did they do so at the end of the 1980s? And why did electoral democracies and neoliberal market economies emerge from the ashes of state socialism?

My answers to these questions rest in the politics of breaking promises. In the global economy that prevailed after the oil crisis of 1973, the only practical purpose of the Soviet empire in Eastern Europe was to insulate socialist states from the pressure of breaking promises. This insulation, which came in the form of subsidized energy and other raw material deliveries, was extremely costly. By the early 1980s, the Soviet leadership decided that protecting its allies from the pressures of the global economy was in fact too costly, and they committed themselves to lowering these costs, even if it meant risking the loss of the empire itself. When Gorbachev informed his allies of the repeal of the Brezhnev Doctrine, he was not self-consciously liquidating the Soviet empire but rather breaking the promise the Soviet Union had made to its allies since the oil crisis to protect them from the disciplining demands of the global economy. When the empire crumbled in 1989, Soviet leaders peacefully accepted the result because they no longer believed that protecting Eastern Europe from the challenge of breaking promises was in the Soviet Union's national interest.

The loss of Soviet imperial protection from the global economy, however, did not automatically lead the holders of authoritarian power in the Eastern Bloc to peacefully give up their power within communist states. Instead, they gave up their power in the late 1980s in order to gain the political legitimacy they believed was necessary to implement the politics of breaking promises within their own countries. Beginning with Gorbachev's launch of perestroika and glasnost and extending through the roundtable negotiations in Poland and Hungary, communist leaders proactively tried to legitimize their power so they would, in turn, be able to discipline their domestic social contracts. When it became clear to communist leaders that their attempts to legitimize their power would, in fact, result in their loss of power, they chose not to violently prevent that loss because they understood that the challenge of breaking promises would still remain. Under the politics of breaking promises, there were no spoils for the powerful and victorious, only costs. Communist leaders chose to let their successors bear the burden of the costs that came with breaking promises.

These stunning events in the Soviet empire and within communist states happened when they did because the global history of energy and capital markets made the challenge of breaking promises unavoidable within the Eastern Bloc by the late 1980s. Access to Soviet energy and Western capital markets allowed bloc governments to delay the task of disciplining their social contracts throughout the 1970s. But the advantage of Soviet oil deliveries to Eastern Europe and Western capital markets' confidence in the region peaked in the early 1980s and never fully recovered. Thus, the timing of the end of the Cold War was a product not only of individual agency and historical contingency but also of structural developments in the international system dating back to the oil crisis.

Electoral democracy and neoliberal market economies emerged in the East after the collapse of communism for the same reason they survived in the West during the last two decades of the Cold War—they were the best political and economic systems for breaking promises. Democratic capitalist states were not immune from the challenges that befell the communist world in the late Cold War. They too had to rewrite their postwar social contracts in the 1970s and 1980s. But they succeeded where the East failed because their political systems and ideological traditions gave them a number of decisive advantages.

First, although Western governments made numerous promises to their people during the first three decades of the Cold War, they never promised to control every aspect of their society and economy. Even at the height of postwar Keynesian planning, democratic capitalist governments maintained a distinction between "the state"—an area of society they controlled—and "the market"—an area of society they regulated but did not fully control.[32] This stood in stark contrast to their communist counterparts, who proudly claimed that the very foundation of their power and legitimacy rested precisely on their control of the *entire* state, society, and economy. Democratic capitalist governments made fewer promises to their people, and this meant they had fewer promises to break.

Breaking promises nevertheless did not come easy in the West. Indeed, over the course of the 1970s, many of the smartest observers of Western governments believed that democracies' persistent inability to impose economic discipline might prove to be their fatal flaw.[33] The experience of the 1980s proved the exact opposite to be true. The rise of Margaret Thatcher in the United Kingdom and Ronald Reagan in the United States demonstrated that the potent combination of electoral democracy and neoliberal ideology could produce a stronger and more adaptable state than socialist authoritarianism in the era of breaking promises. Though elections forced democratic governments to respond to the interests of their populations, they also provided democracies with a peaceful and stable way to transform their governing ideology. Thatcher and Reagan radically departed from the ideological paradigms of postwar Britain and the United States, but in both countries, the state itself survived. Authoritarianism provided state socialist governments with no such mechanism for stably reforming and adapting their ideology. As soon as Gorbachev tried to reform the governing ideology of the Soviet Union, it produced severe instability throughout the socialist world and ultimately led to the Socialist Bloc's collapse.

If elections provided Western states the political means to break promises, neoliberalism provided the ideological ends. Once in power, Thatcher and Reagan revived the rhetorical tradition of economic liberalism that had lay dormant in the West during the heyday of Keynesian promise making in the postwar period. With its championing of individualism and criticism of all forms of government intervention, this neoliberalism provided an expedient ideological framework to justify breaking promises. Here, again, state socialism's ideological tradition provided no such recourse. Gorbachev attempted to craft an ideology of breaking promises through perestroika, but he consistently struggled to place it within the tradition of Marxism-Leninism. Eventually, he simply abandoned Marxism-Leninism altogether.

All this suggests a peculiar and troubling kind of Western triumph in the Cold War, but it is the only kind of triumphalism the end of the Cold War can teach us. We should have no problem stating that the West won the Cold War, but we should recognize clearly why it did. Democratic capitalism prevailed because it proved capable of imposing economic discipline on its own citizens. Communism collapsed because it could not. And neoliberal democracy emerged in both East and West from the Cold War's ashes because it was the best ideological system for breaking promises. The triumph of broken promises is a theme to which we will return in the conclusion. But first, we must begin with the crisis that forever changed the global economy and the Cold War. In the early 1970s, the price of oil suddenly quadrupled, and the world was never again the same.

PART ONE

THE PRIVATIZATION OF THE COLD WAR

CHAPTER 1

The Oil Shock to the Cold War

ON DECEMBER 10, 1976, East German prime minister Willi Stoph was leaving Moscow disappointed and empty-handed. He had come to the Soviet capital seeking an increase in Soviet oil deliveries to the German Democratic Republic (GDR), but his Soviet counterpart, Alexei Kosygin, had roundly rejected his request. "We don't have the resources for it," Kosygin had said during their meeting in the Kremlin. "We have an acute energy shortage in our country. . . . You must get your mind out of the clouds." "My mind's not in the clouds," Stoph shot back. "But you want us to increase our deliveries," Kosygin responded. "We cannot meet that level of demand. No one in the world can do that."[1]

Now, as the two men drove through the streets of the Soviet capital on their way to the airport for Stoph's departure, Kosygin tried to lighten the mood by reminding his comrade of the overriding advantages of the socialist system compared to the chaos that currently prevailed in the capitalist world. "We understand that the situation in the GDR is not easy," the Soviet premier said, but "compared with the predicament in capitalist states, all socialist states—the USSR as well as the GDR—[are] in an incomparably better situation." To him, the advantages were clear. The socialist countries were "in a position to plan" their economies "until 1980, 1985, and beyond" as well as "agree on the course of our development." In contrast, Kosygin said, "capitalist states couldn't even plan for the next three months." Perhaps shaken from his disappointment by Kosygin's comparison, Stoph piled on the criticism of their ideological foes. "All of the planning efforts of capitalist states have only led them into crisis," he said. Kosygin agreed and concluded, "Our situation is a thousand times better."[2]

In the mid-1970s, one did not need to be a communist ideologue to share this view. Indeed, many in the West believed that the economic crises of the early 1970s had exposed fundamental flaws in both capitalism and democracy. The combination of widespread unemployment and high inflation throughout the West confounded both the professional economists who studied market economies and the democratically elected leaders who governed them. The reigning economic doctrine of Keynesianism offered few answers in this world of "stagflation," and those it did put forth—increased government spending and accommodating monetary policy—appeared to only make the problems worse. Because democracy subjected Western governments to the demands of all their citizens, it was widely believed that Western welfare states were doomed to chronic high inflation because politicians needed to promise their citizens too much of the good life in order to get elected. In foreign policy, a new buzzword—interdependence—dominated discussions of the West's place in the world and appeared to portend an end to Western societies' control over their own fates. What could the developed West do in the face of dependence on oil from the Middle East? To many on both sides of the Iron Curtain, the answer appeared to be nothing at all. Could democratic leaders solve the riddle of stagflation if it meant inflicting pain on those they governed? Smart money said no.

The Eastern Bloc was thought to be different. Socialist states appeared to Western observers to be largely immune to the crises afflicting the capitalist world. As the exchange between Kosygin and Stoph shows, socialist leaders maintained a similar confidence in the superiority of their own system. Because the Soviet Union was one of the world's largest producers of energy resources, the fourfold increase in the price of oil at the end of 1973 and early 1974 first arrived as a financial windfall rather than a structural economic challenge for the leadership in Moscow. The socialist states of Eastern Europe had little oil themselves, but under the generous patronage of the Soviet Union, they received large and growing deliveries of Soviet energy during the 1970s at highly subsidized prices. Because almost all trade and prices were fixed under five-year plans within the bloc, socialist states appeared exempt from the violent gyrations of inflation and commodity price shocks that crippled the Western world. And if democracies' penchant for promising their citizens too much was the cause of Western inflation, then the socialist states' authoritarian structure appeared to make them helpfully unresponsive to the demands of their populations. Taken together, these traits were enough to keep Kosygin and Stoph brimming with confidence as they drove through the Soviet capital that day in 1976.

And yet we begin with their exchange because beneath the professions of confidence, the discussion also pointed to the problems upon which state socialism itself would founder. Stoph had made the initial request for more Soviet oil for a very particular purpose: to lower the GDR's ballooning sovereign debt to Western banks and governments. With more oil, the GDR would be able to produce more petrochemicals and export them to the West for hard currency. This, in turn, would lessen the need to take out Western loans to pay for imports and service old debts. In the first half of the 1970s, Western banks had been eager to loan money to the Socialist Bloc for the very reasons socialism appeared ascendant to all manner of Western observers in the 1970s: it had energy, authoritarianism, and no inflation. But by 1976, the first inklings of doubt had begun to bubble up in the minds of Western bankers: Would socialist states really be able to pay them back? Seen in this light, it becomes clear that Stoph's pilgrimage to Moscow in search of oil was, in fact, an indirect effort to put the minds of Western bankers at ease and keep the flow of Western capital running smoothly.

The GDR's predicament was far from unique; all states in the Council of Mutual Economic Assistance (CMEA or Comecon) shared the East German dependence on both Western capital and Soviet oil to varying degrees.[3] Thus, Kosygin's rejection of Stoph's request points to the second problem lurking in the background of their discussion: after a ten-year period of dramatic growth, Soviet energy resources began to plateau in the mid-1970s and were projected to decline after 1980. The Eastern Bloc's apparent imperviousness to the travails of the global economy rested on these two foundations: easy access to Western capital and an ever-increasing supply of Soviet energy resources. If either or both of these faltered, as they would around 1980, the entire bloc would be forced to reckon with the social, economic, and political problems that beset the West after 1973.

Thus, this chapter tracks the response of both the industrial West and the socialist East to the oil crisis to make one overriding point clear. Although the crisis at first appeared to validate the fundamental differences between democratic capitalism and state socialism, in time it demonstrated that both blocs were subject to the pressures of the same world market. It was a market neither side could fully or even partially control, so how the states within each system reacted to the whims of the global economy became the key determinant of their success and survival. The dramatic expansion of global capital markets after the crisis presented both sides with a means of softening the blow of adjustment to the new market conditions. But the fundamental challenge the crisis posed to both the democratic capitalist states of the West and the state socialist systems of the East could not be permanently avoided. The crisis challenged governments on both sides of the ideological divide to domestically distribute the economic losses caused by the oil price shock, transition their societies to more profitable and energy-efficient systems of production and consumption, and maintain access to the global capital markets that rapidly expanded after the oil shock. All these pressures, in turn, threatened the legitimacy of both the welfare states in the West and the communist states of the East. At first faintly felt and then stridently resisted, the crisis began the transition from making to breaking promises for both blocs.

◆ ◆ ◆

On October 6, 1973, war came once again to the contested lands of Israel and its neighbors. Early that afternoon, Egyptian armed forces crossed the Suez Canal into the Israeli-occupied Sinai Peninsula, and Syrian forces pushed from their homeland to confront Israeli forces occupying the Golan Heights. Over the next three weeks, the Arab coalition and the Israeli Defense Forces fought pitched battles in what would come to be known as the Yom Kippur War. In the early days of the fighting, the Soviet Union resupplied its Arab allies, and on October 14, the United States responded with its decision to resupply Israel. For the Arab Gulf states that supported the Egyptian and Syrian campaign, the American decision demanded a response equal to the perceived injustice of supporting Israel. Thus, they unsheathed "the oil weapon" and unilaterally announced a 70 percent increase in the price of their oil to $5.11 a barrel. The next day, they committed themselves to a rolling embargo against supporters of Israel, chief among them the United States. After US president

Richard Nixon announced a new aid package to Israel on October 19, King Feisal of Saudi Arabia upped the ante considerably by imposing a complete embargo on oil supplies to the United States.

By the end of October, the guns had fallen silent, but the effects of the price increase were only beginning to ripple outward. In December, ministers from the Organization of Petroleum Exporting Countries (OPEC) met in Tehran to discuss where to peg the oil price going forward. At the urging of their host, Shah Mohammad Reza Pahlavi, the group settled on an even higher price target of $11.65, one that would have been unfathomable only months before.[4] As recently as 1970, OPEC had only been able to fetch $1.80 per barrel on the world market. With the breakdown of the Bretton Woods system in 1971 and the resulting devaluation of the US dollar (in which oil was priced), some of the oil price increase could be accounted for by producers' desire to recapture the value they had lost with the dollar's decline. But the fourfold increase from $2.90 in mid-1973 to $11.65 at the end of the year represented more than that. Economically, it reflected the fact that the development of affluent industrial societies in the West had increased oil demand sixfold since 1950 and had pushed the United States beyond energy autonomy to dependence on foreign oil in the late 1960s.[5] Politically, the price increases represented a precipitous culmination of decades of struggle on the part of developing nations to increase the value of the commodities that formed the basis of their national wealth. When they collectively called for a "New International Economic Order" at the United Nations in May 1974, they did so with the winds of long-sought wealth at their backs.

The boon for the oil producers of the world delivered a bust to the developed world on a scale unknown in the postwar years. The oil crisis arrived in a Western world already beset by a burgeoning list of economic problems. Chief among them was inflation. The rising price level had a diverse set of causes, including US president Lyndon Johnson's attempt to fund his Great Society programs and the war in Vietnam without a tax increase, an explosion of real wage increases across the West from 1968 to 1972, and the 1971 American decision to suspend the convertibility of the dollar into gold. Washington had abandoned the Bretton Woods system of fixed exchange rates in response to the continued economic rise of Western Europe and Japan, which increased competitive pressure on US industry and decreased America's relative standing in the world economy. The devaluation implicit in the 1971 decision, and the floating exchange rate system that soon followed, restored a measure of US competitive-ness.[6] But it also produced persistent monetary instability in the capitalist world and freed the United States from the nominal constraint of limiting its money supply to amounts that could be converted into gold at thirty-five dollars an ounce. In combination, these forces had pushed consumer price inflation in Organization for Economic Cooperation and Develop-ment (OECD) countries to an annual rate of 8.2 percent in 1973.[7] With prices already galloping ahead at a steady pace, the fourfold increase in the price of the commodity that formed the basis of industrial society was bound to have dramatic economic effects.

In short order, in 1974–1975 the West experienced its worst economic downturn since the Great Depression.[8] Unemployment across the OECD reached 5.5 percent in 1974 and peaked at 8.9 percent in the United States in May 1975.[9] Under the economic conditions that had prevailed since 1945, a downturn of such scale would have nipped the problem of inflation in the bud. But the skyrocketing oil price made this contraction different, and consumer price inflation increased across the West to 14.1 percent in 1974 and 11.8 percent in 1975.[10] And so, in defiance of postwar economic theory and experience, "stagflation" was born.

In the realm of public policy, the years since 1945 in the West had un-folded in the long shadow of British economist John Maynard Keynes and the body of economic theory that bore his name. During their heyday in the 1960s, Keynesian economists who populated Western governments had declared victory over the business cycle and professed the ability to prevent economic downturns through changes in monetary and fiscal policy. "Recessions are now considered fundamentally preventable, like airplane crashes and unlike hurricanes," Arthur Okun, Lyndon Johnson's chief economist, declared in 1970.[11] On the European continent and in Japan, two decades of almost uninterrupted economic growth from 1950 to 1970 lent the credibility of lived experience to such claims. Even in the United States, where recessions had been a recurrent, if mild, part of postwar life, economists in the 1960s found reason to think that economic performance was ultimately subject to government control. The Phillips curve, named for the New Zealand economist, A. W. Phillips, who had first theorized its existence in 1958, purported to show that inflation and unemployment were inversely related—the more one went up, the more the other would go down. With this knowledge in hand, economists argued in the 1960s that governments could control the level of both inflation and unemployment through fiscal and monetary fine-tuning.

Using this line of thinking, postwar governments had based their policy and built their legitimacy on the promise of optimizing the social effects of the economy. From this, the central economic goal of the Western welfare state emerged: full employment. As Charles Maier has written, "a full employment 'standard'" emerged after 1945 as the measuring stick by which all Western governments were judged. Under this standard, it was now the responsibility of government to ensure that everyone who wanted a job had one. This commitment was a dramatic departure from the responsibilities of democratic capitalist governments in the prewar years, when, under the gold standard, the nations of the West prioritized their international solvency over the interests of their domestic working classes. The horrid experience of the Great Depression, Europe's descent into fascism, and the emergence of a Socialist Bloc that purported to govern in the interest of the working class all forced democratic capitalist governments after the war to adopt the interests of the working class as their own. The result of this fusion of interests between the working class and its governments was full employment. As Maier has written, "Accepting the primacy of full employment meant that a major priority of the working class had become that of society in general."[12]

Stagflation, quite plainly, called into question the entire promise of Keynesian governance and, with it, the legitimacy of Western welfare states too. If the basic task of postwar government was to *do* something to protect the interests of the working class, it was not clear after 1973 what that should be. Inflation appeared to signal that governments and the unions they supported had already done too much. As a financial phenomenon, inflation was straightforward to understand—the price level increased when there was more money than goods in an economy. But as a social phenomenon, inflation was a signal of unresolved conflicts within a society over how wealth should be distributed. Workers believed they should get a greater share, so they demanded wage increases. Capital, unwilling to see its profits decline, responded by increasing prices, and the process continued without resolution until there was more money than goods. More than simply a monetary phenomenon, inflation appeared in societies where competing social groups had been promised more than the market could deliver.[13]

In Western societies, the culprit of the accumulated promises was widely believed to be the postwar welfare state and its foundational promise of full employment. Inflation was caused by "the worldwide commitment to full employment and maximum production," the American magazine *Business Week* wrote in October 1974. This view was not confined to the spokesmen of the business community. Even those sympathetic to the interests of labor and the welfare state, such as Keynesian economist Paul Samuelson, agreed that the 1974–1975 crisis signaled that governments were doing too much to protect workers from market realities. Inflation "is deep in the nature of the welfare state," he concluded, because "even when there is slack in the system, unemployment doesn't exert the downward pressure on prices the way it did under 'cruel capitalism.'" The problem, he wrote, was that no one wanted "to turn the clock back."[14]

This is precisely what made defeating inflation so difficult. It implied someone would have to lose. The oil crisis compounded the challenge by bringing about the situation the Phillips curve had proclaimed impossible—high unemployment and inflation at the same time. Governments could fight one or the other, but not both at once. The stability of Western societies and the legitimacy of their governments depended on the restoration of economic growth, but the fight against inflation required that this restoration not add more claims on societies' resources to those already going unfulfilled.

In Europe, this predicament threatened to destroy the fragile order that had emerged since 1945. "The postwar era is over," the historian Fritz Stern declared in a May 1974 article. "For some twenty-five years . . . a steadily expanding economy protected Europe from major political upheavals." In the upheavals of 1968, students and radicals may have rebelled against the conformity of bourgeois life, but the core constituents of postwar politics—the workers—had been appeased with ever-increasing promises of prosperity. "The workers of Europe found *embourgeoisement* a novel and, on the whole, exhilarating experience," Stern wrote. "Each year, in every European country, more workers were able to afford cars, take vacations, dream of country bungalows, hope for a better life for their children." That world was now gone. With Europe headed toward "'zero growth'—at best," Stern believed democracies on the continent would be robbed of the premise of prosperity that had underpinned them since the Second World War. Without prosperity, no one could be sure there would still be peace.[15]

The promise of the postwar order therefore had to be kept alive, even as its economic foundation crumbled all around it. Across the West, governments and the unions they supported ensured that the living standards of the working class were protected as the oil price shock took hold in 1974. In the United States, workers' pay increases for the year outpaced inflation.[16] In West Germany, the first public employees strike in the country's history in May brought workers across the board a 3.4 percent real wage increase for the year.[17] In Great Britain, a tense national election in February 1974 yielded a weak Labour government that immediately granted the nation's industrial workers a 29 percent nominal wage increase.[18] In Italy, where all salaries were indexed to inflation through a system called the *scala mobile,* workers even received a 10 percent increase in real wages in 1975.[19] In Japan, where inflation ran at an astounding 24 percent in 1974, workers easily covered the increase with a 32 percent increase in wages.[20] Across the West, the first reaction in every political system was to protect the nation's workers from the changing global market.

Since the promises of postwar politics were not easily jettisoned, new sources to fund them had to be found. The oil crisis transferred roughly 2 percent of the world's wealth to the oil-producing nations, and if life in the West was to go on as it had before, a way needed to be found to bring these funds back into Western economies.[21] "Looking out to 1980 and beyond," the US Treasury noted in August 1974, "the World's capital requirements will be massive by historical standards."[22]

The Euromarkets—the forerunners of today's unregulated global capital markets—presented one possible avenue for distributing world savings from oil producers back to oil-consuming nations. Founded in London in 1955 using Europeans' surplus US dollars, the Euromarkets were made up of all currency held outside its country of origin and thus subject to little regulation. Because the US dollar was the most important and widely used currency in international trade, Eurodollars represented the overwhelming majority of liquidity in the Euromarkets, though West German deutsche marks, Swiss francs, and British pounds played a role as well. Throughout the 1950s and 1960s, the United States heavily regulated the interest rates banks could apply to their deposits within the United States, so increasing numbers of companies, banks, and central banks began to keep their US dollar holdings abroad and receive a higher rate of return in the Euromarkets. Neither the US nor the British government was eager to regulate this activity, so the Euromarkets continued to grow.

By 1970 the markets were valued at $80 billion, and by the time the oil crisis struck, they represented one option for mediating the world's rapidly growing financial interdependence.

They were far from the only one, however. Many financial observers and policy makers believed that governments or the International Monetary Fund (IMF) would have to manage the recycling process rather than leave such an important element of the global economy to the volatility of the marketplace. In the first ten months of 1974, OPEC nations deposited $16.5 billion of their $45 billion surplus in the Euromarkets compared with just $10.5 billion in the United States.[23] This was a strong boost for the unregulated markets, but most doubted it could last long. On June 26, 1974, West Germany's largest private bank, Herstatt, collapsed under the pressure of speculative foreign exchange losses. Many within the financial community itself believed the crash would be just the first of many dominoes to fall if the recycling process remained the responsibility of banks and the Euromarkets. Banks were using short-term deposits from OPEC countries to make loans to oil-importing countries with maturities ranging from seven to ten years. That was, as the *Wall Street Journal* noted days after the Herstatt collapse, "borrowing short and lending long, the bankers' classic formula for trouble." Given what appeared to be an untenable situation, the *Journal*—not usually known for its advocacy of governmental control—concluded that governments and the IMF would have to take over the primary task of petrodollar recycling. "The only other choice is an ominous one," it noted, "drastic reductions of imports, currency devaluations and sharp economic slowdowns at the cost of rising unemployment."[24]

Once more, events defied expectations. By late 1974, it became clear that oil producers had no interest in using finance to destabilize the countries that purchased their oil, and they moved to secure their deposits with Western banks on a longer-term basis. Banks, in turn, found fewer reasons to worry about lending to countries. By the summer of 1975, a US Treasury official could report that "the financing problems due to the OPEC financial accumulations now are generally recognized by most banks as manageable."[25] If the private banking system could manage the recycling process, there was little role for the IMF or governments to play. From the start of 1975 onward, government efforts to control the recycling process waned, and the vast majority of sovereign borrowing stayed on the Euromarkets, which continued their skyrocketing growth for the remainder of the 1970s (Figure 1.1).

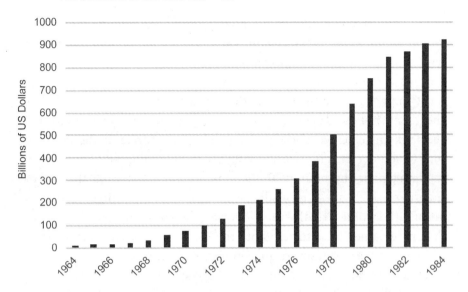

Figure 1.1 **The growth of the Euromarkets from 1964 to 1984.**
Data source: Benjamin Cohen, *In Whose Interest? International Banking and American Foreign Policy* (New Haven, CT: Yale University Press, 1986), 23, table 2.2.

This was, for the history of both democratic capitalist and state socialist governments, a fateful development. With the world's surplus capital now at its disposal, the international financial community became an arbiter of politics around the world. Neither bankers nor most politicians were eager to see the role of finance in these terms, but it was true nonetheless. Any nation-state, East or West, that relied on borrowed capital to fund the products of its domestic politics was now subject to the capricious confidence of capitalists. As long as markets remained convinced that borrowed capital would be repaid on time and with interest, politics within states could proceed normally. Politicians could continue to promise their people prosperity, and the legitimacy of the government could survive unquestioned. But should market confidence ever falter, the domestic politics of borrowing states would be thrown into immediate disarray. In both East and West, the temptation to use borrowed capital to support domestic living standards proved too strong to resist. This meant there was now a direct connection between the promises governments made to their citizens and the capital markets they used to fund them.

As the importance of global capital markets rose after 1975, the importance of central banks increased in equal measure. If governments could not control the capital markets to which they were now subject, central banks still could control how much liquidity pulsed through those markets on a daily basis. This made the reaction of the most important central banks in the world to the escalating economic crises of the 1970s as important as the response of governments. At the US Federal Reserve, the most important central bank in the world because of its control over the liquidity of the US currency now circulating the globe as petrodollars, the bank implemented a brief period of high interest rates in the spring of 1974 to counter the oil price shock, but it quickly returned to an accommodating policy by autumn. This left interest rates at or below the level of inflation, which, in turn, made the real cost of borrowing US dollars around the world virtually zero. With minor variations, the real cost of dollars remained close to zero until the late 1970s.[26] Needless to say, this encouraged the global sovereign lending process a great deal.

Other central banks tried harder to restrict the growth of money and reduce inflation in their societies. West Germany and Japan both adopted forms of monetarism in the mid-1970s that brought them a measure of success in controlling inflation within their borders. But as long as the real engine of global liquidity, the US Federal Reserve, failed to attack inflation with all its might, governments would continue to have little trouble financing the race to make promises. Until the Federal Reserve adjusted, political systems throughout the world would not be forced to adjust either.

This made any governmental attempt to defeat inflation a political choice—and an extremely unpopular one at that. Three days after assuming the presidency in August 1974, US president Gerald Ford told the nation in a nationally televised address, "inflation is our domestic public enemy No. 1," and proceeded to launch a campaign to WIN (Whip Inflation Now), under which he encouraged Americans to grow their own food, balance their budgets, and use credit sparingly. Doing little to halt inflation, the only real effect of the WIN campaign was to contribute to the record losses of the Republican Party in the November 1974 midterm elections. Chastened by defeat and dealing with massive Democratic majorities in both houses of Congress, Ford signed a series of simulative tax cuts in 1975 and left the challenge of government-imposed austerity to another day.[27]

Throughout the rest of the West, governmental attempts to prioritize fighting inflation over restoring full employment were ground to pieces by the forces of political opposition. Only in West Germany did Chancellor Helmut Schmidt, a social democrat who enjoyed strong ties with the West

German trade unions, succeed in passing a contentious austerity package in 1975. He did so by leaning on his stature as a representative of the workers who was merely delivering the economic bad news the new market conditions demanded. As he told the nation the year after the austerity measures passed, "Nothing will ever be like it was before 1974."[28]

Most Western politicians and the constituents they served did not want to believe Schmidt's fatalistic conclusion. Even those who did found that their message was deeply unpopular in democracies that favored those who promised a return to the glory of the postwar golden age. Perhaps no other work captured the prevailing mood across the West like the British economist Fred Hirsch's 1976 *The Social Limits to Growth*. "Economic liberalism," Hirsch wrote, is "a victim of its own propaganda: offered to all, it has evoked demands and pressures that cannot be contained." The promise of affluence had been extended to everyone in Western societies because of the "principle of universal participation" and "the demands of political legitimation." Although "the spread of bourgeois objectives downward through the social scale strengthens the political legitimacy of liberal market capitalism," Hirsch wrote, "the same process proves ultimately disruptive to economic performance." The fundamental economic problem of "advanced societies," he wrote, was now "a structural need to pull back the bounds of economic self-advancement." The prospects of this occurring were dim because the "central fact of the modern situation is the need to justify" policy choices to the population. That, Hirsch wrote, was "its moral triumph and its unsolved technical problem." The fact that resolution to the West's economic problems needed to be "ethically defensible" imposed "drastic limits on the set of feasible solutions." This meant the biggest challenge to industrial societies was not formulating policies to solve the crisis of stagflation but rather gaining "the public acceptance necessary to make them work."[29]

Public acceptance was indeed the challenge of the hour, and few Western states appeared capable of fostering it. If social consensus would forever evade Western democracies, perhaps political systems that discarded it altogether would fare better in the post-1974 world. If nothing would ever be the same after the oil crisis, perhaps the future at last belonged to state socialism.

◆ ◆ ◆

Quite understandably, the socialist leaders of the Eastern Bloc wanted to avoid the problems vexing their democratic capitalist counterparts at all costs. At first glance, they appeared well positioned to do so. Until the mid-1970s, prices within Comecon were fixed as part of the five-year planning process. Thus, in 1970, the USSR had set the price for its oil within Comecon for the entire period 1971–1975 at roughly 14 rubles per ton, about $2.43 per barrel.[30] At the time, oil prices on the world market hovered around $2 per barrel, so Comecon states paid a slight price premium for Soviet oil. It was a premium they were happy to pay because trade with the Soviet Union was not conducted in hard currency—currencies that were freely convertible, such as the US dollar, British pound, or West German mark. Although Soviet oil was priced in rubles for accounting purposes, Comecon trade was conducted on a barter basis within the five-year plans. Before the oil crisis, planners would use the five-year planning process to determine that Soviet oil was worth a certain amount of East German television sets, Polish ships, or Czechoslovak engineering equipment, and then trade for the entire period would proceed at that price.

For Eastern Bloc countries, which generally imported raw materials and exported finished products, this arrangement had two overriding advantages compared to the trade they conducted on Western markets: their products had a guaranteed buyer and could be sold without regard for their quality. Soviet officials could (and did) protest about the quality of East European goods sent their way, but without radically altering the structure of Comecon, there was little they could do to stop the flow of inferior goods. These advantages for Eastern Europe notwithstanding, trade within Comecon before the oil crisis was not fundamentally different from trade on the world market. The barter system did not emphasize quality, but the economic value ascribed to goods (as seen in the rough parity of Comecon and world oil prices) was basically in line with world market values.

The commodity price explosion of the early 1970s fundamentally altered this dynamic. Within a matter of months from late 1973 to early 1974, the world market value of the Soviet Union's energy resources quadrupled, and with it, the country's dominion over the rest of the bloc became an enormous economic liability. As long as world oil prices remained above ten dollars a barrel, any deliveries of Soviet oil to Eastern Europe at two and a half dollars a barrel would represent a breathtaking loss on the sale of the country's most valuable asset. But if the Kremlin adjusted Comecon prices to reflect the new world market prices, Eastern Bloc countries would have to dramatically increase their exports to the Soviet Union to pay the new prices. This increase in exports would have to come at the expense of domestic consumption, and thus it had the potential to disrupt the unwritten social contracts of late socialism and produce severely destabilizing social unrest. This was a prospect all Eastern Bloc leaders hoped to avoid, so they used all the tools at their disposal to insulate their domestic social contracts from changes in the world market and Comecon. After the oil crisis, a new tension defined relations among the "fraternal allies"; the economic interests of the Soviet Union now stood in stark opposition to the political, economic, and social priorities of the bloc as a whole.

This tension first appeared in 1974 after the Soviet leadership proposed a new Comecon pricing system that would dramatically increase the price of Soviet energy resources in order to bring them more in line with the new world market prices. The Soviet Politburo debated the issue on numerous occasions that year, and Soviet general secretary Leonid Brezhnev "personally attache[d] great importance to this question," Gosplan chairman Nikolai Baibakov told his East German counterpart, Gerhard Schürer, in December that year. The Soviet leader believed "that no socialist country, nor the Soviet Union, should have a setback in national economic development due to price regulation." For the leadership, the issue of oil prices was "fundamentally a political question, not just a purely economic problem," Baibakov said. Soviet leaders knew that a transition to current world market prices "could lead to the emergence of chaos in the economies of the socialist countries, as is currently the case in capitalist countries." At the same time, however, they believed the socialist countries could not "completely separate themselves from the development on the world market" because the price changes were "an objective [and] irreversible process." This meant that the Socialist Bloc could not "escape the prevailing price increase on the world market."[31]

Escape was precisely what Eastern European leaders believed the bloc should do. For them, the oil crisis was the clearest sign yet that capitalism was prone to crisis and doomed to failure. Official East German policy maintained that the oil price shock was "influenced to a large degree by speculative and inflationary factors" that arose "out of the intensification of the general crisis of the capitalist system, especially from the chronic energy, currency, and financial crisis."[32] Similarly, the Hungarian Socialist Workers' Party concluded that "manipulations of international capitalist monopolies" had produced the commodity price shock. "The general crisis of capitalism deepens," party documents declared.[33]

Faced with capitalism's evident failures, Eastern European leaders thought it foolish to willingly import the effects of capitalism's crisis through changes to Comecon prices. As GDR policy makers told their Soviet comrades, the bloc "should under no circumstances" incorporate price increases into the Comecon price system based "on speculative . . . factors of the imperialist system." Such a move would only "transmit the effects of capitalist inflation into our economic relations." This would not only have "economic effects," they warned. "We must also recognize that political problems could arise if price increases for raw materials trigger a general price increase within our community of states."[34]

Soviet leaders understood the explosive social potential of price changes, but they remained firmly convinced the oil price increase was something to be celebrated, not admonished. Far from signaling the power of monopolies and speculators in the capitalist world, the commodity price shocks represented a resounding victory for the global forces arrayed against Western imperialism. "Something fundamental has happened in the world," Nikolai Patolichev, the Soviet minister of foreign trade, told his East German colleagues. "Developing countries have achieved their economic independence in recent years. 1973 was the conclusion of this struggle. This is not an imperialist process but an anti-imperialist development." The socialist community had "supported developing countries in their political struggle, and now they have triumphed," Patolichev said. This meant that "by their very nature, the new commodity prices are the result of the anti-imperialist struggle."[35]

The differences in ideological interpretation between the Kremlin and its allies reflected differences in national self-interest and domestic politics exposed by the oil crisis. As the Soviet foreign trade minister Patolichev rhetorically presented it to GDR officials, "How are we to explain to our people that we are selling our oil 30 rubles below the world market price?" The allies needed to understand, Patolichev said, "what it would cost the Soviet side to sell the raw materials so cheaply." The Soviets could not go on providing such a subsidy because they could no longer "explain it to the Soviet people." This made it "absurd to reject" the Soviet Union's "authority (*Berechtigung*)" to revise the Comecon price structure.[36]

Bloc governments equally felt the pressure to please their people. As East German leader Erich Honecker wrote in a 1974 letter to Brezhnev, the GDR leadership felt it could not allow "a reduction of the population's standard of living" because the state's "class enemies" in the West led "a daily ideological diversion against the people of the GDR." To counter this threat, the East German leadership thought it "necessary to solve a series of social questions (increases in pensions, the minimum wage, support for young families, aid for children, [and] acceleration in the construction of housing, hospitals, and schools, etc.)."[37] The same governing strategy defined the regimes of János Kádár in Hungary, Edward Gierek in Poland, Gustáv Husák Czechoslovakia, Todor Zhivkov in Bulgaria, and Nicolae Ceaușescu in Romania. Higher Soviet energy prices would mean fewer houses in Leipzig, lower wages in Gdánsk, emptier shelves in Sofia, and more political instability everywhere.

Ultimately, it was the Soviet Union that had the oil, so it was the Kremlin that set the policy. At first, the Politburo decided that energy prices within Comecon for 1975 should be set based on an average of the world market price in 1973 and 1974. Because these two years contained the dramatic price increases, this would have served Soviet economic interests handsomely. But after hearing loud protestations from their allies, the Politburo decided that the two-year price average would be "too difficult for the socialist countries." Instead, they chose to base the 1975 price on an average of 1972, 1973, and 1974 in order to include "one year each with low, medium, and high price[s]." After 1975, Soviet officials decreed, the Comecon price system would adjust based on a rolling average of the previous five years of world market prices.

It was a decision worth billions of rubles—and, by extension, billions of dollars. As Baibakov explained, if Comecon had moved immediately to world market prices, the socialist countries would have had to export an extra 16 billion rubles worth of goods to the Soviet Union during the 1976–1980 Five-Year Plan. Under the system of flexible prices, the 16-billion-ruble burden on Eastern Europe would fall to 7 or 8 billion rubles.[38] Patolichev described the new sliding price system as "an optimal compromise, which splits the necessary strains between the USSR and the other CMEA countries." Optimal did not mean easy, however. Everyone involved in the negotiations throughout the bloc knew that the consequences of their decisions would be vast and long lasting. As Patolichev told Honecker in the midst of a particularly testy exchange, "The current change in Comecon prices is the most difficult task of my life. . . . The system of sliding prices is not only a question for the USSR, but also politically and economically important for the entire socialist community."[39]

What appeared difficult to Soviet officials appeared life threatening to Eastern European officials. Even under the sliding price system, it was now clear the price of energy for bloc countries would dramatically increase in the years ahead. Upon hearing of Moscow's move to change the pricing system, Erich Honecker called an emergency meeting of the East German leadership to formulate a response. There were domestic and international dimensions to the Soviet decision that needed to be discussed. Internationally, the general secretary observed that the oil crisis had fundamentally, and perhaps permanently, changed Eastern Europe's economic value to the Soviet Union. "Until now," he said, "we have paid more for a ton of oil from the USSR than the FRG [Federal Republic of Germany]. That may have changed as a result of the price increases in the West."[40] For the foreseeable future, Eastern Europe would now be an economic burden on Moscow.

Domestically, the sliding price system presented the prospect of social and political disruption. The first estimate of the economic losses for the GDR under the new price system projected an additional cost of 7–8 billion marks in 1975 and 8–9 billion marks per year during the period 1976–1980. To put the scale of these costs in perspective, state planners warned the Politburo that the new annual costs for Soviet oil were "more than the annual increase in national income." Günter Mittag, Honecker's deputy and the chief economic official in the GDR, understood immediately what this would mean for the country: "an absolute fall in living standards in the GDR." He was furious. If prices were not fixed, then insulating the GDR from world market volatility would be impossible and the inflation pervading the capitalist world would creep into the Eastern Bloc. For Honecker, preventing this from happening was a top priority. "We have no intention of letting inflation penetrate the socialist camp," he told the group. Budget subsidies were the only way to turn flexible and rising import prices into stable and cheap domestic prices, so the fight against world inflation would come at the expense of the state budget.[41] Honecker gave the new marching orders to his state planning commissioner, Gerhard Schürer, in early 1975. "The main task," he said, was to achieve economic growth "by means of intensification"—the socialist term for increases in productivity—and to ensure that "social security is placed at the center of the development of working and living conditions." Social security meant, "above all, stability of prices . . . implementation of the housing program, preservation and expansion of health care capacities, and safeguarding of the school program."[42] Progress in the land of real existing socialism would go on, Honecker had decided, no matter the consequences.

Progress would also go on in Hungary. In 1972, the Hungarian Polit-buro had decided on the need to further improve the position of the working class and increase real wages. A capitalist crisis like the oil price shock was not going to stand in the way of this goal. János Kádár told the country in his speech to Eleventh Party Congress in 1975, "Despite the external difficulties it is possible for our national economy to develop in the coming years at approximately the same rate as it has in recent years and for living standards to continue to rise."[43] The party program adopted at the 1975 congress still insisted the final stage of communism could arrive in Hungary in the next fifteen to twenty years.[44]

The bloc governments' decisions to leave the social contract untouched in the face of the oil crisis was born of searing historical memories. Ger-hard Schürer, the head of the East German State Planning Commission, wrote of the East German leadership, "Since the sugar price increase of June 17th, 1953,"—when price increases had sparked an uprising that was violently suppressed by the Soviet Army—"the fear of price increases on basic goods sat so deep in the bones of policymakers that no one achieved a change."[45] In Poland, dangerous history was much closer at hand—Edward Gierek owed his ascension to the pinnacle of the country to the repeal of the 1970 price increases and the start of his "New Development Program," which promised workers a better life. In Hungary, Kádár had secured the political acquiescence of the population after the national trauma of 1956 with a single promise: ever-increasing living standards. Gustáv Husák was detested in Czechoslovakia, but after 1968 he drove a similar bargain. Throughout the bloc, higher living standards were the price of social peace.

But if history and politics provided the impetus for stabilizing the so-cial contracts of late socialism, they were not what made it possible. For that, the particular configuration of the global capitalist economy that emerged after the oil crisis was required. In a supreme irony, it was only the development of global finance capitalism that allowed late socialism to exist. Without the explosive growth of global capital markets after 1970, and particularly after 1974, the governing model of late socialism would have been impossible. Had there been no transnational pools of capital on the Euromarkets in the 1970s, or had those pools been more highly regulated and thus less easily accessed, the entire time line of socialism's denoue-ment would almost certainly have looked completely different. Rather than speaking of the rise of Solidarity in the Polish Crisis of 1980 and 1981, we might instead be writing about a Polish, Hungarian, or East German Crisis of 1974 or 1975.

Günter Mittag, the East German party leader for economic policy, admitted as much in his memoirs. In his words, because in the 1970s "it was regarded as an indisputable axiom that the standard of living should increase, loans were taken out to bridge supply shortages." Had these loans not been available, the Unity of Economic and Social Policy—the East German name for their policy of raising living standards and expanding social welfare—would have quickly become untenable. Abandoning this policy, Mittag wrote, would have "been a funeral for the GDR in the 1970s." Upending the social contract would have produced "social conflicts with political consequences, which would probably have affected more than just the former GDR." In the 1970s, "a possible political destabilization in the GDR through a restriction of social policy was connected with an incalculable political risk. In this respect, the guarantee of economic and social stability was a basic premise of all political action."[46]

In the same way, a basic yet unexamined premise of our histories of the last period of the Cold War is the intimate relationship between the globalizing financial capitalism of the 1970s and the fragile stability of late socialism. It was a relationship that quietly underwrote everything from the daily lives of Eastern Europeans, who unknowingly depended on it to put food on their tables and goods in their stores, to the high politics of the Cold War, where it was the prerequisite for détente on the European continent. Its power was really only apparent once it was gone, as it would be in 1980, at which point the broken connection between finance capitalism and late socialism would produce a crisis in Poland that would disrupt both the daily lives of Eastern Europeans and the high politics of the Cold War.

A closer look at the situation of the GDR at the moment the oil crisis struck illustrates this interdependence. Just as the oil crisis was beginning to unfold in November 1973, members of the East German Ministry of Finance produced a projection of the GDR's sovereign debt out to 1980 if the country maintained its trajectory under the rapidly rising world prices. The results were frightening. The GDR's debt to the West at the end of 1974 was projected to be 8.7 billion "valuta marks" (VM), the East German accounting unit used for foreign trade and finance and pegged at roughly the value of a West German deutsche mark (DM). This converted to roughly $3.5 billion.[47] Even under optimistic hard currency export assumptions, the projection anticipated the hard currency debt growing from VM 12.1 billion in 1975 to VM 25.5 billion, or roughly $10 billion, in 1980. Officials believed such a level of debt would simply not be possible to attain. They estimated that over the entire period of 1974–1980, VM 18 billion of planned borrowing on global capital markets was simply "not financeable." As they wrote, "All calculations show" that the nation's economic trajectory "is not viable" because "of the development of the debt and the impossible financing [requirements]." If the debt was to be controlled, they wrote, the social contract would have to be disciplined.[48]

In its first months, the oil crisis only seemed to make the prospects for substantial Eastern Bloc borrowing worse. As discussed previously, many Western observers did not think the Euromarkets could sustainably manage the process of petrodollar recycling for any period longer than a couple of months.[49] This sentiment was immediately and urgently echoed within the East German leadership. In March 1974, there were "fundamental differences of opinion" among the economic leadership on the question of whether "the necessary sources of credit for financing the planned imports of 1975–1980" could be found. It remained an open question because East German bankers had recently been forced to meet existing debt payments by taking out new loans. This was "already a tense goal because the existing sources of credit [were] largely exhausted." Foreign banks were "increasingly questioning the liquidity of the GDR." The first months of higher commodity prices had made the availability of credit worse, not better. Markets, it seemed, might force a change in Eastern Bloc domestic policy whether communist leaders wanted one or not.[50]

Throughout the tumultuous summer of 1974 in the West, the debate over the sustainability of the bloc's access to global capital markets continued. As the Soviet Union worked to change Comecon oil prices in September, a newly formed group of top economic officials in the GDR discussed a Marxist-Leninist analysis of the Euromarkets that was designated "Top Secret." In the first section, titled "The Nature of the Eurocurrency Market and Its Risks," the author detailed how the markets had begun in the late 1950s when surpluses of US dollars ended up in Europe due to the "unrestricted political and economic predominance of US imperialism on the world capitalist market." Then, in the late 1960s, "objectively acting laws of the capitalist mode of production" such as the "uneven economic development of capitalist industrial states" and "the excessive expenditure of US imperialism on financing its aggressive global strategy" led to a breakup of the Bretton Woods system in 1971. The report reminded the working group that the party had recently decided that "the general crisis of capitalism has reached a new stage" and declared that this conclusion was "fully applicable to the development of the Eurocurrency market." The upshot was clear: "With its inherent risks, the Eurocurrency market does not provide a long-term basis for financing balance of payments deficits."[51] If this was true, then all bloc states would confront a highly precarious situation. As 1975 approached with Eastern European leaders determined not to let increases in Soviet energy prices lead to a fall in domestic living standards, bankers throughout the bloc had no choice but to test how much money Western capital markets would let them borrow.

To universal surprise, it turned out to be a great deal. Once it became clear that private banks could manage petrodollar recycling on a permanent basis, economic plans across the world that had been deemed "not financeable" in 1973 became eminently so by 1975. The rapid expansion of the Euromarkets that began in 1974 pushed the horizon for living on credit to a level that would have been deemed dangerous and impractical just one year earlier. OPEC nations accumulated a $60 billion current account surplus in 1974. Of this $60 billion, $21 billion was deposited with Eurocurrency banks, and the total assets of the five largest US banks grew at an unprecedented annual rate of 40 percent in 1974.[52] Western banks were, in short, flush with cash and eager to find places to put it. The time was ripe for a marriage of convenience, and in 1975, the Eastern Bloc as a whole borrowed more money than they ever had before. Eurocurrency loans to the bloc—the type East German officials had feared would suddenly become scarce—more than doubled from 1974 to 1975, rising from $1 billion to $2.4 billion. Quite literally, the surplus capital generated by a global crisis in capitalism was now funding state socialism's defense against the global capitalist system.[53]

Indeed, by the beginning of 1976, the growth of socialist borrowing was so notable that *Euromoney* magazine, the publication of record for the Euromarkets in the 1970s, put the Eastern Bloc on the cover of its January issue. "It is customary to begin the new year with a backward look," the lead article noted, "and if we focus on the Euromarkets, the number and nature of Comecon borrowings in 1975 are striking."[54]

There was so much Comecon borrowing in 1975 that by early 1976, Western financial and political leaders were beginning to question the bloc's creditworthiness. The January 1976 *Euromoney* article noted it was "inevitable" that "the magic" would eventually "go out of lending to Comecon countries."[55] In May, a widely discussed article in *Business Week* quoted Zbigniew Brzezinski, soon to become Jimmy Carter's national security advisor, on the political dimensions of the increase in the Eastern Bloc's debt. "We are dealing with both an opportunity and a threat," Brzezinski told the magazine in a quintessential expression of the logic of interdependence. "Indebtedness often increases the leverage of the debtor and decreases the leverage of the creditor," he said. "If a Comecon country defaulted, it could create considerable problems" for Western European banks that had lent out the most money.[56] This threat of interdependence was the concern of US secretary of state Henry Kissinger, who warned a gathering of OECD officials in June 1976 of "possible efforts" by socialist states "to misuse economic relations for political purposes inimical" to the West.[57]

The flurry of commentary in the West caught the ear of officials in the East who were now highly sensitive to changes in global market sentiment. "The capitalist national and international banks," East German officials wrote in early 1976, "have recently expressed doubts about the creditworthiness of the socialist countries. That was not always so. A few years ago . . . insolvency from a borrower in a socialist country was as unthinkable, for example, as an insolvency from the American automaker General Motors."[58]

But if the dangers of a Comecon default had become thinkable for both sides by the spring of 1976, that did not stop the banks from lending.[59] By the start of 1977, the bloc was once more the star of the Euromarkets and reappeared on the cover of *Euromoney*. "Any concern over the rapid increase in the level of indebtedness of the CMEA countries has not restricted the volume of lending," journalists for the magazine wrote. "On the contrary, 1976 was a vintage year." Banks seemed to agree they had lent Comecon too much, but they couldn't help themselves from lending more. Eurocurrency credits to the communist world had increased 33 percent in 1976 to $3.2 billion, and there was no end in sight.[60] As Figure 1.2 makes clear, the debt burden of the Socialist Bloc would continue to rise through the end of the 1970s and would remain onerous for the rest of the Cold War.

Why did the banks continue to lend? The potent combination of surplus capital and erroneous assumptions pushed their enthusiasm beyond rationality. "On any normal criteria," one London banker told *Euromoney*, the Eastern Bloc was "certainly overborrowed." But banks were not holding

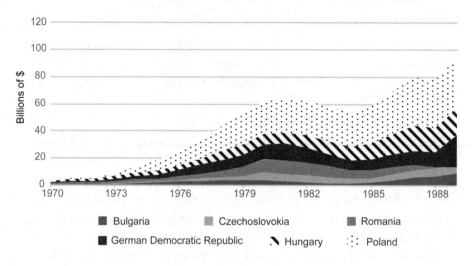

Figure 1.2 **Eastern European sovereign debt (net of hard currency reserves) from 1970 to 1990.**

Data source: United Nations, Economic Commission for Europe, *Economic Survey of Europe in 1990-1991* (Geneva: United Nations, 1991), 250, appendix table C.11.

the bloc to high standards of creditworthiness "because they're so flush with funds," another said.[61] Bankers' confidence in the wisdom of their own cause compounded the enticements of easy liquidity. Citibank CEO Walter Wriston, the leading proponent of the global movement toward sovereign lending in the 1970s, notoriously proclaimed, "Countries don't go bankrupt."[62]

Above and beyond "normal" capitalist countries, bankers believed socialist countries had three other advantages. First, they had a pristine record of timely payment and had never defaulted on their debts. Second, bankers assumed that socialist states' authoritarian structure meant they had the "ability to control domestic consumption and investment," which would put them "in a better position" to exercise "restraint."[63] Unlike capitalist democracies, which promised their citizens too much, socialist authoritarianism was assumed to be adept at implementing austerity. Should that fail, however, bankers saw a strategic reserve behind the Eastern Bloc unparalleled throughout the rest of the global economy—the Soviet Union. Over the course of the decade, they came to believe in what was termed "the umbrella theory," whereby they anticipated that the USSR would "come to the rescue" of its allies if they ran into financial trouble.[64] Under the Soviet umbrella, Eastern Europe seemed safe from financial harm.

On top of favorable ideological and financial structures, a group of very talented communist bankers represented their countries on Western financial markets with aplomb. To read the Western press coverage of these men is to sense the potent mix of intrigue and respect with which Western bankers looked upon their communist counterparts at the time. Standing at the head of this group, and on par with any financial official in the West, was János Fekete, the deputy vice president of the Hungarian National Bank. Fekete had earned his venerable reputation in Western financial circles for accurately predicting a devaluation of the US dollar in 1971 and the global recession of 1974–1975. By the time he was profiled in *Euromoney* in 1977, the magazine treated his opinions with what verged on oracle-like reverence. There was an entire separate article on the topic of "What Fekete Says About the West," presumably to help the magazine's readers glean insight into the future of capitalism from this astute "Marxist economist." Described as "bespectacled and ebullient," Fekete told *Euromoney* that the Eastern Bloc was vastly underborrowed, not overly indebted. "If you take the economic potential of these countries, their debts are ridiculously low," he said. Playing on the Western notion of an umbrella theory, he seamlessly shifted questions about Eastern Europe's problems to a discussion of the Soviet Union's material strength. "In a year, [the Soviet Union] is producing 480 million tons of petrol, it is producing about 300 billion cubic metres of gas, and 700 million tons of coal. It is an enormously strong economy."[65] With such strength in Soviet natural resources, it was implied that the debt of the rest of the bloc hardly mattered. For the time being, Western banks couldn't help but agree.

If Fekete projected self-confidence, Poland's Jan Wołoszyn, the first deputy president of Bank Handlowy, the Polish foreign trade bank, projected stately elegance. The same 1977 *Euromoney* issue described him as a "distinguished, elder statesman of Polish banking who would look equally at home in the boardroom of any bank in the West."[66] Bankers had nothing to fear with "Mr. Poland," a later profile concluded. Wołoszyn was "credible, knowledgeable, and . . . impressive," had never joined the Polish communist party, and had thought more than once about leaving banking for more leisurely bourgeois pursuits, gardening foremost among them. "This is a people business," bankers reported to *Euromoney,* and Wołoszyn was "the one who, through his own charisma, standing, and personality, persuades many banks to lend to Poland."[67]

In East Germany, two men, Werner Polze and Horst Kaminsky, ran the country's public financing efforts on the Euromarkets. Both men went about their business in the West without the fanfare of Fekete or Wołoszyn. After the Cold War, their actions receded further into the background in Germany after the revelation that another man—Alexander Schalck-Golodkowski, known simply as Schalck—had been running an organization within the East German government called *Kommerzielle Koordinierung*. KoKo, as it was referred to, was charged with creating hard currency for the East German state using any means available. From the late 1960s to the collapse of the state in 1989, this mission led KoKo into all manner of activities, including currency and commodity speculation, hotel management, consumer goods stores, garbage disposal services for West Berlin, and weapons sales to developing countries. Along the way, Schalck became one of the most important people within the East German leadership because he was the state's chief negotiator with West Germany on all financial matters.

And there was a great deal to negotiate. After the launch of Willy Brandt's *Ostpolitik* in the late 1960s and the signing of the Basic Treaty normalizing relations between the two German states in 1972, the West German government began to use its financial resources as a tool of its détente policy. East Germany was granted access to a "swing" credit with West German banks, under which it could borrow deutsche marks without interest up to a negotiated limit, which ranged from DM 500 million to DM 800 million in the 1970s and 1980s. Bonn also made an annual transportation payment to the GDR that was ostensibly for the maintenance of the roads running between the Federal Republic and West Berlin but was, in fact, free for the East Germans to use as they pleased. Most spectacularly of all, the Federal Republic began buying East Germans' freedom, transferring increasing sums of money to the East German government in exchange for the release of dissidents (and eventually many others) to the West. Schalck played a role in all these negotiations while still organizing KoKo's varied commercial activities, so his influence within the East German hierarchy steadily grew over the last two decades of the Cold War. Once the Berlin Wall fell, the public revelations of KoKo's dubious activities led many in the newly reunited Germany to label Schalck "public enemy #1."[68]

The East German situation was an especially vibrant example of how the politics of détente further eased the reigns on sovereign lending beyond their already lax hold. Gierek's regime in Poland proved particularly adept at using Western governments' interest in better relations with the Eastern Bloc to unlock Western state coffers. Each US president in the 1970s—Nixon, Ford, and Carter—visited Poland under the banner of détente, and each time they landed in Warsaw, they brought with them increases in US government loan guarantees as a sign of goodwill and a means of boosting US exports.[69] In 1975, on the sidelines of the meetings to sign the Helsinki Accords, Gierek and West German chancellor Helmut Schmidt signed an agreement granting Warsaw a "jumbo credit" of DM 500 million in exchange for the Polish government's willingness to let its German minority emigrate to the Federal Republic.[70] In Romania, Nicolae Ceaușescu parlayed his reputation for independence from Moscow into membership in the International Monetary Fund in 1972, which, in turn, helped his country gain broader and cheaper access to Euromarket credit. The Kádár government in Hungary generally refrained from using détente to gain politically motivated credits from Western governments, but it nevertheless used its reputation in the West as the most liberal and reform-minded country in the bloc to great financial effect.

Even if the question of access to Western credit markets turned out to be surprisingly easy for Eastern Bloc states to solve, the question of how to use the borrowed capital proved infinitely vexing. Every foreign borrowing strategy in the Eastern Bloc was at least officially premised on a single idea: using the hard currency to import Western technology, modernize domestic production, and develop industries capable of producing exports to the world market that would earn enough hard currency to pay off the loans.[71] In Poland, for instance, Gierek's New Development Strategy had augmented the country's traditional export strengths in copper and coal with new hard currency investments in heavy industry, chemicals, aircraft, construction equipment, and auto parts on the assumption that these industries would produce exportable goods by the end of the decade. In East Germany, planners had funded a massive expansion of the petrochemicals industry in the late 1960s and early 1970s to take advantage of growing Soviet energy supplies to produce more exports of refined petroleum products to the West. In each case, some of the imported capital made it all the way to improving the quality of Eastern European factories and production processes, but much of the rest merely presented rampant opportunities to expand domestic corruption and patronage networks.

More importantly, the decision to base long-term development on future exports to the world market broke an important barrier between Comecon and the rest of the world economy. In order to win in global export markets, Eastern Bloc countries would have to compete with the developing countries of Latin America and East Asia to sell their goods in the developed West. This competition subjected Eastern Bloc goods to direct competition with capitalist goods and pitted socialist methods of production against the capitalist methods the bloc had long eschewed. Implicit in the Eastern Bloc's choice to borrow on global capital markets was also the choice to compete on global trade markets.

It was a competition the bloc would lose time and again in the 1970s. Despite constant exhortations from the very top of each state's governing structure about the importance of increasing exports and eventually producing hard currency trade surpluses, the Eastern European members of Comecon (excluding the Soviet Union) ran a cumulative hard currency trade deficit from 1970 to 1977 of roughly $26 billion.[72] Eastern Bloc officials liked to blame their inability to increase exports on the slow growth and high inflation of Western economies as well as discriminatory Western trade policies that prevented their goods from reaching Western consumers. But the reality was that they simply were not producing goods Westerners wanted to buy. "While the world economy is based partly on a socialist and partly on a capitalist social system," Fekete would write in 1982, "there are not two world markets, there are no 'capitalist and socialist' machines and products, but only good or bad machines, modern or obsolete products."[73] By the late 1970s, the Eastern Bloc was most assuredly producing flawed obsolescence. And if the trade surpluses required to pay back the debt could not be created through increases in exports, they would need to be created through decreases in imports. That, in turn, meant only one thing: the challenge of austerity lurked just around the corner.

CHAPTER 2

Years of Illusion and Reckoning

BY THE SUMMER OF 1976, the rapid rise in Eastern debts and Western doubts led Edward Gierek to alter his plans for Poland. Although the Socialist Bloc as a whole remained credible in the eyes of Western bankers, Poland was setting a torrid pace for debt accumulation that appeared to be unsustainable. From 1971 to 1975, the nation's debt to the West had exploded from $764 million to $7.4 billion, and it showed no sign of slowing down unless the country's economy underwent dramatic changes to lower imports and increase exports.[1] To that end, on June 24 the Polish government announced a plan to increase food prices across the country by an average of 60 percent.

Two glaring problems stood in the way: the increases would make Polish citizens poorer, and they would undercut late socialism's foundational promise to always increase living standards. Recognizing that the proposal would be unpopular, the government committed to holding "public consultations" to discuss the plan with the population. The fact that the consultations were scheduled to take place in the course of a single day signaled the propagandistic intent underlying them, but Polish workers nevertheless took the invitation to express their opinion of the decision seriously. On June 25, strikes and street demonstrations broke out in industrial centers, and countless smaller work disruptions rippled through the rest of the country. Shaken and unwilling to risk a full reprise of the events of 1970, the authorities claimed by nightfall to have held productive consultations with the working class and rescinded the price increases indefinitely.[2]

In what context should these events be placed? Normally, the events of June 1976 are placed at the midpoint of a narrative about the rise of the labor union Solidarity that begins with the food price strikes of 1970 and ends with the formation of the union in the summer of 1980. Seen in this light, the attempted price increases signal the ineptitude and injustice of the Gierek regime and mark an important moment in the construction of a unified Polish opposition that would unleash the full power of its resistance under the banner of Solidarność in August 1980.[3]

But there is another way to describe the events of that June. Removed from their particular Polish context, they were emblematic of phenomena occurring across the industrial world as nations adapted to the economic crises of the 1970s. First, they exemplified the power of financial markets to force changes in domestic policies. Second, they reflected how torturous it was for governments to attempt to legitimize changes in domestic policy that would harm the interests of their populations. And finally, they spoke to the potential power of the working class to thwart governmental plans for domestic austerity. Described in this way, the Polish attempt to increase prices represents just one of many instances of the basic riddle at work in both Eastern and Western politics in the late 1970s: how could governments extract economic sacrifice from their people?

It was a challenge few governments mastered and most tried to avoid until they had no other choice. Throughout the 1970s, the power of the working class was, if anything, stronger in the West than in the East, and most governments on both sides of the Iron Curtain waited as long as financial markets would allow before asking their citizens to sacrifice. Because Western currencies were internationally convertible and Eastern currencies were not, crises in the West appeared under a different name than in the East. Currency crises bedeviled Western societies, while debt crises came to haunt Eastern ones. But Western currency crises and Eastern debt crises were different manifestations of the same thing: international capital's loss of confidence in the viability of a nation's economy. As such, they required the same response which can broadly be defined as austerity—government policies that intentionally lower the living standards of the domestic population to restore financial markets' confidence in the national economy. Calling this austerity economic or structural "adjustment," as financial officials did in the 1970s and 1980s, disguised the policy's fraught social and political consequences. In both East and West, economic "adjustment" was nothing short of a direct challenge to the legitimacy and governing ideology of any government that tried to implement it.

This chapter chronicles the fraught moments of economic crisis that rolled across the Western and Eastern world over the course of the late 1970s. Governments of the Eastern Bloc continued to rely on their access to cheap Soviet raw materials and Western credit markets to avoid the disruptive adjustments austerity brought to Western societies beginning in 1976. But both of these economic lifelines ran out in the late 1970s, and austerity became unavoidable. In 1977, the Kremlin announced that the Soviet Union would no longer be able to increase energy deliveries to the rest of the bloc after 1980. This weakened one of the crutches Eastern European governments had used to defer the effects of the oil crisis since 1973 and left them overwhelmingly reliant on the continued flow of Western capital, and particularly US dollars, from the Euromarkets to defer the encroaching demands of the world market.

Because the US dollar was controlled by the US Federal Reserve, Western capital would continue to flow easily only as long as US monetary policy remained loose, as it had been throughout the 1970s. The United States, like the communists of the Eastern Bloc, deferred adjustment as long as possible. But by the late 1970s, its time, too, had run out. Severe runs on the US dollar in 1978 and 1979 forced the Federal Reserve to implement domestic austerity at the decade's end to restore global-capital holders' confidence in the currency. US Federal Reserve chairman Paul Volcker's resolution of the 1979 dollar crisis through the imposition of domestic austerity brought an end not only to the United States' years of deferring the effects of the oil crisis but also to the days of easy money on the Euromarkets. The centrality of the US dollar to the entire world economy meant that when the United States finally decided to face *its* reckoning with broken promises, the rest of the world, including the communist states of the Eastern Bloc, had no choice but to reckon with broken promises too.

◆ ◆ ◆

Her Majesty's Government in London was the first government to fall into austerity's grip. Like its counterpart in Warsaw, the

British Labour government of Harold Wilson had borrowed heavily on international credit markets after the oil crisis to defer adjustment. But by March 1976, international capital holders had begun to doubt the long-term viability of the British economy, and they started moving their wealth out of the British pound. This precipitated a run on the currency, and the Bank of England was drawn into supporting the pound on international currency markets. With its resources soon exhausted, the government was forced to approach other Western central banks for a loan. The US Treasury and the Bundesbank granted the British a $5.3 billion loan, but they attached the condition that the Wilson government reach a "high-conditionality stand-by agreement" with the International Monetary Fund (IMF). A package of measures was agreed to in July, but it failed to stem the flow of capital out of the country.

By November, the Labour government, now under the leadership of James Callaghan, was back at the IMF with a request for further assistance. The conditions of the deal that emerged were stiff: 3.5 billion pounds in government spending cuts over the next two years, a reduction in the state borrowing requirement, limits on domestic credit creation, and the adoption of an "incomes policy" under which British workers' wage increases would barely match inflation. Callaghan lobbied the US and West German governments to get the IMF to ease its terms. But both US president Gerald Ford and West German chancellor Helmut Schmidt demanded Callaghan accept the IMF's dictates. Out of international lifelines, Callaghan had no choice but to move ahead with the IMF plan, which was adopted in December 1976.[4]

The country's arrival at the precipice of insolvency led to further diagnoses of democracy's ultimate propensity to promise more than it could deliver. "The greatest sacred cow of all—unfettered representative democracy—will have to be questioned," the British financial writer Samuel Brittan concluded in his 1977 book *The Economic Consequences of Democracy*. "The basic trouble is *the lack of a budget constraint among voters*," he wrote. "Is it possible," he went on to doubtingly ask, "to create or evolve a consensus, so far missing, on a legitimate social order which would appeal to people's sense of justice and persuade them to moderate their pursuit of private interest, both in the ballot box and in their other collective activities?"[5] The prospects appeared bleak.

At the highest levels of the British government, the resolution of the crisis began to fundamentally alter the Labour Party's views on the role of government. IMF austerity made budget constraints the order of the day and led to a rejection of Keynesianism in the economist's home country. As Callahan famously declared in a speech to the Labour Party conference in September 1976, "We used to think that you could just spend your way out of a recession . . . I tell you in all candor, that that option no longer exists and that in so far as it ever did exist, it only worked . . . by injecting bigger doses of inflation into the economy, followed by higher levels of unemployment." Coming as they did from the political standard-bearer of the British working class, Callaghan's words stood as a profound rejection of the Keynesian economics that had dominated British politics since the Second World War.[6]

As global financial markets battered the postwar social contract in Great Britain, they also mounted a sustained assault on Italy. Since the oil crisis, Italian unions had brought their workers significant gains in real wages under the automatic wage indexation mechanism of the *scala mobile* and protected their members from the threat of labor "redundancy" as firms moved to become more efficient through layoffs. By 1976, Italian workers were expensive and difficult to fire, and the ruling coalition, led by the Christian Democrats, was at a loss for how to slow labor's momentum. To cover the yawning gap between national production and consumption, the government had borrowed heavily on the Euromarkets and from the IMF in 1974 and 1975, but financial lifelines had run out by the start of 1976. Negotiations with both the IMF and the European Community early in the year produced demands that the government slow the growth of real wages, domestic monetary creation, and government spending. Lacking enough credibility with labor to get unions to agree to voluntary wage restraints and facing a tough election in June against the Italian Communist Party, the Christian Democrats balked at international capital's demands.

In the context of the Cold War, the possibility of a communist victory in the elections appeared to signal that the Italian Left was dangerously ascendant. But in the crucible of financial crisis, it became clear that, like their counterparts on the British Left, the Italian communists would also accommodate international pressures for austerity. After narrowly winning the June election, the Christian Democratic leader, Giulio Andreotti, formed a government of "national solidarity" that relied on the communists to make the internationally demanded austerity policy "socially acceptable."[7] The Communist Party leader, Emilio Berlinguer, embraced what he described as the "ideology of austerity" in the hope of leading the nation out of its financial crisis. After the passage of deflationary measures in the fall of 1976 that were estimated to reduce domestic demand by 3 percent of GDP, the leading Italian industry and labor groups signed a "social compact" in January 1977 that began to restrict the use of the *scala mobile* and marginally boost labor mobility within firms. The social compact marked a turning point in Italian politics. From then on, labor was on the defensive. With the support of the communists and over the objections of many Italian unions, the government reached an agreement in 1977 with the IMF on cutbacks in public spending and domestic consumption.[8]

The disruptive legacy of austerity in Western democracies reinforced socialist governments' reluctance to implement restrictive policies. For Erich Honecker and János Kádár, it also pointed the way to how their regimes could lay claim to superiority over their Western rivals. Austerity, they believed, was for capitalists whose system was evidently failing. Socialist countries, by contrast, had to appear as lands of economic serenity. "Many people admire the GDR," Honecker told a meeting of East German officials in November 1976 as the crises in London and Rome were unfolding. "Under capitalism there is the path of deflation or inflation. We don't use either one. We go the way of methodical, proportional development of the economy to ever higher levels." Any economic reform must be sure not to "break the backs of the workers," he told his comrades.[9] In a Hungarian Politburo meeting the same month, financial officials warned the country's rapid debt buildup from 1974 to 1976 might not be sustainable without revisions to the national plan. Kádár, however, remained committed to the necessity of raising workers' standard of living. After a pause in the increase in real wages in 1976, Kádár returned the country to a 3.5–4 percent increase in 1977. The debt, in turn, increased apace.[10]

After the price increase debacle of 1976 in Poland, Edward Gierek undertook what he termed an "economic maneuver," which would supposedly lower the nation's debt to the West without lowering domestic standards of living by cutting back investment instead. Polish rates of investment were extremely high, so there was room for restriction, but unless the remaining investment was used more effectively, the new policy would only worsen the long-term debt picture by lowering future economic growth. Polish officials were well aware of this, but like their counterparts in both East and West, they chose the policy that guaranteed present social stability, no matter the long-term consequences.[11] In March 1977, financial officials within the Polish Central Committee warned, "The level of Poland's indebtedness to capitalist countries at the turn of 1976/1977 should be seen as the maximum. Its further growth threatens to negatively impact Poland's socio-economic development throughout the current five year plan."[12] But the political mandates of the moment prevailed over the economic concerns of future years. As long as the nation could borrow money and import subsidized Soviet resources, political expediency would be the order of the day.

By the spring of 1977, the gap in East Germany between the political priorities of the party and the economic capacities of the state had grown so large that the chairman of the State Planning Commission, Gerhard Schürer, and the party's economic leader, Günter Mittag, wrote a secret letter to Honecker pleading for an adjustment. "For the first time we are experiencing acute payment difficulties," they wrote in March 1977. "The hard currency income from our exports . . . is already insufficient to finance new imports." The recurrent fear since the first moments of the oil crisis that credit would suddenly become unavailable was once again at the forefront of their minds. To ward off the threat of looming insolvency, the two men urged their boss to undertake an immediate export offensive and restriction of imports.[13]

Honecker took their warning as a personal affront. Referring to his cherished Unity of Economic and Social Policy, he scolded his two deputies in a face-to-face meeting.[14] Social and price stability were the hallmark advantages of socialism over capitalism, and Honecker was not about to give them up. In describing the Schürer/Mittag proposal later that year, he told the Central Committee the two men had "submitted a plan which would not allow for the continuation of the social policy program. But the path of restriction is not possible." Under such "capitalist conditions," he said, "we would have great complications."[15] Chastened by the browbeating, the two men beat a hasty retreat, and the challenge of asking the nation to sacrifice was delayed another day.[16] In its place, the nation's bankers returned to the Euromarkets to continue financing real existing socialism on credit. They could only hope the days of easy money would not soon run out.

Lucky for them, 1976 was a "vintage year" for the socialist states on the Euromarkets, as *Euromoney* termed it, and all indications were that 1977 would be the same.[17] So long as Western capital and Soviet oil kept flowing freely, the day of reckoning could continue to be deferred. For the moment, state socialism had defied the laws of economic gravity that dragged the rest of the industrialized world down. But in 1977, cracks in the foundation of Soviet oil production signaled that the reckoning would not be long in coming.

. . .

"The Soviet oil industry is in trouble." So began a bombshell March 1977 report from the Central Intelligence Agency titled "The Impending Soviet Oil Crisis." The CIA kept close tabs on the industry that formed the economic base of Soviet power, and they now projected that Soviet oil production would "soon peak, possibly as early as next year and certainly no later than the early 1980s." Soon after that, they augured, the decline in production would be "sharp." The giant Samotlor oil field in western Siberia, which had accounted for most of the growth in Soviet oil production since the late 1960s, was projected to reach peak production by 1978 and maintain that level for only four years. The country had large amounts of coal and natural gas that could compensate for the drop-off in oil, but, the agency noted, these were "east of the Urals," so "distance, climate, and terrain will make exploitation and transport difficult and expensive."[18]

Taken together, the picture was bleak and the repercussions "profound." With plateauing oil production, the Soviet Union would "find it extremely difficult," the agency concluded, "to continue to simultaneously meet its own requirements and those of Eastern Europe while exporting to non-Communist countries on the present scale." These were "important considerations" for the leadership in Moscow because the Kremlin currently supplied three-quarters of Eastern Europe's oil, and "it undoubtedly wishes to retain the political and economic leverage that goes with being their principal supplier." At the same time, however, oil exports to noncommunist countries were "the USSR's largest single source of hard currency."[19] Thus, as the Soviet Union's era of exceptional oil growth came to end, fundamental political choices awaited Leonid Brezhnev in Moscow.

The CIA's timing was impeccable. At the very moment the report was published, the Soviet government was itself grappling with the knowledge that its oil production might soon begin to decline. As early as 1973, Soviet oil specialists had been warning the political leadership that the western Siberian oil boom was temporary and would not provide a basis for growth after 1980. General Secretary Brezhnev had rebuffed the warning signs even as Prime Minister Alexei Kosygin began to call for greater oil and gas conservation in the mid-1970s. By the end of 1977, the signs of impending crisis forced action, and Brezhnev decided on emergency changes to the five-year plan to redirect investment to the oil industry to ensure the output targets through 1980 were met. This bought the country some time and prevented the CIA's prediction of plateau and decline from coming to fruition, but it did so at significant costs to the efficiency of the oil industry and the productivity of the rest of the economy, which lost out on precious investment resources.

Even with the emergency investment plan, the challenge of energy stagnation after 1980 remained unsolved. A fierce debate broke out within the Soviet leadership around how to rectify it, but all sides agreed on two things: the future would not be like the past, and the time of energy abundance had come to an end.[20] As a Soviet official told his East German counterpart in early 1978, "The question of raw materials is very difficult. . . . As of today . . . one cannot expect an increase in oil resources. There are also comrades in our country who cannot believe it. We had grown accustomed to having an increase of around 100 million tons of oil in each five-year-plan and not 0% growth, as it will be for the five-year-plan from 1981–1985."[21]

As the CIA anticipated, the crisis had immediate effects on Moscow's relations with its allies. At a meeting of Comecon ministers in June 1977, Premier Kosygin told a room full of officials hoping for increases in Soviet energy supplies that the growth of Soviet oil production after 1980 would be "considerably lower" than in the 1970s. The problems in the Soviet energy industry were numerous, Kosygin told the group, and under such conditions, the only answer for the bloc was to increase its energy efficiency. He framed the challenge as global in nature, one equally shared by East and West: "The fuel and energy problem is one of the sharpest problems of economic development in the world. All countries are looking for their solution by increasing the effectiveness of energy consumption through substantial savings of energy resources." To adapt to the new environment, the Soviet Union had made increasing its energy efficiency a priority as well.

The same could not be said, Kosygin believed, for the rest of the bloc. Satellite governments had put forth woefully inadequate plans to increase their energy efficiency. Given the wastefulness of the Soviet economy, this had more than a tinge of the pot calling the kettle black. Nevertheless,

Kosygin had come to the meeting to scold his allies into action. In preparation for the gathering, each nation had submitted projections of their energy needs out to 1990 to the leadership in Moscow. The resulting picture of the bloc's energy situation over the next decade was sorry indeed. "It is clear from these materials," Kosygin said, that "most countries are planning to increase the rate of growth in energy consumption over the period up to 1990." Though the allies collectively planned to increase their energy demand by 47 percent through 1990, they only planned to increase their energy production by 23 percent. To the Soviet leader, it was clear they planned to make up the difference "mainly by an increase in petroleum and gas supplies from the USSR." This, Kosygin firmly told them, was not possible. The numbers simply did not add up. When considered together, the Eastern Europeans were counting on a 74 percent increase in Soviet oil deliveries, a 130 percent increase in Soviet natural gas, and a 135 percent increase in Soviet electricity from 1980 to 1990. "We have made thorough calculations," Kosygin told his audience, and those calculations made clear that "energy supplies from the Soviet Union at such levels are not possible."

Soviet energy could no longer be the bloc's economic elixir. "The CMEA [Comecon] countries' fuel supply problem cannot be solved only through an increase in supplies from the Soviet Union," Kosygin said. Instead, each country would have to look inward, to their own economies, and figure out how to use resources more efficiently. "We must say," he concluded, "that so far this work is insufficiently accomplished in all Comecon countries, including the Soviet Union."[22]

The news that Soviet energy deliveries were likely to peak in 1980 sent shock waves through the bloc. For states whose economic growth depended on ever-increasing inputs of energy rather than the more efficient use of energy, Kosygin's message was nothing short of an existential threat. The GDR's reaction illustrates the broader bloc's dynamics. Throughout the 1970s, East German policy makers had closely linked the fate of their nation to the supply of Soviet raw materials. The changes in Comecon prices announced in 1974 had altered the price of these raw materials, but they had left their year-over-year growth rate untouched. Even at higher prices, it was clear to the leadership that the continued growth of Soviet resource deliveries was essential to their survival. "It was and is an invaluable advantage for our national economy," the State Planning Commission wrote in 1975, "that we import the majority of our raw materials from the socialist economic area, especially from the USSR, at long term contract rates that are below the capitalist world market price."[23] A year and a half later, as planners began to work on the 1980–1985 plan period, they returned to the fundamental importance of increasing Soviet deliveries. "The questions of covering [our] demand for raw materials and energy," planners wrote at the end of 1976, occupied "a central place" in the Soviet–East German relationship. The GDR would "continue to depend on growing imports for many energy sources and raw materials." Even under the country's plan to make "the most efficient use of fuels and energy," the planning commission stressed that "we need further increases in oil and natural gas supplies from the USSR." To that end, the policy makers asked that annual oil deliveries be raised from their 1980 level of 19 million tons to a level of 22 million tons by 1985 and 25 million tons by 1990. Similarly, they requested that annual natural gas deliveries be raised from the 1980 level of 6.5 billion cubic meters to 9 billion cubic meters in 1985 and 11 billion cubic meters in 1990.[24]

Kosygin's announcement in the summer of 1977 clearly threw a significant wrench in these plans. Without the increases in energy after 1980, the GDR would have two options: it could either figure out a way to use energy resources more efficiently or make up for the lost Soviet deliveries by taking out more debt from the West in order to purchase the raw materials on the world market. With regard to the first option, East German officials who studied the problem knew that despite the leadership's commitment to undertaking "great efforts" to save energy, their planned economy stood little chance of using energy more efficiently.[25] Even after domestic energy prices were raised in 1980, the basic structure of the planned economy led firms to hoard input materials, rather than try to save them.

At a loss over how to increase energy efficiency, officials quickly recognized they would have to make up for the shortfall in Soviet deliveries with imports from the West. This would, in turn, worsen their already serious sovereign debt problem. Indeed, this connection was so strong that East German officials began to quantify the link between a decline in Soviet energy and raw materials and increasing hard currency imports from the West. First, they tallied the gains they had already received in the 1970s from the Soviet Union's patronage. In 1977, planners concluded (and underlined for emphasis), "If the GDR had been forced to buy the amount of oil it received from the Soviet Union from 1974–1976 on the world market, it would have been forced to pay about 4.5 billion VM more than it paid the Soviet Union." Even that figure, the planners recognized, understated the benefit because rather than paying for the oil with hard currency, East Germany had been allowed to pay for the Soviet oil "with goods from the GDR, which as experience shows, would have been difficult to sell on the capitalist market."[26] In countless other areas like grain, natural gas, and steel, the planners well understood that Soviet price patronage had directly lowered the country's debt to the West. As high as the debt was, it was clear it would only have been higher without Soviet raw materials.

This was a point East German officials tried to make over and over to their Soviet counterparts in the late 1970s. After numerous conversations in 1977 in which the Soviet side emphasized that there could be no increase in deliveries after 1980, East German officials opened 1978 by stressing that Soviet shortfalls would only drive them further into the arms of the West. After being told, yet again, in a February 1978 meeting that increases were not possible, a member of the State Planning Commission told his Soviet counterpart that if "the supplies of the USSR cannot be increased," the GDR "would have to buy the raw materials in the West."[27]

This back and forth continued between the two sides until October 1978, when Kosygin informed his East German comrades that rather than level off their deliveries after 1980, the Soviet Union would, in fact, have to cut them back. The East Germans were furious. They immediately told him such a decision would either "call into question" the economic development of the GDR or force the country to carry out "a politically and economically unacceptable increase in hard currency imports." In response, Kosygin told them that Soviet deliveries had given the GDR the luxury of being "largely independent from raw material imports from capitalist countries." Because the development of raw materials in the Soviet Union had become "increasingly difficult and expensive," it was a luxury the bloc could no longer afford.[28]

Back in East Berlin, planners quickly calculated that the Soviet decision to cut back deliveries would lead to VM 10.7 billion more in imports (and debt) from the West.[29] Such an alarming number meant the time had come to take their case to the highest court. In late 1978, Honecker made a direct appeal to Brezhnev to hold energy and raw materials at their 1980 level during the next five-year plan. By the time East German premier Willi Stoph returned to Moscow in December to meet with his old friend and comrade Kosygin, Honecker's appeal had worked. Kosygin announced that the 1980 levels would be maintained because "Comrade Brezhnev has decided to find possibilities to help the GDR in this matter."[30]

The announcement removed a contentious issue from the agenda but left a simmering tension between the two sides that boiled over in the remainder of the meeting. Socialist solidarity could no longer mask the widely divergent economic interests of the allies. Kosygin launched into an extended tirade about how easy the GDR had it in the grand scheme of the global economy. "I would like to . . . say that the entire economy of the GDR is in a rather privileged position," the Soviet premier said. "You will not think about that sometimes, but I would like to remind you of it." Posing what he termed "a foundational question for the entire economy," Kosygin asked: "Where can you find, Comrade Stoph, such a situation in the world, where oil and also natural gas come by pipelines practically to your front door?" Pushing the thought further, he said, "The economy of [your] country is in paradise. The GDR [is] in a much better and more privileged position than the economy of Italy, France, or the Federal Republic." Stoph shot back angrily, "What do you mean Italy, France, and the Federal Republic? We're not them at all. We are the GDR!" Kosygin responded, "I understand that you are not Italy or France. But very often you hear—'We have different conditions.'" On the question of energy, this was not so. Every country, whether capitalist or communist, now had to use energy more efficiently.[31]

As Stoph left Moscow, the worst-case scenario had been averted. The Soviet leadership had committed to maintaining deliveries at the 1980 level for the 1981–1985 period. But there were few reasons for optimism. The basic dilemma remained the same—either the GDR could achieve radical advances in energy efficiency or it would have to increase its Western imports and debt. In 1979, the State Planning Commission tried to formulate a realistic estimate of how the burden of stagnating Soviet supplies would be split between these two elements. The results were a lopsided reflection of the problems with the planned economy. Frozen at their 1980 levels, Soviet oil deliveries to the GDR from 1981 to 1985 would be 19.5 million tons below what the GDR had planned. Of these 19.5 million tons, planners believed only 3.8 million could be saved through increased efficiency. That meant 15.7 million tons of oil, worth about $3.2 billion, would have to be imported from the West for hard currency.[32] More borrowing clearly would be required.

But just as Soviet stagnation was increasing the GDR's demand for Western loans, warning signs were appearing in the West that financial markets' confidence in the Socialist Bloc was wearing thin. While officials from the State Planning Commission were busy shuttling back and forth to

Moscow to try and secure more Soviet oil, officials from the East German Foreign Trade Bank were making the rounds in the nerve centers of global capitalism to secure more Western loans. In May 1978, the president of the bank, Werner Polze, made a two-week trip around North America to drum up support for a new round of credits. Upon his return, Polze filed an ominous report. Many bankers had told him that there was "now no absolute confidence in the future repayment capacity of the socialist countries." Western bankers could see that the situation was starting to become untenable. "The question was continuously raised," Polze reported, of how the GDR planned to "balance its trade and payments accounts" in the face of "considerably higher import prices, poor export opportunities to capitalist markets . . . and the stable domestic price level, which leads to constantly increasing domestic demand." The same questions could have been (and surely were) asked of all bloc countries.[33]

In the eyes of Western banks, the most pressing problem was Poland. Since the aborted 1976 price hikes, the country's debt had continued to rise at a torrid pace. Polish officials, led by Jan Wołoszyn, had returned to the Euromarkets over and over again. By the fall of 1978, this search for Western capital led them to announce that they would seek to organize a $500 million loan on the Euromarkets, an unprecedented and shocking amount for a socialist country. Polish officials tried to minimize the growing financial difficulties in public, but in private, the truth was plain enough to see.[34] Just as Poland was getting set to announce its new loan, Polze returned to the West to once more test the waters for East German credit. In meetings in London, "the question of socialist countries' debt again played a clear role in the negotiations," he reported. "Almost all banks emphasized that Poland's frequent appearance in the market had led to a certain distrust of granting further credit to the Poles." In the shadow of Warsaw's spiraling financial needs, the banks "warned [against] a country or a bank entering the market for finance loans too often."[35]

Thus, with Soviet raw material deliveries about to level off and Western financial confidence hanging by a thread, the task confronting all Eastern Bloc countries at the dawn of 1979 was daunting. Perhaps best summed up by the East German State Planning Commission that summer, "the basic problem" for their economies was that "despite the fraught task of increasing performance under extremely limited commodity supplies" and despite efforts to raise exports and lower imports from the world market, "a significant unresolved financial deficit . . . remains."[36] The "unresolved financial deficits" in different bloc countries varied in magnitude, but the basic problem was the same. Try as they might to cut their dependence on Western capital, policy makers in East Berlin, Budapest, and Warsaw remained more dependent than ever on the financial markets of the West to finance their societies. Moscow could no longer be relied on to shield the bloc from the world economy. The times were changing, as Brezhnev demonstratively told Honecker in the fall of 1979. Pounding his fist on the table during a meeting with the entire East German Politburo in East Berlin, the Soviet general secretary declared, "Those who say that you can only consume what you produce are correct." In a thinly veiled warning, he continued, "None of us wants to live at the expense of others or declare ourselves bankrupt."[37]

Only the US Federal Reserve could tip the scales and turn this array of warning signs into a full-blown crisis. As Fed chairman Paul Volcker would one day say of the US dollar, "Our money is the world's money."[38] So long as the Fed, the engine of global monetary creation, kept real interest rates low and US dollars flowing easily around the world, socialist governments would be able to retain their veneer of tranquility amid the choppy waters of the world market. A shining example of this fact came in the spring of 1979, when, despite their profound misgivings about the Polish economy, Western bankers pooled their capital together and granted the Polish request for the $500 million loan anyway.[39]

But if events ever conspired to force the Fed to change its policy and restrict the easy flow of capital around the world, the bloc would be exposed to the crisis it had fought to avoid since 1973. It was a frightening prospect, but as late as 1979, it also remained an unlikely one. A significant increase in the Federal Reserve's interest rates would surely bring austerity to the United States, and just like the communist states of Eastern Europe, the American government had shown little inclination and no ability to impose austerity on its own people in the 1970s. By the end of the decade, most American officials had come to question whether their democracy would ever be able to solve the country's riddle of austerity. Inflation, the telltale sign of too many promises chasing too few goods, was running at 13 percent in 1979 and showing no sign of slowing down. "Can a democracy discipline itself?" Alfred Kahn, a prominent American economist and advisor to US president Jimmy Carter, weightily asked in the late 1970s.[40] The answer would have implications on both sides of the Iron Curtain.

◆ ◆ ◆

In the fall of 1978, the future of the US dollar hung in the balance. After menacing Great Britain and Italy with currency crises in 1976, international capital holders had turned their attention to the United States and forced the dollar to severely depreciate against the Japanese yen and the deutsch mark from September 1977 to October 1978. As with the more acute crises in London and Rome, capital holders' departure from the dollar signaled their doubts about the long-term viability of the US economy. After declining to 4.9 percent at the end of 1976, inflation had risen back to 9 percent by 1978, which led capital holders to worry that the future value of their US dollar holdings would be frittered away over time.[41] Their departure from the currency sent policy makers across the West scrambling to support the dollar in foreign exchange markets. Over the course of 1978, the Federal Reserve gradually raised interest rates from 6.5 percent to 9.5 percent, but these moves barely brought interest rates in line with inflation. It was clear more aid would be needed, so on November 1, Western central banks unveiled a dollar "rescue package" aimed at saving the currency. For a time, the coordinated efforts worked, and the dollar stabilized at the end of the year. But for everyone involved, the crisis was a wake-up call and a harbinger of the far-reaching crisis that would come if American domestic policy did not soon change.[42]

The dawn of 1979 brought renewed challenges, as the crescendo of revolution in Iran led to the ouster of the shah, Mohammed Reza Pahlavi, in January and a wave of uncertainty on world oil markets. Iran, the world's second-largest oil producer, had stopped exporting oil in December 1978, and the social instability that followed the shah's departure provided reason to think those exports would not return anytime soon. Panic ensued, and OPEC members took the opportunity to engineer another massive increase in oil prices. From December 1978 to December 1979, crude oil prices rose 150 percent, this time from thirteen dollars a barrel to more than thirty. Gas prices within the US climbed 55 percent in the first half of 1979, and inflation quickly followed suit, rising to 13.4 percent. If it was allowed to continue to rise, there was no telling when international capital holders might again lose confidence in the United States and precipitate another run on the currency.[43]

Thus, like the pressure they had applied to many smaller governments since 1973, oil and capital markets conspired in the spring of 1979 to put pressure on Washington, DC to implement austerity. The question, as always, was how to make this policy socially acceptable to the domestic population. The administration of Jimmy Carter thought about the challenge in precisely these terms. "How best to sell publicly a policy of long-term economic austerity" read the cover sheet of a memo sent from Treasury Secretary Michael Blumenthal to President Carter in the spring of 1979. Blumenthal considered the "continuation of tough and austere macroeconomic policies requiring sacrifices by many" to be "the only viable course" for the nation going forward. However, this path would create "political dissatisfaction among a broad array of interest groups." Therefore, the administration would have to find a way to make austerity domestically palatable. "I freely concede," Blumenthal wrote, "that this is no easy task." To be successful, Blumenthal believed, a program of austerity needed "an overarching theme that engages the imagination and deep convictions of the people." Carter would have to tell the nation that "as individuals, a national economy, and as a government, we have been borrowing and consuming—living off deficits in our personal, governmental and trade accounts." The message had to be, "We can no longer afford this." In order to return the United States to its former economic preeminence, Carter would have to tell the country, "We must now sacrifice and rebuild."[44]

For Carter, the question of how to regain control of the country's economic fortunes quite literally produced a period of deep soul-searching. For ten days in the summer of 1979, he withdrew to Camp David, the presidential retreat in the foothills of Maryland. There he discussed the nation's dilemmas with a wide array of experts and considered his own journey to that point. He was a Democrat who had risen to the presidency in 1976 on promises of enacting full-employment legislation, fiscal stimulus, and labor law reform to strengthen the bargaining power of unions. And yet circumstances now appeared to dictate that he transgress the interests of the constituents who had elected him. There were three options for controlling inflation—cutting government spending, inducing wage restraint through negotiations with the nation's labor unions, and tightening monetary policy. At various points during his first two and a half years in office, he had half-heartedly tried all three. But the challenge remained undiminished. Indeed, with Americans now waiting in lines at gas stations across the country, inflation running at 13 percent, and GDP contracting at a rate of 3 percent in the second quarter of 1979, the task of steadying the American economy amid the volatility of the world market appeared more intractable than ever before.

The crisis, Carter decided, was spiritual. When he descended from the mountains of Maryland, he took to the nation's airwaves to tell Americans they were collectively experiencing "a crisis of confidence" in a nationally televised address. Amid a wide-ranging diagnosis of the nation's ills, the president told the nation that "too many of us now tend to worship self-indulgence and consumption."[45] Although he did not directly say it, the undertone of Carter's speech was a call for the nation to live within its means. Little did he know, it would be the exact message Brezhnev would deliver more bluntly to his East German comrades a few months later in East Berlin. A healthy nation could only consume what it produced—everybody could agree on that. Both sides in the Cold War believed they had consumed too much, both were distinctly aware of their dependence on global capital and foreign energy to fund their way of life, and both believed their time was running out. The question now was how to remedy these conditions.

Like Western European governments before him, Carter had come to believe that managing the relationship between business and labor held primacy of place. If unions could be made to moderate their wage demands, Carter and his advisors believed, the long road back to low inflation could slowly begin. To that end, in the summer of 1979, the president launched an initiative to bring business and labor together around a program to moderate wage growth. At the end of September, he signed a "national accord" with representatives of the American labor movement that aimed to ensure that "the austerity arising from battling inflation is fairly shared." Modeled on the social contracts that had been used in Western Europe to try and restrain real wage growth in the 1970s, the national accord was seen in its immediate aftermath as a decisive step in shifting the country to a more austere footing. As Jefferson Cowie has written of the accord, "It stood as an inverted homage to the triumphs of the thirties and forties. Rather than FDR's compact for working-class plenty, the accord looked to shared austerity to overcome political hostility."[46]

Rather less consequential in Carter's mind was the nation's monetary policy. In the days following the "crisis of confidence" speech, he shook up his cabinet and asked a number of people, including Treasury Secretary Blumenthal, to resign. He replaced Blumenthal with the current Fed chairman, William Miller, which left a vacancy at the helm of the central bank. Many names from the world of private business and banking were floated for the job, but Carter eventually settled on Paul Volcker, the head of the Federal Reserve Bank of New York. By all accounts, the president chose Volcker with little sense of his vision for monetary policy beyond a vague knowledge that he was "very tough on inflation."[47]

Carter was not alone in paying relatively little attention to monetary policy and the role of the Fed chairman. Most observers in the late 1970s believed there was little central banks could do to stem the tide of inflation in the face of the well-entrenched habits of postwar democratic governance. The politics of the welfare state simply would not allow it. None other than a former chairman of the Federal Reserve, Arthur Burns, proclaimed as much in a speech to global financial elites in the fall of 1979. Over the course of the postwar period, he said, "rising economic expectations, wider citizen participation in the political arena, and governmental commitment to full employment" had driven governments across the West to perpetually promise more than their economies could deliver. "Once it was established that the key function of government was to solve problems and relieve hardships . . . a great and growing body of problems and hardships became candidates for governmental solutions." In such an environment, Burns concluded, central banks "will be able to cope only marginally with the inflation of our times."[48]

Volcker understood the purpose and power of his new office very differently. Inflation, he believed, was a product of people's expectations about the economy. By 1979, rising prices had become such a standard part of life people had begun to factor them into their behavior. Workers asked for higher wages, consumers borrowed more money, the government ran a larger deficit, and speculators bet against the US dollar because they universally accepted it as fact that US dollars would be worth less tomorrow than they were today. These actions, in turn, produced a self-fulfilling prophecy; they created the very inflation they anticipated. Higher wages, higher borrowing, and higher government spending increased the demand for goods, and prices inevitably rose as a result. Therefore, if inflation was to be vanquished, Volcker believed that expectations would have to be altered.

To alter expectations, one first had to understand them. Where did they come from? What assumptions underlay the universal confidence that inflation would always continue? The answer was, in short, the politics of making promises. If inflation was an inherently political phenomenon, then inflationary expectations were, by definition, assumptions about politics. They signaled widely shared and unconsciously held beliefs about what society and government valued. By 1979, people had come to believe instinctively what intellectuals in the West had been writing since the mid-1970s: the government—and, by extension, its central bank—was incapable of breaking its promises and imposing economic discipline. For reasons of public morality and electoral expediency, governments were unable to turn a blind eye to the fates of their constituents. Given the choice between preventing unemployment and fighting inflation, postwar governments had always chosen to prevent unemployment, and there was no reason to think they would not continue to do so.

Volcker believed he had to change precisely this line of thinking. He and the Federal Reserve had to convince the country and the world that they were willing to let Americans suffer economic hardship. As he privately told his colleagues at the Federal Reserve in 1980, "When we take on this inflation fighting job . . . we should not look around for much of a constituency. If we . . . go to the brink or let some . . . things happen that we have not allowed to happen during the entire postwar period, people . . . are not going to be very happy." But, he said, they could not "change inflationary expectations without it happening." To illustrate the point, he recounted a recent conversation he had had with a banker in Chicago. The banker, when pressed on why his bank was aggressively expanding despite the poor economic conditions, responded, "If we get in trouble, the government will protect us." If there was "a real problem in the economy," Volcker concluded, people thought the Fed was always "going to give way."[49]

Thus, changing inflationary expectations entailed nothing short of changing citizens' assumptions about what they could expect from their government. It was the most political of tasks. Inflation would end once people believed that the Federal Reserve cared more about price stability than it did about full employment or economic growth. The United States government's commitment to breaking promises had to become credible.

If that was the end goal, what were the means by which it could possibly be achieved? As Volcker told his colleagues, it was a task that would invite intense political backlash. During any economic downturn, the popularity of political leadership suffers because people expect the government to do something to fix it. Austerity was different because the source of the economic pain was the government itself. In the Federal Reserve's case, every time it voted to raise interest rates, it would look like (and it would indeed be) a conscious decision to inflict economic pain on the American people. With inflation running at 13 percent and inflationary expectations firmly entrenched, no one at the Federal Reserve knew how high they would have to raise rates or how long they would have to keep them elevated in order to get people to believe they really were comfortable inflicting pain on American society. All they knew was that every one of their decisions would create a political blowback.

It was best, then, to minimize the number of decisions they had to make. Monetarism, the school of economics promoted in the 1970s by University of Chicago economist Milton Friedman, posited that the sole responsibility of a central bank was to ensure a constant annual rate of growth in a nation's money supply. Friedman held little faith in the powers of central bankers to accurately understand the economy, so he argued they should give up trying to influence it. The Federal Reserve should simply set a simple target for annual monetary growth—3 percent was Friedman's ideal—and call it a day.

Volcker, and most of the other members of the Federal Reserve, found the economic fundamentals of monetarism to be woefully simplistic. The idea that monetary policy was as easy as setting an annual target offended both their self-regard and their life experience. But in the face of the horrendous politics of the anti-inflation fight, Volcker became attracted to monetarism because it offered an escape from political culpability. If, under monetarism, the Fed could simply commit to growing the monetary supply at a constant low rate, then the dramatic increases in interest rates that would inevitably result would appear to the public not as active and mean-spirited decisions of the Fed but rather as unfortunate by-products of market forces. President Carter's chief economist, Charles Schultze, said of Volcker's embrace of monetarism, "This whole move was, in the broadest sense, a political move, not an economic move. In theory, the Fed could have kept on raising the bejesus out of the interest rates, but that's what it couldn't do politically. The beautiful thing about this new policy was that as interest rates kept going up, the Fed could say . . . 'We're not raising rates, we're only targeting the money supply.' This way they could raise rates and nobody could blame them."[50]

For his first month on the job, however, Volcker found most of his colleagues at the Fed leery of both monetarism and higher interest rates. At a meeting on September 18, 1979, the Federal Reserve Board publicly split its vote 4–3 on whether to raise the discount interest rate it charged to US banks. The interest rate was raised, but because the board normally reached decisions by consensus, the public dissent appeared to signal to the market that the effort to implement a more restrictive monetary policy would eventually fail. Faced with a political system that appeared unable to implement austerity, speculators did what they always did: sold the currency in question. In the weeks following the September split decision, markets lost confidence in Volcker's ability to control inflation, and a second run on the dollar began. The price of gold soared more than $25 in a day, and by early October, it reached $442 an ounce. "There was a genuine flight from the currency," Fed vice chairman Fred Schultz recalled. At the Fed, the need for radical change now beckoned.[51]

On Saturday, October 6, Volcker called a secret emergency meeting of the Federal Open Market Committee, the Fed's main governing body, and gained its assent for the switch to monetarism. The recent wild speculation in the markets had convinced previous doubters that change was needed. The implications of their decision were clear to everyone who gathered around the table. "There wasn't any question that the board knew that recession would follow" the vote, Federal Reserve governor Phillip Coldwell recalled.[52]

At a press conference that evening, Volcker announced the change in policy. A reporter asked him if the new policy meant the federal funds rate would be "completely free to go as high as it might." The Fed chairman responded, "I don't know what you think is as high as it might. There will be substantial freedom in the market."[53] The fate of the nation, Volcker now told Americans, rested in the hands of the marketplace. This was not actually true, of course. By controlling the money supply, Volcker was still controlling the total amount of liquidity in the system and thus controlling interest rates, growth, and employment. But the language of monetarism had now given him a way to shift responsibility for policy outcomes to the market.

The effects of Volcker's actions were hardly limited by national borders or ideological boundaries. Across the Iron Curtain, bankers and policy makers in the communist world watched as their last lifeline of external support begin to slip away. On October 25, three weeks after Volcker's decision, Horst Kaminsky, the president of the East German State Bank, wrote in a memo to Günter Mittag, "Recently a dramatic increase in interest rates has commenced on the capitalist financial and credit markets. The current interest rate on the Euromarket stands at about 16%. Further increases in the coming weeks cannot be ruled out."[54]

Two weeks after Kaminsky's warning, an event halfway around the world that had nothing to do with the Cold War, socialism, or even finance caused the Eastern Bloc's financial predicament to go from bad to worse. On November 4, 1979, Iranian students stormed the American embassy in Tehran and took fifty-two Americans hostage. Ten days later, the Carter administration responded by freezing all Iranian assets in US banks: roughly $11 billion at the time. As the diplomatic crisis between Tehran and Washington played out over the next year, the frozen Iranian assets caused significant uncertainty in the international financial community and further limited its willingness to lend to socialist states.[55]

The Soviet Union itself then hammered the final nail into the coffin of the Eastern Bloc's access to Western capital. At the end of December 1979, Soviet forces invaded Afghanistan, and President Carter responded by placing a grain embargo on the Soviet Union and asking all US banks to review their credit policies toward the Eastern Bloc. He also announced a new US defense posture in the Middle East, dubbed the Carter Doctrine, and requested corresponding increases in the US military budget. The renewal of superpower tensions over Afghanistan destroyed the last semblance of normalcy for socialist borrowing on the Euromarkets. In early February, Polze and Kaminsky produced a new confidential report, which began, "The situation on the international finance and credit markets . . . has significantly tightened in the last few weeks." Because of "the uncertainty arising from the blockade of Iranian assets in the USA" and the US government's "blackmail" (*Erpressung*) against the Soviet Union in response to Afghanistan, banks "temporarily could not grant any new loans" or were "demanding higher credit costs due to the increasing risk." Leading capitalist banks believed, Polze and Kaminsky wrote, that "credit granted to socialist countries in the future would be considerably restricted." The "arms buildup in the USA and other imperialist states" in response to the Soviet invasion of Afghanistan, they noted, would "lead to interest rate increases in the future" because it would force Western governments to borrow and spend more money. Thus, they concluded, "a decline in the high interest rates can hardly be expected in 1980."[56]

The arrival of spring brought no change. As always, the telltale sign of market sentiment was Poland. Since the June 1976 price increases, Gierek had avoided, at all costs, asking Polish citizens to sacrifice, but he could avoid it no longer. At the end of May 1980, the Polish State Planning Commission urgently warned the party leadership that the "conditions for implementing the national plan" had "deteriorated markedly." They wrote, "Notably, the payment situation has worsened" because of "credit difficulties." The "main problem" was "the issue of obtaining financial loans for the purchase of raw materials." Even for the loans they did receive, the interest rate had "greatly increased, at times exceeding 20%." These conditions led the commission to project a financing shortfall for the remainder of the year of $4.1 billion. In order to compensate for this difference, the ministers proposed to increase exports to the West by about $3 billion and to restrict hard currency imports by $1–$1.5 billion. If these corrections could be achieved, the planners wrote, they would compensate for the current "deterioration in credit possibilities."[57] The challenge of breaking promises had now arrived in the Socialist Bloc.

Even in these first moments of the onrushing crisis, a decisive difference was already apparent between the neoliberal capitalism emerging in the West and the state socialism struggling to survive in the East. When contemplating the fate of democratic welfare states in the doldrums of the mid-1970s, Fred Hirsch had approvingly written of the capitalist system, "A great strength of liberal capitalism has been its ability to dispense with an explicit ethical standard for the distribution of awards. Justification is provided by the benign outcome of autonomous unregulated processes."[58] Under the postwar ethos of the welfare state, this "great strength" had been submerged under explicit government promises to distribute economic gains fairly and broadly throughout society.

Those promises were now being broken, and appeals to "the market" to justify the distribution of economic outcomes were returning to prominence. Volcker's fight against inflation had dispensed with Washington's commitment to full employment, and his embrace of monetarism had allowed the Fed (and the broader national government of which it was a part) to claim it was no longer responsible for social outcomes. Once more, American officials could say that markets were producing social outcomes, even if, in reality, they remained in full control of policy. As a member of the Fed put it, "Everyone could say: 'Look, no hands.'"[59]

Under state socialism, by contrast, the party's hands were in everything, and explicit ethical standards for the distribution of economic benefits formed the ideological foundation of the state. The communist parties of the Eastern Bloc had spent the entire postwar period purposefully creating states in which they were responsible for everyone's fate, and this would make their promises immensely more difficult to break.

CHAPTER 3

A Tale of Two Crises

BY THE LATE 1970s, the challenge of breaking promises could no longer be deferred in both East and West. As Paul Volcker began his monetary crusade against inflation in the United States, global markets pushed governments in the two economic laggards of Europe—Great Britain and Poland—to undertake their own fraught campaigns to remake the economic and social foundations of their countries. Within their respective blocs, Britain and Poland had taken on ignominious titles in the 1970s that reflected their hapless circumstance. In the West, "the British disease" had become shorthand for the profound problems of economic management afflicting democratic capitalism—low growth, high inflation, industrial strife, and high unemployment. In the East, "the Polish disease" had become a moniker for all that was wrong with state socialism—high sovereign debt, low export growth, and government subsidy of all manner of economic activity. The worst part about both diseases was that they appeared to be terminal. After the British and Polish populations rejected attempted reforms through popular protest in 1970, 1974, and 1976, most observers concluded that the national diseases were simply incurable on account of popular resistance to the necessary cures.

The fundamental challenge for British and Polish politicians, therefore, was not identifying the policy outlines of a cure—though that was fraught enough—but rather gaining the domestic political support to implement it. Under the leadership of Margaret Thatcher in Britain and Wojciech Jaruzelski in Poland, the question of popular support was definitively but divergently decided in the early 1980s. Thatcher received and maintained the support, or at least the acquiescence, of the British population as she implemented economic discipline, while Jaruzelski never received the same from the Polish population. This chapter seeks to explain these divergent outcomes, primarily through the story of John Hoskyns and Mieczysław Rakowski. Hoskyns and Rakowski, respectively, were two of Thatcher's and Jaruzelski's most important advisers, particularly on the issue of building popular support for economic reform. So through their stories, we can gain a broader understanding of the divergent histories of their countries during this period.[1]

As we have seen, many people in the West in the 1970s assumed that state socialism had a distinct advantage in imposing economic discipline precisely because popular support appeared to be an irrelevant factor in socialist authoritarian governance. If an iron fist was good for anything, it was thought, surely it was good for imposing unpopular solutions on a resistant domestic populace. Electoral democracies were assumed to be fatally flawed for precisely the opposite reason. How could democratically elected leaders ever hope to carry out unpopular economic policies in political systems where their power depended on gaining and maintaining the approbation of their people? As the Cold War transitioned from a race to make promises to a race to break promises in the 1970s, state socialism appeared, in this regard, to have the upper hand.

Thatcherism and the Polish Crisis turned this prevailing wisdom on its head. These two crises command our attention not merely as the most vibrant case studies of broader dynamics occurring throughout the East and West but also as events that changed the Cold War in a fundamental way. The course of events in Warsaw and London, in Gdańsk and Orgreave, demonstrated for policy makers around the world the merits and demerits of implementing the politics of breaking promises in democratic and anti-democratic political systems. They demonstrated the ways in which the potent combination of electoral democracy and neoliberal ideology could produce a stronger state than socialist authoritarianism in the era of breaking promises.

Margaret Thatcher was able to achieve what her Polish counterparts could not because of the manifold benefits multiparty democratic elections and neoliberal ideology bestowed upon her government. Elections allowed her to credibly claim no responsibility for past government policy and instilled in most British people a confidence that their government was legitimate. Neoliberalism's embrace of individual freedom as the highest moral good and critique of government intervention in the economy provided an ideological framework that painted the politics of breaking promises in a virtuous light. To be sure, there were many people within Britain who despised Thatcher and all she stood for, but after 1979 they failed to win the hearts and minds of a national majority.

These points come into sharper relief when juxtaposed to the situation in Poland. Because Wojciech Jaruzelski sat atop an antidemocratic state and a Communist Party that monopolized power, he could not credibly distance himself from past policy, rely on popular belief in his legitimacy, or gain society's trust. Because he led a Communist Party that proudly proclaimed its control over society and the economy, he struggled to frame the politics of breaking promises in propitious ideological terms. The fundamental roadblock standing in the way of reform was also the reason Solidarity garnered widespread national support: most people believed they lived in an unjust society under the rule of an illegitimate government and therefore did not trust the Communist Party to carry out economic reform. Despite Jaruzelski's numerous efforts to overturn these beliefs, it became clear in the crucible of crisis that he could not do so without liquidating the communist state itself. So he chose martial law instead. As Britain returned to growth under Thatcherism and Poland faltered under martial law during the rest of the 1980s, the lessons for the world were clear enough: the politics of breaking promises worked best when citizens viewed their government as legitimate and when governments found an ideological basis for defining austerity as virtuous. These lessons would redound in their effects all the way to the revolutions of 1989.

◆ ◆ ◆

As the economic fate of both Poland and Britain faltered in the 1970s, the fraught prospects of reform became the subject of a broad and diverse national debate. Countless economists, policy makers, and public intellectuals proposed ways of reversing national decline, but it was John Hoskyns in Britain and Mieczysław Rakowski in Poland who rose above the general din of the debate to fundamentally influence the course of their nations. Both men had spent their lives in a profession other than politics—Hoskyns had built a successful career in business as the CEO of a computer company, and Rakowski was the longtime editor of the reformist weekly Polish newspaper *Polityka*. But because their ideas offered persuasive ways of overcoming the nations' crises, they became influential advisors to Thatcher and Jaruzelski as their governments tried to implement economic discipline.[2]

By his own admission a man of mixed political allegiance (he had voted Labour through the 1970 election), Hoskyns's engagement with British politics grew in equal measure with his dismay over the political system's failure to fix the British economy. After watching Edward Heath's government fall in the 1974 election, caused by the powerful National Union of Mineworkers (NUM) strike, he became convinced the key to solving all of Britain's economic problems lay in breaking the power of the country's trade unions to resist economic discipline. With this conviction, he went in search of a political party.

The choice was not as clear at the time as it appears in retrospect. Both the Labour and Conservative Parties had followed the same broad Keynesian consensus throughout the postwar period, and their trade union policy varied between the confined limits of outright support and quiet accommodation. Neither party stood against trade union interests because neither believed the trade unions could be defeated. Indeed, it was assumed across the political spectrum that Britain could only be governed with the permission of organized labor. The fall of the Heath government appeared to be proof that any policy that transgressed the interests of the working class would not only fail but would also bring down the government that proposed it. As Thatcher herself recounted in her memoirs, for most of the 1970s, "the conventional wisdom was that Britain could only be governed with the consent of the trade unions. No government could really resist, still less defeat, a major strike."[3]

Thatcher, of course, shared the broad outlines of Hoskyns's view, and thus it was in her ascendant radical wing of the Conservative Party that Hoskyns found a home. In the wake of the 1974 Heath defeat, Thatcher and her closest political ally, Keith Joseph, set up a think tank, the Centre for Policy Studies (CPS), to transform the Tories' postwar policy of Keynesian economic management and trade union accommodation. The following year, she was elected party leader and became leader of the opposition in Parliament. Through Joseph, Hoskyns met Thatcher in the summer of 1976 and joined the ranks of the CPS to study how the nation's economic decline could be reversed. As the country descended into the fraught politics and strict economics of the International Monetary Fund (IMF) crisis that fall, the time for fresh thinking about cures for the British disease was indeed propitious.

It did not take long to identify the root of the problem: policies that would solve the country's economic problems were politically impossible, and policies that were politically possible would not solve the country's economic problems. Thus, expanding the horizons of political possibility lay at the heart of any attempt at reform. In a June 1977 letter to Joseph, Hoskyns wrote that turning around the British economy would require "a complete change in the unions' role; a further fall in living standards; yet more unemployment (unless wages can fall further still)." This whole package was "obviously a political non-starter," and "the dilemma of government (of either party)" was therefore "absolute." A government could "either face up to the real measures which might just turn the economy around, but which are politically impossible: or it can select measures which, however sensible, cannot save the UK economy, but are at least politically permissible." The key question confronting the Tories, therefore, was political rather than economic. "What political innovation is needed to remove the political constraints on government's freedom to pursue such policies?" Hoskyns's letter asked.[4] It was the question that would define the Conservatives' time in opposition. In response to the letter, Joseph latched onto the theme of "political innovation" and discussed Hoskyns's views with Thatcher. Liking what she heard, Thatcher tasked Hoskyns and his collaborator, Norman Strauss, with developing their thoughts into "a coherent plan" to campaign and govern.[5]

The result was the *Stepping Stones* report of November 1977. Widely regarded as the blueprint for Thatcherism, the report had two objectives. First, it aimed to develop a communications strategy that would "begin the long process of convincing the public that radical change would have to come, that it would be pretty uncomfortable, and that the alternative would be something much worse."[6] The Tories needed to focus on "the selling of new policies" because "creating the necessary understanding of the need for reform" would ensure "that the reform itself did not provoke what many feared might be physical revolution."[7] Second, *Stepping Stones* aimed to unite the party itself around the set of policies that would need to be implemented to transform the economy. The array of policy changes was vast. The inflation rate, the exchange rate, interest rates, tax rates, nationalized industry policy, and public sector spending would have to be altered. But all of them revolved around the central and politically radio-active issue of trade union reform. Numerically, if not ideologically, the Tories were still dominated by politicians who believed the trade union issue should be left alone (in time, they would become known as the "wets"). Those, led by Thatcher, who favored tackling the issue head-on (later called the "dries") were a powerful minority, but a minority none-theless. Firmly uniting the party around a policy platform that included union reform was therefore essential.[8]

The *Stepping Stones* report fostered no illusions about the challenge that lay ahead. The task of the next government would be "of a different order" than that facing any other postwar government. Economic re-covery would require "a sea change in Britain's political economy." To achieve this sea change, a "landside" victory in the next election would not be enough if it only reflected "the electorate's material dissatisfaction." Instead, the electoral victory would have to represent "an explicit rejection of socialism" and "the demand for something morally and economically better." It had to produce a mandate to deal with the country's "one major obstacle—the negative role of trade unions." Gaining such a mandate would not be easy, but if the union question was "skillfully handled," the "rising tide of public feeling" could transform the issue from a political liability into a strength.[9]

How could the party effect such a dramatic change in public opinion? The report drew on theories of advertising to lay out nothing short of a grand theory of social change. First, it posited that "in politics, the party and its policies are all aspects of the 'Product,' which the voter, or the 'User,' buys with his vote." Each voter had a "Mental Set"—"a more or less stable set of opinions, values, interests and purposes"—they used to choose a Product, and as long as voters' Mental Sets remained unchanged, their behavior would "tend to be predicable and to follow a fixed pattern." Only "New Data"—new information about the Product's (or party's) function, effects, or psychological impact—could disrupt Users' Mental Sets and put them in a state of "Cognitive Dissonance," which Users would find stressful and attempt to resolve by changing their behavior. If enough voters reached a state of cognitive dissonance, the electorate would recog-nize that the country had reached "Discontinuity": "a point at which solu-tions to our problems simply could not be found without breaking constraints (either political or economic) which had previously been ac-cepted as unalterable 'facts of life.'"[10]

This was all a rather elaborate way of saying the Tories had to get people to change their minds on the issue of organized labor. But when taken out of the realm of jargon and made concrete, the scale of the challenge before them began to emerge. "There must be a national realization that the unions must modify their behavior so as to be less combative, more flexible and genuinely helpful," the report concluded. "We must ensure that [voters] feel an aversion to current union values. . . . They must be made to dislike them so intensely that their fear turns to anger."[11]

Although *Stepping Stones* serves as a convincing interpretation of how Thatcherism actually won popular support, it garnered only lukewarm support among the Tory leadership in late 1977 and 1978. Thatcher called it "the best thing we've had for many years" and ordered the formation of working groups to study how it could be implemented. But as those groups began their work in the spring of 1978, the career Tory politicians who had survived by not provoking conflict with the trade unions slowly buried the *Stepping Stones* agenda under deafening silence. Rather than strategically raising the issue in public forums in ways that would "invite" voters to reorganize their "Mental Sets," most of the party leadership relied on the tried-and-true method for dealing with uncomfortable topics: simply not talking about it.[12]

But if it was not a slick, strategic communications strategy that engineered a broad public recognition of "Discontinuity," what did? A more banal but also more effective cause was lurking in the wings—unforeseen events. In the summer of 1978, the Labour prime minister, James Callaghan, decided to delay the next election from the fall of 1978 to the spring of 1979. In the intervening months, Callaghan's IMF-sponsored "incomes policy," which mandated nationwide levels for annual pay increases as a means of fighting inflation, broke down under popular pressure, and trade unions of all stripes went on strike for higher wages. In what came to be known as the Winter of Discontent, British society virtually ceased to function in the months surrounding the turn from 1978 to 1979. Bernard Donoughue, a senior advisor to Callaghan, recalled:

> By the second week of January [1979] . . . there was a serious shortage of food and medical supplies—ministers considered sending tanks into the ICI medical headquarters to retrieve drugs and essential equipment. . . . The nightly television pictures of violence and the brutal face of trade unionism were doing terrible damage to the government and to the trade union movement itself.

. . . a million and a half public service workers went on strike, closing hospitals, schools and local authority services across the country. The railways came to a halt. . . .

NUPE [The National Union of Public Employees] publicly and without apology or sign of compassion announced that they would not allow the sick into hospital; and an official stood before the television cameras and stated that "if people died, so be it."[13]

The Winter of Discontent was, in the vibrant and depressing color of lived experience, precisely the "New Data" that *Stepping Stones* had called for. Britain arrived at a moment of "Discontinuity," and people immediately began to search for a way out of what had only recently seemed to be the unalterable facts of life. On January 18, 1979, Hoskyns recorded in his diary that "the party [is] in grip of mild euphoria, I think, because country beset by strikes. . . . Union issue is now top of the list."[14] At the end of March, Callaghan lost a vote of confidence in the House of Commons, which led to the first general election forced by the House of Commons since 1924. Just over a month later, on May 3, 1979, the Conservatives returned to government with a forty-three-seat majority, and Thatcher became prime minister with a mandate to fight inflation, limit public spending, and curb trade union power.

While Hoskyns was developing *Stepping Stones* in Britain, Mieczysław Rakowski was hard at work on reform plans for Poland. From his editorial perch at *Polityka,* Rakowski watched the 1970s unfold in a political and economic system both radically different and strikingly similar to the one in the United Kingdom. Where Edward Heath had fallen in 1974 after trying to impose discipline on British unions, Władysław Gomułka had fallen in 1970 after trying to impose discipline on Polish workers through consumer price increases. Like the Labour men who replaced Heath in Britain, the man who replaced Gomułka, Edward Gierek, legitimized his leadership after 1970 by championing rather than disciplining the interests of the Polish working class. Even the mid-decade crisis point in Poland arrived the same year as the IMF crisis in Britain.

This left the fundamental problem of Polish and British society in the late 1970s essentially the same: the political impossibility of economic reform. As in Britain, pressure to appease the working class had pushed wage increases in Poland during the first half of the 1970s far beyond increases in workers' productivity. This had left the Polish population with lots of money to spend and too little to spend it on. In Britain, where prices freely moved in response to market pressures, this monetary overhang manifested itself in crippling inflation. In Poland, where prices were administratively fixed, this overhang took the form of equally crippling shortages of consumer goods. Where Hoskyns and the Tories sought to solve this problem in Britain through monetarism, subsidy cuts to nationalized industries, and trade union discipline, policy makers in Poland sought similar solutions in price increases, enterprise independence, and campaigns to increase work discipline. In both countries, the results of these reforms would be significant declines in national living standards, bankruptcies of prized nationalized companies, and greater job insecurity for the working class. In both countries, then, the results would threaten political stability.

The question in Poland, as John Hoskyns might have posed it, was what political innovation would allow the government to pursue policies that were seen as economically necessary but politically unpopular. It was here that Rakowski emerged as an important voice on the Polish scene. Rakowski was not an economist, but he was an astute observer of the nation's politics. By the late 1970s, it had become clear to him that the government's future economic reform efforts would forever be crippled by two glaring weaknesses: its lack of legitimacy in the eyes of the Polish people and the population's consequent lack of trust in the government. Drawing attention to these weaknesses drove him in 1978 and 1979 to compose a book-length critique of communist leadership in the 1970s, *The Republic on the Threshold of the Eighties* (*Rzeczpospolita na progu lat osiemdziesiątych*).

After beginning the book with the requisite praise for the achievements of socialism in Poland, Rakowski quickly arrived at the problem that had motivated his work. By 1979, the economy had already been performing poorly for three years, and it was likely to show no significant improvement for at least two more. Half a decade would therefore be defined "by serious economic difficulties." Five years of troubles meant the country's economic problems "were no longer a trivial matter" and ensured that the country was "not only dealing with an economic problem but also with a political one."[15]

The country's economic problems had produced two worrying social phenomena. First, the Polish people increasingly viewed their society as an unjust one. "Many people are increasingly aware of the growing gap between their life situation" and the life situation of those who were "considered privileged in society," Rakowski wrote. Social policy had begun to depart from "the basic principles of social egalitarianism and the simplest principles of social justice." Second, a widespread distrust of the current government and the nation's Communist Party, the Polish United Workers' Party (known by its Polish acronym, PZPR), had taken hold in the population. As shortages of consumer goods and long queues at stores had become depressingly familiar in the late 1970s, the "accumulating difficulties of everyday life" had caused large sections of society to "lose confidence" in the party's constant declarations of socialism's benign advance.[16]

Because of these two trends, Rakowski feared that a "majority of society" did not believe in "the idea of jointly leading Poland out of the difficulties it had fallen into." As the party tried to "carry out large and not at all easy economic and social tasks" in the coming years, it would be forced to do so amid a deepening "crisis of public trust in our policy." If such an environment persisted, he wrote ominously and presciently, "the time may come when society, or some of its factions, will fiercely question our ability to take a leading role in framing the country's development directions." The consequences of such a development would be "tragic."[17]

In search of a way to prevent this looming tragedy, Rakowski then posed a very Hoskynsian question. "What then should be done to open the way out of the current, highly unfavorable situation?" he asked. He offered many answers, but they all centered around a common theme— indeed, around a political innovation: it was time for the PZPR to enter into a "partnership" with society to solve the nation's problems. Rakowski defined this partnership as an agreement between the PZPR and other societal forces that would establish the partners' "co-responsibility" for reform policies and "for the country's fate." The Catholic Church and the country's trade unions headlined the list of possible partners. The church was "one of the guarantors of peace in Poland," and the trade unions could "fulfill the role of an authentic intermediary between the working class and the centers of power." If both could be brought on as partners, Rakowski believed the party would benefit from a "real distribution of shared responsibility for the development of the country." But they had to act fast. Rakowski warned that inaction would bring even greater problems to the fore. If the party did not "meet the growing striving of society for real participation in government," Rakowski concluded, then "life will force us to do so anyway."[18]

However perceptive Rakowski's judgments appear in retrospect, they received no quarter in the Polish halls of power in 1979. Because of his book's extended criticism of the Communist Party, Rakowski could not find a publisher to print it, though he was allowed to circulate it among his friends and associates.[19] The economy contracted at a rate of 2 percent in 1979, and instead of confronting the mounting problems proactively, Gierek's party apparatus assumed a pose of political paralysis. Like the fate of *Stepping Stones* in Great Britain, it would take a moment of national crisis before Rakowski's views would receive full consideration. Only after a moment of "Discontinuity" would people (in this case, in the Communist Party) search for a way out of what had only recently seemed to be the unalterable "facts of life."

The moment of crisis was not long in coming. Shut out of global capital markets by the stinging combination of Volcker's interest rates, the Iranian hostage crisis, and the Soviet invasion of Afghanistan, Gierek's government attempted to raise food prices for the third time in a decade on July 1, 1980. Within three weeks, strikes consumed the nation's industrial centers. In mid-August, unrest returned to the Lenin Shipyard in Gdańsk, where activists made both economic and political demands, including the reinstatement of two workers who had been fired for union organizing. One of these workers, Lech Wałęsa, went on to lead the local strike committee and worked to unite the strikes under a single umbrella organization, the Inter-Factory Strike Committee. The speed and size of the protests overwhelmed the state systems of repression, and soon the newly united workers published a list of twenty-one demands to end the strikes. Sensing the weakness of its own position, Gierek's Politburo decided to negotiate with the strikers, and on August 31, the government and the fledgling opposition signed the Gdańsk Accords, which acknowledged the workers' rights to form independent trade unions, strike without reprisals, and express themselves freely in the public sphere. Similar agreements were signed in other parts of the country in the days that followed, and in mid-September, the workers joined their groups together into one national organization, the Independent Self-Governing Trade Union "Solidarność." Poland had arrived at its moment of discontinuity, and the national search for ways out of previously unalterable facts of life promptly commenced.

As in Britain, the first step in Poland was to throw out the leader who had steered the country into crisis. In early September, Gierek was swiftly deposed by his own Politburo in a desperate attempt by the party to distance itself from the policies of the 1970s. However, his replacement, Stanisław Kania, was almost equally implicated in the mistakes of the past, and few Poles looked upon his appointment as a fresh start. The latter months of 1980 produced further bouts of tension between the PZPR and its newfound opposition. In October, Solidarity organized a one-hour general strike to protest delays in the wage increases that had been promised at Gdańsk, which forced Kania to pledge adherence to the Accords the next day. In November, as the party dragged its feet on officially recognizing Solidarity's existence, the union leadership threatened another, longer general strike unless its registration went through. Again, the party caved. In December, workers in the city of Piotrków Trybunalski went on strike to protest a drop in their meat rations. The government said the economic crisis necessitated the meager rations, but as Rakowski had feared, the workers had lost all confidence in the credibility of government statements. Indeed, a widespread belief had taken hold that the party was purposefully manufacturing the economic crisis (including, it was believed, withholding food from the population) to discredit Solidarity in the eyes of society. Only when local officials agreed to allow Solidarity to supervise the food distribution system in the area did the workers return to their jobs.[20]

Upon such vacuous foundations of social trust, a program of economic reform and discipline could not be built. Rakowski, who had long believed this, viewed the strife of late 1980 as a chance to finally build support for his position. In November, he took to the pages of *Polityka* to advocate for a change in the party's course. Under the title "Credibility," he told the Polish people, "We are witnesses of the end of a certain era—the epoch of the PZPR autonomy. In place of autonomy, partnership enters as a prospect." The party's rule could no longer be based "on suspicion towards partners" because those potential partners now enjoyed "the support of major factions of society." The "decisive factor" in the creation of Solidarity had been "the tiredness of the working class and the whole society with [the party's] way of exercising power." If the PZPR wanted to continue to govern Poland, it first had to regain society's trust.[21]

Amid the crisis, these views at last caught the eye of a very important person, Wojciech Jaruzelski. As Kania's standing faltered in late 1980, Jaruzelski began to take on an expanded role in the party leadership. Already the head of the army and the defense minister in the fall of 1980, he became prime minister in February 1981. After reading Rakowski's articles throughout the fall of 1980, he asked Rakowski to send him his unpublished book manuscript. In his memoirs, the general recalls sharing Rakowski's conviction that Solidarity had to be viewed "as a valued partner" and believing that their views generally "corresponded."[22] As a result, he offered Rakowski the post of deputy prime minister for trade unions in his new government and charged him with implementing his vision of partnership between the PZPR and society. As in Britain, a moment of social crisis had brought about a change in government and in government thinking. What remained to be seen was whether the new governments and the new thinking could produce the unpopular change that had eluded all predecessors.

◆ ◆ ◆

The first year of the Thatcher revolution was, in fact, not much of a revolution at all. To resolve the labor disputes at the heart of the Winter of Discontent, the outgoing Labour government had granted a generous set of wage increases across the economy, and Thatcher chose not to spend her first moments in office refighting the labor battles that had won her Downing Street in the first place. In combination with the pressures produced by the second oil crisis, these wage increases only deepened the inflationary problem hanging over Britain. In addition, while Thatcher's first budget was certainly not a Keynesian spending spree, it nevertheless stimulated more than disciplined the economy through income tax cuts. The result was that by the fall of 1979 inflation was running at 17.4 percent, and the British welfare state and trade union system remained virtually untouched.[23]

It was left to those who controlled the printing presses to impose the discipline that Thatcher's cabinet avoided. Under Geoffrey Howe, the new chancellor of the Exchequer, the government adopted a monetarist policy aimed at breaking inflationary expectations among the population. Like Volcker in the United States, the government would now set a target for monetary growth every year and then adjust interest rates to meet that target. Theoretically, this meant the government put no cap on the interest rate levels it would set in pursuit of its monetary goals, but in practice it simply meant interest rates would go much higher than they ever had in the past. And go up they did. Howe raised rates from 12 to 14 percent in June 1979 and again from 14 to 17 percent in November. The toll on the economy quickly showed. The British pound sharply appreciated to an average value of $2.40 in the second half of 1980 (up from $1.57 in the depths of the IMF crisis), and the resulting competitive disadvantage for British industry on world markets led to massive layoffs in the private sector. Unemployment, which had numbered 1.4 million people when Thatcher entered office, began a steady and excruciating climb to 3 million by January 1982.[24]

Hoskyns and his allies expected a popular backlash. With memories of the Heath government in 1974 and the Winter of Discontent in 1979 fresh in their minds, they started to plan for what they believed would be the inevitable response of the working class: strikes. In the summer of 1979, Hoskyns began what he called the "Quick" and "Long" campaigns to change working-class thinking. The basis of both campaigns was what he and his Policy Unit colleague Norman Strauss termed "event-led communications." This theory was motivated by the conviction that "public attitudes were not much affected by speeches and articles because most people are not in the habit of visualizing differing future situations." Instead, "what changed their minds . . . was the direct observation—or better still, first-hand experience—of actual events and actions." In practical policy terms, this meant the Thatcher government should use "principled argument" to state its economic positions publicly and "then be ready to let the strikes happen." Once strikes were "causing wide-spread hardship" and "stress in the minds of the public," the "moral and intellectual bankruptcy" of union leaders would be exposed. Only then would public attitudes toward unions, including among rank-and-file union members, begin to change.[25]

There are two important points to make about this line of reasoning. First, as with the *Stepping Stones* report in opposition, most of Thatcher's ministers found this policy of purposeful provocation to be politically reckless and chose instead to keep quiet. Most ministers simply did not share Hoskyns's faith in the mutability of public opinion. After a few stern speeches by Thatcher and Howe in the fall of 1979, the "Quick" campaign petered out, and by the spring of 1980, Hoskyns himself had abandoned the "Long" campaign on account of internal opposition.

But second, and more important, even if the Tory cabinet did not place much hope in "event-led communications," leaders across the Iron Curtain in the Polish Politburo did. Throughout their own long battle with a union, Polish leaders consistently hoped that the public's "first-hand experience" with the "material hardships" produced by Solidarity's actions would expose what they believed to be "the moral and intellectual bankruptcy" of the union leadership and sway public opinion in their favor. In this hope, of course, they faced a rather significant problem: in their antidemocratic and unjust socialist authoritarian system, it was difficult to convince any Pole that it was Solidarity, rather than the party, that was morally and intellectually bankrupt. Although there is some evidence to suggest that the Polish population grew tired of the material hardship and uncertainty of daily life by late 1981, these feelings never translated into a widespread turn of public opinion against Solidarity. The PZPR never did take the steps that would have given it the moral and intellectual high ground required to change public opinion because it could not do so without liquidating the communist system itself. For that reason, events always "communicated" a different message to the Polish population than they did to the British.[26]

Despite Hoskyns's ambition, by the start of 1980, the Thatcher government still had not done anything to change the structure of British government and society. A number of policy innovations in the spring and summer of that year converged to begin to produce such changes. In March, the Treasury announced a new policy of long-term monetary planning called the Medium Term Financial Strategy (MTFS). A further elaboration of the government's monetarist vision, the MTFS announced annual goals for growth in the money supply and committed the government to lowering the budget deficit in order to meet those goals. Many exceedingly smart civil servants and politicians in the Bank of England, the Treasury, and 10 Downing Street thought this was an exceedingly stupid idea.[27] The growth of the money supply, they reasoned, was extremely hard to measure, let alone predict, and any time it looked as though a target would be missed, the government would be boxed in. As Nigel Lawson, Howe's deputy at Treasury who first proposed the idea, put it, "That of course was the point of the whole exercise." The MTFS, he wrote, "was intended to be a self-imposed constraint on economic policy-making, just as the Gold Standard and the Bretton Woods system . . . had been in the past."[28] In the end, both sides in the debate proved to be right. The targets were often missed (sometimes wildly), and yet their very existence pushed the government to adopt politically difficult policies that otherwise would have been avoided.

Evidence of this began to show almost immediately. With the announcement of the MTFS, the government faced pressure of its own making to cut public expenditure. Throughout the summer and fall of 1980, this pressure manifested in various technical debates over public sector pay settlements, the deindexing of public spending from inflation, and the determination of "cash limits" for each government ministry and nationalized industry. Collectively these debates show a government searching for a way to make politically possible what it now deemed economically necessary.

As the government's chief strategist, Hoskyns's counsel in these debates proved decisive. With inflation running at double digits in 1980, any government decision to deindex pay increases from the price level was sure to deliver workers a significant decline in real wages. Everyone knew this might cause trouble and even lead to a strike in the Civil Service, but Hoskyns confidently advised Thatcher to make the change.[29] If it led to a strike, so be it. Hoskyns, of course, believed that changes in public opinion were really "events led," so perhaps a strike would be just what the Thatcher government needed. "There is a strong case for doing it early," he wrote, "in order to allow maximum 'protest time' so that the ensuing debate can expose the moral and intellectual bankruptcy of the union position." As he had been writing since first crafting his grand theory of social change in *Stepping Stones*, he repeated, "You won't get *new behavior* unless you have *new attitudes*. And you won't get new attitudes without *new information* and enough *elapsed time* for it to be put across, explained by the media and understood by the public."[30]

Decoupling social security payments from inflation presented a similar disciplinary challenge. Hoskyns's memo on the issue immediately noted "the political difficulties" inherent in the decision, but it encouraged Thatcher to press ahead anyway. To make society's bitter pill go down easier, Hoskyns suggested the deindexing be folded into "a bigger package" that would include a signal of the "fair distribution of sacrifice." He surmised that something like "a symbolic surcharge" on the highest tax brackets would do the trick. "People will accept almost anything," he concluded, "provided they are persuaded that it is (a) necessary; (b) fair."[31] By this point in her premiership, Thatcher was known the world over for her mantra, "There is no alternative." For Hoskyns, the phrase only encapsulated half the challenge: people not only had to be convinced that there were no alternatives to the government's discipline, but they also had to be convinced that the burden of the discipline would be distributed fairly throughout society.

These questions of necessity and fairness came to a head at the end of 1980. Despite months of work on preparing policies of economic discipline,

Thatcher and her government still had not introduced enough reform to change the country's outlook. Indeed, by November 1980, most observers both inside and outside the government had concluded that the government had struck the wrong balance between fiscal and monetary policy in its first two years. The combination of high interest rates and loose fiscal policy had produced the worst of all worlds—high interest rates that had led to an over-valued pound; an overvalued pound that had decimated British industry; a decimated industrial sector that had subsequently laid off hundreds of thousands of workers; a rise in the number of unemployed workers, which had driven up government social insurance spending; and an increase in government spending that had increased the budget deficit and pushed already high interest rates even higher. It was a vicious spiral from which there appeared to be no politically easy exit. All the apparent options that would solve the crisis—cutting public spending further, repealing the tax cuts that had defined Thatcher's governing agenda, or allowing nationalized industries to go bankrupt—looked like political suicide of one form or another.

It was precisely the moment of political impossibility Hoskyns had long seen on the horizon. Beginning in late November 1980 and extending through the next budget's publication in March 1981, he undertook a sustained campaign to get Thatcher to disregard all political constraints and do what he deemed economically necessary. "We must now be approaching the point . . . when we have to choose between one of two routes," he wrote her in November. "On the one side, we can start to move increasingly towards what is 'politically possible' but simply inadequate for solving the problem. On the other, we will have to find ways of doing things which appear to be 'politically impossible' but which are essential."[32] By the end of the year, he had extended the scope of his message to the entire postwar period. Britain's postwar decline had been caused by "politicians who have never understood what is economically *necessary,* only what appears to be 'possible.'" In late 1980, very few things seemed politically possible because of a long list of constraints—an inability to cut social security spending, an inability to reform trade unions, an inability to handle strikes, and an inability to liquidate state-owned enterprises. But Hoskyns pleaded for persistence: "Acceptance of these constraints is tantamount to saying: 'On reflection we've decided we can't succeed.'" He implored Thatcher to convince her cabinet that each of these constraints "*has* to be broken" and then to focus on "the right political communications to gain public acceptance."[33]

Ever the politician, Thatcher had long been focused on plucking the rhetorical strings that would make the British public's heart sing. Throughout her speeches, she appealed to liberal themes of individualism, independence, and self-reliance to ennoble her crusade against government intervention in the economy. In her telling, she was not imposing economic discipline on a resistant population but rather liberating a captive population from the growing tyranny of the state. "It is not the State that creates a healthy society," she told the nation in October 1980. "The State drains society, not only of wealth, but of initiative, of energy. . . . A healthy society is not created by its institutions." Instead, "a great nation" was "the voluntary creation of its people," and prosperity was the product of "countless acts of personal self-confidence and self-reliance."[34] This was no mere cover story whipped up for public consumption; Thatcher was an effective promoter of her vision because she truly believed in it.

This sincerity of conviction proved decisive when—as in fall 1980—everything about Thatcher's deteriorating circumstances suggested she should abandon her beliefs. Indeed, most observers believed it was only a matter of time before she would change course, and talk of a Thatcher "U-turn" became widespread. The Iron Lady relished defying their expectations. "To those waiting with bated breath for . . . the 'U' turn," she said in her October speech, "I have only one thing to say. 'You turn if you want to. The lady's not for turning.'"[35] Neither this confidence in the righteousness of economic discipline nor liberalism's lexicon of individualism and self-reliance was available to Jaruzelski and Rakowski in Poland.

Righteous confidence still needed to be attached to particular policies, so in early 1981, a small group of leading officials gathered at Chequers for a weekend retreat to discuss their next steps. It was at this retreat that the 1981 budget—the defining landmark in the fiscal history of Thatcherism—was born. When the group assembled on January 17, Geoffrey Howe brought with him some very bad news: the budget deficit was growing with no end in sight.[36] Unless the growth in government borrowing was reversed, interest rates and the pound would continue to rise, industry would continue to shed workers, and public spending would continue to grow. To prevent this slide, it was now clear the government would have to propose a draconian deflationary budget in the midst of an already severe recession. The ministers returned to London late in the day, where a battle for the future of the Thatcher experiment awaited.

In her memoirs, Thatcher wrote, "I shall never forget the weeks leading up to the 1981 budget. Hardly a day seemed to go by without the financial scene deteriorating in some way."[37] Indeed, every time Howe produced new forecasts, the projected size of the budget deficit only grew larger and further over the government's stated goal in the MTFS. The debate within the government, therefore, aimed to balance the interests of the two groups most important in the politics of breaking promises: capital holders on global markets who bought British debt and the citizens of the country the government served. Through much of February, the debate over how to balance the competing interests of these two groups raged within the government. After one such meeting, Hoskyns and the Policy Unit warned, "This budget is the turning point." Economic constraints had forced a confrontation with brutal political reality, they concluded, and Thatcher's political future now rested on her choice. "IN SHORT, WE BELIEVE THAT THE BUDGET PRESENTED ON 10 MARCH WILL LARGELY DETERMINE WHETHER WE WIN OR LOSE THE NEXT ELECTION."[38]

In the end, Thatcher chose economic discipline over political felicity and introduced a deflationary budget of tax increases and spending cuts. She publicly tried to explain that in prioritizing the reduction of the deficit, the budget aimed to lower interest rates, improve the exchange rate, and thereby eventually return Britain to economic growth. But it was a tough sell. Across much of the political spectrum and the academic world, the budget was condemned for holding to a blind faith in the power of monetarism over the obvious suffering of the British people. Most famously, a group of 364 economists from across Britain published a letter in the *Times* declaring, "There is no basis in economic theory or supporting evidence for the government's belief that by deflating demand they will bring inflation permanently under control." The 1981 budget, they declared, "will only deepen the depression."[39]

There is a significant academic debate about the ultimate effects of the 1981 budget, but two things are clear and important for our purposes.[40] First, whether caused by the budget or merely correlated to it, the recession of the early 1980s reached its trough in the first quarter of 1981, and economic growth returned thereafter. As Nigel Lawson wrote of the 364 economists' letter with evident satisfaction, "The economy embarked on a prolonged phase of vigorous growth almost from the moment the letter was published. So far from launching the economy on a self-perpetuating downward spiral, the Budget [sic] was a prelude to eight years of uninterrupted growth."[41]

Second, whatever the scale of the budget's economic effect, the limited scale of its political and social effect was even more important. In the spring and summer of 1981, socially troubling and politically difficult riots broke out in the Brixton district of London and the Toxteth district of Liverpool. Hundreds of police and protesters violently clashed, more than one hundred buildings and police cars were burned, and hundreds of arrests were made.[42] But Britain did not descend into revolution. Such a statement may seem outlandish in the contingency it grants to the course of British history. But one only needed to look across the Iron Curtain to see potential scale of popular revolt that waited in austerity's wings. As Jaruzelski and Rakowski were about to find out in Poland, implementing economic discipline in a political system with no popular legitimacy was a recipe for national revolution.

＊　＊　＊

The two Polish leaders began their quest at almost exactly the same moment Thatcher announced her 1981 budget. In his first speech to the Polish Sejm after assuming the position of prime minister in February 1981, Jaruzelski called for a three-month moratorium on strikes so the government could "take the first steps toward the introduction of a program for economic stability" and "prepare wide ranging economic reforms." In exchange for its compliance, Solidarity was offered participation in a "Permanent Committee" on government-union relations, to be led by Rakowski.[43] Two days later, Wałęsa met Rakowski for the first time and welcomed the call for social peace and consultations. On February 15, Rakowski gave his first speech in the Sejm, telling the gathered officials, "We have begun the difficult and arduous path of regaining credibility with voters." It was, he said, "not possible to imagine the construction of a partnership agreement in Poland without 'Solidarity.'"[44]

Wałęsa met Rakowski and Jaruzelski again for meetings in early March. Rakowski told the union leader of the government's "fatal" assessment of the economic situation and expressed concern over local Solidarity groups' recent anti-Soviet and antigovernment statements in various parts of the country. Wałęsa agreed to quiet those elements of his coalition, but Rakowski and Jaruzelski could not be sure he would be able or willing to follow through.[45]

The first test of the Solidarity leader's intentions came in the city of Radom, where the local union had gone on strike in early March with a mix of political and economic demands. Wałęsa traveled to the city and urged the striking workers to call off the strike and give the new government more time. "We should take a different style of struggle," he said, "we cannot destroy ourselves. . . . Our Prime Minister wants to do something [good] . . . we must remember that we must have a wise and strong government, which must have time" to undertake reforms. Upon reading the speech back in his office in Warsaw, Rakowski concluded, "If Wałęsa can impose this way of thinking on his people, maybe we can build something good."[46]

The optimism did not last long. In March 1981, in what came to be known as the Bydgoszcz crisis, tensions between the party and Solidarity reached a boiling point that nearly ended all hope of partnership and almost triggered a Soviet invasion of Poland. The crisis began when police in the city of Bydgoszcz forcibly removed a group of Solidarity activists from a government building. Three activists were injured, and within days, Solidarity members across the country were pressing for a union-wide response to the government's provocation. As tensions increased, Wałęsa called for a general strike, and Soviet planners hinted at invasion. For nearly two weeks, the country hurtled toward a final confrontation until, at the end of the month, Wałęsa and Rakowski worked out a compromise that left neither side happy but both sides intact.[47]

Even as Rakowski's idea of partnership survived the Bydgoszcz crisis, the country's political and economic constraints continued to tighten a noose around the idea with each passing day. First and foremost, the country was now out of money. Since Polish bankers had first struggled to raise money on global capital markets in the spring of 1980, they had been fighting an increasingly improbable battle to keep the nation solvent. The Gdańsk Accords and all of Solidarity's activism since then had not helped, as they only increased the government's promises at a time when promises needed to be broken. The Soviet Union had provided at least a billion dollars in hard currency support in 1980 to help the country stay afloat, but it was not enough to meet the country's mounting debt payments.[48] So, in February 1981, Warsaw announced to the West its desire to reschedule its debts. In April, fifteen Western governments signed a rescheduling agreement with Poland that deferred most of its 1981 debt payments for five years, and in June, Western banks followed with similar terms. The agreements deferred

Poland's obligations to its creditors temporarily but did nothing to reopen the country's general access to global capital markets. Western banks' confidence in the Polish system was now lost, and until significant and painful domestic reforms were implemented, it would not return. Even with its debts rescheduled, the state still had precious little hard currency to buy the food and basic goods it needed to fill the country's shops and assuage the population's concerns.

The result was rationing. In April, the government was forced to introduce ration cards for meat, butter, and grain products, which only furthered the population's suspicion that it was being starved for political purposes. Soon cigarettes and alcohol were added to the list of controlled goods.[49] If economic reality was bad, economic reform would only make it worse. Everyone agreed that any package of reforms in Poland would involve significant and extended hardship for the population. One Western economist writing in the *Socialist Register* in 1981 estimated that food prices would have to go up 100 percent, rationing would have to continue, work hours would have to be lengthened, and 1.2 million Poles would have to lose their jobs for economic growth to return.[50] Solidarity's own economists reluctantly agreed. They eventually arrived at similar projections for price increases and layoffs that would produce an average drop in Polish living standards of 25 percent.[51]

Unlike Hoskyns's Britain, however, the government had no credibility with society that it could use to gain acceptance of austerity. For that, it needed Solidarity. This left the union in a powerful position that it was slow to recognize and embrace. Through most of 1980, the Solidarity leadership had said that economic reform was the government's responsibility. Solidarity was only a trade union, its leaders maintained, and therefore could take no position on an issue that was clearly the purview of politicians. As the economy continued to deteriorate, however, this position became increasingly untenable. With rumors swirling that the party was starving society for political purposes, it became clear that only Solidarity could be an arbiter of any potential reform. So, by spring 1981, the union changed its tune. It would use its credibility to gain popular acceptance of economic discipline, but only if it was granted the power to oversee the reform's implementation alongside the government. In theory, this accorded with Rakowski's concept of partnership. After all, he had defined it as an agreement between the PZPR and societal forces for "co-responsibility" of the country's fate. But could it work in practice?

The second half of 1981 would prove that it could not. When Jaruzelski declared martial law on December 13, Rakowski fully supported the decision. By that time, the man who had originally proposed partnership as a means of overcoming the nation's economic challenges had abandoned the idea as unworkable and threatening to the state's very existence. In tracing his change of heart, we can gain insight into why imposing economic discipline in the antidemocratic systems of the Eastern Bloc proved to be so difficult and unstable. With each new blow to the economy, the Solidarity leadership felt compelled by popular pressure to demand more social and political power in return for its sponsorship of austerity and reform. And with each new Solidarity demand for more power, Rakowski came to view the union not as a partner but as a threat. The only thing that could have stopped this escalating cycle of forced demands and perceived threats was social trust, the very thing Rakowski had first sought to create. The final months of the Polish Crisis revealed that social trust was partnership's premise rather than its product. Without it, the road to martial law proved unstoppable.

The downward spiral began in August when the two sides convened for their first general negotiations since the Bydgoszcz crisis. The backdrop for the talks was grim. The government's announcement of a further cut in meat rations at the end of July had led Solidarity to sponsor "hunger marches" across the country. Because the union was not consulted about the change, its leadership refused to recognize the legitimacy of the government's decision. They once again accused the PZPR of withholding food from the population in order to weaken its opponents.[52] Such accusations understandably left Rakowski angry and disappointed. He confided to his diary, "If the warehouses were bursting at the seams with excess food, the government, struggling to gain public support . . . would throw all the strategic supplies on the market. There is nothing more important to us than social peace." Alas, he noted, "the people unfortunately believe Solidarity."[53] The cutback in rations and the hunger marches had also led some Solidarity members to conclude that the government could not lead the country out of the crisis, so the union had to "take the helm."[54] Rakowski perceived these claims as growing calls to overthrow the state. Even as he held out hope that some in the Solidarity leadership shared his idea of partnership, he wrote in the days before the negotiations began, "I have the impression we are approaching a confrontation."[55]

These mutual doubts predictably made the negotiations an acrimonious affair. Solidarity arrived at the meeting in Warsaw with just one primary demand: that it be given control and supervision of the country's food supply. Rakowski saw this as a threatening bid for power.[56] Despite their rough beginning, the two sides whittled away at their differences over the next three days until they reached the outlines of an agreement that would give Solidarity supervisory rights over food distribution and increased media access in exchange for the union's guarantee of social peace. As the two sides worked late into the night on August 6, Rakowski presented Wałęsa with a final draft of the communique that included small changes not previously discussed. Two parties that trusted each other might have been able to look past these changes or would not have proposed them in the first place. But trust was nowhere to be found. Wałęsa refused to sign it. Infuriated and exhausted, Rakowski stormed out of the room, and the negotiations ended without agreement.[57] "The talks ended . . . with a fiasco," he wrote later that night. "I expected everything, but not such a finale."[58]

The breakdown in negotiations only strengthened Solidarity's conviction that the union had to take on a greater role in governing society. In its first national meeting after the negotiations, union leaders spoke openly for the first time about the necessity of changing Poland's political system along with its economic one. Some proposed demanding free elections to local government and the Sejm; others thought it was time for a new second house in the Sejm, a "House of Labor" that would represent the interests of society alongside those of the government. Still others believed that the union should simply begin managing the economy without consulting the government and, in so doing, signal that it did not need the PZPR to govern. It was this last idea that led the union to publish an "Appeal to Society," in which it called on the people to end all strikes and work longer hours for the good of the nation. Solidarity would now lead a "self-managing reform," the appeal proclaimed, while it awaited the establishment of "institutions that will guarantee working people influence in the socioeconomic policy of the state."[59]

The nature of these institutions became the subject of further debate at Solidarity's first National Congress in September and October 1981. The congress proposed to create a Social Council on the National Economy to oversee implementation of the country's economic reforms. The program adopted at the congress noted that "a condition for the successful struggle against the crisis lies not only in drafting a program acceptable to society, but also in public control over the implementation of the program."[60] The

Social Council would serve this controlling function. The council would be composed of twenty economists and other professionals who maintained "social confidence," and it would be given the power to propose its own economic reforms and to veto plans passed by the government. The congress program affirmed that, over time, the council should lead to "a new Sejm" that would enjoy the confidence of the people.[61] To observers both within Poland and abroad, it was clear that the scope of Solidarity's demands and ambitions had grown a great deal.

Rakowski looked on with mounting dismay. His language began to change in telling ways. "Our partners, or rather now our opponents," he wrote in his diary on October 6, "underestimate the real threats from the outside [the Soviet Union], and in internal affairs publicly take the position that if the government agrees to give them control over the economy and government policy, then the economic misery and severe shortages . . . will disappear like morning fog." Jaruzelski too began to believe that Solidarity was turning away from the possibility of partnership. The Solidarity Congress had "disregarded" the "line of agreement," he told a meeting of the government on October 13. "The outstretched hand of the authorities was left hanging in a vacuum," and the economy had "become an arena for the struggle for power," he concluded. Neither Rakowski nor Jaruzelski took joy in their perception of Solidarity's turn toward confrontation. "The disaster will not spare anyone—neither 'Solidarity' nor the authorities. We sail in one boat," Rakowski wrote in his diary.[62]

Despite their growing despair, Rakowski and Jaruzelski did not abandon efforts to build a social basis of support for economic reform. To counter Solidarity's Social Council on the National Economy, which he viewed as a proposal for a second government, Jaruzelski proposed a Council of National Accord among the PZPR, Solidarity, and the Catholic Church. The sincerity of this proposal is often doubted in histories of the Polish Crisis that see it as a propaganda ploy on the road to martial law, but Rakowski's diary tells a different story. On October 22, Jaruzelski met with the Polish primate, Cardinal Józef Glemp, to introduce the idea of a national front and share his conviction that "to overcome the crisis, one must create a broad platform of national agreement." Even as he described himself as "rather skeptical," Rakowski recorded that "the General clung to the hope" that the national accord "could stop the unfavorable and very dangerous course of events." To further explore the possibility of an accord, Jaruzelski convened an unprecedented meeting with Glemp and Wałęsa on November 4 to discuss the idea.[63]

The meeting only served to expose the growth in Solidarity's demands and the growth in the party's perception of Solidarity's threat to the state. When Wałęsa announced to Solidarity's National Coordinating Committee that he would meet with Jaruzelski, the radical wing of the leadership attacked him for playing into the hands of the party. Then, while he was attending the meeting in Warsaw, the committee adopted a resolution threatening a general strike if the Social Council on the National Economy was not formed within three months. At the meeting, Wałęsa tried to assure Jaruzelski that the Social Council on the National Economy was not intended to be a second government, but the general remained unconvinced.[64] He had now made up his mind about Solidarity's intentions. In a Politburo meeting on November 10, he told his comrades, "You cannot have any illusions about the strategic goal of the 'S' leadership, which is to take power and change the system." Nevertheless, to demonstrate that the party was exhausting all peaceful options and to win the hearts and minds of undecided Polish citizens, he believed the party should continue to publicly pursue a national accord, even as it readied other measures.[65]

Negotiations between the two sides continued throughout November, but the die had now been cast. Discussions in both camps in the month before martial law reveal the stark, incompatible differences that had come to separate Solidarity and the PZPR. After the government forcibly broke up a strike in Warsaw in early December, Solidarity's National Committee convened a meeting in Gdańsk, where the full scope of their expanding demands and intentions emerged. Wałęsa began the meeting by saying he had long pursued partnership and compromise with the authorities because it was a strategy that would win hearts and minds. But the time for that strategy had now passed. He stated, "Today the society must learn that a confrontation is inevitable." Others seconded their leader's conclusion and even expressed confidence that the Soviet Union would accept a Solidarity government as long as the union guaranteed Moscow's security interests. When Jacek Kuroń took the floor, he stated that society's need for "a government with social trust" compelled Solidarity to demand the immediate implementation of free elections, a free press, and the Social Council on the National Economy. Activist after activist followed with calls for some form of "social control" over politics and the economy, and when the meeting ended, the union issued a list of "minimal conditions" the party had to meet in order for negotiations to continue.[66]

In good Communist Party fashion, the PZPR had its security services wiretap the proceedings, so Rakowski and Jaruzelski soon found themselves listening to tapes with every word of Solidarity's meeting. After the tape finished, "there was silence for a moment," Rakowski wrote. Then Jaruzelski said, "Well, yes . . . I did not expect that." Rakowski was more dramatic, confiding to his diary that he listened to Wałęsa's speeches "with the feeling of a disappointed lover." They decided the tapes should be discussed the next day in the Politburo. As Rakowski returned home in a "grim mood," he convinced himself that he and Jaruzelski had given the idea of partnership a real shot. "It is beyond doubt that we recognized 'S' not only as a real but lasting force in Polish socialism." It was the union rather than the party, he thought, that had destroyed the idea of partnership, and now it threatened the existence of the Polish state. He concluded, "What I heard cannot be called anything else but a call to overthrow the legal power of the state and its institutions. Is it possible to imagine any government in the world idly watching calls to overthrow it by force?"[67]

The next day in the Politburo, the party plotted its final move in light of the new strength of Solidarity's demands. One member, Stanisław Ciosek, began with a summary of the tapes. Solidarity now demanded, he said, uncontrolled access to the mass media, a political transformation of the state, and economic reform. "Consent to the introduction of [economic] reform is subject to [our] consent to the first two conditions," he reported. "So it is political transformation as a price for agreeing to economic reform." When Rakowski took the floor, he made his private views from the evening public for the entire party leadership.[68] The possibilities of partnership had been "exhausted," he said. "Our partner decided to fight us. . . . We thought we would force him into limited co-responsibility. 'S' does not want it. . . . The 'S' leadership has gone from a union and social movement to the opposition party with a counter-revolutionary countenance."[69] After the discussion went around the room, the last word fell to Jaruzelski. "Faith in the omnipotence of martial law is mythology," he told the group.[70] It would not solve all their problems immediately. Their fight to regain the country would be long and hard, but at this point they had no choice, he believed. They had to defend the state. He asked the group to grant him the power to declare martial law at a time of his choosing, and everyone readily acceded. As Rakowski left the meeting, he shared the general's conclusion: "There is nothing left for us except strength."[71] With that, his transformation was complete.

On the night of December 12, 1981, Jaruzelski brought discipline to Poland. Just before midnight, security forces surrounded a meeting of the Solidarity leadership in Gdańsk and arrested the entire group. Wałęsa was placed under house arrest, and within hours, thousands of the union's middle ranks had been arrested across the country. Tanks rumbled into the center of Warsaw and Gdańsk, and at six the next morning, Jaruzelski appeared on national television to declare a "state of war." Poland "was on the brink of an abyss," he told the nation, and the new Military Council of National Salvation would impose the order and discipline on society that had been sorely lacking since August 1980. Under the cover of martial law, the difficult economic reform that had eluded the country for so long would finally be implemented.[72] As the national anthem began to play in the background, he repeated its "immortal words" and asked all patriotic Poles to do their part to save the country.[73]

In the months that followed, prices went up, real wages went down, and many Poles were "redistributed" into new jobs. Estimates of the fall in Polish living standards put the decline at 20–30 percent. The economic reform program was officially introduced in early 1982. Under the banner of three new S's—self-reliance, self-governance, and self-financing—the reform program announced that a new "criterion of economic activity" would govern Polish enterprises. "It is profit," a government report proclaimed. Supposedly freed from government control and government subsidy, Polish enterprises would now be guided by "economic rationality," which would "lower production costs," "improve quality," and force them "to strive for competitiveness."[74]

Even as martial law gave Jaruzelski the blunt power of force to implement economic reforms, it sapped the last vestiges of legitimacy the Polish communists enjoyed at home and abroad. Accurate measures of Polish public sentiment in the aftermath of martial law were difficult to produce, but one comprehensive study of Polish public opinion in this period concluded, "The regime had destroyed Solidarity, but had also discredited itself, and the socialist ideology from which it claimed legitimacy."[75] The promise of socialist Poland had been broken, but as long as martial law ruled the land, a new vision for a just society and a legitimate state could not take shape.

◆　◆　◆

As tanks rumbled into Warsaw, Margaret Thatcher faced long odds across the Iron Curtain. The immediate aftermath of the 1981 budget yielded only economic hardship and political unpopularity. The hot summer of riots that followed in its wake further dented Thatcher's political popularity, and the threat of a run on the pound in the autumn called into question her government's economic credibility. In order to prevent capital from fleeing the country, Chancellor of the Exchequer Geoffrey Howe was forced once again to increase interest rates, which was precisely the type of monetary discipline the 1981 budget had been meant to avoid. In September, the stock market fell to a seventeen-year low, and at the dawn of the new year, the number of unemployed Britons crossed the dreaded threshold of three million.

On top of these economic hurdles, a new and potent political force had appeared on the British scene: the Social Democratic Party. Led by a group of disaffected Labour Party ministers known as the Gang of Four, the SDP disrupted the political landscape by taking ideas from both the Left and the Right in the hopes of occupying the increasingly wide-open political center. Unlike Labour, which continued to oppose Thatcher's efforts to reform trade unions, the SDP favored limits on unions' political power. But unlike Thatcher, the new party did not stridently oppose the welfare state and, in fact, sought to use the state vigorously to ease the nation's adjustment to the global economy. Against the backdrop of Thatcher's austerity and the Labour Party's uncompromising opposition to any change in the old economic order, this centrist blend appeared to be an effective political combination. It was widely believed that in a general election, the SDP would combine forces with the minority Liberal Party, and a September 1981 Gallop poll found that such an SDP/Liberal alliance would receive 40 percent of Britons' support, while the Conservative Party would only get 16 percent.[76]

Polls like these understandably made Conservatives nervous, and the numbers were made worse by the fact that the economy provided the Tories no riposte. "The Conservative Party faces grimmer prospects than at any time since the end of the second world war," cabinet minister Peter Walker wrote to Thatcher early in 1982. "We are presiding over 3 million unemployed and, now, falling living standards for those still at work. . . . We are the first post-war government to have produced a substantial drop in the nation's real output." The SDP/Liberal alliance was the "most ominous third-party threat in modern times," he wrote, and its existence put Britain "on the verge of one of those junctures in which a familiar political landscape is radically rearranged."[77] Walker's judgment was a gloomy but hardly solitary opinion. As Thatcher's biographer has concluded, in the early months of 1982, "few far-sighted observers . . . imagined that she was likely to win the next general election."[78] Almost three years into the Thatcher experiment, the results were meager, and the Tories' political fate looked dire. If, as Walker sensed, the country was on the verge of a radical rearrangement, it seemed unlikely Thatcher and Thatcherism would find a place in the new political landscape.

But then history took yet another unexpected turn. Eight thousand miles away from London in the South Atlantic, Argentine armed forces under the direction of the military junta in Buenos Aires invaded the Falkland Islands on April 2, 1982. The Falklands had been a British colony for a century and a half, but by the early 1980s, they were a largely forgotten piece of a mostly bygone empire. Confronted with the Argentine invasion, however, Thatcher and the country at large quickly recaptured the nation's imperial self-image and committed to reclaiming the islands and freeing the 1,800 British inhabitants from the tyranny of their newfound oppressors. Over the next two and a half months, the prime minister played the central role in a most improbable drama of tense international diplomacy and deadly military conflict. After bilateral negotiations broke down, a British expeditionary force invaded the Falklands while the Royal Navy and Air Force engaged the Argentines in the surrounding seas and skies; 255 British servicemen and 649 Argentines died in the ensuing battles, but British forces steadily retook the islands in late May and early June. On June 15, the Argentine high command surrendered, and the Falklands returned to full British control.[79]

The scale of the triumph on the battlefield was only surpassed by the magnitude of Thatcher's newfound standing on the domestic political scene. Though her premiership had been teetering on the brink of failure before the conflict, she emerged from the war in resolute command of her own fate and that of the nation. "The Prime Minster has complete freedom of action now," Alan Walters of the Policy Unit told a colleague on the day of victory. Thatcher, in Walters's estimation, now had complete "freedom in imposing domestic, foreign and defense policies."[80] All three main parties—Conservative, Labour, and Liberal/SDP—went into the Falklands in a virtual dead heat for popular support, but the Conservatives emerged from the conflict with a roughly 15 percent advantage.[81] The obvious question now was: how would the Tories use it?

Before providing an answer, Thatcher thought it best to win the next general election. Although some advisers were tempted to call an election while the post-Falklands glow burned bright, Thatcher concluded that such a decision would smack of opportunism and decided to postpone the election until 1983. The trade union issue remained unresolved, but politics demanded patience. "Democratic institutions and the need for a high degree of consent," Thatcher wrote to Friedrich Hayek in 1981, made the reform process "painfully slow."[82] The economy required further restructuring, but it would have to wait for the election. The government had "to reduce the burden of the loss making state enterprises," John Vereker of the Policy Unit wrote in a strategy memo in late 1982. The British Steel Company survived "in the face of all economic logic" for "political reasons," he wrote, and British Rail also needed to be downsized. But the government would "do well," he concluded, to wait until "after the election" to make any decisions.[83]

And then there was coal. In both political and economic terms, restructuring the British coal industry was the government's most significant economic challenge.[84] Since the start of the Tory government in 1979, both Thatcher and the National Union of Mineworkers had been biding their time, waiting for the right moment to strike the decisive blow to the other side. Both camps viewed a reprise of the events of 1974, when the NUM had brought down the Heath government through a strike, as inevitable. They had come closest to confrontation in early 1981, when the National Coal Board's initial lowball wage offer to the NUM had brought the miners to the brink of calling a national strike. But against the backdrop of the dismal politics surrounding the 1981 budget, Thatcher had concluded she did not have the strength or support to win a strike and assented to the NUM's wage demands.

Losing that battle only hardened the prime minister's determination to win the wider war. In the wake of capitulation, the government launched a multifaceted strategy to prepare the British state for the next time the miners threatened to act. The strategy had three primary prongs: increasing the nation's electricity endurance during a potential strike by building up surplus coal stocks at power plants, fortifying and coordinating the nation's police force to keep working mines open during a strike, and molding public opinion to prevent other workers and unions from taking up the miners' cause. John Hoskyns summarized the confrontational mentality that underwrote the strategy: "We cannot win a war of economic survival by pretending it's peacetime."[85] The government needed, in his view, to build up the physical infrastructure and state capacity to withstand a strike and then let the strike unfold for the entire country to see. "We believe as a *general* rule . . . the only way to end the strike-culture," he wrote in another memo, "is to *let it happen*." Rather than try to prevent a strike, Hoskyns believed the government should concentrate its efforts on "mobilising public opinion to win the battle for us."[86]

For its part, the NUM girded for action by electing a new, more militant leader—Arthur Scargill. Scargill had made his name as the local leader of the NUM at the so-called Battle of Saltley Gate during the 1974 strike, during which the miners had overwhelmed the police at Birmingham's Saltley Coke Works and shut the plant down. Within weeks, Heath had capitulated to the miners' demands and was soon out of office. Scargill believed—and the Tories feared—that he would be able to do the same thing to Thatcher. After his election to NUM president in December 1981, he pressed the union to strike twice in 1982 and again in early 1983, but each time the miners voted to keep working. Government ministers took this as a sign of "reluctance on the part of the miners themselves to strike," but they nevertheless understood, on the cusp of the election, that Scargill was "by no means a spent force."[87]

Thus, by the time the *Economist* declared simply, "The Issue Is Thatcher," on the cover of its May 1983 election issue, the British people were sure to have a weighty sense of the implications that lurked beneath the name. At the time of the vote, 46 percent of the population believed the Conservatives had the best policies for the country (compared to 23 percent and 22 percent for Labour and Liberal/SDP, respectively), and 55 percent of the population believed the Conservatives had "the best team of leaders" (compared with 16 percent for Labour and 23 percent for Liberal/SDP). Such sentiments were a recipe for a landslide election. The Tories picked up thirty-eight seats in Parliament, while Labour lost fifty-two, and Thatcher returned to government with the largest majority of the postwar era.[88]

With a new mandate in tow, Thatcher set about unleashing the full breadth and depth of her vision for reform. This meant, above all, finally taking on the NUM. By the fall of 1983, the country's endurance in the face of a prospective coal strike had reached six months, leaving no reason to delay any longer. "There is no case for making a special effort to avoid a miners' strike this year," an advisor wrote to Thatcher in September.[89] The head of the National Coal Board (NCB), Ian MacGregor, agreed, and in September he laid out a vision for accelerating pit closures and downsizing the mining workforce over the next two years. He anticipated closing seventy-five pits and decreasing the size of the workforce from 202,000 to 138,000 miners by 1985.[90] The plans were not made public in order to limit popular backlash, so industrial peace was maintained through the winter of 1983–1984. But on March 6, 1984, MacGregor at last made public his plan to cut 20,000 jobs over the course of the coming year, and soon the government was receiving reports of "the temperature . . . rising in the coalfields."[91] The miners of Yorkshire and Scotland, who would be particularly hard-hit by the closures, were soon on strike, and by mid-March about half the country's miners had followed. The question now was whether Scargill would ballot his members to launch an official national strike.

He never did. Having already been turned away by the NUM membership three times, Scargill decided he could not risk another ballot. It was an enormously consequential decision that robbed the NUM's cause of legitimacy and made it difficult for other unions to justify supporting the miners with parallel action. Scargill enthusiastically tried to turn the strike into a national coalition against Thatcher's government, but the absence of a ballot gave his calls to action a hollow ring. "The NUM is engaged in a social and industrial Battle of Britain," he wrote to the country in March. "What is urgently needed is the rapid and total mobilization of the Trade Union and Labor Movement."[92] Unable to mobilize even a majority of his own union, it proved difficult for him to attract a majority of the country. Three months into the strike, 71 percent of the country believed it was "sensible" to close "uneconomic" coal pits; only 25 percent favored Scargill to win, and 51 percent wanted the NCB to emerge victorious.[93]

The yearlong strike that followed crystalized in almost pure form the politics of breaking promises and the way in which those politics took on divergent meanings on either side of the Iron Curtain. Much as Wałęsa eventually did in Poland, Scargill declared the overthrow of the government "the explicit objective" of his efforts.[94] But unlike the ten million Poles who flocked to join Solidarity's ranks, the NUM was never able to develop a popular base of support, and Scargill's exhortations to take "extra-parliamentary action" against the government fell on deaf ears.[95] Large majorities of the British public disapproved of both any attempt by

striking miners to force working miners to join their strike and any prospect of other unions joining the miners to start a general strike against the
government.[96] A full 69 percent of the country believed Scargill's motives
were political, but unlike in Poland, this was not a good thing.[97]

Just as Jaruzelski did in his declaration of martial law, Thatcher painted
the actions of her government and the police as the state's appropriate response to lawlessness and violence. But whereas martial law destroyed the
Polish communists' legitimacy both at home and abroad, the miners'
strike only served to cement Thatcher's image around the world as the
determined and *legitimate* Iron Lady. "What we have got is an attempt to
substitute the rule of the mob for the rule of law, and it must not succeed,"
Thatcher told the nation as a battle between thousands of strikers and police unfolded at the Orgreave Coke Works in May 1984.[98] The British
people by and large agreed with her. Even though only 40 percent of the
country approved of Thatcher during the strike, an overwhelming 92 percent approved of the police who were upholding her policies on the
ground.[99] The country may have been deeply divided, but the state remained overwhelmingly legitimate.

For twelve months, the strike raged on, but the country never ground
to a halt. The electricity endurance built up over the previous three years
kept the economy supplied with power, the police protected working
mines and miners, and public opinion never deserted the government.
Scargill's obstinate refusal to compromise ensured that when defeat came,
it would be complete, so when the miners at last returned to work on
March 3, 1985, they did so without any commitment from the coal board
to secure at least some of their jobs and mines in the future. Within five
years, more than half of the NCB's 170 coal mines would close and 79,000
miners would lose their jobs. These losses were only the proverbial canary
in the coal mine of industrial and working-class Britain. During Thatcher's time in office, manufacturing employment fell from 30 to 22 percent
of the country's workforce, and union membership fell from 54 to 42 percent of workers. All told, unions lost three million members across the
1980s.[100]

The defeat of the miners' strike signaled the culmination of the process Hoskyns had first laid out in the *Stepping Stones* report eight years
before: enough citizens' "Mental Sets" had been disrupted by "New Data"
to produce a change in the horizons of political possibility. Democratic

institutions and neoliberal ideology proved decisive in facilitating this process. At the height of the strike, Thatcher infamously described her adversaries as "the enemy within." By the time he declared martial law, Jaruzelski could not have dreamed of a better epithet for Solidarity than "the enemy within," but he failed to convince the Polish people that this was true. Without the sense of legitimacy or distance from past policy that democratic elections bestowed on Thatcher in Britain, Jaruzelski struggled to get the Polish population to trust his government. And without the precepts of neoliberalism to make a virtue out of discipline, Jaruzelski struggled to justify his actions in Marxist-Leninist terms. Poles made their acceptance of a new, more disciplined social contract conditional on greater control over the political process. This was a deal Jaruzelski could not accept, so martial law became his only choice. Like Thatcher, he defeated Poland's "enemy within," but the means he employed to do so ensured that the enemy would one day rise again.

CHAPTER 4

The Capitalist Perestroika

BEFORE PERESTROIKA TRANSFORMED the socialist world, it swept across the capitalist world to profound effect.[1] That, at least, was the view of Soviet officials in the 1980s. In 1983, for instance, officials from the Soviet state bank, Gosbank, wrote that the International Monetary Fund (IMF) required debtor countries to carry out "a perestroika of the economy" before it would grant the debtor states financial relief.[2] For Soviet analysts, the word "perestroika"—translated most directly in English as "restructuring"—was so intimately tied to processes of capitalist economic reform that it even anchored the Russian phrase (*strukturnaya perestroika*) for "structural adjustment," the loaded idiom the IMF used to describe the promarket reforms it attached as conditions of its financial aid.[3] Even after Mikhail Gorbachev had claimed "perestroika" as his own and instilled it with particular socialist and Soviet meanings, both he and Soviet officials continued to use the word to describe economic change in the capitalist world. As we have seen, Gorbachev told his Politburo in 1987 that many capitalist countries in Western Europe, including Great Britain under Margaret Thatcher, were "also carrying out a perestroika."[4] And officials from the Soviet Union's influential United States and Canada Institute echoed their leader's judgment. The "current structural perestroika of the economy of developed countries has far-reaching consequences," they wrote in 1989.[5]

Indeed it did. This chapter looks at the causes and consequences of the perestroika that swept the capitalist world in the early 1980s. The capitalist perestroika included three processes. First, US Federal Reserve chairman Paul Volcker launched the capitalist perestroika through his shock to US dollar interest rates from 1979 to 1983. We saw earlier the onset of the Volcker Shock and will now carry the story forward from 1980. Throughout the capitalist world, the Volcker Shock set off a wave of deflation, bankruptcies, and unemployment on a scale without precedent in the postwar period. This wave of broken promises, in turn, produced a variety of long-term disciplinary effects in economies throughout the Western world. In the United States, capital firmly regained the upper hand over labor, wages permanently fell behind productivity growth, and inequality dramatically increased. In Western Europe, governments did more to protect labor rights and income equality, but unemployment rose steeply and remained high for the remainder of the twentieth century. Most importantly, while the East remained a world of heavy industry, Western governments embraced deindustrialization and shrank the size of their industrial working classes. In total, Western governments after 1979 provided their citizens with some combination of the rising incomes, job security, and full employment that had defined the politics of making promises. But they could no longer provide all three at the same time. The promise of the postwar social contract was broken.

Second, in the early 1980s, Ronald Reagan unwittingly but fundamentally altered the flow of capital in the global economy by transforming the United States from a net exporter of capital to the world's largest debtor nation. Reagan's unyielding pursuit of both the largest tax cuts and the largest peacetime military buildup in the nation's history created massive US budget and current account deficits. In defiance of all expectation, these deficits were funded by a deluge of foreign capital. Capital poured into the United States in the 1980s at a rate previously unimaginable. This "Reagan financial buildup" erased the US government's traditional choice between guns and butter and underwrote the renewal of economic growth at home and the projection of American power abroad. The same policy instrument that disciplined American workers—high interest rates—held the key to unlocking these capital inflows from abroad, so only by breaking promises at home did the United States renew its power in the world.

Third, the capitalist perestroika ended the economic interdependence of the 1970s and initiated a new era of Western economic leverage over the rest of the world. The Reagan financial buildup produced this fundamental transformation in the world's political economy. The buildup not only enhanced the projection of American power by funding the military buildup, but it also fundamentally altered the geopolitics of the decade by *preventing* the flow of capital to other countries. The more the United States monopolized the world's surplus capital, the harder other governments found it to attract capital to their countries. Capital scarcity, in turn, altered the power relations between lenders and borrowers in the world economy and allowed the Reagan administration and the IMF to impose their economic vision on the rest of the world. The sovereign debt crisis that followed initially threatened to bring down the entire global financial system because debtor and creditor countries found themselves in a state of mutually assured financial destruction—if the debtor nations defaulted, the creditor nations would plunge into economic depression. But the leaders of the global financial system at the Federal Reserve, the IMF, and within the US government adroitly unwound this interdependence and made debtor countries fully dependent on their creditors. In so doing, Western policy makers discovered how to use sovereign debt as leverage, and through debt, they began to impose neoliberal economic programs on countries around the world.

The cumulative effect of the capitalist perestroika on both the United States and the world was profound. In the five short years from Volcker's appointment in 1979 to Reagan's reelection in 1984, the United States went from a country beset by financial limits, international interdependence, and domestic government weakness to a country with no discernable material limits that wielded the leverage of financial dependence and military superiority over the rest of the world. Unlike the Soviet government under its own perestroika, the US government renewed its power during the capitalist perestroika by disciplining its own citizens and tapping the wellspring of foreign capital that has sustained the American imperium ever since.

◆ ◆ ◆

Though Paul Volcker announced the Federal Reserve's move to monetarism in November 1979, he held the brunt of his attack on inflation in reserve until after the 1980 presidential election was complete. Volcker was fully aware of the deleterious effects higher interest rates would have on the real economy, and he did not want to be perceived as having tipped the election against Jimmy Carter by deepening the country's economic woes on the eve of the vote. So he waited. And with Ronald Reagan's election in November 1980, he finally had the opportunity he had been waiting for.

In choosing Reagan, the American people consciously elected someone who was committed to fighting inflation, even if it came at the price of working-class jobs. In fact, 42 percent of union households pulled the lever for Reagan at the ballot box.[6] Frustrated by a decade of economic crisis and attracted to the religious and cultural appeals of Reagan's "New Right," many white, working-class voters who had traditionally formed the cornerstone of the Democrats' New Deal coalition were willing to give Reagan's promarket, antigovernment conservatism a chance. These so-called Reagan Democrats delivered the Republican candidate an Electoral College landslide, as Reagan defeated Carter by a staggering 489–49 margin.[7]

Volcker believed that the months immediately following Reagan's victory presented the country with a "rare opportunity" to "come to grips, in a fundamental and decisive way, with the inflationary problem."[8] As he told Congress in the early days of January 1981, "the fact is we now have one of those rare opportunities to marshal a national consensus" in prioritizing inflation over the traditional priorities of full employment and economic growth.[9] It was an opportunity he was sure not to miss. For the next year and a half, US dollar interest rates breached 20 percent for weeks on end and never dipped below 15 percent.[10] Even after Volcker began to ease rates in the second half of 1982, his determination to vanquish any hint of inflationary expectations led the Federal Reserve to keep interest rates unprecedentedly high for the remainder of the decade. After languishing below zero for most of the 1970s, real interest rates (nominal interest rates minus inflation) skyrocketed to 5 percent in the early 1980s and remained staunchly positive for the remainder of the twentieth century.[11]

As Volcker's shock set in, the politics of making promises gave way to the politics of breaking promises across the country. Factories closed, unemployed lines swelled, and the nation's industrial backbone shuttered out of existence. Between 1979 and 1983, fixed investment in manufacturing in the United States plummeted at its steepest rate on record, and employment in durable goods manufacturing declined by over two million jobs.[12] Real output contracted 3.3 percent, and unemployment reached a postwar peak of 10.8 percent.[13] Even when national economic growth returned in 1983, the good old days for American industry did not. In 1983, for instance, U.S. Steel, a bellwether of America's industrial might, announced it was shutting down nearly 20 percent of its capacity and laying off 15,000 workers. This was just one bleak moment in a broader decade of despair for the American steel industry, which saw the employees in its ranks fall from 450,000 at the start of the 1980s to 170,000 at the decade's end.[14]

For Reagan, Volcker's monetary discipline was a necessary antidote to what he perceived to be the profligacy of the politics of making promises. The high taxes, regulation, and social spending of the postwar period had, he believed, destroyed Americans' incentives to work hard and demolished American companies' reasons to invest in new equipment and expand production. His rhetoric suggested the economy needed to be freed from the shackles of the government. "Government is not the solution to our problem; government is the problem," he famously told the country in his first inaugural address.[15] In place of the promissory paradigm of the postwar period, Reagan embraced supply-side economics, a school of thought that proposed to solve the riddle of stagflation by cutting taxes and government regulation in order to unleash a new economic boom. Why work hard and invest in the future, supply-siders asked, if the government was just going to confiscate the fruits of success through taxation? How could companies and individuals take risks and chase innovation when the government increasingly regulated every facet of the marketplace? Amid the stagnant production, nosediving productivity growth, and low savings and investment totals of the 1970s, these questions had begun to resonate, and with Reagan's election, they prevailed. Supply-siders confidently assured the country that individuals would save more, businesses would invest more, and the economy would grow more if taxes and regulations were cut back.

Once in government, these convictions led the Reagan economic team to embrace a cavalcade of deregulation already well underway. In the last years of the Carter administration, bipartisan efforts to deregulate most facets of the American economy had gained traction. By the early years of Reagan's term, rules controlling competition and pricing in sectors ranging from airlines and railroads to telecommunications and trucking had been abolished. The financial sector soon followed suit. In a pair of laws passed in 1980 and 1982, Congress removed all interest rate caps on bank deposits, deregulated the savings and loan industry, and allowed banks to lend at variable rates. In one sector after another, lawmakers limited the government's power to moderate and regulate the marketplace.

All told, the percentage of the economy subject to some kind of price regulation dropped from 17 percent in 1977 to 6.6 percent in 1988.[16]

To this burgeoning trend of deregulation, Reagan added his own dash of anti-labor militancy. After the federal minimum wage had increased 127 percent in real terms from 1950 to 1980, it fell 26 percent in real terms while Reagan was in office.[17] In his first year in office, he made it more costly for workers to defend their economic position by declaring those who went on strike ineligible for food stamps.[18] And in the summer of 1981, he publicly signaled his intention to discipline American organized labor by abruptly firing 11,000 members of the Professional Air Traffic Controllers Organization (PATCO) who had walked off the job on strike and banning them from federal employment for life. Both labor and management quickly viewed PATCO's demolition as a turning point in the country's labor relations. President of the AFL-CIO (American Federation of Labor and Congress of Industrial Organizations) Lane Kirkland described Reagan's heavy-handed response as having the "massive, vindictive, brutal quality of the carpet bombing."[19] By the letter of the law, Reagan's action was perfectly legal, but it was a step few corporate leaders had been willing to take since the New Deal.[20] Now corporate leaders were quick to take their cue. "Managers," *Fortune* magazine reported in November 1981, "are discovering that strikes can be broken . . . and that strikebreaking . . . doesn't have to be a dirty word."[21] Broad changes in public sentiment drove the removal of this taboo. Reagan's action was popular, even among union members: 64 percent of the country supported the president's decision, including 52 percent of those in unions.[22] As in Britain, the American public clamored for an end to economic crisis and malaise, even if it came at the expense of organized labor.

The combination of the Volcker Shock's wave of mass unemployment, the rising tide of deregulation, and Reagan's firing of the air traffic controllers broke the resistance of American labor to economic discipline. Rather than fight for further gains, many workers simply rushed to secure what they already had. In 1982, for instance, the International Brotherhood of Teamsters—a potent union that many feared could bring the economy to a halt with a national truckers' strike—agreed to a three-year freeze in wages for more than 300,000 long-haul drivers.[23] Across the nation, the number of days workers spent on strike plummeted. During the heyday of the politics of making promises from 1950 to 1973, the number of large strikes per year averaged 325. But from 1982 to 1990, that number fell to roughly 60. As unions' militancy dissipated, so did their presence in the workplace. Though unionized workers were 21 percent of the private sector labor force in 1979, they only comprised 12 percent a decade later.[24] A less organized labor force was also a less well-compensated one. Real hourly compensation in the private economy flatlined during the 1980s, growing at an average annual rate of just 0.1 percent from 1979 to 1990.[25]

In total, the early 1980s marked a sea change in the compensation the American working class received for its labor. As shown in Figure 4.1, until the early 1970s, the relationship between workers' productivity and hourly compensation in the United States had moved in unison throughout the postwar period. The economic crises of the 1970s put a dent in this relationship, but it was only with the Volcker Shock, the deregulation push of the late 1970s, the rising import competition of the early 1980s, and the empowerment of management over labor in Reagan's first term that wages and productivity became permanently severed. The average American worker saw virtually no increase in real wages from 1979 to the end of the century.[26]

American workers were far from the only ones to bear the burden of high interest rates. The Federal Reserve's actions forced other central

Figure 4.1 **The divergence between American productivity growth and average hourly compensation.**

Data source: Economic Policy Institute (EPI) analysis of unpublished Total Economy Productivity data from Bureau of Labor Statistics (BLS) Labor Productivity and Costs program, wage data from the BLS Current Employment Statistics, BLS Employment Cost Trends, BLS Consumer Price Index, and Bureau of Economic Analysis National Income and Product Accounts. "The Productivity–Pay Gap," EPI, accessed June 21, 2021, https://www.epi.org/productivity-pay-gap/.

banks around the world to dramatically increase interest rates in order to protect their currencies. West German chancellor Helmut Schmidt, therefore, had a right to complain when he lamented that Volcker had caused interest rates in Europe to rise to their highest levels "since the birth of Jesus Christ."[27] High real interest rates, in turn, squeezed excess capacity and labor out of all the industrial economies of the West with ruthless effectiveness. After falling below 2 percent on the eve of the first oil crisis, unemployment across Western Europe ballooned to over 10 percent in the mid-1980s and remained over 8 percent well into the 1990s.[28] The potent combination of high unemployment and high interest rates put a very low ceiling on wage growth. After rising 3–5 percent per year in the 1960s and early 1970s, real wages in Western Europe and Japan grew only about 1 percent per year in the 1980s and 1990s.[29] As in the United States, employment in manufacturing and heavy industry was hit particularly hard. Even in an industrial powerhouse like West Germany, work hours in manufacturing fell by 10 percent from 1979 to 1985, and the growth of unit labor costs was cut in half during the 1980s.[30] The dismantling of the industrial working classes was broad based across Western countries and proved to be a decisive difference between democratic capitalism and state socialism. As Figure 4.2 shows, while Eastern Bloc governments continued to add workers to heavy industries in the 1980s, Western governments were able to deindustrialize their workforces.

Much of this "de-manning," as it was often called, occurred through the privatization of state-owned assets and enterprises. Few other Western leaders matched Thatcher's and Reagan's millenarian zeal for neoliberal solutions, but that did not stop them from embracing privatization as a means of making their countries' legacy industries leaner and more competitive. Over the 1980s, a veritable wave of privatization swept across Western economies.[31] Everything from Dutch airlines to Japanese telecom companies to German electric utilities found their way into private hands. Even the socialist government of Spain joined the action. In the late 1980s, some eighty Spanish companies were privatized—a number that would only grow larger by the end of the century.[32] When Gorbachev told the Politburo in 1987 that Spanish prime minister Felipe González was among the Western leaders "also carrying out a perestroika" of their economies, he was referring to a socialist presiding over the full-scale privatization of an economy where almost 20 percent of Spaniards were unemployed.[33]

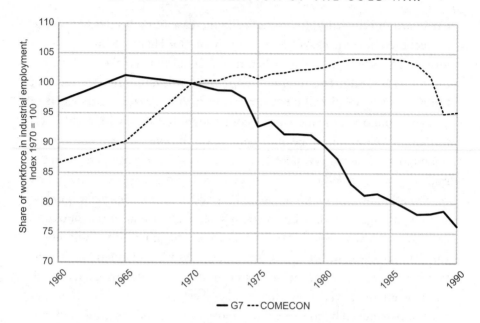

Figure 4.2 The rise and fall of industrial workforces in the East and West.

Reformatted with permission of University of Chicago Press Journals from Maximilian Krahé, "TINA and the Market Turn: Why Deindustrialization Proceeded under Democratic Capitalism but Not State Socialism," *Critical Historical Studies*, 8:2, Fall 2021, Figure 1; permission conveyed through Copyright Clearance Center, Inc.

As Western governments pulled back from owning the means of production, they did not affect a similar decline in the size of their welfare states. The large increase in unemployment even slightly increased social spending across the OECD (Organization for Economic Cooperation and Development) from 14.5 percent to 16.5 percent of GDP during the 1980s.[34] But high interest rates and globalized financial markets did place strict limits on how much public welfare and state intervention Western leaders could pursue in their domestic economies. Global capital holders tolerated the survival of the welfare state as a way of providing basic necessities for the workers made redundant by economic restructuring, but they did not tolerate any expansion of the state's role in regulating the economy or providing economic and social security for its citizens.

These new limits became most starkly apparent in France. In 1981, French voters bucked the conservative trend spreading through the Anglo-American world and elected the socialist François Mitterrand president. As the first directly elected socialist head of state in Europe, Mitterrand's election was a historic achievement for the European Left. Socialists within France and around Europe viewed his victory as a long-awaited chance to use the reins of state power to institute a "rupture with capitalism" and bring the economy fully under government control.[35] Mitterrand's campaign platform contained all the hallmarks of the politics of making promises—industries would be nationalized, government jobs would be created, and the welfare state would be resolutely expanded. In a governing coalition with the French Communist Party, the Socialists quickly delivered on these promises in their first year in office. Public spending jumped 27 percent, and the government borrowed money to raise wages and pensions, lower the retirement age, and reduce work hours. Thirty-eight banks and financial companies, five of France's largest industrial corporations, and the country's two giant iron and steel conglomerates were nationalized.[36] And for a brief moment, the politics of making promises in the West reached their postwar apogee.

But capital holders did not like what they saw, and they wasted little time in signaling their displeasure. As inflation, spending, and taxes on wealth increased within France, investors did everything they could to get their money out of francs. Capital flight forced French authorities to devalue the currency in October 1981 and June 1982 and caused Mitterrand to begin his own search for new economic thinking. In support of the second devaluation, he announced what became known as his "U-turn": a domestic austerity package of wage and price freezes, tax increases, and spending cuts that directly contradicted the thrust of his earlier policies. But with industry still nationalized and communists still in the government, this austerity did little to restore capital's confidence. Faced with the prospect of further devaluations and capital flight, Mitterrand abandoned his socialist crusade completely in 1983 and embraced a policy of *rigueur,* a code word for prioritizing price stability and fiscal austerity over socialist domestic policy. By the spring of 1984, the communists were gone from the government, and Mitterrand was calling for a modernization of the French economy *à l'américaine.*[37] Over the remainder of the decade, the government joined the privatization craze sweeping the West and led the global charge to eliminate national capital controls and give finance free reign to roam across state borders.[38]

Thus, we can conclude that although the size of the Western welfare state remained largely unchanged in the 1980s, its *meaning* in Western societies changed dramatically. The postwar welfare state had emerged as part of Western governments' broader commitment to regulate the economy in pursuit of higher living standards and equitable distribution across their societies. But its persistence in the 1980s signaled a trimming of government's aspirations. As high unemployment or stagnant incomes became enduring failings of many Western economies, the welfare state became an ally of the politics of breaking promises by providing subsistence to the millions of workers deindustrialization had made superfluous. Indeed, in a place like Britain, the government actively encouraged healthy people to apply for disability benefits simply so they would not show up in the state's unemployment numbers.[39] As governments' ability or willingness to raise wages and ensure employment diminished, so too did citizens' confidence in the state's power to shape the economy toward just and prosperous ends. As Tony Judt has written, there was a "cumulative unravelling" in the Western world during the 1980s of the postwar assumption "that the activist state was a necessary condition of economic growth and social amelioration."[40] No longer self-confident architects of equality and progress, Western governments became tools for socializing the human costs of economic restructuring.

◆ ◆ ◆

The static size and diminished expectations of government were nowhere more evident than in the United States. Despite his assertive rhetoric about getting the government out of Americans' lives, Ronald Reagan failed miserably to shrink the size of the American state. "The true Reagan Revolution never had a chance," David Stockman, Reagan's first budget director, wrote in his 1986 memoir, *The Triumph of Politics: How the Reagan Revolution Failed*. What started as an "ideas-based" movement to create "minimalist government" turned into "an unintended exercise in free lunch economics," Stockman wrote. Reagan's tax cuts and military spending increases combined with the government's inability to reduce domestic spending "unleashed" a "massive fiscal error . . . on the national and world economy."[41] The Reagan Revolution was "only a half-revolution—and a fiscal disaster."[42]

The budget director's views had not always been so dour. Stockman burst onto the American political scene in the late 1970s as an ardent proponent of supply-side economics, and he became Reagan's budget director with the firm intention of cutting taxes and shrinking the size of the state. A central tenet of at least the rhetoric of supply-side economics was that tax cuts would pay for themselves by spurring a boom in economic growth. In the first budget forecast of the Reagan presidential campaign in August 1980, Stockman appeared to provide proof of this tenet by producing budget projections that led to a budget surplus in 1985. These projections included Reagan's plan for a 30 percent cut in income tax rates, a 7 percent annual increase in military spending, and no significant cuts in entitlements. Stockman would later call these projections "neither logical, careful, nor accurate within a country mile," but he achieved such a logic-defying budget miracle because of the dramatic effect of inflation on tax revenue through a process known as "bracket creep." As the inflation of the 1970s raised Americans' incomes, it also pushed them into new tax brackets, which led them to pay a higher share of their income in taxes.[43] Critics ranging from Jimmy Carter in the White House to George H. W. Bush in the Republican presidential primary painted Reagan's program as inflationary "voodoo economics" that would explode the budget deficit. But with double-digit inflation showing no sign of slowing down, Reagan's economic team could produce budget projections to refute the charge. Most importantly, the more the Reagan team told itself and the country that it could cut taxes, increase military spending, and balance the budget, the more they actually believed such a combination was possible.[44] Reagan sincerely proclaimed, in the early moments of his first inaugural address, "For decades we have piled deficit upon deficit, mortgaging our future and our children's future for the temporary convenience of the present." Normal citizens, he said, "can, by borrowing, live beyond our means, but for only a limited period of time. Why, then, should we think that collectively, as a nation, we're not bound by that same limitation?"[45]

Before 1981, there was little reason to think the nation was not bound by the same limitation. But the events of Reagan's first term would permanently alter this line of thinking. Change began with Volcker. As the Federal Reserve's skyrocketing interest rates brought the liquidity engine of the 1970s to a screeching halt, inflation began an unexpectedly precipitous retreat—from a high of 13.5 percent in 1980 to 3.9 percent in 1982. The economic engine of bracket creep that had fueled Stockman's forecasts quickly evaporated.

As it did, Congress passed the Economic Recovery Tax Act (ERTA), which included a 25 percent reduction in personal income tax rates over three years, a significant cut in the capital gains tax, and an enormous reduction in corporate taxes through extremely favorable changes in depreciation rules. Combined with financial innovations taking place on Wall Street, including the creation of the collateralized mortgage obligation, the ERTA created two economic conditions that would define the Reagan financial buildup—an extremely hospitable environment for debt investments and an unprecedented hole in federal tax revenues. In retrospect, the Reagan economic team estimated that the ERTA reduced the effective tax rate on capital by 50 percent,[46] and the Office of Management and Budget calculated the cumulative federal revenue loss of the ERTA over the course of the 1980s at almost $1.5 trillion.[47]

This decline in tax revenue only became apparent once Volcker's sky-high interest rates had their unexpectedly quick effect on inflation. As inflation began its steep decline, administration officials ran new budget projections in the fall of 1981 based on lower inflation and economic growth numbers. They discovered, to their surprise, that the fiscal policy they had just enacted would produce, in Stockman's memorable formulation, "deficits as far as the eye can see." The new projections were "horrifying," Stockman recalled. They "showed cumulative red ink over five years of more than *$700 billion*. That was nearly as much national debt as it had taken America two hundred years to accumulate. It just took your breath away. No government official had ever seen such a thing."[48] In his diary, Reagan called the new deficit projections a "bomb." He wrote with apparent surprise, "Inflation is a tax. We have brought down inflation so much faster than we anticipated that tax revenues will be lower than we figured."[49] By December 1981, he had resigned himself to the fact that "we who were going to balance the budget face the biggest budget deficits ever."[50]

The question on everyone's mind in the fall of 1981 was how these deficits could possibly be funded. In a closed national economy, economic theory posited that government budget deficits would harm the economy by "crowding out" private investment, driving up interest rates, and killing economic growth. No less an authority than Volcker himself firmly held to this position, and most of the administration's own economists agreed.[51] Larry Kudlow, a staff economist on the Council of Economic Advisors at the time, concluded at the beginning of 1982, "Excessive Federal and federally-assisted borrowing will compete with private demands, absorbing much needed capital resources and generating additional upward interest rate pressures."[52]

The stakes of this funding question for Reagan's presidency could not have been higher. If the massive deficits Reagan had created through tax cuts and military spending increases in his first year had crowded out domestic investment and killed off economic recovery in the remaining three years of his first term, the political effects on his presidency would have been resoundingly negative: he would have had to either retreat on his signature policy achievements and repeal his income tax cuts while cutting back on military spending or run for reelection in 1984 with the economy still mired in a deep recession. Put simply, if traditional economic theory had held true in the early 1980s, the Reagan Revolution itself would have been crowded out of the American political scene, and Reagan's military buildup would have been an inconsequential blip on the radar of the long-running Cold War conflict.

By the early 1980s, however, glimmers of change in the global economy suggested that Reagan's day of financial reckoning might forever be deferred. International capital flows were on the rise, and there were faint indications the United States was uniquely positioned in the global economy to use these flows for its lasting benefit. Governments had long faced a fundamental choice between guns and butter, but perhaps with the aid of the world's capital, the United States could transcend that choice for good.

Of this, no one could be sure. But in the summer of 1981, some members of the Reagan administration were eager to find out. In June, the administration created the Cabinet Council Working Group on International Investment to review US policy toward foreign investment because it had become "an important and rapidly growing source of capital to the U.S. economy."[53] By the fall of 1981, the chairman of the Council of Economic Advisors was writing that "foreign portfolio flows are potentially useful in easing deficit financing pressures in domestic markets."[54] But this was far from certain, and smart minds across the political and economic spectrum doubted its feasibility.[55] William Niskanen, a member of the Reagan economic staff, speculated to an audience at the American Enterprise Institute in December 1981 that "the opportunity to import capital" might save the economy from the harm of the deficits. But, he recalled, "the audience rejected the plausibility of net capital inflows in any substantial magnitude."[56]

Throughout 1982, the question of the role of foreign capital in funding the US deficits lay dormant as the economy entered the deepest recession of the postwar period. In this gloomy economic climate, there was little danger of government borrowing crowding out private investment because there was little private investment to speak of. The public debate was instead about the future. The now widespread recognition that the ERTA would lead to unprecedented deficits led to loud political debates in 1982 and a number of piecemeal efforts to close the gap between revenues and expenditures, including the Tax Equity and Fiscal Responsibility Act of 1982 (TEFRA).[57] Though accompanied by a great deal of consternation and fanfare, these efforts left the long-term picture basically unaltered: budget and current account deficits as far as the eye could see.

Something would have to give. And in 1983, Reagan administration officials began to notice that it was the old rules of economics, rather than their own policies, that were changing. Over the course of the year, they came to understand and tentatively embrace the fact that the newly globalized financial system would allow them to borrow foreign capital in far larger quantities than anyone had ever dreamed possible. The United States ran a current account deficit of $8 billion in 1982 and was projected to run one of $25 billion in 1983. This meant that after being a capital exporter for most of the postwar period, the United States had made the fundamental shift to being a net importer of capital from the rest of the world. Volcker's high interest rates and Reagan's tax cuts, labor discipline, and budget deficits had created a perfect storm of attractive conditions for capital, and foreigners were flocking to US markets in response.

The result was the so-called Super Dollar. From its nadir in the fall of 1978, the US dollar began a rapid and virtually constant ascent through 1985.[58] The Super Dollar was a potent double-edged sword for the US economy. For many economists, exporters, and workers throughout the country, the dollar's rise was a disturbing trend because it made foreign goods cheaper within the United States and priced American exports out of foreign markets. The higher the dollar rose, the more American workers lost their jobs, the more downward pressure was placed on wages, and the more businesses went bankrupt. But for capital holders and consumers, a rising dollar meant greater returns, more access to borrowed capital, and cheaper goods. And for the government, the rising dollar allowed US officials to solve their fiscal problems without having to raise taxes or cut spending to balance the budget. Foreign capital inflows transformed the hard budget constraints of traditional economy theory into a brave new world of no budget constraints at all.

Martin Feldstein, one of the most influential economists within the administration, noted in an internal memo in spring 1983 that the rising dollar was a "safety valve" that reduced the competition for capital and inflationary pressures within the United States. The United States could utilize this safety valve because the dollar had become "a portfolio asset for international investors." Now that Volcker's interest rate policy had restored capital holders' confidence in the US capacity to impose discipline, foreigners were chasing dollar investments because of the currency's central role in international trade and financial flows. As a result, Feldstein wrote, the administration did not need to worry in the short term about the country's turn toward relying on foreign capital to meet its domestic needs. "A country cannot expect to go on running a current account deficit forever," he wrote. "But why should we expect or want a current account balance every year?"[59]

Treasury Secretary Donald Regan very much agreed. In the summer of 1983, he established a number of working groups in the administration to study international capital flows as well as the country's trade and current account deficits.[60] The resulting studies cautiously embraced the new reality. "Traditionally the current account was thought to drive international transactions," officials noted in September 1983. "Currently, however, there are reasons to believe the capital account is the driving force, as foreigners seek to invest in the United States. As they exchange their currencies for ours, the value of the dollar is pushed upward." Foreigners sought out US financial markets because of the "marked reduction in inflation" in the United States and because US markets were "the largest and most liquid in the world." This left the United States in a uniquely benign international position, officials tentatively believed: "If it is true that the rest of the world is intentionally seeking out the United States as a capital investment location, there could be a beneficial impact on U.S. credit and equity markets and a valuable supplement to domestic savings."[61]

Volcker and his colleagues at the Federal Reserve fully understood the crucial role they played in unlocking the nation's access to foreign capital. All the leading members of the Federal Reserve in the 1980s later admitted that attracting foreign capital to the United States played a key role in their decision-making. Vice Chairman Preston Martin explained, "We have to have rates high enough to bring in the capital. All of us have to consider the government financing very seriously." Governor Charles Partee concurred. "We stayed above the foreign interest rates so that foreign investors would be attracted to the U.S," he said.[62] Japanese investors were by far the most important to attract. Martin explained how the Federal Reserve set interest rates just high enough to attract Japanese capital. "How are the Japanese reacting to these new thirty-year securities?" he would ask his colleagues. "What mattered was the Japanese. Are the Japanese buying? Fine, if they are, we don't have to raise rates."[63]

The combination of Volcker's interest rates and Reagan's deficits produced a financial buildup in the United States of massive proportions: $85 billion in net foreign capital entered the United States in 1983, followed by $103 billion in 1984, $129 billion in 1985, and $221 billion in 1986. The federal budget deficit in these years ranged from $208 billion in 1983 to $221 billion in 1986, so by the end of this period, foreign capital inflows were directly or indirectly covering *all* the federal government's borrowing.[64]

By the dawn of 1984, the US economy was booming and inflation had been vanquished. But the turnaround had not happened in the way Reagan had anticipated. Rather than defeating inflation by balancing the budget and cutting spending, the administration had exploded the federal deficit and unexpectedly discovered a way to pay for American guns and butter with foreign capital. The two economic phenomena that supply-side policies were supposed to encourage—increased savings and investment—had not materialized and, in fact, had gotten worse.[65] Instead, an administration economist noted in early 1984 that "large flows of foreign funds into the United States have helped finance our Federal budget deficits and partially alleviated upward pressure on domestic interest rates." This meant that the "continuation of the current trends" would make "the United States a debtor nation in the international economy" for the first time since 1914.[66] Those trends did continue, and in 1986, the United States became the largest debtor country in the world.[67] Foreign capital was now sustaining the renewal of American prosperity at home and the projection of American power abroad. It is a trend that has continued to this day (Figure 4.3).

The resurgence of the American economy in the 1980s was also a profoundly unequal renewal of fortunes. The potent tonic of high interest rates, low taxes, capital inflows, and booming asset prices made the 1980s a dynamite decade to be wealthy in the United States. Over the course of the decade, the wealthiest 10 percent of Americans saw their share of the country's total income grow 16 percent; the wealthiest 1 percent saw their share increase 43 percent; and the wealthiest 0.1 percent saw their share surge 71 percent. This inaugurated a long-term redistribution of income upward in US society, as the top 1 percent's share of total national income exploded from 10 percent in 1980 to 23.5 percent on the eve of the 2008 financial crisis.[68]

The less fortunate were, well, less fortunate. Wages stagnated, job security decreased, and entire occupations virtually disappeared from the

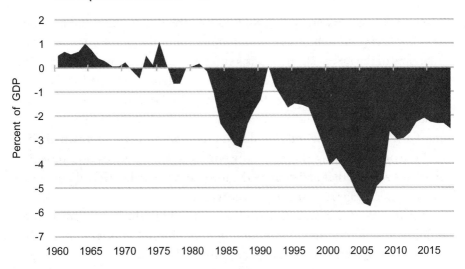

Figure 4.3 **The US current account balance as a percentage of GDP.**
Data sources: Federal Reserve Bank of St. Louis and IMF World Economic Outlook.

American landscape. In place of the postwar social contract of rising in-comes, job security, and full employment, working- and middle-class Americans were offered a new deal of debt-fueled consumption. Outstanding consumer credit loans doubled during the 1980s, and two-thirds of American households had a credit card by the end of the century.[69] Cheap imports from abroad, rising home prices, and access to all manner of credit became the new foundations of a decidedly more precarious American way of life.

◆ ◆ ◆

Just because the US economy was not suffering from crowding-out effects did not mean that crowding out was not happening. It only meant that it was not happening in the United States. As capital began to pour into the United States in the early 1980s, governments around the world that had borrowed heavily on global capital markets in the 1970s suddenly found it difficult to maintain their solvency. The petrodollar recycling system that had fueled the global economy for almost a decade ground to a halt. The G7 countries' cumulative capital outflow of $46.8 billion in the 1970s turned into a cumulative capital inflow of $347.4 billion in the 1980s.[70] It is strictly true in theory and roughly true in practice that international current accounts must balance out at a global level. International finance in the 1980s was Newtonian: every action produced an equal and opposite reaction. The equal and opposite reaction to the Reagan financial buildup was the sovereign debt crisis that came to dominate the global political economy of the 1980s. The debt crisis empowered lenders over borrowers in the global economy, and because the United States controlled the world economy's lender of last resort—the IMF—the US government came to hold a particularly powerful position during the crisis. The potent combination of the Reagan financial buildup and the administration's own financial diplomacy during the crisis unwound the relationships of economic interdependence that had defined the 1970s and opened powerful points of American leverage over the rest of the world.

The first sign of crisis came—as it often would in the last decade of the Cold War—from Poland. As we have seen, the Polish Crisis was intimately linked to developments in the global financial system. From the vantage point of global capital holders, events in Warsaw and Washington moved in opposite directions in 1981. As commercial bankers watched Volcker's burgeoning success in defeating inflation and imposing discipline on the American economy, they also saw the Polish government struggle to do the same on the other side of the Iron Curtain. While they watched Reagan fire the air traffic controllers with surprising speed and popular support, they also saw Solidarity grow ever more resistant to the communist government's attempts to trade domestic austerity for limited political reform in Poland. And as they saw Reagan's tax cuts create massive new demand for capital within the United States by the end of the year, they also watched Wojciech Jaruzelski declare martial law in Poland on December 13, 1981, with his country in de facto bankruptcy.

The result was a collective rethinking of the sovereign lending system that had propped up governments across the developing and communist worlds since the oil crisis of 1973. "Fundamental change is sweeping the Euromarkets," *Euromoney* reported in May 1982. "The era of the government borrower, the main prop of international bank lending in the 'seventies, is dying." Bankers reported that "the Eastern European economic situation" had generated "a change in attitude" among banks toward the sovereign loan market.[71]

In turning away from their previous state clients, the banks were unwittingly sowing the seeds of their own potential destruction. A decline in sovereign loans did not mean a decline in sovereign debt. By 1982, debt among non-OECD countries sat at $600 billion, more than enough to bring down the global financial system if the debtors defaulted on their loans.[72] This meant the Western financial system was fully interdependent with the debtors of the developing and communist worlds. The prospect of default became all too real in August 1982 when Mexican officials informed the international financial community that the country could no longer service its debts. Argentina and Brazil soon announced the same, and by autumn the world was hurtling toward the largest financial crisis since the Great Depression.

Officials in the US government, the Federal Reserve, and the IMF quickly came to believe that resolving the crisis would require large amounts of two things: structural adjustment from the borrowers and more money from the lenders. Structural adjustment—which, the reader will recall, Soviet officials termed *strukturnaya perestroika*—was an umbrella term for a whole series of policies with one primary goal: to turn a debtor country into a net exporter of capital and thus begin the process of paying off the debt. To do this, Western officials told debtor countries to devalue their currencies and eliminate foreign exchange controls, reduce their government budget deficits through cuts in investment and public subsidies, raise domestic interest rates to encourage domestic saving and halt inflation, privatize state-owned industries, lower import tariffs, eliminate domestic price and wage controls, strengthen bankruptcy laws to eliminate inefficient enterprises, and eliminate barriers to foreign investment. This long list of policy prescriptions would affect the debtor economies in diverse ways, but it pointed in one overarching direction: economic discipline. To solve the burgeoning sovereign debt crisis, Western officials believed that debtor countries would have to implement the politics of breaking promises.

But discipline alone would not be enough. Breaking promises would take time, but the debts needed to be paid without delay if the system was to avoid a general financial crisis throughout the capitalist world. Banks counted sovereign loans as assets on their balance sheets because, under normal circumstances, the principal and interest payments on loans offset the banks' obligations to their depositors (the banks' liabilities). If debtors defaulted on their debts and those sovereign loans became "nonperforming," the banks would have to write those loans down as losses on their balance sheets. One or many sovereign defaults, therefore, had the potential to turn billions of dollars in bank assets into billions of dollars in losses virtually overnight. And if that happened, it was not difficult to imagine how economic depression across the capitalist world would soon follow.

Unwinding this interdependence would not happen overnight. Banks would need years to build up reserves on their balance sheets that could sustain the blow of writing down their sovereign loan portfolios as losses. In order for the banks to have more time, the borrowers needed to have more money. Only new money from Western banks, governments, and international organizations enabled the debtor countries to continue to service their debts. And only the debtor countries continuing to service their debts allowed the banks to continue to treat their sovereign loans as assets on their balance sheets. In short, unless debtor countries received a fresh infusion of capital to pay off their old debts that were coming due, the accounting ruse that propped up the banks' house of cards would collapse in a downward spiral of defaults, write-offs of losses, insolvencies, and bank runs. Therefore, Western officials also believed that they— and the commercial banks whose reluctance to continue lending had precipitated the crisis in the first place—would have to provide debtors with a fresh round of capital to pay off old debts.[73]

Western financial institutions and the Reagan administration came to believe in this two-pronged approach of austerity and capital infusion very early in the crisis. Indeed, members of the administration were planning for it as soon as signs of trouble emerged in the spring of 1982. At that time, the Federal Reserve began circulating proposals to dramatically increase the IMF's capital base (known as its quota). The Reagan administration supported this proposal because, as one NSC official noted in April 1982, "although most . . . vulnerable countries have implemented austere stabilization programs, it will probably take between 4–10 years until the major economic adjustments entailed can . . . sharply curtail or eliminate borrowing requirements."[74]

In the meantime, new capital would need to be pumped into the international financial system. Western central banks kicked this off with a $1.85 billion loan from the Bank of International Settlements to Mexico just days after the government declared insolvency, and the US Treasury followed with $2 billion in further credits and financial support. The central banks and the Treasury Department only extended their financial aid on the condition that Mexico negotiate an adjustment program with the IMF, so in November 1982, the Fund and the Mexican government signed a three-year agreement that granted Mexico $3.7 billion in exchange for a domestic economic plan that would dramatically cut the budget and current account deficits through 1985. New government money and debtor austerity went hand in hand. But the

IMF, the Fed, and the Treasury also aimed to ensure that commercial banks contributed their fair share to keeping the financial system afloat. So, even as the IMF agreed to the terms of the bailout in November, its managing director, Jacque de Larosière, shocked the banks by forcing them to supplement the public financing with an additional $5 billion of their own capital.[75] This combination of fundamentals—short-term bridge financing from central banks and governments, the negotiation of an austere IMF structural adjustment program, and the commitment of new bank capital to the debtor country—became the standard formula for addressing the many national debt crises that roiled the world economy over the next decade.[76]

With this standard formula in hand, the Reagan administration, the IMF, and the Federal Reserve continued to strengthen their leverage by buying time to decrease the interdependence in the international financial system. The trick was to create enough new liquidity to prevent sovereign defaults and banks failures without setting off new inflationary pressures in the global economy. In this way, Volcker's program of high interest rates at home was intimately linked to the Fed's and IMF's handling of the debt crises abroad. Beginning in the fall of 1982, Volcker and the Fed began to moderate the draconian interest rates of the previous two years to provide a modicum of liquidity to the financial system. Throughout 1983, administration officials and Reagan himself stridently lobbied Congress to increase US funding of the IMF. Despite a slew of domestic opponents who claimed that increasing IMF funding would merely bail out the big banks who had engaged in reckless lending, Congress passed a significant expansion of IMF funding into law in the fall of 1983.[77] Not for the last time, the US government bailed out Wall Street despite the resistance of Main Street because it believed that the banks were too big to fail.

Across the Global South, debt crises begat more debt crises as the banks pulled back on their lending to sovereign borrowers. By the end of 1984, only two Latin American countries—Colombia and Paraguay—had not rescheduled their debt, and all told, thirty countries across the world had fallen behind on their debt payments and were seeking help from the IMF (and, by extension, the United States). With each passing day, Western banks were able to set aside more reserves to cushion the potential losses on their sovereign loans, and as they did, the interdependence of the 1970s waned and the US government's leverage waxed in equal measure. As the Western financial system became ever more insulated from the threat of sovereign default, US officials grew to understand that they now held all the cards. As Treasury

Secretary Regan brashly recognized as quickly as November 1982 in a meeting of the National Security Council, debtor countries would "look to us for help." The question was, "What do we want in return?"[78]

Structural adjustment and austerity were what they wanted, and over the course of the 1980s, that is exactly what they got. In country after country, the Reagan administration and the IMF restructured the economies of the Global South. Even as the administration presided over unprecedented budget deficits in the United States and turned the country into the world's largest borrower, the US Treasury and the IMF demanded that borrowing countries in the developing world act differently. Budget deficits were slashed, austerity of all kinds was imposed, and state intervention in the economy was beaten back at every turn. Poverty and economic dislocation spiked throughout debtor countries, and austerity inevitably bred political resistance. Most governments that entered debt crises failed to survive them, and a wave of political change followed in debt's wake. Across Latin America, military dictatorships and authoritarian rulers who had survived the 1970s by borrowing on global capital markets collapsed in the 1980s as the economic basis of their rule precipitously crumpled. In their stead, US, IMF, and domestic officials within debtor countries looked to democratic elections as a means of building popular support and legitimacy for austerity. As one Brazilian business publication warned while the country faced economic crisis, "The dark clouds accumulating on the horizon . . . will only be dissipated with an authentic and democratic government."[79] Many throughout the region agreed, and over the course of the 1980s, Latin America experienced a wave of democratization directly tied to the region's sovereign debt crisis.[80] Just as in Thatcher's Britain and Reagan's America, governments in the Global South that had received a stamp of democratic legitimacy found it easier to break promises, so electoral democracy and the debt crisis rippled through the global economy hand in hand.

Thus, by 1985, the world economy had undergone a dramatic restructuring in the six short years since Paul Volcker had assumed his post at the Federal Reserve. The United States had emerged from the malaise of the 1970s to recapture its dominant position in the global economy, and the Reagan administration had discovered an unexpected way to renew economic growth at home and project power abroad with a seemingly endless supply of foreign capital. The Volcker Shock had simultaneously imposed the politics of breaking promises on the United States and a resistant world, but the Reagan financial buildup had quickly allowed the United States to write a new, but lopsided, social contract funded by borrowed foreign capital. And in buying time for banks to insulate themselves from defaults during the early years of the sovereign debt crisis, the Reagan administration and the IMF had unwound the financial interdependence of the 1970s and established new and potent points of American leverage over debtors in the world economy.

Through it all, the Cold War conflict between East and West persisted, but it was hardly insulated from the effects of the capitalist perestroika. The Reagan administration entered office with a keen sense of the Communist Bloc's economic weakness and an intense desire to exploit that weakness for geopolitical gain. Had the capitalist perestroika not fundamentally restructured the world economy in the early 1980s, it is likely this intense desire would have come to naught. But because the Volcker Shock, the Reagan financial buildup, and the sovereign debt crisis starkly transformed the world economy in the United States' favor, Reagan and his administration were able to wage an effective economic Cold War against the Soviet Bloc in the early 1980s and set the stage for the socialist perestroika that was to come.

CHAPTER 5

The Economic Cold War

"WE WERE UNDER attack," János Fekete, the Hungarian state banker, told *Euromoney* in 1982 in reference to his country's fate.[1] Amid the rising Cold War tensions of the early 1980s, Fekete could have been excused for using such language to describe the military policies of Ronald Reagan. The new US president had campaigned on a policy of strident anticommunism and had launched a massive expansion and modernization of the US military in his first year in office. Both the United States and the Soviet Union had recently developed a new generation of intermediate-range nuclear weapons—the so-called Euromissiles—that were capable of hitting their targets, and thus starting World War III, in less than ten minutes. Cold War tensions were at their highest point since the early 1960s, and people across the world had begun to consider the prospect of superpower war to be all too frighteningly real.

But the attack Fekete was referring to had nothing to do with military hardware, and the attackers he identified had no connection to the United States. They were, instead, the central banks of Libya, Iran, and Iraq, and their weapon of choice had been money. In late December 1981, each had withdrawn the $200–$300 million in hard currency they had on deposit in Budapest, precipitating a general run on the Hungarian National Bank. Soon, financial institutions from every corner of the world were pulling their money out of the Communist Bloc as a whole. "The door to the Euro-market," *Euromoney* noted, "had closed on Comecon: quietly, politely, but firmly. Sometime during the winter, banks across the globe had . . . decided . . . that they wished to cut their exposure to Comecon by as much as possible."[2] By the time spring arrived, foreign banks had withdrawn $1.1 billion from Hungary and left Budapest with a measly $374 million to make the country's mounting debt payments.[3] Fekete found it difficult to stomach the injustice the global financial system had visited upon his country. "We were attacked," he lamented, "without any reason."[4]

There were, in fact, many reasons why international capital holders attacked Hungary and the rest of the communist world in the spring of 1982. The bank run on Budapest was just one piece of an economic Cold War that unfolded in the early 1980s against the backdrop of the capitalist perestroika. Beginning with the Polish Crisis in 1980 and extending through Mikhail Gorbachev's accession to power in the Soviet Union in 1985, the two superpowers renewed their military competition and once again looked to energy and finance to influence their allies and adversaries.

This new economic Cold War had three components. First, faced with mounting economic problems at home and geopolitical crises on their imperial periphery, Soviet leaders came to the historic decision that the burden of empire had become too much to bear, and they committed themselves to lightening that burden, even if it meant risking the loss of the empire itself. The Polish Crisis was a watershed moment in this respect. In the crucible of the crisis, Soviet leaders decided they would not invade Poland to crush Solidarity and even expressed a willingness to accept a Solidarity-led government in Warsaw. They decided, in other words, to repeal the Brezhnev Doctrine, their long-standing policy that they would intervene in allies' affairs to "protect" socialism from foes both foreign and domestic. At the same time, in recognition of the growing limits of their material capabilities, they cut back the energy resources they delivered to the rest of Eastern Europe. Allied governments in the region stridently protested the Soviet decision and warned that the cutbacks would leave them dangerously exposed to Western financial and political pressure. But Soviet leaders held firm to their conviction that the interests of the Soviet domestic economy were now more important than the political stability of their allies. It was a historic revision of Soviet national interest that would have profound effects on the last decade of the Cold War.

Second, the Reagan administration entered office with a keen awareness of the growing limits of Soviet material capabilities and aimed to exacerbate them. Reagan and his team attempted to force the Soviet leadership to choose between the three competing demands on its diminishing resources: its military, its allies, and its own population. Through the military buildup that bore his name, Reagan aimed to compel Soviet leaders to choose between continuing the arms race and maintaining support for their allies and domestic population. And through a coordinated campaign to limit Soviet access to Western financial markets and restrict Soviet energy sales on the world market, the administration aimed to cut off the Kremlin's access to the energy and financial wealth required to fund its military, diplomatic, and domestic commitments. They aimed, in short, to force Moscow to confront the politics of breaking promises.

It was a strategy that produced decidedly mixed results. The military buildup did have its intended effect on Soviet decision-making when Gorbachev began to seek arms control agreements on American terms in the mid-1980s to free up resources for the Soviet civilian economy. But the administration's efforts to restrict Soviet access to financial markets and energy wealth proved to be an abject failure. The United States' allies in Europe and Asia roundly rejected Washington's plans to restrict the Communist Bloc's access to capital markets, and they continued to buy Soviet energy in exchange for billions of dollars in hard currency. At this level of diplomacy and policy, the administration's energy and financial efforts produced little more than transatlantic rancor.

And yet, as Fekete described so indignantly, the Communist Bloc still lost access to international capital markets, and the Soviets were nonetheless forced to choose among their military, their allies, and their own people in the early 1980s. At the same time that the Reagan administration was mounting its failed campaign to restrict the Communist Bloc's access to global capital markets, the forces at the heart of the capitalist perestroika—the Volcker Shock and the Reagan financial buildup—were achieving this result of their own accord. The international financial system attacked the communist world for the same reason it attacked debtor countries in the Global South at the same time: the high interest rates and budget deficits in the United States began to monopolize the world's capital, and there was little left for everyone else. And though the administration failed to restrict Moscow's energy sales on the world market, the Soviets' own domestic economic problems forced them to confront the choice of breaking promises to their military, allies, or citizens, just as the administration hoped.

The result was a perfect storm of crisis that produced the third element of the economic Cold War: the bailouts of Eastern Europe. The decline in subsidized Soviet energy and the scarcity of global capital left debtor countries of the region unable to pay their debts and in search of a lifeline. Time and again, they turned to the Soviet Union for aid, only to be spurned by Moscow. This left them with no choice but to seek Western aid, and in the early 1980s, Western governments and institutions bailed them out of their financial distress. These bailouts signaled a dramatic shift in the Cold War balance of power. If, through the 1970s, Eastern Europe had been within the Soviet Union's economic sphere of influence—as the bankers' "umbrella theory" posited—then from the early 1980s onward, the region came to rest under the economic umbrella of the West. From that point on, it was Western governments and institutions rather than the Soviet Union that provided decisive economic aid to the region, and it was policy makers in Washington and Bonn who attached conditions to their support. This conditionality would, in time, provide the West with a powerful tool to force the communist leaders of Eastern Europe to confront the politics of breaking promises.

◆ ◆ ◆

By the late 1970s, the Soviet economy had ground to a halt. After averaging 5.2 percent from 1966 to 1970 and 3.7 percent from 1971 to 1975, economic growth had slowed to an anemic 0.8 percent in 1979. A string of three consecutive bad harvests forced the Kremlin to buy massive amounts of grain on the world market. After importing only $100 million worth of grain in 1970, Moscow was forced to import $3–$4 billion of grain every year by the late 1970s just to maintain Soviet citizens' meager standard of living. To pay for this rising import bill, the Soviet leadership had relied on the simultaneous boom in their energy production and world market prices to export oil and natural gas for mountains of hard currency. Soviet hard currency export revenues from oil and natural gas had risen from $444 million in 1970 to $3.6 billion in 1975 to $11 billion in 1979.[5] But by the end of the decade, the domestic oil industry found itself in crisis. Its problems were both geographical and technological: Soviet oil men had tapped all the country's easily accessible oil, and future growth would have to come from regions geographically and technologically more difficult to exploit.[6] The rapid expansion of the Soviet natural gas industry partially offset oil's stagnation, but the oil industry remained far larger, so its troubles could not be papered over.

Much like the first oil crisis of 1973, the second oil crisis of 1979 arrived in Moscow as a potent double-edged sword. The sudden 150 percent increase in world oil prices boosted the value of Soviet energy exports at precisely the moment Moscow needed hard currency to keep its faltering economy afloat. But it also, once again, exploded the size of the subsidy the Soviet Union was providing to its allies for energy deliveries. Indeed, the size of the Soviet energy subsidy reached its peak in the late 1970s and early 1980s (Figure 5.1). The combination of rising costs of energy extraction, rising energy demands from Eastern Europe, and now the rising subsidy for energy deliveries combined to produce an overwhelming material burden on Moscow.[7]

If the Soviets' allies in Europe presented a long-term structural challenge, their new enemies in Afghanistan constituted an immediate and debilitating threat. When the Politburo reluctantly authorized the Afghanistan invasion in December 1979, it committed 30,000 troops to what was expected to be a quick and easy campaign to overthrow the government and stabilize a loyal socialist government in its place. Events quickly defied expectations. From virtually its first day in the country, the Soviet Army faced widespread resistance from broad swaths of Afghan society and a ruthlessly determined insurgency that would become known the world over as the mujahideen. Within a year, Moscow had committed 115,000 troops and spent an estimated $2.7 billion on military operations, but the conflict settled into a stubborn stalemate with no end in sight.[8]

Amid these dreary conditions and darkening horizons, the onset of crisis in Poland in August 1980 was a most unwelcome development. Initially, Soviet officials were happy to bear the traditional burden of supporting an ally at a time of need. The USSR should "lend all possible economic assistance to enable the Poles to make it through this trying time," Brezhnev told his Politburo colleagues in October 1980. "No matter how burdensome it will be for us, we should do it."[9] In line with the general secretary's conviction, officials put together multiple aid packages in the fall of 1980 and early 1981 that eventually totaled some $4 billion worth of energy, raw material, and food deliveries as well as debt deferrals and hard currency aid.[10]

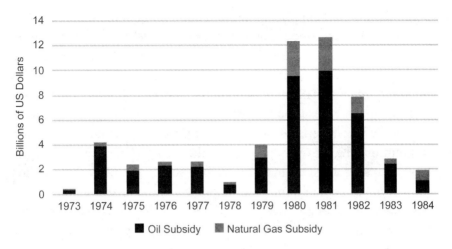

Figure 5.1 **The estimated annual Soviet oil and natural gas price subsidy.**
Data sources: "Übersicht über die Preisentwicklung für Erdöl ab 1972," undated but 1985, DE/1/58747, BArch Lichterfelde, and PlanEcon, Inc., *Soviet and East European Energy Databank* (Washington, DC: PlanEcon, Inc., 1986).

In doing so, however, they also repeatedly bumped up against the limit of their material capabilities, which spurred them to fundamentally rethink the place of Eastern Europe in the country's national interest. The first limit arrived in October 1980, when the Poles asked the Kremlin to increase their oil and hard currency support so Warsaw could meet its mounting debt payments to the West. The Politburo decided it could meet the request, but only if it simultaneously decreased oil deliveries to other bloc countries for the coming year. There simply was no extra capacity in the Soviet economy to draw on.[11] The allies were none too pleased, but they eventually acquiesced on the understanding that the cutbacks were a temporary measure that would be repealed once Polish leaders had defeated Solidarity's "counterrevolution." With the extra hard currency from oil sales on the world market, Soviet officials kept the Polish government precariously afloat through the depths of the 1980–1981 winter.

But as they did, they continued to notice and lament the limits, burdens, and opportunity costs of supporting their ally. In late March 1981, as the Bydgoszcz crisis came to a head and observers both in Poland and the West feared that Soviet military intervention was imminent, officials in Moscow had money, rather than guns, on their minds. Ivan Arkhipov, first deputy prime minister in charge of economic affairs, told the Politburo his ministers could not meet all the Polish requests for raw materials because they were "simply unable to give a larger quantity." The Poles had asked for a further $700 million to service their debt to the West, but "of course," Arkhipov said, the USSR could not "possibly come up with such a sum." The endless stream of requests was beginning to weigh on even the most ardent socialist internationalists. Foreign Minister Andrei Gromyko complained that the Poles did not "attach much importance to the supplies of raw materials from the Soviet Union." This spurred Arkhipov to point out the massive opportunity the Soviet Union was missing by providing subsidized oil to its allies. "We supply Poland with 13 million tons of oil at 90 rubles per ton. If one considers that the world price per ton is 170 rubles, then we receive from the Poles 80 rubles less per ton. We could sell all that oil for hard currency and the earnings would be colossal."[12]

This was also true for the oil Moscow was delivering to the rest of the bloc. And in the spring and summer of 1981, the Soviet leadership decided the burden of these deliveries had become too great, and they resolved to rebalance socialist economic relations in their favor. For too long, they reasoned, the Soviet economy had suffered in the name of allied stability; the time had come to prioritize their own economic interests. Oil was the linchpin of Soviet support for its allies, so it would also be the linchpin of economic rebalancing. As we have seen, Soviet officials had already informed bloc leaders in the late 1970s that they could not continue to increase annual oil deliveries in the 1980s. Now, in 1981, they told their allies they would, in fact, have to substantially reduce annual oil deliveries in the years ahead. Well aware of how important oil was to the economic and political stability of the bloc countries, the Kremlin worked throughout the summer to prepare its allies for the news.

Brezhnev's annual summer meetings in Crimea with each bloc leader provided the perfect opportunity to lay the groundwork. "The healthy economic development of the . . . allies is vitally important," the general secretary told Erich Honecker in August, but "just as vital, we think, is the economic health of our own country." The current Soviet subsidy of Eastern Europe was not striking the right balance between these vital interests. "Our economists, Erich," Brezhnev continued, "have calculated that the fraternal countries' direct benefit from imports of fuel and raw materials from the USSR in the last five years amounted to 15 billion rubles and will amount to almost 30 billion rubles over the coming five years." The Soviet economy could no longer bear this "big sum." Brezhnev promised to do everything he could to aid the German Democratic Republic (GDR)'s continued economic development but also admitted he was "seriously concerned" the USSR would not be able to meet its scheduled energy deliveries in the years ahead.[13]

Four weeks later, the general secretary confirmed that his fears had come true. In letters to East Berlin, Budapest, Prague, and Sofia, Brezhnev reported that the Soviet energy industries would miss their production targets and the Politburo had decided to cut back energy deliveries to the rest of the bloc in the years ahead. He tried to make both the Kremlin's burden and its bind clear. "As you know," he wrote Honecker, "we supply the European member states of the CMEA [Council of Mutual Economic Assistance] with more than 72 million tons of crude oil per year, 7 million tons of petroleum products, 29 billion meters of gas" as well as coal, coke, and electric energy. "As you also know, we are forced to sell substantial quantities of crude oil and petroleum products to capitalist countries in order to obtain currency for the purchase of grain and food." With Soviet agriculture on the verge of its third consecutive bad harvest, officials in Moscow had concluded they would need to sell some of the oil previously meant to go to Eastern Europe on the world market in order to get the hard currency required to continue their massive grain imports. The Kremlin's commitments to their allies and their own people had come into direct conflict, and Brezhnev had chosen the Soviet people. He pleaded for the allies' understanding. "I beg you, Erich," he wrote to Honecker, "to show understanding. . . . The current situation forces us to take such a step."[14]

None of the allies took the news well, but Honecker was particularly upset. Even the slightest cutback in Soviet oil deliveries would, he wrote to Brezhnev, "undermine the foundations of the existence of the German Democratic Republic."[15] When Soviet Politburo member Konstantin Rusakov arrived in East Berlin to try and calm the East German's fears, Honecker got straight to the point: the oil decreases would lead directly to austerity in the GDR, and with the economic powerhouse of West Germany right next door, that was simply unacceptable. The oil reductions were such a monumental setback that "the stability of the GDR is no longer guaranteed," he told his Soviet counterpart. Soviet bureaucrats had announced that the reduction would amount to two million fewer tons of oil per year for the GDR (a reduction from nineteen to seventeen million tons annually), and this quantity quickly took on political and social significance in Honecker's mind. "I request that you ask Comrade Leonid Ilyich Brezhnev," he concluded bitterly, "whether these two million tons of oil are worth destabilizing the GDR and destroying our people's trust in the party and state leadership."[16]

Rusakov arrived ready with a litany of retorts. The Soviet Union was "almost in last place in comparison to the standard of living in all socialist countries," he reminded the East German leader. The leadership in Moscow could no longer justify asking the Soviet people to sacrifice for the good of other socialist countries. "If we need to tighten our belts even more, our people may ask us: what about the socialist brother countries? Why do the Soviet people always have to stay in such a bad position?" And that was not all. The USSR also had to provide military security for all the nations of the Socialist Bloc, so austerity in the Soviet Union would not just be a threat to "the standard of living of the population, but also the weapons of our army."[17] Soviet leaders were not unsympathetic to the East Europeans' plight— Brezhnev had "cried" while signing the letters announcing the reductions, Rusakov said—but bloc leaders needed to remember that the USSR had helped them many times in the past when they faced troubles. "Now we are asking you all for your help," Rusakov said. "We . . . don't see any other way."[18]

Rusakov returned to Moscow, and the Kremlin went ahead with the energy cutbacks in spite of their allies' protests. As we will see, it was a decision laced with significant implications for the allies' financial and political relations with the West and thus the Soviet Union's control over its sphere of influence.

Against the backdrop of this growing material burden, the question of military intervention in Poland continued to hang over Soviet deliberations through the spring of 1981. In the heated early months of the crisis, Brezhnev and the other leaders of the Warsaw Pact had come to the brink of authorizing a joint invasion of Poland in December 1980 before ultimately deciding to give the Polish leadership more time to resolve the situation. During the Bydgoszcz crisis in March 1981, Soviet leaders had again allowed the Poles to think they were on the verge of invading, even though they never seriously considered it.[19] In April, they continued to hold menacing meetings with Polish leaders that were meant to galvanize them to mount a decisive crackdown by implying a Soviet invasion was imminent.[20]

But was it? Through the spring, not even Soviet leaders themselves knew the answer. That changed in June 1981 when the political and

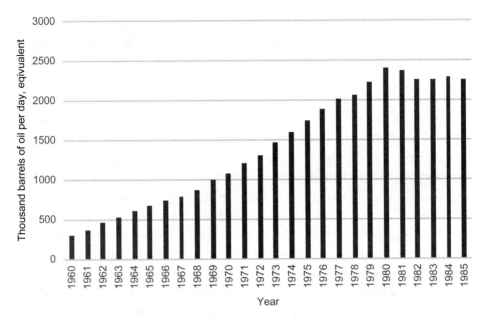

Figure 5.2 **Soviet energy exports to the so-called CMEA Six: East Germany, Hungary, Poland, Czechoslovakia, Bulgaria, and Romania.**
Data source: PlanEcon, Inc., *Soviet and East European Energy Databank, Vol. II*, Table "USSR–Primary Energy Balance," U-3.

military leadership met to resolve the question once and for all. In two separate meetings, the Soviet General Staff and Politburo decided the burden of intervention would be too great. The combination of Solidarity's grassroots support in Polish society, the growing burden of the war in Afghanistan, economic problems at home, and the specter of crippling Western sanctions convinced Soviet leaders that military intervention in Poland was not in the Soviet Union's national interest. As Mikhail Suslov, the chief ideologue of the party and a leading conservative, reportedly said, "Under no circumstances, even if the Polish leadership requests, will we send Soviet and other troops into Poland. If a new leadership comes to power [Solidarity], we will cooperate with it. . . . Introduction of troops would be a catastrophe for Poland and, yes, for the Soviet Union."[21] To maintain the illusion of military pressure, Soviet leaders did not inform their Polish counterparts of this decision, but internally the die had now been cast. No matter the circumstances, Soviet troops would not enter Poland.[22]

With the military option off the table, Soviet leverage over Poland came to rest primarily in the economic sphere. Soviet officials attempted to use economic aid as a coercive lever to force the Polish leadership to implement martial law.[23] Poland's hard currency debt, however, made economic leverage work both ways. Because Poland was shut out of global capital markets and the Soviets could not cover all its financial needs, the Polish leadership was reliant on Western governments for the hard currency needed to pay for grain imports and debt service. They had to be ever mindful of Western opinion when dealing with Solidarity.[24] Polish officials maintained constant contact with Western diplomats about further economic aid, and in Washington, the National Security Council even began to consider the merits of a multiyear aid package worth billions of dollars.[25]

It was plain to see that if Polish leaders cracked down on Solidarity, no Western aid would be forthcoming. So, as he prepared his plan for martial law, General Jaruzelski made its implementation contingent on increases in Soviet aid to compensate for the Western shortfall that would surely follow. On December 7, 1981, six days before he would declare martial law, Jaruzelski told Brezhnev on the phone that he "would need to be sure of [Soviet] economic assistance" before making a final decision.[26] Brezhnev immediately sent the chairman of the State Planning Committee, Gosplan, Nikolai Baibakov to Warsaw to see what the Polish leader had in mind; he returned to the Politburo on December 10 with a long list of 350 items totaling some 1.4 billion rubles. When combined with the aid the Soviet Union already planned to give to Poland in 1982, this would bring Moscow's total aid to 4.4 billion rubles in the year ahead. Baibakov informed his comrades that they would only be able to meet the Polish request by taking resources "from state reserves or by limiting supplies to domestic markets." To make matters worse, Jaruzelski had delayed the date of implementing martial law and hinted he would only go through with it if he could count on Soviet military support. At the eleventh hour, the question of military intervention had been reopened, and responsibility for defeating Solidarity's "counterrevolution" appeared to have fallen back into the Kremlin's lap.[27]

But the Soviet leaders did not budge. Unlike previous crackdowns in 1953, 1956, and 1968, they maintained their newfound commitment to prioritizing developments within the Soviet Union over those within the broader Socialist Bloc. Yuri Andropov, the formidable head of the KGB and future general secretary of the party, delivered the definitive declaration that drew the unanimous support of his Politburo colleagues:

Jaruzelski is rather persistently placing economic demands before us and conditioning the implementation of Operation "X" [martial law] on our economic aid; and . . . he is raising the question, albeit indirectly, of military assistance. . . . As far as economic assistance, of course it will be difficult to do that on the scale they are requesting. Apparently something needs to be done. . . . [But] we do not intend to introduce troops into Poland. That is the proper position, and we must adhere to it until the end. I don't know how things will turn out in Poland, but even if Poland falls under the control of Solidarity, that's the way it will be. . . . We must be concerned above all with our own country and about the strengthening of the Soviet Union. That is our main line.[28]

The Brezhnev Doctrine was now dead. After claiming the stability of socialist governments in Eastern Europe to be in the Soviet Union's national interest for over three decades, Soviet leaders had come to accept the possible overthrow of a socialist government in order to focus on development at home. They were willing to countenance limited economic aid to their ally in a time of need, but even that willingness had been called into question by the broader decision to cut back energy supplies to the rest of their allies in the region. The burden of empire had grown too great, and Soviet leaders were now committed to extracting themselves from that burden, whatever the political costs and risks might be.[29]

◆ ◆ ◆

The declaration of martial law in Poland kept the world from learning of this historic revision to the Soviet national interest. News of martial law arrived in Washington not as a sign of Soviet retreat but as an omen of renewed Soviet aggression. Upon hearing of the crackdown, Ronald Reagan confided to his diary, "Our intelligence is that it was engineered & ordered by the Soviet[s]. If so, and I believe it is, the situation is really grave."[30] As tanks took up positions on the streets of Warsaw and thousands of Solidarity members were summarily arrested, the president and his team began to debate what response would match the gravity of events.

They did so against the backdrop of their own long-running effort to develop a more aggressive American strategy toward the Soviet Union and the broader Communist Bloc. Reagan had risen to the presidency as a strident critic of the superpower détente that had developed in the 1970s.

In his mind, the diplomatic effort to improve East-West relations and stabilize the Cold War had only weakened the West militarily, subsidized the Communist Bloc economically, and provided Moscow with diplomatic cover to spread its influence abroad and continue its military buildup at home without fear of Western retribution. Using all the tools of American hard and soft power, Reagan entered the Oval Office determined to rectify what he perceived as a decade of relative American decline and subsidized Soviet advance.

The strategy that emerged was well attuned to the dynamics of the privatized Cold War. Though the administration did not, of course, use the term, its Cold War strategy was premised on exploiting the relationship at the heart of the privatized Cold War: nation-states' access to guns and butter had become dependent on finance and energy. Reagan and his cabinet understood that communist governments in general, and the Soviet government in particular, relied on finance and energy to fund foreign and domestic promises, and they believed they could use the tools of American statecraft to force the communist world to confront the politics of breaking promises. If Soviet leaders had to choose between the three competing demands on their increasingly scarce resources—their military, their allies, and their citizens—then American officials believed that one day, they just might choose their own citizens over their arms and allies.

This strategy played out to greatest effect in the military arena. Reagan wasted little time in delivering on his campaign promise to significantly increase US military spending. Though it was, in fact, Jimmy Carter who began to increase US military spending in the wake of the Soviet invasion of Afghanistan, Reagan significantly extended and accelerated Carter's initiatives. The US defense budget surged over 40 percent from 1980 to 1986, and the Pentagon developed a new generation of conventional and nuclear weaponry. B-1 and B-2 bombers, the MX intercontinental ballistic missile, Trident nuclear submarines and their Trident II nuclear weapons, F-117 Stealth fighters, and Apache attack helicopters became the cornerstones of a new, more technologically advanced global fighting force.[31]

To be sure, these weapons were meant to serve real security purposes and restore the strategic leverage Reagan believed the United States had frittered away over détente's decade. But they also served a critical economic function by drawing the Soviet Union into a new round of the arms race that it would not be able to afford. US intelligence agencies had concluded by 1981 that Soviet economic performance had "deteriorated to the point that, if military expenditures continue to expand as in the past, there will be few if any resources left with which to raise living standards."[32] Reagan and his cabinet meant to exacerbate Moscow's guns-versus-butter dilemma by applying the full weight of the United States' economic capacity to the task of military modernization. Indeed, for US officials the arms race was ultimately an economic, rather than military, competition. As Reagan said in late 1981, the purpose of the military buildup was to "threaten the Soviets with our ability to outspend them, which the Soviets knew we could do if we chose. Once we [have] established this, we [can] invite the Soviets to join us in lowering the level of weapons on both sides."[33]

All they needed was time. Demonstrating the full depth of the United States' pockets would take many years, so the administration felt little urgency, upon entering office, to immediately engage the Soviets in arms control negotiations. In the wake of the Soviet invasion of Afghanistan, Jimmy Carter had withdrawn the second Strategic Arms Limitation Treaty (SALT II) from Senate consideration, and Reagan saw no reason to reintroduce it. The president also reaffirmed the North Atlantic Treaty Organization (NATO)'s 1979 "dual-track" decision to deploy a new generation of intermediate-range nuclear forces (INF) in Europe by 1983 while also negotiating INF limitations with Moscow. He put his own stamp on this process in November 1981 when he offered to forgo deploying new American intermediate missiles if the Soviets would remove those they had already put in place, a proposal that became known as the "zero option." Many arms control advocates accused the president of intentionally proposing something unrealistic so the United States would be able to go ahead with the deployments when the Soviets inevitably rejected the offer. But Reagan had long been convinced of the ultimate irrationality and inhumanity of nuclear weapons, and he entered office with a sincere conviction to one day reduce and eventually eliminate them altogether. This motivated his decision to discard the concept of Strategic Arms Limitation Treaty (SALT) negotiations, which had dominated the arms control agenda in the 1970s, in favor of Strategic Arms Reduction Treaty (START) negotiations, which were launched in 1982.

All the while, Reagan remained in no hurry to reach a bad, or even merely an inconsequential, arms control deal with the Kremlin. The more time his military buildup had to strain Soviet resources, Reagan reasoned, the more convinced Moscow would become that it needed to conduct arms negotiations on American terms. If the Soviets "saw that the United States had the will and determination to build-up its defences [sic] as far as necessary," he told Margaret Thatcher in 1983, "the Soviet attitude might change because they knew they could not keep up."[34]

Reagan's economic approach to the military buildup and his genuine belief in nuclear abolition came together in his 1983 announcement of the Strategic Defense Initiative (SDI). Quickly dubbed "Star Wars" by its critics, SDI aimed to make the Soviet nuclear threat obsolete by developing a ballistic missile shield capable of shooting down incoming Soviet nuclear weapons. Reagan declared it his "personal hope" that SDI could "bring an end to nuclear war,"[35] but most of his advisors were simply interested in it as an extension of their broader effort to spend the Kremlin into submission.[36] The program would play to all the United States' strengths—technology, research and development, and, most importantly, money—and the Soviets would find it very difficult to keep up. "SDI gives us a great deal of leverage on the Soviet Union," Reagan told his own National Security Council (NSC), and his advisers very much agreed.[37] In a world where Moscow was already struggling to feed its people and fight the Cold War at the same time, countering the American attempt to gain the upper hand through strategic defenses was a budgetary challenge the Kremlin could ill afford.

Here, too, the effects would not be immediate. Administration officials understood that SDI would only challenge the Soviet Union if it could be sustained over many years, so it could not be counted on to immediately bring the Soviets to the bargaining table. What could have an immediate effect on Soviet decision-making, however, was the Kremlin's access to hard currency through energy and financial markets. As they waited for their military buildup to restore the strategic balance and strain Soviet resources, Reagan administration officials zeroed in on energy and finance as a means of crippling their foe. "The period of U.S. military vulnerability," National Security Advisor Richard Allen wrote to Reagan in November 1981, "can to some extent be offset by Western exploitation of Soviet Bloc economic and social vulnerabilities." Limiting the Soviets' access to hard currency, he wrote, "will make their civilian vs. military choices more difficult and increase the likelihood of internal unrest in the satellites."[38]

This was no mere guesswork. Throughout the early 1980s, American intelligence agencies provided the administration with a stream of reports that discussed the deteriorating Soviet material predicament with astonishing accuracy. At the same time that officials in Moscow were dealing with their allies' blowback over the announced cuts in energy supplies in the fall of 1981, the Central Intelligence Agency (CIA) delivered a report to the Reagan administration that concluded the Soviet Union's growing economic problems would force the Kremlin to make "increasingly tough and politically painful choices regarding resource allocation."[39] After overzealously projecting in 1977 that Soviet oil production would peak in the early 1980s, the CIA now foresaw stagnant production through the middle of the 1980s and a decline thereafter. Though the growth of natural gas production would offset some of oil's decline, analysts knew—like Soviet planners in Moscow—that it would not fully compensate for the loss. To make matters worse for Moscow, energy prices were now widely expected to decline in the 1980s after their decade of explosive growth in the 1970s.[40]

For intelligence officials, these structural trends meant Western countries could have a real impact on Soviet behavior by restricting Moscow's access to credit and not buying its energy. "The reduced availability of hard currency and energy," the CIA concluded in 1982, "would make more difficult the decisions Moscow must make among key priorities in the 1980s—sustaining growth in military programs, feeding the population, modernizing the civilian economy, supporting its East European clients, and expanding (or maintaining) its overseas involvements."[41] The Soviet economic situation was so bad, and its resulting political implications so acute, that intelligence officials even concluded in the early 1980s that "a new leadership by mid-decade will feel greater pressure to reduce the growth of defense expenditures to free up labor, capital, and materials—resources urgently needed in key civilian sectors."[42] The world did not yet know the name Mikhail Gorbachev, but American intelligence officials believed that a figure like him might soon emerge.

This was music to the administration's ears. The sum total of this intelligence presented American policy makers with a simple conclusion and an important question. "The Soviet economy is in trouble," CIA director William Casey told the National Security Council. "The question is do we want to make it harder for them?"[43] Their answer was most assuredly yes. As the crisis in Poland dragged on during their first year in office, officials at the highest level of the administration debated how best to combat the Soviet Union politically by hurting it economically.[44]

Foremost at issue was a massive new natural gas pipeline Western Europeans were building to increase Soviet natural gas deliveries to Europe. Since the early 1970s, Western European companies and banks, led by the West Germans, had participated in four pipeline developments that brought increasing amounts of Soviet natural gas to the continent. East-West energy trade had become a cornerstone of European détente and West Germany's *Ostpolitik*. Even as the Soviet-American détente collapsed in the late 1970s, Soviet and West German officials pushed ahead with their negotiations on a new Siberian pipeline, finalizing an agreement in 1981. For both sides, this new pipeline held immense political and economic significance. Politically, it was the cornerstone of Western European governments' attempts to keep détente alive in Europe even as it evaporated between the superpowers. Economically, the pipeline was expected to double the Soviets' annual natural gas deliveries to Western Europe and provide Moscow with an additional $6 billion a year in hard currency when it came online in 1984.[45] Everything about it, then, looked disastrous to a Reagan administration intent on ending the economic interdependence of détente and diminishing the Soviets' hard currency earnings.

The question in Washington was whether the United States should risk a rift with its European allies in the hope of delivering a decisive blow to Moscow's economic prospects. Advocates of halting the pipeline in the Department of Defense and CIA believed the potential benefits far outweighed the risks. Led by Defense Secretary Casper Weinberger, this group saw preventing the pipeline's construction as a strategic necessity on par with the US military buildup. "The pipeline is just as militarily significant as a plane," Weinberger told the NSC.[46] The administration's entire attempt to strain Soviet decisions about resource allocation would make little sense if Washington allowed the construction of a pipeline that would ease those constraints by giving the Soviets billions of dollars every year in energy sales.[47]

Secretary of State Alexander Haig led the charge in opposition. Though he shared Weinberger's desire to weaken the Soviet Union economically, he believed that Western European governments would view any attempt to halt the pipeline as an infringement on their sovereignty. Moreover, he was not at all convinced it was within the administration's power to stop the pipeline. European banks and companies had more than enough capital and technology to build the pipeline without American involvement, so it was not clear to Haig that placing American sanctions on the pipeline's construction would have a material effect. Throughout 1981, these two poles within the administration fought a pitched bureaucratic battle to determine American policy.

Jaruzelski's declaration of martial law tipped the scales in Weinberger's direction. Because Reagan and most of the world believed Jaruzelski's actions were directed from Moscow, the administration's debate following the crackdown centered on how it could weaken both Warsaw and Moscow in response. At the end of 1981, Reagan announced sanctions against Poland and prohibited US companies from participating in the Siberian pipeline. This, however, left an important issue unresolved, because it became clear in early 1982 that the key question was whether or not Reagan's sanctions on the pipeline applied "extraterritorially"—that is, to US subsidiaries and licensees in Europe that were actually involved in the pipeline's construction. In a world of multinational corporations and complex technology licensing agreements, it meant little for Reagan to prohibit companies in the territorial United States from participating in the pipeline. Administration officials quickly realized, therefore, that the question of extraterritoriality was where the rubber would actually meet the road. If not extended to US subsidiaries and licensees in Europe, the sanctions would be useless; if the sanctions were extended, they would compel the Western Europeans to halt the pipeline against their will.[48]

Recognizing the political ire such a move would surely spark in Europe, Reagan delayed his decision on extraterritoriality and instead launched a diplomatic effort to restrict Moscow's access to the other great pool of global wealth: international capital markets. If the Europeans did not want to stop buying Soviet energy, perhaps they would instead agree to restrict Moscow's access to credit. In March 1982, the president sent senior diplomat James Buckley on a tour of Western European capitals to drum up support for this alternative method of weakening the Kremlin's hard currency position. Though the quid pro quo was not made explicit, it was plain for all to see: if the Europeans agreed to restrict Soviet access to credit, the administration would not extend their pipeline sanctions to US subsidiaries and licensees in Europe.

European officials politely received Buckley but firmly and consistently rebuffed his entreaties.[49] They quickly pointed out the hypocrisy of the United States asking Europe to suspend its energy ties to Moscow while its own grain sales to Moscow went untouched. The previous summer, Reagan had repealed the grain embargo Jimmy Carter had placed on the Soviet Union after the Afghan invasion, and in the months following martial law, there had been no mention of bringing the restrictions back. If the White House was so intent on hurting Moscow, European leaders concluded, perhaps it should limit its own trade before asking Europe to do the same.[50] Buckley optimistically reported to the NSC after his trip that he sensed a growing understanding in Europe "that easy money helps the USSR solve its critical problems," but it was clear that no one across the Atlantic shared Washington's urgent desire to use finance or energy as weapons in the ever-chillier Cold War.[51]

This left Reagan in a difficult position. Since the declaration of martial law in December 1981, he had told the world he would use the tools of economic statecraft to punish the Soviets and Poles for what he took to be their shared aggression against Solidarity. And yet as spring came to Washington in 1982, martial law remained in effect, Lech Wałęsa remained in jail, and Moscow's access to energy wealth and capital markets appeared to remain unimpeded. If his administration allowed the pipeline sanctions to remain toothless *and* failed to restrict Moscow's access to credit, Reagan told the NSC, "we will lose all credibility." Not only that, but a golden opportunity would be lost to cripple the Kremlin at its most vulnerable. "The Soviet Union is economically on the ropes," he continued. "This is the time to punish them."[52]

So punish them he did. American and European diplomats made a last-ditch effort to find a satisfactory compromise on the issue of credit controls at the Versailles G7 summit in June 1982, but Reagan remained unsatisfied. In a now-famous speech to the British Parliament after the summit, he laid out his economic understanding of the Soviet predicament. "In an ironic sense Karl Marx was right," he told British lawmakers. "We are witnessing today a great revolutionary crisis, a crisis where the demands of the economic order are conflicting directly with those of the political order. But the crisis is happening not in the free, non-Marxist West, but in the home of the Marxist-Leninism, the Soviet Union." Brimming with confidence in the moral and material superiority of democratic capitalism, he concluded, "The march of freedom and democracy . . . will leave Marxism-Leninism on the ash-heap of history."[53] Upon his return to Washington, he announced that American sanctions on the Siberian pipeline would indeed apply to US subsidiaries and licensees in Europe. If the Soviet Union was in a "great revolutionary crisis" on account of its abysmal economy, Reagan had decided the West should push it into full-blown revolution.

There was just one problem: it didn't work. The only revolts the expanded pipeline sanctions caused were within the US government and among US allies. Because Reagan failed to consult Secretary of State Haig before making his decision, Haig resigned immediately. And because Reagan went ahead with the sanctions in spite of the reservations of his European allies, they all howled in revolt and soon defied the American order. As the summer wore on, they began construction on the pipeline in defiance of the sanctions. Reagan came to regret the transatlantic dispute he had caused, and when he brought George Schultz on as his new secretary of state in July 1982, he charged him with finding a face-saving way out of the diplomatic crisis. In the first of many delicate rounds of diplomacy during his tenure at Foggy Bottom, Schultz got the Europeans to agree to cosmetic changes and future consultations on their credit and energy policies, and in return, Washington repealed the pipeline sanctions in November 1982. By all appearances, East-West economic policy returned to the way it had been.[54]

Beneath the surface, however, major changes were afoot. Structural shifts in the global economy produced exactly what Reagan's statecraft could not. The Volcker Shock and the Reagan financial buildup denied the communist world more capital than Reagan could ever have dreamed of restricting through diplomatic channels, and the long-term decline in global energy prices that began in 1980 weakened Soviet energy wealth far more than the pipeline sanctions ever would have.

The macro effects of this story can be seen in Figure 5.3. After running substantial current account deficits in the 1970s, the Communist Bloc began running significant current account surpluses in the 1980s. This meant that after being a substantial capital importer for most of the 1970s, the communist world—like the Global South—became a capital exporter in the 1980s when the Reagan financial buildup began to monopolize the world's capital. After importing a net total of $40.5 billion from 1973 to 1981, the Soviet Union and Eastern Europe exported a net total $31.2 billion from 1982 to 1989.[55] The same broad transition in global capital flows that allowed the United States to erase its choice between guns and butter in the 1980s significantly hardened that choice for the communist world. The pivotal year was 1982. At the very moment the Reagan administration

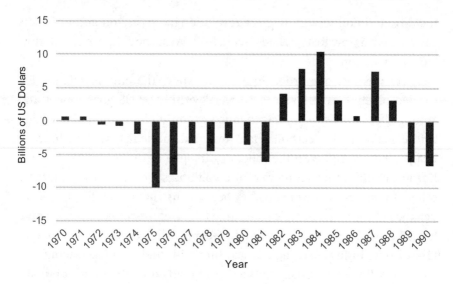

Figure 5.3 **The collective current account balance of the Soviet Union and the CMEA Six. A negative value signifies a net annual capital import, and a positive value signals a net annual capital export.**
Data source: Appendix table C.10 in United Nations, Economic Commission for Europe, *Economic Survey of Europe in 1990–1991*, 249.

was trying and failing to *diplomatically* restrict communist access to energy wealth and capital markets, the unexpected course of its *domestic* economic policy—the potent combination of high interest rates and massive tax cuts—was achieving the very same result at a magnitude far greater than anyone on the National Security Council could have ever hoped.

What the Volcker Shock and the Reagan financial buildup did for capital flows, market forces did for energy wealth. Capitalist societies had spent the years after the 1973 oil crisis trying to conserve energy and develop new energy sources, and their collective efforts began to pay off in the early 1980s. Global energy supply began to outstrip global demand, and prices began to fall.[56] After peaking at a nominal price of $39.50 a barrel in the summer of 1980, oil prices began an almost decade-long slide, dropping to $13.50 a barrel in the fall of 1988. Punctuated by a precipitous collapse in fall of 1985 that would come to be known simply as "the counter shock," this decline in prices deprived oil-exporting countries, including the Soviet Union, of billions of dollars every year in hard currency earnings.

The combined effect of these two historic transformations in capital flows and energy prices for the Communist Bloc was profound. Within the span of a few short years in the early 1980s, the favorable trends on global capital and energy markets that had lifted the bloc in the 1970s evaporated, and highly adverse trends took their place. As much as capital and energy markets *helped* the Communist Bloc in the 1970s, they equally *hurt* the bloc in the 1980s. Indeed, though no one could know it at the time, we can conclude in retrospect that the material capabilities of the Communist Bloc peaked in 1980 and never again recovered. Through the Volcker Shock and the Reagan financial buildup, American policy makers had a significant hand in spurring this historic transformation. They simply did not realize how they were doing it.

◆ ◆ ◆

For the governments of Eastern Europe, these structural transformations arrived not as gentle shifts in long-term trends but as wrenching crises fraught with political and economic consequences. Warning bells began to sound in the weeks before Jaruzelski declared martial law. Ten days before tanks rolled into Warsaw, Alexander Schalck-Golodkowski, the shadowy leader of East Germany's Kommerzielle Koordinierung (KoKo) department, which was charged with earning hard currency for the state coffers, informed the leadership that foreign banks had begun withdrawing their short-term deposits from the state bank at an alarming rate. To "prevent the insolvency of the GDR," he wrote, the country would have to take extraordinary measures to reduce imports, increase exports, and gain access to more hard currency.[57] Around the same time, the central banks of Libya, Iran, and Iraq began their flight from the Hungarian National Bank, and soon the bloc as a whole found itself under sustained attack from the international financial system.[58] By the early months of 1982, hard currency was fleeing at such a rate that even Czechoslovakia, which had built up very little debt in the 1970s, was on the brink of insolvency.[59]

Communist officials quickly concluded the capital flight was a coordinated Western attack in retribution for the declaration of martial law in Poland. Reagan's diplomatic efforts to stop the Siberian pipeline and coordinate Western credit restrictions in response to martial law lent credence to their conclusion. "The USA's policy of confrontation," Schalck wrote Honecker in March 1982, "has led in recent weeks to the imposition of a total credit boycott . . . the enemy is now concentrating all its efforts on quickly achieving the insolvency of the GDR."[60] Vladimir Alkhimov, chairman of the Soviet state bank, Gosbank, echoed his East German counterpart at a bloc meeting in April. "The U.S. is currently conducting a comprehensive currency war against the socialist countries," he told his comrades. "The aim is to organize the insolvency of the socialist countries."[61]

We have already seen, however, that Reagan's economic diplomacy in response to martial law failed on all counts. Though Reagan certainly intended to use energy and finance to weaken the Soviet Union, his allies did not share his goals, and they rejected his efforts at every turn. Instead of the Reagan administration, it was, in the words of one International Monetary Fund (IMF) official, "a couple hundred panic stricken bankers" from commercial and central banks around the world who launched the financial assault on the communist world.[62] They did so not out of Cold War animus—they had, after all, gleefully loaned money to communist countries for over a decade—but rather out of frightened concern for their balance sheets. As a group of commercial bankers explained to a gathering of Polish and Western officials, "Western banks cannot be asked to make political and social judgements. The financial community must be concerned solely with problems of economics." Bankers reacted to the political context of the Cold War, but they did not themselves care about the West's fight against communism. They were only interested in "stability and predictability," the bankers said, and the crisis in Poland had demonstrated that the communist world might not be able to ensure either. Reagan's bellicose rhetoric in the wake of martial law only added to their uncertainty about the future of East-West economic relations. Banks "remain, in the final analysis, financial, with responsibilities to their shareholders," they told the gathering. "They are not political and social agencies."[63] Communism had simply become a bad bet, and the banks were now looking to take their money elsewhere.

Even if communist officials mistook the ultimate source of the attack, there was no mistaking its ultimate effect: the threat of imminent bankruptcy. Communist financial officials regularly produced projections of their country's future hard currency needs and resources, and as hundreds of millions of dollars fled the bloc in the early months of 1982, those projections quickly turned sour. In East Germany, for instance, Schalck ran the numbers in March and concluded there was a 1.5 billion valutamark (VM) (roughly $700 million) financing gap in the first half of the year that could not be filled through new credits from Western banks "because of the credit boycott." He informed the leadership that he could use the state's hard currency reserves to cover the gap until June but stated that the day when the country would run out of money was now in sight. "At the end of the second quarter, there will be no more credits available," he wrote, "and we will have to declare the insolvency of the GDR to capitalist banks."[64]

Only a miraculous infusion of new capital could thwart the inexorable drive toward insolvency, and only one country in the Socialist Bloc was capable of making such miracles happen: the Soviet Union. As their countries hemorrhaged capital in early 1982, Eastern European financial officials rushed to Moscow in the hope of receiving financial reinforcements. After the oil cutbacks of the previous summer, they knew that the provision of new economic aid was unlikely, but they hoped the gravity of their predicament would change the Kremlin's calculus.

It was not to be. Having already stretched their resources to the limit to help Jaruzelski restart the Polish economy after martial law, the Soviet leadership now confessed that they simply did not have the resources to help any further. "The USSR can no longer step into the breach," senior Soviet financial officials told their bloc comrades in March 1982. "The Soviet people no longer understand why we give credits to all [other] countries when the shelves in their own shops are empty."[65] A month later, as Reagan ramped up plans to restrict communist access to capital markets, Soviet officials recognized the need to coordinate a bloc-wide response to the American initiative, but they stopped short of doing so because they knew it would stoke their allies' hopes for more aid. "It would be seen by some as paternalism," Alkhimov, the Gosbank chairman, said, "and all countries would come with the expectation that the SU [Soviet Union] will provide financial aid, which is not possible."[66] In what would prove to be the start of a trend that spanned the 1980s, Eastern European officials were forced to return from Moscow empty-handed and deal with their crises on their own.

This left the communist governments of Eastern Europe with an uninviting set of options. Declaring insolvency was theoretically possible, but the Polish government's fate had demonstrated the dangers of admitting to the world that debts could no longer be repaid. Since Warsaw had done so in early 1981, it had not received any new loans without the help of Western governments, and even those had been for the barest of essentials, like grain. All Western financing for capital investments that might actually improve the Polish economy had long since ceased to flow in Warsaw's direction. A more radical option was the possibility of coordinating a bloc-wide default in order to damage the Western financial system and gain leverage over the banks. Like the debtors of the Global South, the Communist Bloc was in a state of mutually assured destruction with its Western creditors in 1982. Communist debt occupied enough space on Western banks' balance sheets that many banks (particularly West German banks) would likely have become insolvent if forced to write down communist debt as a loss.[67] But no evidence has emerged to suggest that communist leaders even remotely considered the possibility of declaring a collective default.[68] Some Western financial policy makers worried about this eventuality, but most concluded it was unlikely because, as one British central banker wrote, default "would take Comecon decades to live down."[69] Communist leaders apparently shared this perception, concluding that insolvency was to be avoided at all costs.

Maintaining solvency would require two things that were as unpalatable as they were unavoidable: domestic austerity and Western aid. Both carried significant risks. The more austerity communist governments imposed on their people, the more they ran the risk of sparking another Polish Crisis. Western aid would lessen this risk by providing a fresh infusion of capital and reopening access to global capital markets. But it came with its own peril of surrendering the nation's sovereignty to the Communist Bloc's ideological and geopolitical enemies. The choice between austerity and Western aid, then, was a matter of deciding which risk—domestic instability or the loss of international sovereignty—was the lesser of two evils. Each government in the region navigated this choice differently in the 1980s. Hungary, Poland, and East Germany pursued greater Western aid to minimize the risk of austerity, while Romania chose the path of draconian austerity to maintain its sovereignty. But in each case, the government's decision was primarily driven by its opinion of one institution: the International Monetary Fund.

At first glance, the IMF represented everything about the capitalist system the communist world sought to resist. It was the institutional embodiment of capitalist class power and generally sought to impose a capitalist perestroika on debtor economies.[70] But the IMF also had money and was willing to share it, two traits not easily scoffed at in an environment of financial scarcity. So, as foreign capital fled and Moscow failed to answer its allies' pleas for help, a wide-ranging debate broke out within the bloc on the merits and demerits of turning to the IMF for help.

Hungary pressed the issue. Since the heady early days of détente, János Fekete had carried out a decade-long dalliance with the Fund to lay the

groundwork for a potential membership.[71] But János Kádár had always declined to take the final step on account of Soviet resistance. Since Joseph Stalin
had declared the IMF a tool of Western imperialism in the early postwar period, the Kremlin had maintained a standing prohibition on any member of
the Communist Bloc joining the Fund, and only maverick socialist states like
Tito's Yugoslavia (a member since 1945) and Ceaușescu's Romania (a member
since 1972) had dared to defy the Kremlin.[72] The oil cutbacks in summer 1981
directly led to a change in Kádár's thinking. Upon hearing of the cutbacks, he
authorized Fekete to move forward with final membership negotiations. And
in an important sign of how the energy cutbacks had diminished Moscow's
political power within the bloc, he did not ask Soviet leaders for permission
but simply informed them of his decision after the fact.[73]

The Kremlin did not like the insubordination but could do little apart
from register its objection. "The IMF is an instrument entirely under the
influence of the aggressive forces of the United States," Alkhimov lectured
a meeting of bloc officials in the spring of 1982. Trying to solve the bloc's
financial problems through the Fund would prove "illusory," he warned,
because the United States was only interested in seeing socialist countries
declare their "insolvency." The Hungarians begged to differ. They not only
believed that the IMF was not interested in seeing socialist countries become insolvent, but also that it was, in fact, the only way for the socialist
countries to avoid insolvency and the extreme austerity that would come
with it. The head of the Hungarian National Bank told his comrades that
the choice facing the Politburo in Budapest could not have been any
clearer. The party leadership either had "to drastically reduce living standards or try to obtain further loans through the IMF. They have chosen
the latter."[74]

Western financial institutions rewarded them for their choice. From
1982 to 1984, the West provided Budapest with the financial bailout the Soviets no longer could afford. The first infusion of $210 million came in
March and April 1982 from the Bank for International Settlements (BIS),
an institution that acted as a sort of central bank for central banks. Fekete
used these funds to fight off the Libyan, Iraqi, and Iranian capital flight,
and the country successfully maintained its solvency through the summer
by the skin of its teeth. Under pressure from the IMF and Western governments, commercial banks then stepped in with a new syndicated loan in
August to stem the tide even further.[75] In December, Hungary came to
terms with the IMF on its first short-term financing agreement, and the

Fund dispersed roughly $500 million from its coffers.[76] With the Fund on board, banks' confidence in Budapest temporarily returned in 1983, and when it again began to falter later that year, the IMF stepped in once again with a fresh infusion of $450 million in January 1984.[77] When Hungary joined the Fund, it also joined the World Bank, which granted it over $700 million in loans from 1982 to 1985.[78] All told, Western institutions funneled almost $2 billion to Budapest in its moment of greatest economic need. While the world watched tensions between Moscow and Washington descend to new lows in the early 1980s, few noticed as Western financial institutions quietly completed the first bailout of Eastern Europe and, subtly but fundamentally, shifted the balance of power in the Cold War.

All the while, a single question dominated Hungary's negotiations with the IMF. Indeed, it would define the last decade of the communist state's existence: how much austerity could the government get the Hungarian people to peacefully accept? The BIS, the IMF, and the World Bank relieved Budapest of the most extreme austerity pressure associated with insolvency but did not eliminate it entirely. As with any country, the IMF's primary goal in Hungary was to turn the country into a net capital exporter—in financial parlance, to create a current account surplus—so the country could begin to repay its debts, which would require the imposition of domestic discipline. The essence of a relationship with the IMF, then, lay in striking a balance between the austerity and adjustment the Fund wanted and the domestic stability the government needed.

Negotiating this balance was a political process with political implications, so Hungary's relationship with the IMF ultimately revolved around questions of political power. In their talks with Budapest, IMF officials proposed a number of ways to achieve what was, in essence, the politics of breaking promises: price increases, subsidy cuts, the closure of loss-making enterprises, a reduction in the state budget deficit, and a devaluation of the national currency, the forint.[79] Each of these policies carried with it a risk of domestic unrest, and it was by this political standard that the Hungarian leadership decided which measures it could implement and which it would resist. The government "needed to think over the social-political implications" of each IMF demand, József Marjai, the deputy prime minister in charge of the Hungarian economy, told the Fund in 1982. The leadership "did not want to jeopardize political stability. They wanted to choose those policies against which social opposition was the least strong."[80] In Hungary's case, this meant the government was reluctant to reduce its financial support for housing, transportation, and consumer prices but was willing to devalue the forint, reduce business investment, and hold down workers' wages.[81] These measures were enough to garner the two short-term financing agreements from the IMF in late 1982 and early 1984, but they precluded agreement on a long-term arrangement that would have provided Budapest with larger sums.[82] The Fund stood ready to pay Hungarian leaders to take the politics of breaking promises as far they wanted to go, but the leadership consistently balked at the political implications of economic discipline.[83]

Then, in the spring of 1984, Kádár rejected a continuation of the politics of breaking promises altogether. "Believe me," he told the party's Central Committee in April 1984, "we cannot exist with 0.5% growth in national income, and it cannot win the support of the masses." In place of IMF austerity, he ordered a return to the 2.5–3 percent growth that had prevailed in the 1970s and asked Fekete to find a way to make it happen.[84] Lucky for them, the two IMF agreements and World Bank funding had been enough to reestablish Hungary's creditworthiness, and the country was able to return to its former borrowing ways.[85] By the time 1985 dawned on the Danube, the good life had returned to Hungary. All that remained to be seen was how long global capital markets would allow it to last.

Events unfolded very differently in East Berlin, primarily because the East German leadership held a very different view of the IMF. Where Hungarian leaders saw the Fund as an important, if also problematic, source of capital, East German leaders saw it as nothing other than an existential threat to the very existence of the GDR. "To be or not to be, that was the question," Alexander Schalck wrote in his memoirs in reference to his country's fate in the early 1980s. "We did not want to expose socialism to the dictates of the International Monetary Fund."[86] Both during the Cold War and after, it was taken as axiomatic that East Germany was financially dependent on West Germany. This dependence was real, but it was also a choice. The East German leadership chose to increase its reliance on Bonn in the late Cold War to avoid having to deal with the IMF. As in Hungary, maintaining solvency in the GDR required some combination of domestic austerity and foreign aid, and the Federal Republic's aid was much preferable to the IMF's because it came with dramatically different strings attached.[87]

The Fund, as we have seen, sought to impose the politics of breaking promises on debtor economies in order to turn them into capital exporters. The West Germans, by contrast, were not interested in reforming the East

German economy but rather in opening East Germany's borders. *Ostpolitik* was premised on the idea that greater flows of goods, people, and information across the intra-German border would produce a more peaceful European continent and one day reunite the German people. Bonn therefore attached conditions to its aid aimed at increasing these flows across the German divide. The choice between the IMF and the Federal Republic of Germany (FRG) was a matter of determining which condition—the politics of breaking promises or more open German borders—was a bigger threat to the stability and legitimacy of the state. Choosing between open borders and breaking promises would prove to be the defining challenge of the GDR's final decade.

For East German leaders, there was much not to like about the idea of more porous German borders. They were, after all, the ones who had built the Berlin Wall precisely to eliminate the border's pores altogether. But they believed that breaking promises was worse. Throughout the last decade of the Cold War, they would continuously choose to increase the porousness of their borders in order to avoid disciplining their domestic social contract. That was how difficult and dangerous the challenge of austerity was—even the men who had built the world's most infamous symbol of border security proved willing to sacrifice that security to avoid breaking promises at home.

In the early 1980s, the full consequences of this choice were only dimly felt, but they did influence the form of the West's bailouts of East Germany. While Fekete negotiated with the IMF to exchange Fund financing for domestic austerity in Hungary, Schalck negotiated with the FRG to exchange West German deutsche marks for a more porous German border. On orders from Honecker himself, Schalck was quick to make the GDR's allergy to austerity clear. Any credit "must come without conditions such as those issued by . . . the International Monetary Fund," he told his West German interlocutor, Franz Josef Strauß, in one of their first meetings. The GDR had not joined the Fund, he said, precisely because "that would mean lowering the standard of living." Instead, he could offer the FRG two concessions that would make intra-German travel marginally easier and the militarized German border marginally more humane: West German schoolchildren would no longer have to make the minimum hard currency payment required to enter the GDR, and the East German government would dismantle the automatic shooting devices that barbarically populated its side of the border.[88]

Strauß, the head of the West German conservative party in Bavaria and the country's leading Cold Warrior, was willing to accept these paltry concessions in pursuit of his larger purposes of stabilizing the GDR at a time of rising Cold War tensions and, as he later said, getting "the GDR as dependent on the D-Mark as a drug addict is on heroin."[89] The result was two billion-mark loans (the so-called *Milliardenkredite*) to the GDR in 1983 and 1984. Officially, the West Germans attached no conditions to the loans, but when the GDR eliminated the minimum exchange requirement for children in late 1983 and dismantled the last of the automatic shooting devices in late 1984, everyone on both sides of the Iron Curtain knew why.[90]

Eliminating a few guns along an already heavily militarized border and allowing children to enter the GDR for free may not sound like much in exchange for 2 billion deutsche marks, and in concrete terms, it certainly was not. But symbolically, the loans and their concessions contained immense importance. First, like the Fund's involvement in Hungary, the *Milliardenkredite* signaled to global capital markets that the GDR had a new and very wealthy lender of last resort, the Federal Republic. In the banks' search for "stability and predictability," few countries could match the West German powerhouse's steadfast credibility, and this immediately rubbed off on East Berlin's access to capital. Just a month after the announcement of the first loan, Schalck was already writing to Honecker that the "negotiating environment" between the East German state bank and foreign banks had already "relaxed." The KoKo chief was so confident the billion-mark loans would alter banks' willingness to lend to the GDR that he did not even use them to pay off the country's debt, putting them instead on deposit in KoKo's foreign bank accounts to save for a rainy day.[91]

As in Hungary, this return to creditworthiness on international markets allowed the GDR's leaders to return to the politics of making promises at home. Austerity and all its challenges could once again be deferred. The diplomatic import of the loans was no less profound. The *Milliardenkredite* cemented the terms upon which the future inter-German relationship would rest: since the GDR was resistant to exchanging financial aid for domestic austerity, it would instead bargain over increases in the movement of people across the German border.

Moscow, of course, was none too pleased. For the Kremlin, the loans signaled, yet again, that the West was stepping in to fill the material void in Eastern Europe left by the Soviet Union's diminishing resources.[92] Soviet leaders maintained no illusions about the political meaning of their ally's growing dependence on West Germany. As the third general secretary in three years, Konstantin Chernenko, told Honecker in 1984, the loans represented "additional financial dependence of the GDR on the FRG" that strengthened Bonn's leverage over East Berlin.[93] If the Federal Republic was now going to serve as the GDR's financial protector, who knew what concessions they might one day tie to assistance.

There was a way for the Kremlin to prevent this threatening prospect: repeal the energy cutbacks from the early 1980s and increase them for the remainder of the decade. But like Brezhnev and Andropov, Chernenko viewed this as both materially impossible and strategically unwise. "We understand the significance of Soviet oil and oil products for [Comecon] member countries," he told the Politburo in 1984. "Here we should help them, but only according to our capabilities. They are such that the maximum we can possibly do [for the 1986–1990 Five-Year Plan] is maintain supplies at the 1985 level."[94] The Kremlin therefore had its own material shortcomings to blame for its allies' growing dependence on the West. It was Honecker who had warned Brezhnev that the oil cutbacks risked destabilizing the bloc, and the bailouts of Eastern Europe were merely bloc leaders' attempts to avoid that instability.

The bailouts were also a collective product of the many profound changes that had swept the world since the start of the decade. The tectonics of the global economy and the Cold War had fundamentally shifted. Beginning with the second oil crisis, the onset of the Volcker Shock, and the Soviet invasion of Afghanistan in 1979, a conjuncture of events around the world had conspired to produce dramatic changes in world energy and capital markets that had, in turn, directly affected the material and ideological balance of power in the Cold War. The potent combination of the Volcker Shock and the Reagan financial buildup had at once deprived the world of capital and unbound the United States from material limits. Ronald Reagan had begun to plumb these newfound material depths to produce a military buildup the Soviet Union would find difficult to match. Unfolding side by side, the Polish Crisis and the Thatcher revolution had demonstrated that democratic capitalism could produce a stronger and more legitimate state than socialist authoritarianism in the era of breaking promises. Reagan and Thatcher had introduced the language of neoliberal self-reliance to make an ideological virtue out of government-imposed discipline. And Western policy makers had skillfully managed the capitalist perestroika to unwind the economic interdependence of the 1970s and replace it with a world in which Western creditors—be they the IMF, the US Treasury, or the Federal Republic of Germany—held exorbitant leverage over the many debtor nations of the Global South and the Communist Bloc.

All the while, the Soviet Union was supposed to be the material and ideological fount of opposition to this worldwide turn toward breaking promises. Resisting capitalism's disciplinary pressures had been its founding mission and remained its raison d'être. But its own material failings, in energy and agriculture above all, had deprived it of the resources required to mount an effective resistance, and its ideology of socialist authoritarianism had left it responsible for the promise to control every aspect of the state, economy, and society. The crisis in Poland had exposed the dangers of trying to break promises in a dictatorship of the proletariat, particularly when the proletarians themselves no longer believed they had any say in the dictatorship. The decade-long fall in global energy prices that began in 1980 was compounding the Kremlin's domestic energy problems and had left Soviet leaders with brutally hard choices between funding their allies, the military, or their own people. The financial crises in Poland, Hungary, and East Germany had made the limits of Moscow's support for its allies in Europe clear but had left the Soviet choice between guns and butter untouched. As the Kremlin cycled through three aged general secretaries in Brezhnev, Andropov, and Chernenko, the Soviet Union's response to the new era of breaking promises remained on hold. It would fall to their successor, a young party secretary from the Soviet countryside named Mikhail Gorbachev, to chart a new path. On the eve of his election on March 10, 1985, not even Gorbachev himself knew where this new path would lead. All he did know was what he told his wife that night as he waited to become the leader of the worldwide socialist vanguard: "We just can't go on living like this."[95]

THE END OF THE COLD WAR

CHAPTER 6

The Socialist Perestroika

FOR MUCH OF his adult life, Abel Aganbegian lived on the edge of polite society in the Soviet Union. After becoming the leader of the Novosibirsk Institute of Economics and Industrial Organization in Siberia in 1964, he had used his sharp mind and prolific pen to push his higher-ups in Moscow to reform the Soviet economic system. Two thousand miles away from the capital, Aganbegian turned the Novosibirsk Institute into a hothouse of economic ideas subversive to the Marxist-Leninist traditions that dominated official thinking. By the early 1980s, however, he had little to show for his efforts besides a series of run-ins with party conservatives who beat back his calls for change at every turn.[1]

In 1985, the rise of Mikhail Gorbachev transformed his fate. The new general secretary brought Aganbegian in from the cold, and by the late 1980s, Aganbegian had become one of the leading advocates of the reform project that had set the world ablaze—perestroika. On both sides of the Iron Curtain, people eagerly wanted to know what, exactly, perestroika was, and it fell to advisors like Aganbegian to provide an answer. In his 1989 book, *Moving the Mountain*, he did just that. "The central problem of the new economic system," he wrote, was "to make people care about the results of their work" and "to inculcate . . . feelings of personal responsibility." Over the seventy years of its existence, the Soviet Union had failed to develop "an effective system of individual incentive and responsibility," and the ultimate task of perestroika was to create one. If this sounded like a goal worthy of Ronald Reagan or Margaret Thatcher, the parallel to the capitalist experience was not lost on Aganbegian. "If I were asked my opinion of the new policies of the Conservative government [in the United Kingdom], often labelled Thatcherism," he wrote, "I would generally have to give them quite high marks." Aganbegian believed that Thatcher had undertaken the "reconstruction, the perestroika, so to speak, of Britain's economy," so there were similarities between her predicament in London and the Soviets' own trials and travails in Moscow.[2]

Gorbachev shared his advisor's understanding of the parallels between the capitalist and the communist challenges in the 1980s, and so too does this chapter. Perestroika was an ideology of economic discipline that aimed to achieve a renewal of economic growth by implementing painful domestic reforms. In seeking to launch an economic boom by significantly reducing the state's role in the Soviet economy and society, perestroika was, in fact, a socialist version of supply-side economics. Perestroika aimed to discipline the postwar Soviet social contract of full employment, stable prices, and heavy state subsidy and intervention in the economy.[3] It was, in short, the socialist form of the politics of breaking promises.

Despite its architects' aspirations, however, perestroika failed miserably because Soviet leaders failed to accomplish the task at the heart of their new ideology: to carry out painful economic reforms. Though they recognized the economic need for discipline, Soviet leaders consistently shied away from imposing disciplinary policies like price increases, bankruptcies, and unemployment because they feared the domestic political backlash.[4] Gorbachev tried both to build popular support for the difficulties of economic reform by democratizing the Soviet political system, and he tried to reform communist ideology to account for a more coercive social contract, but he soon found himself unable to transgress the popular will and ideological legacy of Marxism-Leninism. Unlike Reagan and Thatcher, he had no easy recourse to an ideological tradition of liberalism that prized individualism and made a virtue out of economic discipline. The result was an economy that was anything but disciplinary: in the four short years between Gorbachev's accession to power in 1985 and the revolutionary events of 1989–1990, the Soviet economy spiraled into inflationary chaos that left the Soviet leadership wildly unpopular at home and dangerously dependent on capital from abroad.

This descent into dependence played an important role in the end of the Cold War because it significantly weakened the Soviet Union's ability to project power and influence around the world. As Gorbachev sought to break promises at home, he also aimed to do so abroad. As we have seen, by the early 1980s, the Soviet Union's material burden of its allies and the arms race had become too much to bear, and the new general secretary began an urgent search for relief from both. The result was his "new thinking" in Soviet foreign policy and a series of developments that shocked the world: the explicit repeal of the Brezhnev Doctrine in Eastern Europe, a diplomatic campaign to rid the world of all nuclear weapons, the signing of the Intermediate-Range Nuclear Forces (INF) Treaty, and the unilateral withdrawal of Soviet armed forces from the European continent. By the time revolutionary upheaval shook the world in 1989, the Soviet Union was on the verge of bankruptcy, and this dramatically curtailed the Kremlin's ability to slow or stop the changes unfolding in Europe.

◆ ◆ ◆

The aspiration to reform the Soviet economy did not begin with Gorbachev. As far back as the mid-1960s, Soviet premier Alexei Kosygin had introduced a series of economic reforms aimed at decreasing government intervention in the economy; increasing enterprise independence, output, and profitability; and incentivizing workers to be more productive by linking wages to performance. These reforms were met with a wave of resistance from the party and government bureaucracy, and by the end of the decade, they disappeared into the belly of state administration. General Secretary Leonid Brezhnev did his part to bury Kosygin's efforts, and he spent his decade and a half at the helm of the Soviet Union using bureaucratic platitudes and the 1970s oil wealth to smother all attempts to reform the Soviet economy along more disciplinary lines.[5]

Only the conjuncture of the economic crisis of the early 1980s and Brezhnev's death in November 1982 reopened the door to meaningful economic reform. As in capitalist countries, deteriorating economic performance led to a broad-based search for "new thinking" in economics and politics, and many of the ideas Gorbachev would advocate in the late 1980s had begun to be discussed at the highest levels of the party and government early in the decade.

The essence of reform lay in putting the country on a path toward intensive economic growth: the production of more output with fewer inputs through increases in productivity. The Soviet economy had been built on a model of extensive growth—the addition of increasing quantities of land, labor, and capital to economic production to yield increasing amounts of finished products—but as growth of those inputs slowed in the late 1970s and early 1980s, the challenge facing Soviet economic planners became one of designing an economy that grew because of efficiency rather than resources. Though Soviet planners were loath to recognize it publicly, they understood that intensive growth would inevitably require coercing Soviet workers and enterprises into being more productive. As Aganbegian eventually wrote, the country had "not found the mechanism to ensure that people would be highly motivated in socialist conditions."[6] Putting the country on a path of intensive growth would require finding such a mechanism.

Capitalism had four extremely powerful stimuli that motivated workers and corporations to care about their output: private profit, corporate bankruptcy, wage inequality, and unemployment. The power of these stimuli was communicated in the economy through a system of flexible, market-based prices. Everything under capitalism—land, labor, and capital—had a price that, for the most part, responded to changes in supply and demand. Most importantly, when the price of something like oil, labor, or credit went up, economic actors had an incentive to use less of it, so flexible prices drove efficiency.[7]

These four stimuli and the flexible price system that mediated them were the foundations of capitalist economies, but they had traditionally been viewed as anathema to communist theory and practice. Communists had considered private profit, corporate bankruptcy, severe wage inequality, and working-class unemployment to be the foundations of capitalist exploitation and had effectively banished them from their societies. Communist states confiscated most enterprise profits, supported loss-making enterprises to prevent them from going bankrupt, leveled out wages between low-performing and high-performing workers, and guaranteed every citizen the right to employment. Rather than letting prices change in response to supply and demand, communist governments fixed them to rid their economies of what they saw as capitalism's chronic tendency toward instability and crisis. In short, none of the stimuli that drove capitalist growth and efficiency were present in communist economies because the foundational promise of communism had been to protect workers from the exploitation of the capitalist system.

Soviet reformers decided that these stimuli would have to reintroduced, and the 1980s saw a series of progressively more radical attempts to do so. These solutions first began to form under the leadership of Gorbachev's mentor within the party, Yuri Andropov.[8] Upon assuming the post of general secretary in the wake of Brezhnev's death, Andropov made improving the economy his top priority. Fitting his mold as the former head of the KGB, he first sought to fix the economic morass through discipline of a traditional, top-down Soviet variety—more severe penalties for worker absenteeism and drunkenness, greater punishments for criminality, and a campaign to rid the party of waste and corruption.[9] Even as Andropov imposed traditional solutions, however, he also authorized Gorbachev, a rising star in the Politburo, and Nikolai Ryzhkov, a young party policy maker who would serve as Gorbachev's prime minister, to undertake a comprehensive review of the country's economic problems and seek out new solutions from its top economists.[10]

The first reform they considered was one that had haunted communist governments throughout their existence and would haunt perestroika as well: price increases. By 1982, the party and government bureaucracy had readied a set of price increases for the general secretary's authorization, and with Brezhnev's death, it fell to Andropov to make the decision. Though Gorbachev and Ryzhkov recognized the economic reasons for pursing the increases, they counseled Andropov to refrain from moving ahead because of the fraught politics that price increases would entail. Like their counterparts in Warsaw, Budapest, and East Berlin, they feared potential unrest, and on their recommendation, Andropov canceled the price-increase plan.[11] It was but the first in a long string of moments in the 1980s when the Soviet leadership would shy away from disciplinary reforms because of their potential political effects.

The same held true for three other foundational reforms: enterprise autonomy, labor force "rationalization," and social spending. These were the communist ways of referencing profit, bankruptcy, unemployment, and welfare, and during Andropov's time, Soviet officials began to discuss them with increasing frequency and urgency. The party's 1983 economic program committed the government to doubling the economy's productivity over the next two decades and expanding "the economic autonomy of associations and enterprises" to "improve production efficiency and quality of labor."[12] A year later, an economic strategy document prepared for Gorbachev and Ryzhkov encouraged the creation of incentives for enterprises to carry out "production tasks with a smaller number of workers."[13] By one estimate, fifteen to twenty million surplus workers were weighing down a bloated economy, and they would have to be squeezed out of the production process if the country was to begin to grow intensively.[14]

Production with fewer workers would, in turn, require each remaining worker to work harder and more productively. When discussing ways to motivate the workforce, Soviet officials sounded like their ostensible neoliberal enemies on the other side of the Iron Curtain. "Socialism is not collective philanthropy," a senior Gosplan economist wrote to Gorbachev in early 1984. "The view is becoming more and more common among economists," he continued, that the "free provision of goods" like housing, education, and health care "weakens incentives to work." Instead of giving these benefits to workers for free, economists now contended that any "able-bodied person in a socialist society should earn any good through their work."[15] Ronald Reagan or Margaret Thatcher could not have stated their own views about postwar capitalist societies any better.

Revising the social contract, however, was ideologically and politically difficult, so Andropov moved slowly in implementing fundamental changes. He authorized a limited number of enterprises to experiment with independence from the state plan and "self-financing" (i.e., operating without subsidies from the state). Their initial performance under these new conditions was good—productivity went up and costs went down—but the health of the Soviet leadership hindered further reform. Just fifteen months after he took office, Andropov died in February 1984 and was replaced by a bastion of the country's old guard, Konstantin Chernenko. Even older than Andropov and ill from the moment he took office, Chernenko lasted just thirteen months in office before dying in March 1985. Though Gorbachev, Ryzhkov, and their reformist allies were able to continue a modicum of work under Chernenko's infirmed watch, they could not contemplate reforms of the entire system.[16]

Gorbachev's accession to general secretary was meant to change this. Party leaders chose him over older, more conservative options precisely because they wanted to break from the static course set by Brezhnev.[17] His election was the first act of Soviet "new thinking," as the leadership searched for new ways out of their old domestic and international predicaments. "It seems as if we've got a leader at last!" Defense Minister Sergei Sokolov raved to Chief of the General Staff Sergei Akhromeev shortly after Gorbachev's rise.[18] Both men would later have substantial problems with their new leader, but for the moment, they embraced him as a symbol of long-overdue change. For his part, Gorbachev was firm in his conviction that change would come, but he harbored no radical or specific agenda for bringing it about.[19] His opinion of the country's past three geriatric leaders was so dim that he assumed his mere presence atop the Soviet hierarchy and some tinkering around the edges of the system would launch the country to new heights.[20]

Over his first two years in office, he began to use two words, *uskorenie* (acceleration) and *perestroika* (restructuring), to signal the broad outlines of his agenda. He filled in that agenda with a series of measures to increase investment, make workers' wages more responsive to the quality of their work, and increase the quality of Soviet products through stricter government oversight. None of these moves were radical, and none were effective. It is easy, in retrospect, to associate Gorbachev with the fundamental change of his later years, but through the end of 1986, he did little on the domestic front to dismantle the system he inherited.[21]

Instead, three developments during Gorbachev's first eighteen months in office—one very traditional discipline campaign and two events completely out of his control—dramatically altered the fiscal and financial health of the Soviet Union and forced the leadership to reach for radical solutions by late 1986. First, the most consequential policy of Gorbachev's early tenure was his failed anti-alcohol campaign, which began in May 1985. This was, as one author has written, "a full-fledged disciplinary campaign of the old style" that sought to increase workers' productivity by decreasing their access to the bottle.[22] Though it failed to prevent Soviet citizens from drinking (the black-market liquor business boomed), it did open a gaping hole in the state budget by causing tax revenue from alcohol sales to plummet.

Then, in late 1985, the world price of oil collapsed. By March 1986, it was two-thirds lower than the previous autumn. This led to a 9 billion ruble drop in Moscow's export earnings in the first half of 1986 and added 4 billion dollars to the country's foreign debt.[23] Ryzhkov, now prime minister in charge of the economy, diverted oil from the domestic to the world market to stem the government's losses, but this left less energy for domestic production and prohibited the import of Western consumer goods to incentivize Soviet workers to work more productively.[24]

Then, on April 26, 1986, the no. 4 light-water nuclear reactor at the Chernobyl nuclear power plant in Ukraine exploded, leading to the worst peacetime nuclear disaster in world history. Chernobyl was a catastrophe of many dimensions—human, ecological, and ideological—but its economic impact on the Soviet state was profound. A little more than a month after the accident, the costs were already calculated at 3 billion rubles, and they would only escalate over time.[25]

With the setbacks compounding, Gorbachev and his Politburo comrades sounded by the fall of 1986 like they were overseeing an escalating crisis, not a budding revolution. On October 30, the general secretary told his colleagues that the country had lost 13 billion rubles in 1985 from the fall of energy export prices. In the past two years, he continued, imports had declined from 24 to 13 billion rubles. "Never before in the history of the country has this happened," he rued. Yegor Ligachev, who would soon lead the conservative resistance to Gorbachev, could only agree. "The financial economy of the country is in a very difficult situation, to say the least," he said. Gorbachev blamed the crisis on the fact that there was "more money than goods in the country," leaving people with a "weakened interest in work." The entire point of economic reform efforts since the early 1980s had been to motivate Soviet workers, but circumstances had now conspired to make them the least motivated workforce in the country's history. "The situation has us by the throat," he concluded.

At this moment of crisis, Gorbachev professed convictions to his comrades that would come to define his entire foreign and domestic policy. First, with regard to perestroika, he said that "the main thing is do not retreat, do not waver, no matter how difficult" the tasks might be. Where others may have turned back, he was committed to pressing onward. As domestic reform deepened, he believed the country needed to return to economic health by paring down its international commitments. "We must be extremely careful in matters of assistance to other countries," he said. There should be "no promises to anyone." Military spending was also too high and was crippling the domestic economy. "The peculiarity of this five-year plan is that it is necessary to combine 'both guns and butter.' It is difficult, very difficult," he said.[26] Before military spending could be cut back, Gorbachev knew he would have to ease the tensions of the Cold War.

◆　◆　◆

"Perestroika," Gorbachev wrote in his memoirs, "would have been impossible without . . . the creation of propitious international conditions."[27] From his first day in office, he held to this fundamental view.

His foreign policy was meant to serve his domestic plans, which required a de-escalation of the Cold War, a scaling back of the nuclear arms race, and a retreat from the burdens of empire. He was not alone in holding such convictions. Important elements of the party, foreign policy, and military elite perceived a growing divergence between capitalist and communist capabilities, and they welcomed Gorbachev's efforts to relieve the country of these burdens.[28]

The events of the first half of the 1980s had definitively altered the balance of power between the Soviet Union and the United States. The potent combination of the Volcker Shock, the Reagan financial and military buildups, and the fall in Soviet oil production and world oil prices had created two blocs of vastly different material capabilities and economic outlooks. Reagan had found a way to eliminate the choice between guns and butter for the United States by borrowing on a massive scale from foreigners, and some Soviet officials concluded that the limitless material capabilities of the United States would strengthen the Reagan administration's negotiating position on arms control. "It can be assumed," a 1987 report from the influential United States and Canada Institute concluded, "that cost-saving considerations will not be a factor in the coming years that would significantly affect the current position of the US leadership in the field of arms limitation."[29]

For the Soviets, by contrast, cost-saving considerations were the entire basis of their push for arms control. Moscow could, and did, borrow on international capital markets, but no country, let alone the leading anti-capitalist state in the world, could match the advantage the United States derived from its position at the heart of global capitalist finance. If the Kremlin wanted to match Washington by devoting even more resources to its already massive military-industrial complex, it would have to take resources away from investment in its civilian economy and the standard of living of the Soviet people.

From these structural considerations, Gorbachev formulated the foundational goal of his foreign policy: to prevent a new stage of the nuclear arms race. Gorbachev regularly talked about the importance of "the human factor" in his superpower diplomacy with Reagan, and scholars have generally followed his lead to argue that the personal relationship between the two leaders was essential to producing the nuclear arms control agreements of the last years of the Cold War.[30] But while there is no doubt that the warm working relationship between the two leaders was important, the archival record makes it clear that all the breakthroughs in arms control in the late 1980s derived from Soviet concessions that stemmed from the Kremlin's desire to ease the military burden on the economy. "We are at the limits of our capabilities," Gorbachev told the Politburo in October 1986.[31] Therefore, "the most important task" was "to derail a new phase of the arms race." If a new stage began, it would be "a loss everywhere," especially in the "wearing down of our economy. And this is unacceptable. If they impose a second stage of the [arms] race, we will lose!"[32] With a new team of foreign policy advisors, including Georgian reformer Eduard Shevardnadze as foreign minister, Gorbachev pursued nuclear arms control from his first day in office with tactical brilliance, ideological innovation, and a great deal of rhetorical flourish.

It began in Geneva, Switzerland. In November 1985, Reagan and Gorbachev converged on an eighteenth-century chateau on the shores of Lake Geneva to size each other up and present their first proposals. In what would become a recurring (and increasingly untenable) theme of his public diplomacy, Gorbachev stridently denied that the Soviet economy was in any serious trouble and rejected the idea that Reagan's military buildup could force the Soviet Union to capitulate. Both sides agreed that strategic nuclear weapons should be dramatically reduced, but Gorbachev irritably told the president he would never agree to reduce the Soviet Union's defenses as long as Reagan pursued his Strategic Defense Initiative (SDI). The next day, Reagan made a formal proposal to reduce each side's offensive nuclear stockpile by 50 percent and cut back both sides' capabilities in other categories of weapons as well. Gorbachev assented, but only if Reagan committed to abandon SDI. Reagan would not, so the conference ended short on results.[33]

If personal diplomacy was not enough to persuade Reagan, perhaps bold public proposals would pressure him into a deal. On the advice of the chief of the Soviet General Staff, Sergei Akhromeev, Gorbachev announced in January 1986 a proposal to eliminate all nuclear weapons by the year 2000. The plan grabbed global headlines, but the Reagan administration rejected it because it failed their long-standing litmus tests in disarmament talks: it said nothing of the massive Soviet advantage in conventional military forces in Europe, it failed to independently address the intermediate-range nuclear missiles the Soviets had deployed in Europe since the late 1970s, and it continued to insist that the British and French nuclear arsenals be included in the mutual reductions. These had all long been nonstarters for the American side, and they had held up arms negotiations since the early 1980s.

Desperate for progress, Gorbachev gave ground. Over the spring and summer of 1986, as the oil price collapsed, alcohol tax revenues evaporated, and Chernobyl demonstrated the costs and consequences of nuclear fallout, the general secretary matched the drama of his public call for complete nuclear abolition with a series of specific concessions. The British and French arsenals would not have to be included, he told the Americans. Conventional forces could be considered as part of a general reduction and balancing of the two blocs' armed forces. Most important of all, laboratory research on SDI could continue, as long as the Americans renounced external testing and deployment.[34] For Gorbachev, the reasoning behind these moves was clear. "If we don't back down on some specific, maybe even important issues, if we won't budge from the positions we've held for a long time, we will lose in the end," he told the Politburo, "We will be drawn into an arms race that we cannot manage. We will lose, because right now we are already at the end of our tether."[35]

The trail of concessions led to Reykjavik, Iceland, where Gorbachev and Reagan held their second summit in October 1986. Before leaving Moscow, Gorbachev sketched out his strategy to the Politburo: "The United States is interested in keeping the negotiations machine running idle, while the arms race overloads our economy. Therefore, we need a breakthrough."[36] He flew to Iceland with a bold proposal to immediately halve both sides' strategic nuclear weapons and remove all intermediate-range missiles from Europe. The Americans were elated at the extent of the concessions. Over the next two days, the two sides approached the precipice of an agreement to eliminate *all* their nuclear weapons over the next ten years, but it foundered once again on SDI. Reagan could not bring himself to permanently cede the right to deploy the system, and Gorbachev was unwilling to sign away all the Soviet Union's nuclear weapons without such an assurance.[37] The two sides left Iceland stunned at how close they had come to agreement and acrimonious about the mutually perceived absurdities that had kept them apart.

Three weeks later, the Politburo gathered for their October 30 meeting where all agreed that the economy was "in a dire position" and lamented "the necessity to combine both 'guns and butter.'"[38] Reykjavik had now taught them that if they wanted to escape the burden of guns in order to produce more butter, they would have to make more concessions abroad in the years to come.

* * *

As he moved to end the arms race with the United States, Gorbachev looked to shed the weight of the Soviet Union's empire in Eastern Europe as well. The subsidized energy deliveries that had caused so much quiet consternation between Moscow and its allies since 1973 made Gorbachev's blood boil. As he told the Politburo on August 14, 1986, the Soviet Union's imperial role left the country "harnessed into slave labor," extracting raw materials and supplying them to other countries.[39] The clearest solution was simple: jettison the rolling price system and settle trade within Comecon in hard currencies at world market prices. But every Soviet leader since the 1970s had known that doing so was sure to bring about the collapse of their empire and influence in Eastern Europe. The poor quality of Eastern European products would be immediately exposed, and the relative price of Soviet oil would increase dramatically, destroying the economies of all the Soviet satellites. Forcing bloc countries "to pay in hard currency," Gorbachev recognized, "would be catastrophic for them."[40]

Nevertheless, new thinking about Moscow's role in the Socialist Bloc was necessary. As with other areas of his policy, Gorbachev's new thinking for Eastern Europe partially stemmed from his genuine belief in the primacy of "shared human interests" over "class interests," his respect for human rights, and his general aversion to the old, violent methods of Soviet governance. But the cornerstones of his new policy derived not from the inclinations of idealism but from the realities of economics: Moscow would gradually campaign to move the bloc toward mutually beneficial trade, and it would provide no further economic aid under any circumstances. Most of all, it would officially repeal the Brezhnev Doctrine and respect the sovereignty of bloc countries because it could no longer bear the burden of empire.

Gorbachev wasted little time in signaling to his allies that change was coming. At his first meeting of the Political Consultative Committee, the Warsaw Pact's highest governing body, in October 1985, he said to his allies, "The possibilities of the Soviet Union supplying raw materials in exchange for finished products from other countries are exhausted." Going forward, the Soviet leadership would meet its economic "obligations" but would also aim for "balanced foreign trade" in the bloc.[41] In place of subsidized commodity exchange, mutually beneficial economic integration was the only way forward.

As with every other area of policy, the drop in oil prices in late 1985 made this transition more difficult. Just as the five-year average made the intrabloc oil price rise more slowly than the world price when oil prices were rising, it now slowed its fall as well. At nominal prices, this increased the value of Eastern Europe to the Soviet Union by making oil exports to the bloc more valuable than exports to the world market. But real prices told a different story. The average selling price of a Soviet barrel of oil within the bloc in 1987 was twenty-two rubles per barrel. At the official dollar/ruble exchange rate, this valued the oil at thirty-two dollars a barrel, 74 percent higher than the world market price. But because the world valued the ruble much less than the Soviet Union did, the actual dollar/ruble exchange rate was much lower than the official exchange rate, and thus the price of the oil was much lower as well. At the market dollar/ruble exchange rate of sixty cents to a ruble, Soviet oil was only twelve dollars a barrel—quite a bargain compared to the world market price of seventeen dollars. As prices stayed low in the late 1980s, the Comecon price kept dropping too, reaching roughly ten dollars a barrel in 1988 at market exchange rates.[42] The declining price at the official exchange rate meant the Soviet Union fell into annual trade deficits with its allies in the late 1980s. These deficits, rather absurdly, put pressure on Soviet officials to *increase* exports to the bloc, even as every communist official knew the Soviet Union was already providing more resources to the bloc than they ever would at world market prices. A switch to hard currency trade would have solved this problem, but Soviet officials were all too aware of the dire political consequences of such a move.

Needless to say, the Soviet leadership took no pleasure in these perverse dynamics, and in 1986 they began to vent their frustration. In August, Gorbachev told his colleagues that they had "lost their way" in economic relations with the bloc and "now had to clean up this mess."[43] Hanging like dark clouds over their considerations were the bloc's debt problems with the West. As the Poles worked to join the IMF in the summer of 1986, Gorbachev sensed danger but felt powerless to stop it. "If we don't hold Poland, then we can't keep the GDR," he told the Politburo. "We grumble about the Poles' relationship with the IMF. But what can they do? The debt is $30 billion."[44] By October, Ryzhkov was worried but resigned to inaction. The bloc was "crawling to the West—into a trap." In Poland, "everyone can see what has happened there. Hungary is now on the brink. Bulgaria stopped in front of a precipice. Saved by us." The Soviet Union was offering "a way out—their integration," he said, but "they do not want it." They just wanted "electronics" and "delicacies" from the West, while "we keep supporting them with coal, oil, [and] metal."[45]

These economic dynamics led directly to new thinking in politics. In 1986 Gorbachev began to advocate letting the bloc countries deal with their problems themselves, no matter the political consequences. In July, he told the Politburo, "What went on before could not continue. The methods that were used in Czechoslovakia [in 1968] and Hungary [in 1956] now are no good; they will not work!" The economy was now "the most important" factor. The Soviets' influence could "only be ideological, only through example! Everything else is an illusion." They could no longer use "administrative methods of leadership" because "this kind of 'leadership' . . . would mean carrying them on our back."[46]

Lightening the imperial load became the main theme of a meeting of the heads of state of the Comecon countries in Moscow on November 10–11, 1986. Gorbachev arrived ready to scold his allies for relying on Western credit for economic growth. "It was false," he said, "to think that our countries' problems could be solved through the widespread use of loans and technology" from the West.[47] "We lived on credit," he told the assembled leaders. "In the last ten to fifteen years, consumption has grown faster than labor productivity in many countries, which means that [national] income has simply been 'eaten up.'" He recognized the importance of "the social sphere" in communist societies that had, after all, been "created in the interests of the workers." But socialism could not continue to promise more than it could actually deliver. The problem with living on credit, he told his colleagues, was that "sooner or later one must pay for it."[48]

Gorbachev now told his comrades that Moscow would not cover the debt bill when it came due. He discussed the Soviet burden in detail. The expenditure required "to maintain the military-strategic balance with imperialism" was "not small," and "nine tenths of it was covered by the Soviet Union." In the area of energy and raw materials, "Soviet deliveries . . . almost entirely fulfill the needs of the brother countries." The imperial burden of arms, energy, and aid limited "the possibilities for solving social problems and raising the standard of living" within the Soviet Union.[49] At the height of the Polish Crisis, Andropov had concluded that Soviet leaders needed to be concerned with their own country's development above all others. Gorbachev was now putting his mentor's principle into practice.

The burden of economics demanded a new form of politics. Gorbachev informed his comrades that the Soviet Politburo had decided to put "the entire system of political relations between the socialist countries on the foundation of equality and mutual benefit." From now on, the "indispensable principles" of relations among socialist countries would be "the independence of each party, their right to sovereign decision-making about problems of development in their own country, and their responsibility to their own people." Most importantly, no country would now "claim a special role in the socialist community."[50]

After already dying in practice in Poland, the Brezhnev Doctrine was now dead in principle too. Describing the meeting to the Politburo in the days that followed, Gorbachev told the group that he had "opened the way for the radical reconstruction of collaboration within the community. Everything will be based on self-reliance."[51] The days of intervening abroad to protect socialism were over, and this was profoundly within the Soviet Union's self-interest. "We need this," he said two months later. "It is in our interest not to be loaded down with responsibility for what is happening, or could happen, there."[52]

When and why the Brezhnev Doctrine was repealed has important implications. Contrary to those who argue that its repeal stemmed from Gorbachev's unique commitment to self-determination, democracy, nonviolence, and human rights, it is clear that the decision was the culmination of a long-running campaign by the collective Soviet leadership to shed the material burden of empire.[53] A policy of nonintervention in the Eastern Bloc conformed to Gorbachev's idealistic plans for glasnost and perestroika within the Soviet Union, but it also aligned with the economically driven understanding of Soviet national interests that had coalesced within the Soviet leadership since the oil crisis of 1973. In fact, combined with Andropov's decision to foreclose the possibility of military intervention in Poland in 1981, it is possible to conclude that for economic reasons alone, most Soviet leaders in Gorbachev's position would have withdrawn the Soviet Union from its responsibility to "protect" socialism by the mid-1980s.[54] Scholars have long assumed that without Gorbachev's exceptional view of the world, the revolutions of 1989 would not have been possible because the Soviet Union would have intervened to stop them.[55] This has it backward. By the mid-1980s, it was the policy of intervention in Eastern Europe, rather than nonintervention, that was difficult for Soviet leaders to justify. Completing the work his predecessors had started, Gorbachev withdrew the Soviet Union from its leading role within the Socialist Bloc to focus on improving the material prosperity of Soviet citizens at home.

The same held true for the war in Afghanistan. Gorbachev made ending the war an early priority and received the support of party conservatives and the armed forces. In the fall of 1985, he called for a speedy withdrawal of Soviet forces within the Politburo and heard no objection from Defense Minister Sokolov, who had led the Soviet invasion, or Andrei Gromyko, who had been one of the invasion's original advocates. By 1986, withdrawal had become a consensus issue within the leadership. In June, when the Politburo agreed to withdraw 8,000 troops from the conflict, it was Gromyko declaring, "This is not our war," and Gorbachev maintaining that "the result must not look like a shameful defeat." The leadership discussed plans to pull Soviet troops out of Afghanistan over the next two years, and in assenting to withdrawal, Gromyko admitted the initial invasion had been a mistake. The entire leadership now agreed that the war had become an unwinnable drain on Soviet resources and the armed forces needed to come home.[56]

◆ ◆ ◆

The troops came home to a financial crisis that was accelerating without relent. The budget deficit reached 6.2 percent of GDP in 1986, funded entirely by "borrowing" from Soviet citizens' savings at the Soviet state bank.[57] In reality, this meant printing rubles and monetizing the deficit—a surefire recipe for inflation and, in the Soviet system of fixed prices, widespread shortages of basic goods. By the spring of 1987, the finance minister was informing the Politburo that the country's financial situation had "reached the point of crisis." State budget losses from the decline in alcohol sales and the oil price now totaled 30 billion rubles, and state subsidies for food would soon reach 100 billion rubles.[58] The government paid nearly one-third of the cost of every loaf of bread, over half the cost of every gallon of milk, 40 percent of the cost of butter, and 70 percent of the cost of every kilogram of beef.[59]

The state's promises to consumers were only one side of the coin. Its promises to producers—the vast network of state enterprises, collective farms, and the military-industrial complex—were the other. Gorbachev drew the Politburo's attention here. "For the last fifteen years, 25–30% of enterprises have not been meeting their income targets. And yet they continue to 'work' at the expense of the state."[60] The Soviet state's unwillingness to push unprofitable enterprises into bankruptcy and its guarantee of full employment meant few workers were ever fired. Enterprises "are going bankrupt," Politburo member Vitalii Vorotnikov reiterated, "and the state is taking them on its back and keeping them afloat."[61]

The Soviet state was now in fiscal and financial crisis, and Gorbachev sought refuge in radicalism. "There is no alternative to perestroika!" he would often tell his comrades, in words that echoed Margaret Thatcher.[62] In the first half of 1987, he explicitly transformed perestroika into a campaign of "radical reform" for the economy. The reform rested on a cornerstone that was only vaguely hinted at because of its social, political, and ideological implications: breaking promises. By breaking the Soviet state's promises to the country's consumers, workers, and producers, Gorbachev hoped to incorporate capitalism's stimuli into the socialist system. "The chief question in the theory and practice of socialism," he declared to the country's top leadership in June 1987, "is how, on a socialist basis, to create more powerful stimuli for economic, scientific, technical, and social progress than under capitalism."[63]

Perestroika's leading economists framed the challenge in blunter terms. "There are a great many people who receive more than they give to society," Abel Aganbegian said in 1987. "Under the conditions of perestroika . . . they are being called upon to 'earn' their keep."[64] Another leading economist, Nikolai Shmelev, went even further. Soviet citizens' "parasitic certitude about guaranteed work," he wrote in spring 1987, was the source of all the nation's ills. Perestroika needed to replace the "administrative coercion" of the state with the "economic coercion" of the market.[65] It was a prescription that echoed what Reagan and Thatcher were doing in the capitalist world, and a year later, Shmelev distilled his thinking in terms they would have heartily endorsed. "We must teach our people," he wrote, "to understand that everything that is economically inefficient is immoral, as well as the reverse—that efficiency is morality."[66]

Moral efficiency was to be found, reformers hoped, in the centerpiece of Gorbachev's economic reform, the 1987 Law on State Enterprises. The law mandated that beginning in 1988, all Soviet enterprises would become independent from the state. This independence would activate the "powerful stimuli" of market economies by allowing firms to keep their profits and forcing them to operate without state subsidy. In words any capitalist could appreciate, Prime Minster Ryzhkov told the Supreme Soviet that the "central idea" of the law was "to comprehensively satisfy the demands of the national economy . . . at the lowest possible cost." Because enterprises would retain their profits, they would now have "an economic interest" in ensuring the "highest returns" and "maximum yield" on their capital.[67] Gorbachev addressed the issue of wages. "Each worker's actual wages should be made closely dependent" on productivity and "should not be restricted by any limit." Those were the carrots, but there were also hints of sticks. If an enterprise consistently failed to maintain solvency, "it would be possible to raise the question of reorganization or terminating the enterprise's activity." And as enterprises became more efficient, "the scale at which workers are being released will grow considerably."[68] Private profit, corporate bankruptcy, wage inequality, and labor mobility were now on socialism's horizon.

Gorbachev knew that breaking promises would garner resistance from many corners of society. Citizens would fear the loss of their jobs, income, and social security, and the sprawling state and party bureaucracy would fear the loss of subsidies and control over the Soviet economy. Both groups could defeat perestroika if they found a way to resist its economic prescriptions. Therefore, if he wanted to break promises, Gorbachev knew he would have to overcome the resistance of society and the state.

His weapons of choice were glasnost and democracy. At every step, Gorbachev paired his economic reform proposals with increasingly bold moves to democratize Soviet society. At first, this fell within the realm of increasing socialist democracy—expanding worker control over enterprises and holding competitive elections between Communist Party candidates at the local level—and allowing greater freedom of the press. But by 1988, with the economic crisis deepening and reform still not taking hold, Gorbachev jettisoned the confines of socialist democracy and embraced national competitive elections at the Nineteenth All-Union Party Conference.

He did so not only out of high-minded idealism but also out of cold political calculation. Indeed, the first reason democracy and freedom of expression emerged in the Soviet Union was because of their potential *to coerce*. Alexander Yakovlev, the driving force in the Politburo behind democratization, wrote to his colleagues, "There is sometimes a misunderstanding: when people talk about democracy, they presuppose some amorphous notion, like liberalization. . . . However, in reality, democracy is discipline . . . and the development of self-discipline."[69] Gorbachev echoed his chief of ideology. "We have embarked on the path of democracy," he told the Politburo in June 1987, because "it provides the strongest grip on power."[70] At that point, he was only talking about democratization in enterprises and within the Communist Party. But in his memoirs, Gorbachev wrote that he applied much the same thinking to the decision to move to full electoral democracy. He recalled an article published in the Soviet press in 1989 that argued radical economic reform could only be implemented under "the reliable shield of strong authoritarian power." He wrote, "For me and my circle this argument was no revelation. We were not so simple as not to recognize" that "significant transformations could be carried out" only with "a firm grip on the reins of power." He knew he would need political power "to overcome the inevitable opposition to proposed reforms" from the state and party bureaucracy, and the most power was to be found in glasnost and democratic politics.[71]

This was the reasoning underlying his groundbreaking speech at the January 1987 Central Committee Plenum. There he announced a radical expansion of glasnost to include freedom of expression as well as elections within enterprises and between CPSU candidates at the local level. "We think that electiveness, far from undermining, on the contrary, enhances the authority of the leader," he told the party leadership. The Soviet system had always been built on "control 'from above,'" he said, but now it was "of fundamental importance" to increase "control 'from below.'"[72] If democracy made enterprise managers, local party bosses, and eventually the entire government and party leadership accountable to the population, public scrutiny would coerce these authorities into implementing economic reform.

On paper, then, the political and economic reforms of 1987 appeared well positioned to successfully impose the politics of breaking promises. Democracy would coerce Soviet enterprises into implementing the Law on State Enterprises, and the Law on State Enterprises would coerce Soviet enterprises and workers into being more productive. The economic discipline of the marketplace would chasten the Soviet social contract, and the economy would be relaunched on the long-sought path of intensive growth.

In reality, however, the reforms were an abject failure. In allowing enterprises to keep most of their profits, the Law on State Enterprises proved to be, in essence, a massive supply-side tax cut. Enterprises paid an average of 63 percent of their profits to the state in 1986, but that number dropped to 40 percent in 1989.[73] State revenues declined precipitously during the same period, falling from 47 percent of GDP in 1985 to 41 percent in 1989. This was, in turn, reflected in the budget deficit, which jumped from an already dangerous 6.2 percent of GDP in 1986 to 11 percent in 1988 and 9.5 percent in 1989.[74] Rather than imposing discipline on the Soviet economy, Gorbachev's reforms replaced the soft budget constraints of the old command system with no budget constraints at all.

How did a reform that was meant to impose economic discipline end up removing it altogether? Why did Gorbachev's attempt at breaking promises fail while his capitalist adversaries' attempts succeeded? Interest groups, communist ideology, the politics of perestroika, and the inner workings of the Soviet financial system provide the answers. Each made it more difficult for Gorbachev to impose discipline, and collectively, they proved too much for him to overcome.

Throughout perestroika, Gorbachev faced a formidable ideological tension between advocating for market discipline and upholding socialist values. Unlike Thatcher and Reagan, who relished their roles as crusaders against socialism in all its forms, even the most radical Soviet reformers in 1987 and 1988 were not trying to destroy socialism, but rather reinvent it. Though they wanted to introduce many of capitalism's coercive stimuli, they remained uneasy about the social effects and ideological implications of their drive for efficiency. Even as he praised Thatcher's work in Great Britain, Aganbegian still believed that perestroika should accomplish its goals without causing unemployment in the Soviet Union. To do otherwise, he thought, would be to betray socialism's founding promise to serve the working class. "As a country where power is in the hands of the workers," he wrote, "it is natural that we should want to have no unemployment."[75] This conviction carried all the way up to the Politburo. "Foreigners . . . are very interested in how we will deal with unemployment, which will inevitably follow in the course of perestroika," Gorbachev told his comrades in 1987. "We know how they have solved that problem; how will we?"[76] Thatcher and other capitalist leaders who were "also carrying out a perestroika" in their own countries acted "harshly, rudely, the capitalist way, regardless of how it affects the workers," he said. The Soviet perestroika needed to be different because it was based on "different ideas," Gorbachev said, but "we can't flinch either."[77] How to not flinch while still retaining the "different ideas" of socialism was a riddle Gorbachev was never able to solve.

The politics of perestroika reinforced reformers' ideological reluctance to follow through on their disciplinary policies. As long as Gorbachev needed the Soviet masses to exert control "from below" over the obstinate state and party bureaucracy, he could not afford to lose their approbation. This made carrying out unpopular reforms extremely difficult in political terms. Reforming the rigid system of fixed prices, for example, was an economically essential component of perestroika, but it proved to be politically impossible to carry out. "The question of prices is principle, fundamental," Gorbachev told the Politburo in May 1987. "If it's not solved, there won't be . . . self-financing, and perestroika will not work." But he could barely finish recognizing the economic necessity of prices before lamenting their political consequences. If the leadership announced a price reform, "commotion would erupt. And people will ask, 'Why do we need all this?'"[78] Since advising Andropov to refrain from raising prices in the early 1980s, Gorbachev had known that price increases were the easiest way for a Soviet leader to lose support among the masses. The late 1980s were no different. "Hands off prices!" was the first rallying cry of the democratic opposition.[79]

As a result of their ideological uneasiness and political trepidation, perestroika's advocates forced themselves to believe that reforms could be socially painless. This was an ideologically consistent and politically wise position to hold, but economically, it was disastrous. Gorbachev told the Politburo that "the most important thing" about a potential price reform was that it "should not undermine the standard of living."[80] The documents announcing the Law on State Enterprises contradictorily declared that "prices should be given a cost restricting character" but also that "the change of retail prices should not lead to a decline in the living standard of the working people."[81] Similarly, the party announced that the law would "induce the enterprises . . . to trim their excessive workforce" but would "not bring about unemployment."[82] The entire point of intensive growth was to produce more output with fewer inputs, including fewer workers, so considerable unemployment was a virtual certainty if discipline was actually imposed. It never was, and significant price liberalization and unemployment did not emerge until Boris Yeltsin came to power in newly independent Russia in 1992.

Gorbachev, of course, was not the only Cold War leader to unleash a massive supply-side tax cut and explode the budget deficit of his state. Ronald Reagan had done much the same thing in the United States. He too had failed, in many ways, to fully overcome his nation's ideological and political resistance to economic discipline. But Reagan had been saved from the inflationary consequences of his policies by the draconian monetary policy of Paul Volcker. Gorbachev had no equivalent savior. In addition to communist ideology and the politics of perestroika, the Soviet financial system significantly contributed to the defeat of his drive to discipline. Unlike capitalist countries, where price stability became the policy priority of the 1980s, the Soviet government was not able to use monetary policy to control the nation's money supply. Instead, by making enterprises' assets convertible into cash, the reforms of 1987 unexpectedly *removed* the government's control over the money supply and unleashed a tsunami of liquidity. KGB head Vladimir Kriuchkov described the problem in the spring of 1990. "The main culprit" in producing the country's economic problems, he said, "is [the] conversion of very large amounts of what in the past had been non-liquid funds—columns of figures in accounting books—to cash. . . . So now we have hundreds of billions of rubles of 'bad money'—money not backed up by goods—circulating in the system."[83] Gorbachev's economic reforms, therefore, not only gave Soviet enterprises a blank check, but also gave them the right to cash in all the old checks they had accumulated under the command economy.

The result was runaway inflationary pressure. Enterprise financial assets grew an astounding 32.6 percent in 1987 and another 22.5 percent in 1988,[84] while total enterprise spending ballooned from 243 billion rubles in 1987 to 462 billion rubles in 1989.[85] Annual income growth skyrocketed, jumping from 4 percent in 1987 to 13 percent in 1989.[86] The 1987 reforms had unleashed a runaway monetary train in the Soviet economy, one that soon imperiled perestroika's popularity at home and crippled the Soviet state's ability to project power abroad.

◆ ◆ ◆

Gorbachev "always considered every significant action or initiative from two perspectives—domestic and foreign," his aide Anatolii Cherniaev wrote in his memoirs. Therefore, as Gorbachev radicalized his domestic reform, "he simultaneously addressed the problem of restraining the arms race and the place of the military-industrial complex in [the] system—above all, its role in the country's entire economy."[87] Cuts to the military could only be made in an increasingly benign international environment, so Gorbachev went abroad in 1987 to foster the conditions that would make this possible. Through soaring idealistic rhetoric and bold personal diplomacy, he attempted to use new means to keep the international position the Soviet Union had formerly secured with military power.

It began with an internal campaign to reform Soviet defense doctrine. Reducing the size of the military-industrial complex could not be justified so long as the Soviet Union held to the principle that had grounded the country's defense policy since the 1950s—maintaining strategic parity in armed forces with the United States. The Americans, Gorbachev said in May 1987, "clearly want to pull us into another round of the arms race. They are counting on our military exhaustion. . . . Therefore, the approach of one soldier there, one soldier here, they have a bullet we have a bullet, is not our approach."[88] In place of strategic parity, Gorbachev now pushed the leadership to accept a doctrine of strategic sufficiency—the idea that the country did not need to match the United States in armaments, it merely needed to maintain armed forces sufficient to ensure that the Americans would be deterred from launching an attack.

Many in the Soviet armed forces were uncomfortable with such an approach, but a bizarre incident abetted Gorbachev's initiative on May 27, 1987. West German teenager Mathias Rust flew a small airplane from Helsinki, Finland, and landed it on Red Square in Moscow without being turned back by the Soviet military. For Gorbachev, it was an opportunity to clean house within the national defense hierarchy. He forced Defense Minister Sokolov to resign and pushed hundreds of officers throughout the armed forces into retirement. His handpicked replacement to lead the Defense Ministry, Dmitri Yazov, now owed his job to the general secretary, and the Defense Ministry and the armed forces struggled to resist the transition to a policy of strategic sufficiency thereafter.[89]

The move to strategic sufficiency paralleled an evolution in the Soviet position on nuclear arms control. After the close call at Reykjavik in October 1986, the leadership was in the familiar position of having to make further concessions if they wanted to make progress. Since his January 1986 declaration aiming for a nuclear-free world by the year 2000, Gorbachev had tried to attain a comprehensive agreement governing all nuclear weapons. That strategy had failed at Reykjavik due to the American unwillingness to give up SDI. By early 1987, a group of reformers and conservatives— Shevardnadze and Yakovlev as well as Ligachev and Sokolov—banded together to advocate decoupling negotiations over SDI and long-range strategic nuclear weapons from negotiations over intermediate-range nuclear forces (INF) in Europe. They also proposed to support the "zero option" in INF negotiations to remove all intermediate nuclear weapons from Europe.[90] These were significant concessions to the Reagan administration, which preferred to discuss strategic weapons and INF separately and had first proposed the "zero option" in 1981, thinking the Soviet Union would never accept it.

Far from leading the charge to decouple negotiations over strategic and intermediate weapons, as many historians have claimed, Gorbachev was at first reluctant to abandon his comprehensive approach.[91] But with the domestic economy faltering and the Americans showing no sign of easing their negotiating position, he came to agree with other members of the Politburo that they needed to do something to jump-start the arms control negotiations. He soon issued a statement to the West proposing to eliminate all intermediate missiles in Europe without linking it to SDI or strategic weapons limitations. In an additional signal of flexibility, his letter railed against the future deployment of SDI but raised no objection to the prospect of researching and testing the program.[92]

The Americans were happy to pocket the concessions and ask for more. US secretary of state George Schultz traveled to Moscow in April 1987 to negotiate with Gorbachev on the newly decoupled INF zero option. His visit came just one week before the Soviet finance minister would tell the Politburo that the country's financial situation had "reached the point of crisis."[93] Desperate to come to terms on a treaty that would enable cuts in the Soviet defense budget, Gorbachev agreed to three central American conditions for an INF treaty: including Soviet Asia in the agreement so the agreement applied globally, including short-range nuclear weapons in the agreement, and assenting to an intrusive inspections regime to verify the treaty. This led to agreement on the basic shape of the final treaty, and the two sides planned to have Reagan and Gorbachev sign it in December at a bilateral summit in Washington.[94]

As he searched for an escape from the superpower nuclear confrontation, Gorbachev believed that Western Europe held the key to his strategy of securing the Soviet Union's international position through diplomacy.[95] The Soviet leadership had long tried to drive a wedge between Western Europe and the United States through peace offensives, and with peace and disarmament movements gaining strength in Western Europe in the 1980s, the time looked ripe for success. But Western Europeans' perceptions of the Soviet Union as a menacing threat would first have to be transformed into visions of the Soviet Union as a cornerstone of peace. There was a "war of ideas" going on between the superpowers for the hearts and minds of Western Europeans, Gorbachev told the Politburo in March 1987, and if the Soviet Union lost, it would "lose everything."[96]

He hoped his vision of a "common European home" would win this war. Gorbachev had first casually mentioned the idea in a speech to the British Parliament in 1984, but it took on new life as the "all-European house" during his trip to Czechoslovakia in April 1987. "We are resolutely against the division of the continent into military blocs facing each other," he said in a speech in Prague.[97] In combination with the bold Soviet moves on arms control, this call to transcend the military division of Europe served its purpose of changing Western European perceptions of the Soviet Union. By the summer of 1987, Gorbachev's popularity in the West had become a political force unto itself; by year's end, *Time* magazine had named him their Man of the Year.

But the material realities of the Soviet empire remained unchanged. While he publicly proclaimed the need for a common European home in Prague, Gorbachev privately told the Czechoslovak leadership that "we will not conduct our perestroika at [your] expense. But do not expect to live at our expense either."[98] As he reinforced to his Kremlin comrades later that year, the Soviet Union could not use "pressure [or] the slightest manifestation of inequality. . . . Each party must sort everything out itself."[99] This included economic support, which Gorbachev once again told his allies the Soviet Union could not provide. "Jaruzelski is waiting for a lot of help in economic cooperation," he reported after meeting with the bloc allies at celebrations of the seventieth anniversary of the October Revolution. "Zhivkov [in Bulgaria] too."[100]

The Soviet Union had nothing extra to give. On October 9, 1987, Ryzhkov reported to the Politburo a litany of economic dismay. From 1985 to 1987, the country's annual hard currency earnings from exports dropped from $25 billion to $17 billion, even though the government had diverted increasing numbers of goods, including oil, from the domestic market to exports every year. Income from foreign trade had dropped from 66 billion rubles in 1985 to 52 billion rubles in 1987. The state budget deficit was now 84 billion rubles.[101] These numbers not only prohibited support for allies in Eastern Europe, but they also reinforced the main goal of Soviet foreign policy—to reduce defense spending. Ryzhkov told the Politburo just one week before his bleak economic report, "If we hold the current level of spending on defense, we cannot upgrade industry, we will not give the people prosperity. . . . We must reduce defense spending."[102]

Lowering defense spending would require the completion of the INF Treaty. In fall 1987, the Soviet negotiating team made another significant concession to keep progress alive. They formally recognized that the Soviet Union had more short- and intermediate-range weapons in Europe than the United States and thus would have to give up more weapons than the Americans to get to zero. These "asymmetrical cuts" had long been a deal breaker for the Kremlin, but circumstances now demanded they give way. In October, Gorbachev made one final attempt to tie his attendance at the Washington summit to an American willingness to negotiate on SDI, but after Schultz stonewalled this demand, he dropped the linkage once and for all. Only a year after he had broken off the Reykjavik summit over SDI, he would now travel to the next summit without the program even on the negotiating agenda.[103]

The signing of the INF Treaty in Washington on December 8 was a historic event and the crowning achievement to that point of Gorbachev's strategy to secure the Soviet Union's international position through diplomacy in place of military power. He publicly declared that the treaty demonstrated the importance of "the human factor" in building trust between adversaries.[104] Hours of personal diplomacy had contributed to the agreement, but the ultimate source of the treaty lay outside any negotiating room. The Soviet leadership had drawn a fundamental connection between cutting the country's military burden and improving the domestic economy and had made a string of concessions in pursuit of that goal. In the final treaty, the Soviet Union agreed to eliminate 1,846 short- and intermediate-range missiles, while the United States only agreed to eliminate 846.[105] Gorbachev had to stomach these disparities to successfully embed the move to military retrenchment within a superpower treaty and transform the Soviet Union's international reputation from menace to peacemaker.

◆　◆　◆

One year later, on December 7, 1988, Gorbachev stood in front of the United Nations General Assembly to announce a bold new vision for peaceful world order. "Force and the threat of force can no longer be, and should not be, instruments of foreign policy," he declared. "Freedom of choice is a universal principle to which there should be no exceptions." The international system would continue to be defined by the "rivalry of various socioeconomic and political systems," but the Soviet Union now wanted "to impart to this rivalry the quality of sensible competition in conditions of respect for freedom of choice and a balance of interests." To that end, he announced, Moscow would unilaterally reduce the size of its armed forces by 500,000 people over the next two years, withdraw six tank divisions from the Eastern Bloc, and reduce its overall military presence in Eastern Europe by 50,000 soldiers and 5,000 tanks.[106]

The speech was a sensation in the Western world. It was a hint—crystal clear in retrospect but only naively trusted at the time—that the Soviet Union no longer sought to control the political and economic destiny of the nations under its orbit. Redefining the long-standing antagonism between the capitalist and socialist worlds as a sensible competition based on respect for freedom of choice did not sound like the Cold War of old. Indeed, it sounded as though Gorbachev was declaring the Cold War's end.

This was precisely Gorbachev's intention. In planning the speech, he had professed a desire to make his address the "anti-Fulton"—reversing Winston Churchill's claim in a 1946 speech in Fulton, Missouri, that an Iron Curtain had befallen the European continent and divided it into two halves. The speech was the apotheosis of Gorbachev's strategy to use bold vision and idealistic rhetoric to maintain the international standing the Soviet Union had once secured through military might.

Over the course of 1988, the conviction to reduce the burdens of empire had grown to encompass Politburo members on both sides of the growing debate over the domestic course of perestroika. In June, as the party prepared for the Nineteenth All-Union Party Conference, even conservative stalwart Andrei Gromyko had come to view exiting the arms race as a national necessity. The decision throughout the postwar period to produce ever more nuclear weapons "was our mistaken position, absolutely mistaken," he concluded. "Tens of billions were spent on production of these toys." His fellow conservative Vitaly Vorotnikov concurred. "We did indeed let ourselves get pulled into the arms race. We found ourselves on the brink of catastrophe. . . . We are the ones to blame." Gorbachev capitalized on the prevailing sentiment to press his new thinking. Was the party's goal "to race the entire world regarding the levels of armaments: cannon by cannon, plane by plane?" he asked. "Then let us introduce ration cards for food, turn the country into a military camp, and just race and race onwards." With shortages already crippling the Soviet economy, this was a prospect no one welcomed.[107]

As the year progressed, the trade-off between the domestic economy and the military burden became ingrained in the Politburo's thinking. It thus directly informed Gorbachev's internal preparation for his UN speech. He believed in a radically new and nonviolent vision of international relations, which he hoped to demonstrate to the world by pulling Soviet troops out of Eastern Europe. But that vision is not what sold his less idealistic comrades in the Politburo on the idea. To them, the worsening domestic economy compelled military disarmament. At the Politburo meeting on November 3, 1988, Gorbachev reasoned, "Our military expenses are 2.5 times larger than those of the United States. No country in the world . . . spends more per capita on the military sector." As the budget deficit spiraled out of control and citizens struggled to find food and basic consumer goods, this fact hung weightily over the chamber. If troops were not pulled out of Eastern Europe, Ryzhkov warned, "we can forget about any increase in the standard of living. No matter what government you put in place of this one, it won't solve this problem." Sensing consensus, Gorbachev proposed that he announce unilateral cuts in the armed forces in his UN speech. Everyone agreed, and he concluded, "The main reason we're doing this is perestroika. . . . Without reductions in the army and the military industrial complex we won't be able to deal with perestroika's tasks."[108]

Upon returning from the United Nations a month later, Gorbachev held another Politburo meeting to assess the speech and the future direction of perestroika. Yegor Ligachev, his preeminent conservative opponent, praised the policy of unilateral disarmament on the grounds of political economy. "We need disarmament most of all," he said. "We took such a burden upon ourselves with relation to the military budget that it will be difficult to dramatically solve anything in the economy." In the spirit of glasnost, many Politburo members advocated telling the world that the domestic economy had necessitated the military cutbacks. But Gorbachev demurred. "We keep this secrecy for one reason," he said. "If we admit now that we cannot build a long-term economic and social policy without [unilateral cuts], . . . this may reduce to nothing [the effect] of the speech at the United Nations." Gorbachev knew that the idealism of the speech would lose its power if it became clear that it was driven by material considerations.[109] For now, people in both East and West were calling the speech's idealism revolutionary. If the Soviet Union was going to maintain its superpower status in an era of retrenchment, Gorbachev knew that he and the country could not afford to lose those acclamations.

Nor could they lose the regard of their allies in Eastern Europe. Since scolding the allies for "living on credit" and lamenting the scale of Soviet oil deliveries in November 1986, Gorbachev had continuously returned to the questions of oil and indebtedness in discussions of the region. In a March 1988 Politburo meeting, he brought up former Polish leader Edward Gierek, who had tried to spur development in the 1970s by borrowing from the West. "What was it all based on?" Gorbachev said. "On credits from the West and on our cheap fuel. The same goes for Hungary." Going forward, economic relations in the bloc needed to change, Gorbachev said, "because we cannot remain a provider of cheap resources for them forever."[110]

By the fall of 1988, it had become apparent that a general economic crisis of the socialist bloc was fast approaching.[111] Georgii Shakhnazarov, Gorbachev's aide for Eastern Europe, wrote his boss an urgent memo detailing the onrushing problems. "There are multiple signs that certain similar problems are increasingly plaguing fraternal countries," he wrote in early October. In the past, "whenever any of them was in crisis, we had to come to the rescue at the cost of huge material, political and even human sacrifice." But now, "any option to 'extinguish' crises by military means must be fully excluded. Even the old leadership seems to have already realized this, at least with regard to Poland." The current crises were, in any case, financial. "We must reflect on how we will act if one or even several countries become bankrupt simultaneously," Shakhnazarov wrote. "This is a realistic prospect for some of them on the brink of monetary insolvency." The prospect of bankruptcy raised a number of questions the leadership needed to address. "Could the socialist countries come out of the pre-crisis situation without Western assistance? What price will they have to pay for this assistance? To what extent should we encourage such a course of events or put up with it? To what degree are we interested in the continued presence of Soviet troops on the territory of a number of allied countries (excluding the GDR)?"[112]

Gorbachev's UN announcement of troop withdrawals from Eastern Europe began to answer this last question. Answers to the others would emerge in early 1989. In January, Gorbachev told the Politburo, "Comrades, we are on the eve of very serious things, because we cannot give [the Eastern Europeans] more than we are giving them now." He heard no resistance from his colleagues to the idea that the country had reached its material limits. But if the Soviet Union did not provide more economic and technological support, Gorbachev said, "there will be a split and they will run away." As populations and politicians across the Eastern Bloc wondered how far they could push Moscow without inviting a harsh crackdown, Gorbachev now told his colleagues, "The peoples of those countries will ask: what about the CPSU, what kind of leash will it use to hold our countries back? They simply do not know that if they pull this leash harder, it will break." In place of the old policy of domination through economic subsidy, Gorbachev declared it was time to transfer relations with Eastern Europe "to the market." In doing so, he knew the Kremlin "would break the old rule that we keep them attached to us only by means of energy resources."[113] To fully explore the burgeoning crisis in the bloc, Gorbachev commissioned a series of reports from the leading foreign policy institutions of the Soviet state.

The report from the Central Committee was quick to frame the looming crisis in Eastern Europe in economic terms. The Eastern Bloc governments suffered "from a lack of legitimacy," the authors wrote, and "*the economic factor, the ability of a country to join and to assimilate into the world economy, has moved to the top of their priorities.*" Because the ruling parties lacked legitimacy, they could not "*rule in the old way anymore*" and were instead attempting a "smooth movement toward democratization . . . under the leadership of the ruling parties." How should the Soviet Union seek to influence socialist countries under these precarious conditions? "Authoritarian methods and direct pressure have clearly outlived their usefulness," noted the report. Even if there was "a sharp deterioration in one of the countries . . . it is very unlikely that we would be able to employ the methods of 1956 and 1968, both as a matter of principle and because of unacceptable consequences."[114]

The report of the Institute of the Economy of the World Socialist System, written by its director, Oleg Bogomolov, paralleled the Central Committee's analysis. Bogomolov plainly stated that the Soviet government faced "a dilemma": either "thwart the evolution" toward market socialist economies and representative government in Eastern Europe "or take it in stride and develop the policy accepting the probability and even inevitability of this process." The academician's answer to this dilemma could not have been clearer. "Attempts to thwart emerging trends . . . would mean wasting means and resources for an obviously hopeless cause." Fighting to preserve the status quo would "weigh as an excessive burden on our economy." If, instead, the Soviet Union permitted its

Eastern Bloc allies to reform, "the economic burden of the USSR [would] be alleviated." In conclusion, Bogomolov warned that countries where the Soviet Union intervened would "inevitably acquire . . . quasi-dictatorial regimes which would continuously deplete the material resources of the Soviet Union."[115]

For Gorbachev, these reports solidified convictions that had long been hardening. On March 3, 1989, he told the Soviet ambassadors to the Eastern Bloc states, "Do not impose anything on anybody! . . . We reject force in everything, in all our policies." Echoing the "main line" laid down by his mentor Andropov almost a decade before, Gorbachev told the group that the leadership would now "think of our own people" instead of assuming "full responsibility" for the fate of the satellite governments in Eastern Europe.[116] Later that month, a group of senior officials led by Shevardnadze and Yazov confirmed that the Kremlin bore no legal responsibility under the Warsaw Pact to defend its allies from internal instability or revolution.[117]

In July, Gorbachev eloquently couched the new Soviet national interest within a stirring internationalist call for a common European home in a speech to the Council of Europe in Strasbourg, France. "The social and political order in some particular countries did change in the past," he said, "and it can change in the future as well. But this is exclusively a matter for the peoples themselves and of their choice. Any interference in internal affairs, any attempts to limit the sovereignty of states—whether of friends and allies or anybody else—are inadmissible."[118] After being repealed in practice in 1981 and among the socialist allies in 1986, the Brezhnev Doctrine was now revoked for all the world to see.

In the chapters to come, we will see that the political transformation of Eastern Europe in the late 1980s was the result of a transnational struggle among Western banks and governments, Eastern European governments, and Eastern European peoples over who would bear the costs of economic adjustment policies. In this struggle, the Soviet leadership held power only to the extent that it was willing to provide economic assistance to its allies or intervene militarily, which would have had its own significant economic costs. Continuing the foreign policy first set by Andropov in the Polish Crisis, Gorbachev and his Politburo colleagues were unwilling to embrace either option. Motivated to shed the burdens of an empire bequeathed to them by history, they watched idly as a wave of economic adjustment, masked as political revolution, washed over the nations they once called satellites. Contrary to the historical memory that prevails today, this wave had not originated in the socialist world with perestroika but rather in the world economy with the oil crisis of 1973 and the sovereign debt that followed from it. By the mid-1980s, it had already washed over much of the capitalist world and was cresting above the concrete walls and iron curtains that separated East from West. Soon it would wash away the division of Europe completely.

CHAPTER 7

A Period of Extraordinary Politics

FIVE YEARS AFTER communism collapsed in Poland, the man who had picked up the pieces wanted the world to know how he had done it. Leszek Balcerowicz had been finance minister in Solidarity's first postcommunist government and authored the eponymous Balcerowicz Plan that had employed "shock therapy" to transform Poland's communist command economy into a market economy in late 1989 and 1990. Shock therapy had required the imposition of all the calling cards of the politics of breaking promises—extreme price increases, budget cuts, interest rate hikes, bankruptcies, and unemployment. Many policy makers, both within and outside the Polish government, had feared that people would openly revolt against the barrage of economic discipline, but they had not. Though there had been pockets of resistance, the Poles had largely accepted the Solidarity government's rude introduction of the global capitalist economy with stoic acquiescence.

In a 1994 article, Balcerowicz set out to explain why. The key to his success, he wrote, had been the "period of extraordinary politics" that had followed the collapse of communism. In such periods of history, "epochal political change" creates "a special state of mass psychology" within a citizenry that heightens its "readiness to accept radical economic measures." During such moments, "both leaders and ordinary citizens feel a stronger-than-normal tendency to think and act in terms of the common good." This tendency, in turn, creates "political opportunities" for a government to impose measures that would otherwise be too unpopular. Periods of extraordinary politics, in short, gave governments a unique amount of "political capital" that they could use to implement the politics of breaking promises.

The connection between extraordinary politics and economic discipline was strong enough that Balcerowicz felt comfortable providing a general model of their relationship (Figure 7.1). The key variable, r, defined as society's "level of readiness to accept radical economic measures," decreased dramatically once politics returned to "normal," so it was important to use the period of extraordinary politics to enact unpopular policies. The first postcommunist Solidarity government had done this, and as a result, it had successfully imposed the politics of breaking promises without inciting popular backlash.[1]

The last of Poland's communists had not been so lucky. The political order over which they presided was anything but extraordinary, and whatever political capital they once had with the population had been frittered away in the cycles of social unrest and state repression that had defined the 1970s and early 1980s. However, the communists' challenge was the same as Balcerowicz's. They had spent their final days trying to answer the same questions as those posed to the first Solidarity government. How

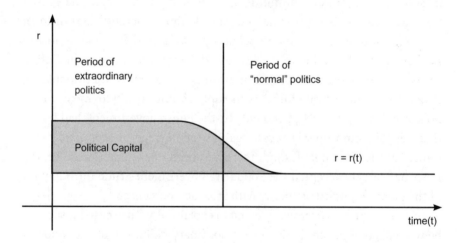

Figure 7.1 The period of extraordinary politics.

Reformatted from Leszek Balcerowicz, "Understanding Postcommunist Transitions," *Journal of Democracy* 5, no. 4 (1994): 75–89, fig. 1. © 1994 National Endowment for Democracy and the Johns Hopkins University Press. Reprinted with permission of Johns Hopkins University Press.

could they get the Polish people to accept radical and unpopular economic measures? How could they impose the politics of breaking promises? Their answer was also a period of extraordinary politics: the roundtable agreement of April 1989. The Polish roundtable was the first step in the collapse of communism and the revolutions of 1989, but its original purpose was to provide the communist government with political legitimacy so it could impose the politics of breaking promises.

By the late 1980s, the Polish state owed its international creditors $39 billion and sat at the mercy of Western governments, banks, and international institutions. These Western entities wielded what we might call "the power of omission": they withheld the considerable resources of Western governments and global financial markets until political and economic conditions on the ground in Poland conformed to their economic and political demands. Capitalist banks and international institutions, led by the International Monetary Fund (IMF), demanded that the communist government impose a capitalist perestroika on Polish society. Western governments, led by the United States, demanded that the government undertake such a perestroika without resorting to violence or a renewal of martial law. The West demanded, in short, that promises be broken in Poland, and broken peacefully.

After years of unrest triggered by austerity, Polish leader Wojciech Jaruzelski and his leading cadre concluded in the early 1980s that they could meet these demands only if they gained the broad support of Polish society. Beginning in the early days after martial law, they therefore undertook a series of political initiatives aimed at regaining popular support. At first, these were blatantly cosmetic alternations that did little to change the structure of political power. But as the economic crisis worsened throughout the remainder of the decade and the need for popular support grew in equal measure, Jaruzelski took ever more radical steps to legitimize the communists' rule by engaging the two most popular institutions in Poland: the Catholic Church and, eventually, Solidarity. Like Poland's Western creditors, the church and Solidarity exerted their own power of omission: they could refuse to endorse any government economic reform proposal that did not also bring real political change to Poland.

The combination of these foreign and domestic pressures eventually led to the roundtable and the collapse of communism in Poland. Scholars have generally shied away from granting economic forces or Western actors any significant role in causing the revolutions of 1989, but this chapter paints a dramatically different picture.[2] By forcing Polish leaders to confront the politics of breaking promises, Western officials, particularly at the White House and the IMF in Washington, played a decisive role in ending communism in Poland and, by extension, spurring the revolutions of 1989. Their pursuit of the politics of breaking promises in Poland was not a conscious strategy of regime change, but regime change was its effect. Jaruzelski did not initiate the roundtable process solely to meet Western conditions, but without them, he would not have been forced to break promises and thus would not have been forced to seek the approval of the church, Solidarity, and, ultimately, Polish society.

The Polish revolution of 1989 was therefore the product of a multisided contest among the communist leadership, the Polish people, and Western institutions to determine just how extraordinary Polish politics would have to become for the Polish people to accept economic discipline and for the West to free the country from its financial shackles. In the end, both the people and the West demanded nothing short of the communist state's full capitulation.

◆ ◆ ◆

Long before there was any talk of roundtables and democratic elections in Warsaw, Poland's communist leaders firmly understood that the economy would ultimately determine their political fate. "Three-quarters of Poland's political problems would disappear," Mieczysław Rakowski told a visiting British diplomat in 1984, "if Polish living standards of 1979 could be restored." He continued, "For anyone governing Poland the primary problems [are] economic. All others [are] secondary."[3] Under the cover of martial law, the government had eliminated the worst inflationary vestiges of the 1980–1981 crisis through draconian budget cuts and price increases, and a semblance of economic stability, if not prosperity, returned. But every member of both the government and the opposition understood that real economic growth would only return once the country again had access to Western capital, technology, and raw materials.[4]

Looking east for help was increasingly not an option. After the declaration of martial law, Moscow announced increased economic support for Jaruzelski to great fanfare, but the reality of its aid turned out to be a meager affair. The Polish Ministry of Foreign Trade concluded in 1982 that the resources the country needed to replace Western imports simply were "not available from other Comecon countries."[5] Jaruzelski continued to lobby Soviet leaders for greater economic aid throughout the early 1980s, but all they offered him was ideological criticism of his handling of Polish society.[6]

Capitalist banks showed even less interest in supporting Poland than the Kremlin. The Polish government's 1981 announcement that it would need to reschedule its debt left the banks with a general feeling of "acute suspicion" toward the country's economic prospects.[7] Most of them sought to cut their exposure, write down their Polish loans as losses, and run for more profitable hills elsewhere in the global economy. As an American banker put it in 1985, the banks' strategy for Poland focused "on draining the country of as much cash as possible."[8] This strategy resulted in four rescheduling agreements between the banks and the Polish government from 1982 to 1985. In each agreement, the banks rescheduled 95 percent of the loan principle but received the interest payments from the government on time.[9] This arrangement paid off as handsomely for the banks as it did poorly for Poland. Each year, the banks received an annual "take out" of interest payments, but Warsaw fell ever deeper into a debt trap, as each rescheduling agreement simply compounded maturing debt payments into new future obligations.[10] Thus, although the country's debt burden grew from $24 billion to $39 billion from 1981 to 1989, Poland received virtually no new capital from the West during the 1980s.

The Poles' only hope for regaining the banks' favor was to come to terms with the International Monetary Fund. As with every other sovereign debtor throughout the global economy in the 1980s, the banks made their reengagement with Warsaw contingent on the Polish government reaching an agreement with the Fund. This left the IMF, and the Western governments that served as its gatekeepers, in an extremely powerful position.

The Reagan administration hoped to use this power to serve both political and economic ends. In the aftermath of martial law, administration officials quickly agreed that vetoing the Poles' outstanding application to rejoin the Fund would be a cornerstone of their effort to sanction Warsaw. The administration also decided in the early days after martial law that it would pursue three political goals in Poland: the end of martial law, the release of all political prisoners, and the renewal of a national dialogue among the government, the Catholic Church, and Solidarity. Until Jaruzelski took these three steps, the Reagan team committed itself to cementing Warsaw's quarantine from the international financial system. Through its IMF veto, a suspension of government-sponsored credits across NATO (North Atlantic Treaty Organization), and an indefinite postponement of negotiations to reschedule Poland's debts to Western governments, Washington ensured that Warsaw would not regain normal relations with the global financial system until it met Western political demands.[11]

But that was not all. In the midst of the ballooning sovereign debt crisis, meeting political conditionality alone would not be enough. In order to receive debt relief and regain financial market access, the Reagan administration made clear that Poland would also have to meet the Treasury Department's global standards for dealing with delinquent debtor nations. As National Security Decision Directive 54, the Reagan administration's policy statement on Eastern Europe, stated, "U.S. policy is to extend debt relief only when it is necessary as a financial measure to ensure repayment and when the debtor country embarks on an economic/financial stabilization program designed to rectify the country's financial position." Such economic and financial stabilization programs would be overseen by the IMF, and nations like Poland would not receive easy treatment simply because they might demonstrate domestic political liberalization or independence from Moscow. "Political and security objectives" would be given "due weight" in determining US support for the IMF's operations in the region, but ultimately economic and financial priorities would be "first among other decision criteria."[12]

Therefore, two levels of conditionality were built into the Reagan administration's Poland policy, and both hinged on the IMF. Washington would first make Poland's reentry into the Fund contingent on Warsaw meeting political conditions like ending martial law and releasing political prisoners. But the simple act of joining the IMF would not give Warsaw access to the Fund's resources. For that, the Polish government would have to come to terms with the Fund on a financing agreement, which would require Warsaw to meet the Fund's strict demands for austerity and structural adjustment.

Administration officials well understood that these two levels of conditionality made the Fund their most important point of leverage over Poland. As one National Security Council (NSC) staffer judged it, IMF membership was the main Western bargaining chip "of active interest to the Poles" because it held out the "promise of hard currency." The West would therefore be "able to use this to press Poles to reform [their] economy." And because granting IMF membership would be a "major concession," the staffer noted, the United States could also "tie political strings" to the lifting of its IMF veto.[13] National Security Advisor William Clark very much agreed. "IMF involvement" in Poland, he wrote to Secretary of State George Schultz in spring 1983, could "speed liberalizing reforms with a positive human rights spillover." The Fund would also have the benefit of "maintain[ing] a neutral character."[14] American officials were under no illusions that the Fund's work would be quick or easy. But in maintaining Poland's quarantine from the global financial system, they hoped to alter the calculus of the communist leadership in Warsaw over time.[15]

There is little evidence this litany of American conditions influenced Jaruzelski's decision-making in the immediate aftermath of martial law. The Polish government fully partook in the mutual acrimony that defined the Polish-American relationship in the early 1980s, and officials in Warsaw saw little reason to bend to Western pressure while the post–martial law economic reforms successfully stabilized the country.[16]

Jaruzelski and his leading cadre, however, shared two beliefs in common with policy makers in Washington: they would eventually have to reconcile with the Polish population to find new sources of legitimacy after martial law, and they would slowly have to introduce market reforms into the economy. The specific types of reconciliation, legitimation, and market reforms Polish officials had in mind in the early 1980s diverged widely from Washington's vision. They firmly believed, for instance, that they would never again negotiate with Solidarity, and they were convinced they could not impose the most extreme forms of IMF-mandated structural adjustment. But they also knew they could not rule the country forever under the iron fist of martial law and the stalled economic system of central planning. The key, then, was to find the tipping point in political and economic reform at which both Western governments and the Polish population would forgive them for martial law and return to business as usual. Through the remainder of the decade, Polish leaders undertook increasingly bold political and economic initiatives in search of this tipping point.

The first efforts in this direction were transparently self-serving and fooled no one into thinking the Polish United Workers' Party (PZPR) was really interested in reform. In the months following martial law, the party announced the creation of the Patriotic Movement of National Rebirth (PRON), an organization composed of minor political parties in parliament meant to create "the appearance of a ruling coalition."[17] After the government officially declared Solidarity illegal in October 1982, it eventually announced the creation of a network of state-sponsored trade unions—the All-Poland Alliance of Trade Unions (OPZZ)—to create a similar appearance of independent workers' representation in the halls of power. In November 1982, Jaruzelski met with the leader of the Polish Catholic Church, Cardinal Józef Glemp, and the two men agreed on an informal quid pro quo: the government would allow the Polish pope, John Paul II, to visit his homeland in 1983 if the church would criticize Western sanctions and publicly encourage the Polish people to refrain from striking. Both sides held up their end of the bargain, and the papal visit was set for June 1983. Then, as 1982 drew to a close, the government took one last step toward a return to normalcy by suspending, if not fully repealing, martial law.

These initial steps toward reconciliation set the stage for a period of bargaining among the government, the church, and the West over an exchange of steps toward limited political reconciliation for relief from Western sanctions. After the papal visit went off without a hitch, the government fully repealed martial law in July. Under pressure from its European allies to restart debt-rescheduling negotiations, the Reagan administration announced that it would rejoin the negotiations if the Polish government moved toward freeing all remaining political prisoners. The church pressed the same demand domestically, and the government, eager to regain society's trust, found itself "desperately anxious to solve the prisoner problem" by early 1984.[18]

Jaruzelski wanted sanctions relief in return, however. So, throughout 1984, the US and Polish governments brokered a series of deals in which all remaining political prisoners were freed in exchange for an end to many American sanctions and, most importantly, a lifting of the American IMF veto.[19] Many Solidarity dissidents were subsequently rearrested, but at the dawn of 1985, the first stage of American conditionality had momentarily been met. Due to a confluence of domestic and international pressures, Jaruzelski had lifted martial law and freed all political prisoners, and in return, the Reagan administration had agreed to open the gates to the IMF. Now the real work of adjusting Polish society to meet the demands of global capital would begin.

◆ ◆ ◆

When Poland officially rejoined the IMF in June 1986, it did not take long for observers, both within and outside the country, to note that Warsaw and the Fund were now "on a collision course."[20] The source of the collision lay in the fundamentally different directions the IMF and the Polish government wanted capital to flow across Poland's borders. As in every debtor country around the world, the IMF's foundational goal in Poland was to turn the country into a net exporter of capital—or, in economic terms, to produce a Polish current account surplus. To produce such a surplus, the Fund aimed to push the Polish government to implement an austerity and structural adjustment program. In a country where austerity had provoked political crises in 1970, 1976, and 1980, this portended future political upheaval. Therefore, the Fund's economic demands confronted Poland's communist leadership with a political challenge: in order to come to terms with the Fund, they would also have to come to terms with the Polish population. What those terms would be defined Polish history from 1986 to 1989.

IMF officials took note of the tension between global capital and the Polish working class in the days after Warsaw rejoined the Fund. IMF staffer Hans Schmitt laid out the challenge ahead in stark and prescient terms. For austerity and structural adjustment to be "tenable in Poland," he wrote in an internal memo, "it must be acceptable both to bankers abroad and labor at home. At the moment the requirements of each seem to be incompatible with one another." The banks and governments seeking to recoup their loans wanted to establish conditions in Poland that would allow for a sustainable outflow of capital from the country. Labor, seeking to improve its plight after years of economic hardship, wanted capital to flow into the country. Schmitt noted the difference. "Bankers require a surplus on external current account large enough to ensure the progressive repayment of debt, and an adjustment in domestic demand (and in wages) large enough to produce it." On the other hand, "labor requires a minimum growth in wages (and in domestic demand) and a deficit on external current account large enough to finance any shortfall in GDP to support it." The IMF, he concluded, "need[s] to find where, if anywhere, the twain can meet."[21]

The Fund was well acquainted with the interests of Polish labor because it was in direct communication with Solidarity. Most labor unions around the world loathed the IMF and the structural adjustment policies it imposed on its members. Solidarity shared in this opposition. The union wrote to the Fund in 1985 that it would "come out strongly against measures leading to the substantial reduction of consumption, increases of prices, freezes on real wages or deterioration in social care."[22] But that did not mean it opposed the IMF altogether. On the contrary, Solidarity declared itself "probably the only labor union in the world" that welcomed its nation's membership in the IMF because it saw the power that Fund conditionality might have to change the political status quo in Warsaw.[23] Therefore, despite their misgivings about the IMF's economic policies, Solidarity's leaders ultimately believed their long-term goals aligned well with the Fund. "Solidarity would like to see Poland in the IMF," the leadership wrote, because "it would be more beneficial for the country to be bound with the West" than with the Communist Bloc.[24]

Nevertheless, the impasse between labor and capital remained, and observers both within and outside Poland began to conclude that resolving it would require a political solution. Specifically, it would require political legitimacy in Poland. On the eve of their country's accession to the World Bank and IMF, two Polish financial officials warned their comrades that "the experience of other countries indicates that IMF programs often encounter serious social resistance, which repeatedly led to their discontinuation and a suspension of subsequent loan installments. We must not allow such an eventuality because it would cause another collapse of our position on the international financial market and socio-political repercussions [domestically]." To overcome society's resistance, the officials recommended that "the arrangements negotiated with the IMF and World Bank should be subject to wide consultation (up to and including a referendum . . .) in order to build a social consensus around the program."[25]

Financial observers in the West very much agreed. Paul McCarthy, an executive at Chemical Bank in New York responsible for relations with the Eastern Bloc, wrote in an article just two months later, "The future actions of Western lenders are interrelated with Poland's handling of its domestic difficulties. New money will be unlikely until the Polish government can assure political stability. Political stability cannot be guaranteed unless the government can fundamentally overhaul the economy. . . . The economy cannot be structurally reformed without the support of the Polish people and workforce." This was where the IMF could play the vital role of catalyst. "The IMF has a major bargaining chip," McCarthy wrote, "in that it controls the single commodity that Poland currently needs the most and is least able to attain. The Fund can provide substantial credits, ranging to $700 million annually." Moreover, "IMF loans could begin attracting new credits from banks and governments." But Western creditors would only change their view once Jaruzelski had gained the popular legitimacy required for austerity. "If Jaruzelski seeks reform without enfranchising the major constituencies, he risks failure," McCarthy concluded. "Meaningful reform will require the support of the Polish people, as further substantial cuts in living standards would be inevitable."[26]

The Fund itself began to press this point in their meetings with Polish officials. In February 1987, the managing director, Jacque de Larosière, sat down to lunch with the president of the National Bank of Poland, Władysław Baka. Baka resisted the Fund's calls for austerity on account of "major political and social obstacles." De Larosière admitted the government was in a tough position but maintained that both Western governments and banks favored austerity, and thus it needed to be "implemented boldly (preferably in one stroke)" in order to convince them "that policies in Poland had changed radically for the better." This would not be easy, and it needed to be "acceptable to the population." Thus, "some preparation of public opinion would be necessary."[27]

Using political maneuvers to prepare public opinion for the hardships of economic reform was not a novel idea for Jaruzelski. As we have seen, he emerged from martial law ready to use token acts of political liberalization to rebuild the government's domestic legitimacy and international standing. By 1986, the question was how far he and the communist leadership were willing to go in this direction. Gorbachev's rise in the Soviet Union widened the Polish communists' political room for maneuver, but it did not immediately affect their strategy toward the opposition. Throughout 1985 and the first half of 1986, the government rearrested countless Solidarity leaders. Both the Catholic Church at home and Western governments abroad did not look kindly on this regression to repression, so alongside the prospect of future IMF-mandated austerity, the government faced renewed calls to free all political prisoners by the summer of 1986.[28]

Polish leaders responded to these pressures by opening a new phase in their search for the tipping point at which Polish society and Western governments would restore their domestic legitimacy and international creditworthiness. In the summer of 1986, the government announced a "second stage" of economic reform that was meant to deepen the moves toward enterprise independence and individual initiative that had first been launched in 1982. On paper, these reforms aligned with the IMF's vision for the country: they aimed to achieve "market equilibrium" through price increases, subsidy reductions, tighter credit policies, liquidation of inefficient enterprises, and the reduction of price and foreign exchange controls. Fund officials reported that they had a "good deal of sympathy" with the goals of these reforms, but they criticized the government's plans for making "virtually no mention" of the Fund's top priority, "balance of payment objectives."[29] Domestic reform was all well and good, in other words, but if it did not produce a sustainable outflow of capital from Poland, the Fund was not really interested in supporting it. To produce such an outflow, Polish officials knew they would have to step up their austerity efforts. They assured the Fund that they would try to reduce subsidies on things like "coal, milk, and foreign trade," but they feared the "social tensions in response to the associated price increases."[30]

To head off these potential tensions, the leadership paired its "second stage" of economic reforms with a new set of political innovations. Most prominent of all, they announced a new general amnesty in September 1986 that set all the nation's political prisoners free. In the Politburo document detailing the reasons for its decision, the leadership recognized that the issue of political prisoners was preventing Poland from sharing in the fruits of Gorbachev's rapprochement with the United States and Europe. "The improvement of relations between the two superpowers . . . has led to a significant increase in East-West dialogue," officials wrote. "However, Poland was not included in this process. The West applied tactics against our country, which make progress in normalizing relations with Poland dependent on assessments of the development of our [internal] situation." Keeping political prisoners locked up would provide the West with further reason to "continue restrictions and hinder the development of economic and diplomatic relations."[31] These were restrictions the leadership could ill afford, so in September 1986, they let all remaining political prisoners walk free.

To build on the amnesty's momentum, the government also augmented the transparently self-serving Patriotic Movement of National Rebirth with a new Consultative Council. Meant to be composed of credible independent voices in Polish public life ranging from Catholic intellectuals to academics to moderate opposition figures, the Consultative Council was charged with advising Jaruzelski on ways to "increase trust" in society, build "social agreement," establish "conditions for economic progress," and develop "current and forward-looking social policy."[32] Like the "second stage" economic reforms, however, the council failed to appease its main audience, Polish society, or divide its main target, Solidarity. Lech Wałęsa quickly denounced it on the grounds that dialogue needed to "be institutionalized, but not in sham institutions."[33] Shunned by Solidarity and meekly supported by the church, the Consultative Council opened in December 1986 to little public approbation.

Though these domestic political initiatives were not enough to sway domestic public opinion, they were enough to win the repeal of the last American sanctions still in effect. In January 1987, US deputy secretary of state John Whitehead traveled to Warsaw for the highest-level bilateral talks since martial law. The following month, President Reagan officially restored Poland's most favored nation (MFN) trading status with the United States and reopened Poland's access to US government-sponsored credits. Having long railed against the all-powerful evil of American sanctions, Jaruzelski believed these steps would at last reopen his nation's access to global financial markets.

What he discovered instead was the harsh reality of life in the privatized Cold War. The mere fact that the US government no longer officially discouraged economic ties to Poland did not automatically mean global capital holders would restore their former friendly ties with Warsaw. For that to happen, the government would have to come to terms with the IMF, impose domestic austerity, and produce a sustainable outflow of capital from the country. Slowly, Jaruzelski began to understand these new ways of the world. "You could say that the sanctions were repealed within the last year," he told East German leader Erich Honecker in September 1987. "Yes and no." The restoration of policies like MFN was fine, he said, but it only boosted Polish export income by about $20 million. Such a sum "requires no comment," he told Honecker. "This is nothing." Similarly, the restoration of Poland's political contacts with Western governments was "important." But diplomatic relations alone did not "put bread on the table." Only the "ban on lending" really mattered, and even though the ban had been formally repealed, "in practice the blockade continues." As long as Poland's debt to Western governments remained in default and the IMF continued to withhold its endorsement of Poland's economic reforms, capitalist banks and Western governments would not reopen their pocketbooks. Even though the United States had formally lifted all its sanctions, Jaruzelski concluded, "as before, economic warfare is being carried out against Poland."[34]

In Moscow, the general's imperial patrons could see very clearly what was happening to their ally but felt powerless to stop it. The size of Poland's debt was a key measure of Soviet impotence. Anatolii Cherniaev,

Gorbachev's foreign policy aide, recalled his boss complaining, "Poland is crawling away from us, and we in Moscow are doing nothing. And what can we do? Poland has a $56 billion [*sic*] debt. Can we take Poland on our balance sheet in our current economic situation? No. And if we cannot— then we have no influence."[35]

Spurned by the Kremlin and rejected by the Polish working class, Jaruzelski had little choice but to expand his search for political legitimacy in the service of economic reform so that he could come to terms with the IMF. In July 1987, he gave an interview to the *Wall Street Journal* in which he discussed the challenges facing his country. "As we've learned in the past," he began, "even the most beautiful and well-constructed decisions and intentions, if they do not command the support of society, they fail." Therefore, he announced that he was considering calling a national referendum on "painful but imperative" steps aimed at bringing the nation into "economic equilibrium."[36] The general specifically intended the interview to signal to the IMF that public opinion preparations were underway. In a meeting with Fund representatives the day after the interview appeared, a Polish official said the referendum would "muster support for economic reform and austerity measures" and that the timing of the interview "was influenced, inter alia, by hopes of a program with the Fund."[37]

There were pressing domestic reasons to propose the referendum as well. Like Rakowski earlier in the decade, Jaruzelski believed in 1987 that the party's domestic political standing was primarily a function of the country's economic performance. "If it was possible to improve . . . the economic situation, above all, the material situation of workers, then there would be no problem," Jaruzelski told Honecker.[38] By 1987, however, the patina of progress in the economy that had followed martial law was fading. An internal government report from August 1987 warned, "Generally, anxiety is rising due to the prolonged economic crisis." Such a situation provided Solidarity with its only hope of reemerging as a potent political force. From the union's perspective, "each action by the authorities in the economic sphere will be favorable to the opposition . . . a full implementation of reform . . . will result in a temporary decline in purchasing power, layoffs, etc." Thus, "the adversary has come to the conclusion that it does not have to bother much—it is enough to sustain a mood of justified anger and wait and join, at the right moment, the eruption of dissatisfaction, as in 1980."[39] Best, then, to head off the dissatisfaction by legitimizing the economic reforms.

The arrival of US vice president George H. W. Bush for an official visit to Warsaw in September 1987 reinforced the connection between economic reform and political legitimacy. In his meetings with Bush, Jaruzelski repeatedly returned to the importance of gaining debt relief, reaching an agreement with the IMF, and receiving new hard currency credits from the West.[40] In return, Bush reminded his host that there were still two prongs to American conditionality—politics and economics. The Poles would have to come to terms with the IMF to reopen access to international financial markets, but only "steps toward democratization would yield a positive U.S. [government] response."[41] The Poles would, in short, have to impose austerity *and* reach the national reconciliation the Reagan administration had demanded since martial law.

Jaruzelski's referendum was officially set for the end of November. By the day of its arrival, Western political and financial pressure had provided the Polish state with ample reason to seek both popular legitimacy and a mandate for austerity. Both priorities were directly reflected in the referendum's two questions to the Polish people. Were they in favor of introducing a "Polish model of deep democratization of political life with the goal of . . . increasing citizens' participation in governing the country?" And were they in favor of a full government program for "radical" economic recovery, "knowing that this will require a difficult 2–3 year period of rapid changes?"[42]

Officially, Poles said they were not in favor of the government's plans. Because the government set the threshold for victory at a majority of all possible voters, and many voters stayed home, the referendum failed even though a majority of those who did vote gave their assent. Jaruzelski emerged disappointed but undeterred. He told the Central Committee and the press that the referendum result did not indicate the population was against reform. Rather, it simply signaled that "a significant and important part of the society" had "doubts and fears" about the pace of change. Despite these misgivings, reforms were "a fact of life" that could not be avoided, he said. Thus, instead of "a one-stroke radical restructuring," reform would be carried out over three years, price increases would be tempered, and the official trade union, the OPZZ, would be allowed to negotiate a wage increase for its workers.[43] It was not long before Polish wages and Polish prices were racing each other into the stratosphere.

This set the stage for the revolutionary year of 1988. On February 1, food, alcohol, and cigarette prices increased by an average of 40 percent, gasoline prices increased 60 percent, and transportation and rent prices were

Table 7.1: Polish public opinion research.

Judgment	Political Situation				Economic Situation			
	1984	1985	1986	1987	1984	1985	1986	1987
Good	18%	28%	35%	36%	11%	12%	12%	6%
Not good, not bad	42%	38%	38%	38%	45%	35%	27%	24%
Bad	25%	15%	19%	18%	38%	46%	59%	69%

Adapted for clarity and translated from Document 10, "Informacja o stanie nastrojów społecznych i działalności przeciwnika w pierwszym okresie n etapu reform," March 2, 1988, in Polska 1986-1989: Koniec Systemu, vol. III, Dokumenty, ed. Antoni Dudek and Andrzej Friszke (Warsaw: Trio/ISP PAN, 2002), 66.

substantially increased.[44] Because the state unions were allowed to negotiate a compensatory wage increase, the higher prices did not so much impose austerity as set off an inflationary spiral. Ever mindful of the foundational connection between their economic and political fate, Polish leaders immediately understood that this was a recipe for political turmoil. In March 1988, researchers in the Central Committee produced a remarkably detailed and prescient investigation of the burgeoning relationship between economic crisis and political upheaval. They began their analysis by presenting data that clearly demonstrated that the nature of the communist government's problem with the Polish population was economic rather than political (see Table 7.1).

In such an environment of economic pessimism, Solidarity posed a very particular kind of threat to the communist system. Because Poles were generally satisfied with the country's political situation, the researchers concluded the union was "not able to lead an effective fight on the level of politics and political demands." But, they hastened to add, "the question arises whether the socio-economic situation, affecting the standard of living of the working people, open such opportunities to it [Solidarity]? No doubt such possibilities exist." Solidarity could "realistically strengthen to dangerous proportions if they are able to control the existing dissatisfaction of various groups with their economic situation."[45] The union's leaders shared the Central Committee's belief that their power ultimately derived from the social costs of economic reform. In February 1988, Solidarity leader Bronisław Geremek proposed in an interview that the government enter into an "anti-crisis pact" with Solidarity, the Catholic Church, and other institutions that maintained society's trust. He framed the necessity of the pact in economic terms. "Without authentic social forces, a break-through cannot be made in the economic situation of the country," he told the magazine.[46] Both sides—the communist leadership and Solidarity—therefore shared the same understanding of the situation: economic reform would bring significant social costs, require domestic political legitimacy, and empower Solidarity.

In the face of the burgeoning turmoil of austerity, Jaruzelski and his advisers began to contemplate opening a new front in their quest to regain domestic legitimacy and international creditworthiness. In a pair of memos drafted in early 1988, a group of senior officials encouraged Jaruzelski to embrace further political liberalization as a means of limiting society's economic frustration and gaining debt concessions from the West. If the party provided "groups of the moderate opposition with limited joint responsibility" and absorbed "the tamest elements of the moderate opposition within our influence and institutions," society would become more amenable to economic reform. This included Wałęsa. The advisers proposed the creation of a new Senate chamber of parliament to complement the existing Sejm, and they recommended the Solidarity leader be offered a high-profile, harmless seat in the new chamber. Just to be sure that these cosmetic changes to the country's political institutions did not alter the actual balance of power, they also proposed the creation of a strong office of the presidency—based on "a French, or even an American model"—to counterbalance the moves toward parliamentary democracy.[47] Maximizing the party's power was, as ever, at the top of their minds.

Indeed, the advisers began to embrace the very logic of extraordinary politics that would come to define Balcerowicz's plans during the first Solidarity government. They warned Jaruzelski that society would view "the increase in freedoms" associated with democratization "mainly as a mark of the authorities' weakness and softness." But that was not their purpose. Democratic reforms were instead meant to give the party a tool it otherwise lacked: the power to carry out unpopular economic reform. "Democratic evolution carried out at an appropriate pace and scope has the power . . . to fulfill the role of a safety valve for [social] moods . . . only when it is a factor accompanying radical, efficient, effective, and resolute actions in the economic sphere. Otherwise, it will be one of the drivers of the crisis."[48] The party would do well, in other words, to use the honeymoon period of political reform to implement the most socially disruptive parts of its economic agenda.

The party would also do well, the advisers told Jaruzelski, to use any moment of domestic political progress to demand debt relief from the West. "Before this whole package of changes is revealed . . . , confidential talks in Washington, and perhaps also the major capitals of Western Europe and the Vatican, seem necessary," they wrote. "The whole package (together with Wałęsa) should be put on the table, and there should be at least tacit approval for the suspension of Polish foreign currency payment obligations." There should also be, they concluded, an improvement in "our credit and other negotiations regarding economic cooperation with the West."[49]

As the country's streets and factories remained at peace in the early months of 1988, Jaruzelski did not yet see a need to embrace the risky strategy of political liberalization. Only the reality of social unrest could shift his thinking, and in April 1988, that reality at last arrived. Strikes ripped through the country as workers sought to keep their wages in line with prices. Generally, the strikes were spontaneous acts of workers hoping to defend their economic interests, but as predicted, Solidarity used the strikes to strengthen its position, and some workers eventually called for the union's reinstatement.[50] The government used a combination of bribery and repression to silence the wave of strikes by early May, but the economic damage had been done. By June, prices and wages were expected to rise 55 percent and 60 percent, respectively, for the year. Far from declining, as the government hoped and the IMF demanded, the real wage of Polish workers was rising by about 5 percent.[51] The conflict between capital and labor IMF officials had anticipated when Poland joined the Fund in 1986 was now fully in motion, and initially, Polish workers maintained the upper hand.

Politically, the news was even worse. Just as they had predicted early in the year, government officials concluded after the strike that Solidarity was "using the public dissatisfaction with the material situation and the poor prospects for its imminent improvement to open a political crisis in Poland."[52] This made austerity very dangerous, as the head of the state-sponsored unions, Alfred Miodowicz, warned Jaruzelski. "It is risky, both from a political and economic point of view," he wrote on May 3, "to continue economic policies resulting in a gradual reduction of real income in the socialist economy."[53]

It was indeed a risk, but because of the country's international financial straitjacket, it was a risk Jaruzelski needed to take. The IMF was disappointed to see wages rising rapidly and outpacing the growth in prices.

This was precisely the opposite of the austerity policies that would produce a sustained outflow of capital from Poland. So, over the summer of 1988, Fund officials changed their tune. Instead of simply encouraging the government to "prepare public opinion," they started to demand the government build a "social consensus" around reform. On June 27, 1988, the Fund managing director, Michel Camdessus, suggested to the visiting Polish deputy prime minister, Zdzisław Sadowski, that "increased popular participation in political decision-making might . . . reconcile the population to the sacrifices required for economic stabilization."[54]

This encouragement only served to reinforce many Polish leaders' thinking about how to overcome society's resistance to broken promises. As Jaruzelski later recalled, "I believe that at that time [the late 1980s] I understood that one can undertake radical reforms and impose unpopular decisions only under two conditions: in an authentic, well-established democracy or in a totalitarian or at least repressive state. We were neither one nor the other."[55] In the spring of 1988, the leadership seesawed between plans to become either one. Jaruzelski's trusted advisor, fellow military general, and minister of the interior, Czesław Kiszczak, twice formulated plans to implement a state of emergency.[56] At the same time, plans to implement some form of limited democratic system gathered pace. In the aftermath of the April strikes, a team of Central Committee experts encouraged the party to appoint a new government "based on the formula of broad national consensus" that would open a "dialogue with all the constructive forces" in society. Such a government was necessary because "the second stage of the reform, which requires social sacrifices and will create social problems . . . , requires much broader public support for the leadership than currently available."[57]

In the aftermath of the April strikes, Jaruzelski was willing to countenance these calls to build a government of social consensus and national reconciliation, but he remained adamantly opposed to relegalizing Solidarity. This left him in search of a different partner that maintained the trust of society, and the Catholic Church quickly became his preferred choice. Throughout the summer of 1988, Jaruzelski's advisers tried to garner the church's support for plans to establish a new Christian Democratic Party that could act as a force of loyal opposition to the Communist Party's leadership. Wałęsa, they said, could even be made chairman of the new Senate chamber actively under consideration. As long as the church would endorse an arrangement that precluded the reemergence of

Solidarity, the communist leadership made clear that it was ready to cut a deal.[58]

The communists' offer put the church in an extremely powerful position. The fate of both the PZPR and Solidarity now lay in its hands. If church leaders endorsed the government's plans to introduce political pluralism without Solidarity, the union likely would have struggled to continue its fledgling resurgence, and the country would have been set on very different path from the one it ended up taking in 1989. If the church withheld its endorsement, however, the government would have little choice but to continue its search for domestic legitimacy by negotiating directly with Solidarity. Therefore, like Western banks and governments, the church possessed its own power of omission: it could withhold its blessing from the communist leadership until their plans conformed to the church's demands. The question in the summer of 1988 was whether the church would stop short of using this power to force the communists to negotiate directly with Solidarity.

The Polish people provided the answer. As the church and state contemplated their arranged marriage, a new wave of strikes broke out in August. Workers across the country went on strike for better wages and the reinstatement of Solidarity. The new wave of working-class revolt made the church's decision much easier and the communists' predicament much harder. On August 20, the church's representative, Andrzej Stelmachowski, told his communist interlocutors that the church would only help end the strikes once the party had announced its intention to begin talks with Wałęsa about trade union pluralism.[59] If the party wanted to renew its legitimacy, it would have to confront its opposition directly.

As the church tightened the screws on the PZPR, the Soviets continued to loosen theirs. In July 1988, Gorbachev arrived in Poland for a meeting of Warsaw Pact leaders. In a speech to the Polish leadership, the Soviet general secretary embraced what he called "socialist pluralism" in relations between socialist countries. In a conversation with Rakowski in early August, one of Gorbachev's top advisors, Georgy Shakhnazarov, made the meaning of this slogan more concrete. If it came to a situation like the Polish Crisis of the early 1980s, Shakhnazarov said, "we . . . would not intervene." Rakowski asked what would happen if Solidarity took power. Shakhnazarov stated, "Well, it [Poland] would probably take on a status close to Finlandization. The USSR would have to accept that."[60]

These signals of acquiescence from the East directly affected the communist leadership's domestic thinking in Poland. Jaruzelski's advisers wrote to him on August 10. "At the moment," they wrote, the Polish leadership's only asset was "Soviet support." This would "weaken, or even disappear," they concluded, "as soon as the ineffectiveness of our actions [in Poland] becomes apparent." Faced with the loss of Soviet support and the challenge of austerity, the advisors felt the PZPR had no choice but to share power with the opposition as quickly as possible. This should happen "early enough to be able to secure the dominant position of the Polish United Workers' Party in the conditions of a successful and transformative division of power."[61] Sharing power today in order to maximize the party's power tomorrow: this was the hallmark of the politics of breaking promises in the Eastern Bloc. By August 1988, its logic had become inescapable for the communist leadership in Warsaw, and Jaruzelski was ready to embrace it.

❖　❖　❖

On August 31, 1988, the eighth anniversary of the Gdańsk Accords that had brought Solidarity into legal existence, Poland's ruling and working classes found themselves face to face once again. Minister of the Interior Czesław Kiszczak sat down with Wałęsa and invited the Solidarity leader to take part in negotiations about launching a roundtable. At the two sides' first official exploratory meeting on September 16 in the Warsaw suburb of Magdalenka, Kiszczak made the party's reason for exploring a compromise abundantly clear. The roundtable could, he said, "respond to and eventually correct the economic model, which should ensure that reforms are effectively realized, achieve economic equilibrium, and resolve the debt issue. The success of the economic reform program . . . depends upon its understanding and social acceptance." Wałęsa agreed that was necessary "to save the country from collapse," but he quickly made his own conditions clear: "union pluralism and the legalization of Solidarity."[62] This was still not something the party was ready to do, so the two sides quickly gridlocked over the nature of Poland's social and political future.

Like Western institutions and the Catholic Church before it, Solidarity now had an opportunity to exercise its own power of omission. The union would only endorse the government's economic plans once the Communist Party had met its political conditions and legalized its right to exist. And like Western institutions and the church before it, the question confronting Solidarity's leaders was whether they would accept anything less than the fullness of their demands before endorsing the party's program. Over the fall of 1988, it became clear they would not. Like Western institutions and the church, Solidarity, too, would hold the party's feet to the fire until the communists agreed to all their demands.

At first, this principled obstinance produced few results. Within weeks, the Magdalenka talks broke down over the issue of trade union pluralism, and it appeared the idea of a roundtable was to be short lived. At the end of September, Rakowski assumed the role of prime minister and announced his intention to form a government of national unity by inviting members of the opposition to become government ministers. Hoping to increase pressure on the party to accept Solidarity's demands, every opposition member turned Rakowski down. Rather than feeling pressure to come to terms with the opposition, however, he proceeded undeterred with the state's most spectacular move against Solidarity since martial law: on October 31, he closed the Gdańsk Shipyard, the union's birthplace, on account of unprofitability.[63]

It was a move laden with intention and significance. Over the course of the 1980s, Rakowski had watched with increasing dismay as successive Polish governments wilted, in his judgment, before the challenge of imposing economic discipline. By 1988, he was the premier advocate within the party apparatus of strengthening and legitimizing the state's power for the express purpose of breaking promises. "The workers have become our enemies," he confided to his diary in the midst of the August strikes. "Our ammunition is weak. We tolerate illegal strikes." The government needed "to get out of trenches" and attack its working-class opposition, he told Jaruzelski two days later.[64] The closure of the Gdańsk Shipyard was his bayonet charge against Solidarity. "I have become convinced that the people want democracy, but also want a strong state," he told Gorbachev in October. It is little wonder, then, that he soon became known in some circles as "the Polish Margaret Thatcher."[65]

As in Thatcher's Britain, unions would play a decisive role in either accepting or resisting the politics of breaking promises. The difference in Poland was that there were two national unions—the legal OPZZ and the illegal Solidarity—vying for the hearts and minds of the working class. By 1988, Alfred Miodowicz, the leader of the OPZZ, could see quite clearly that the party's twin strategies of imposing austerity and engaging Solidarity would destroy his personal power and harm the very working class that communism professed to protect. He also believed quite firmly that

Wałęsa was a simple electrician who had no business leading a national movement. So, in November 1988, he set out to expose the Solidarity leader as a fraud and burnish the party's working-class credentials by challenging Wałęsa to a live debate on national television. Things did not go as planned. Rather than appearing as an overhyped simpleton, Wałęsa projected the calm self-assurance of a man with truth on his side. "We will not make people happy by force," Wałęsa told Miodowicz and the country at large. "Give them freedom."[66] In polling taken immediately following the debate, 68.3 percent of Poles saw Wałęsa as the winner, and just 1.3 percent saw him as the loser. Support for legalizing Solidarity rose from 42 percent in August 1988 to 62 percent the day after the debate.[67]

By changing so many minds in society, the debate also changed the mind of the man who mattered most: Wojciech Jaruzelski. Before the debate, Jaruzelski had held out hope that he could get the Solidarity leadership to join the communist system and take joint responsibility for austerity without actually legalizing the union. In the weeks following the debate, he and his team realized their resistance was futile, and they set about preparing the party leadership for the legalization of its long-time enemy.[68]

The prospect of Western financial assistance was key to overcoming the stiff resistance of the party apparatus. The Central Committee roundly criticized Jaruzelski when he presented the idea of legalizing Solidarity and starting roundtable negotiations in January 1989. In response, the general and his closest advisors threatened to resign and stormed out of the room. Once cooler heads had prevailed, Jaruzelski returned to the chamber and laid out his reasons for supporting this unpalatable step: the roundtable would buy the government a period of social peace; it would enhance the party's legitimacy by increasing popular participation in upcoming elections; and it would unlock Western economic aid. Without the West's "funds, without these various connections, loans, [and] the postponement of some repayments, we will be unable to jumpstart the economy. It is simply out of the question, and it may even get worse." Unable to resist Jaruzelski's logic, the Central Committee approved the plan to legalize Solidarity and open the roundtable.[69]

Polish officials quickly tried to turn domestic political progress into international financial reprieve. "The main purpose of the roundtable talks," a Finance Ministry official told the IMF in early February 1989, "is to offer a <u>political</u> concession so as to facilitate the implementation of the authorities' <u>economic</u> plans."[70] Since the summer of 1988, Fund officials had watched the inflationary turn in Poland with increasing concern, and they had repeatedly told Polish officials that much more discipline would be required before an agreement with the Fund could be reached.[71] But Polish officials were unwilling to risk the imposition of austerity during the roundtable, so the Fund was not optimistic that the politics of breaking promises would soon prevail in Poland. IMF officials heard many times from their Polish counterparts that the roundtable was "an attempt to rally social support for a program of radical economic reform," but there was little immediate evidence to show for it.[72] Instead, Fund officials recognized that if they or the Polish government made an explicit demand for "an 'x' percent reduction in real incomes," they might cause the "breakdown of [the] roundtable discussions."[73] So as the roundtable opened in February 1989, the Fund stayed in the background and let the negotiations play out on their own.

Against the backdrop of the Communist Bloc's long history of state repression, the opening of the roundtable was a truly astonishing, if not bizarre, sight to behold. The American embassy in Warsaw noted the irony of having "a totalitarian regime begging for opposition participation in governing the country, while the opposition resists pressure to become involved." Solidarity was reluctant to play ball with the government's attempt to co-opt their position in society because they knew the purpose for which it would inevitably be used: to legitimize unpopular economic reform. The union only went along with the party's plans because, as Bronisław Geremek said, it viewed the negotiations as "the price they must pay" for the party to legalize the union.[74]

Solidarity began to pay that price on February 9, 1989, when the roundtable opened with a large plenary session. The substantive negotiations were quickly divided into three working groups: one to debate the specifics of trade union pluralism, one to negotiate political reforms, and one to discuss social and economic policy. Before the roundtable opened, Wałęsa and Kiszczak had decided on two foundational points of agreement that would guide the negotiations at the trade union and political reform tables. First, Solidarity would be legalized, not relegalized, so that the government did not have to admit martial law was a mistake. And second, partially free elections would be held for the Sejm to ensure the party retained control of the chamber and Solidarity received a substantial minority. These high-level agreements gave the trade union and political reform tables the outlines of an agreement before they even began.

No similar agreement was reached with regard to the economy. Despite their acceptance of the austerity that would necessarily come in the future, Solidarity officials pursued a policy at the roundtable meant to maintain their credibility with Polish labor. This credibility was in question because, over the course of 1988, Miodowicz had begun to position the OPZZ as the only remaining bastion of resistance in Polish society to the imposition of international capitalist exploitation. In this role, he posed an equal threat to the PZPR and Solidarity. The State Department reported on the eve of the roundtable that Miodowicz "can represent himself as the only true defender of workers' rights against a cabal seeking to introduce free enterprise and impose wage restraints."[75] In the economic reform debates at the roundtable, representatives from the PZPR and Solidarity had to be ever mindful of the ironic prospect that the state-sponsored OPZZ, which had long appeared to be a naked tool of government manipulation, might actually win the hearts and minds of Polish workers.

Advocating for wage indexation was Solidarity's way of maintaining its own credibility. If wages could be guaranteed to move in tune with prices, the union believed it could both reinforce its credentials as a protector of labor and head off a "pay race" between different sectors of the economy.[76] Because they were also interested in winning hearts and minds, neither the government nor the OPZZ was in a position to directly oppose indexation, so the economic roundtable reached an agreement to index wages at 80 percent of the inflation rate.[77]

On other economic and social issues, however, there were signs of Solidarity slowly and reluctantly embracing the politics of breaking promises. To many of the union's leaders, an eventual embrace of austerity and neoliberal economics simply appeared unavoidable by 1989. Solidarity's response to the issues of price and housing reform signaled the beginning of a transformation in the union's thinking. At the second meeting of the working group, the communist representatives called for agricultural and food prices to be freed. Price increases were, of course, the third rail of politics in communist Poland, so a union representative told the American embassy that "taking responsibility for the food price issue" made the Solidarity leadership "very nervous." Nevertheless, the official said, the leadership also knew that prices would eventually have to be liberalized in any final economic reform, which would inevitably mean higher living costs for Polish citizens. Thus, in response to the government promotion of the benign effects of competition under market capitalism, Solidarity turned to the rationale underlying the modern welfare state—the use of government spending to soften the wrenching effects of market transformation. "Food stamps," the Solidarity negotiating team told the roundtable, should accompany any price liberalization.[78]

Similar dynamics affected the roundtable's negotiations over housing policy. Housing in Poland had long been a national disaster. Because of heavy government subsidy, housing prices had long since stopped reflecting the social value and economic cost of the property. There was thus little incentive for construction firms to build new housing at a faster pace. By the late 1980s, Poles had to wait twenty years to move into an apartment of their own. Such waitlists transcended political differences, so everyone at the roundtable agreed radical reform was necessary. The solution was both obvious and painful—raise the price of housing. As with so many other areas of the economy, however, this solution would hurt millions of Polish citizens and force Solidarity to abandon its traditional labor interests. Aleksander Paszynski, the Solidarity negotiator in charge of housing policy, noted the contradictions of reform. Solidarity would have to "brutally" tell society that the era of cheap housing was over and instead work to provide a social "safety net." He lamented that "as trade unionists, Solidarity leaders support higher wages and maintaining standards of living, but as supporters of economic reform, they find themselves backing higher prices and higher rents, even if this leads to greater income disparities."[79] Such were the contradictions of the union's slow embrace of the politics of breaking promises.

In exchange for breaking promises, of course, Solidarity wanted real political control. "If we are to sign a social accord," the Solidarity representative to the economic roundtable, Witold Trzeciakowski, said, "We must control its implementation."[80] Issues of social and political control would ultimately be decided at the highest levels, so on March 2, Wałęsa and Kiszczak met again to address the shape of the final political settlement. In exchange for Solidarity's support of a strong presidency, Kiszczak offered the creation of a wholly new chamber of parliament, the Senate, whose 100 members would be freely chosen in open elections. Although the power to introduce legislation would remain in the Sejm, where the party would maintain control, the Senate would be given "blocking" power on economic, social, and environmental matters. More to the point, it would give Solidarity the ability to engage in politics without being co-opted into government programs with which it disagreed. The new chamber was a momentous concession that met the union's most important demands for both an independent political voice and some form of control over the implementation of reform.[81]

The roundtable negotiations continued through the end of March and were not officially signed until April 5, but the basic structure of the final agreement was now in place. Elections would be held in June, and the PZPR would control the Sejm; 65 percent of the seats would go to the party and its allies, while the other 35 percent would be freely elected. The Senate would also be freely elected, and the president would be elected by a majority vote from the two houses of parliament combined. Because the Sejm was much bigger than the Senate, this would ensure that Jaruzelski became president. The elections were set for early June.

As the parties reached agreement domestically, they also began to present a united front internationally. Solidarity entered the roundtable negotiations with a firm belief that the country's foreign debt was the government's problem, but it had discovered that the debt was its "carrot" in the negotiations. Therefore, as the roundtable progressed, the union threw its support behind a joint appeal with the government for debt relief from the West.[82] When Solidarity leader Jacek Kuroń met with US deputy secretary of state Thomas Simons in early May, the long-time enemy of the communist state told his American counterpart, "The reds deserve some reward for the roundtable."[83]

The appearance of this Polish united front put the US government in an awkward position. Since Reagan's National Security Decision Directive 54 on Eastern European policy, an unresolved tension between US political and economic conditionality had festered beneath the surface of US policy. American officials had long professed to care about both political and economic conditions, but their convictions had never really been tested by events on the ground. Now that the signs of political progress in Poland were undeniable, American policy makers were forced to decide which set of conditions was most important. Would they actually—as George H. W. Bush had told Jaruzelski in 1987—reward political progress in Poland, even if the economy remained unreformed? Or would they hold to the twin foundations of their conditionality and only offer financial relief to Poland once Warsaw had met both Washington's political *and* economic demands? Was the United States' immense power of omission meant to produce a democratic Poland, a capitalist Poland, or both?

These questions consumed the new Bush administration in its first few months in office in early 1989. Condoleezza Rice, a staffer on the National

Security Council, laid out the nature of the debate in a March internal memo. The government's political and diplomatic agencies, led by the State Department and the NSC, firmly believed the United States needed to respond to the political progress of the roundtable with immediate economic support. Rice counted herself in this camp. "The President promised the Polish regime that we would reward <u>political</u> reform with economic flexibility," she wrote. "To now require economic reform first would constitute 'moving the goal posts.'" Moreover, "we have told all of the East Europeans that political reform is a precondition for economic reform because illegitimate governments cannot impose strict austerity measures."[84] For agencies like the State Department and the NSC, which had been fighting the Cold War in Europe under conditions of bipolar political paralysis for four decades, it was political change in Poland that really mattered. Now that it was underway, these agencies believed the administration needed to use its economic resources to reward the choice for political liberalization.[85]

Washington's custodians of the global financial system stridently disagreed. If decades of Cold War competition had made the political situation in Europe appear intractable to the State Department and the NSC, the sovereign debt crisis of the 1980s had made the world's debt problems appear equally intractable to the Treasury Department. Treasury officials therefore viewed developments in Poland through the lens of global debt and saw little reason to adjust their global standards for dealing with debtor nations to encourage political progress in the Cold War. "Arguments about a consistent global debt policy," one NSC official wrote on the eve of the roundtable's completion, "expose a view that there are other regions of equal importance, for instance Latin America, and that Eastern Europe does not deserve special treatment. Current U.S. policy assigns greater weight to economic criteria than political ones in questions of debt relief . . . and in extensions of credits."[86] In the Treasury Department's eyes, even if the roundtable represented "a major political advance," its economic reforms were "likely to be minimal." Therefore, regardless of Poland's importance in the Cold War, the Treasury Department argued that the United States should only "reward economic reform."[87]

George H. W. Bush ultimately agreed with this view. In an April 1989 speech, the new president laid out the United States' response to the astonishing events unfolding in Eastern Europe, and his list of actions left much to be desired for those focused on supporting political reform. The United States would "facilitate cooperation and direct contacts between U.S.

firms and Poland's private business sector" and pursue "imaginative exchange, educational, cultural, and training programs," Bush said. But his administration would not press the IMF for leniency. "A stand-by agreement should be subject to the usual IMF standards," he told the Poles, because "IMF conditionality can help Poland pursue needed economic reforms."[88] The United States would, in short, demand both democracy and capitalism in exchange for access to the manifold blessings of global financial markets. The Poles would, in the end, have to conquer the challenge of breaking promises before they could rejoin the world economy.

Solidarity's strong showing in the June elections initially complicated this task. When Poles went to the polls on June 4, Solidarity won a surprising landslide victory in the new Senate chamber (ninety-nine out of one hundred seats). In the Sejm, the party's candidates, who needed 50 percent of the eligible voting population to avoid competing in the second round of elections, failed to achieve their threshold even though they ran unopposed. Though the PZPR and its allied parties achieved enough support to form a government after the second round of voting on June 18, the overall election results were a stunning rejection of the PZPR's leadership and authority. By the end of the month, Kiszczak, the communists' choice for prime minister, was unable to form a government on his own, and talk of Solidarity joining the government began to surge.

This left the union's leadership with the familiar choice of determining how much power to demand in exchange for its participation in the political system. On July 3, Adam Michnik offered a bold answer: "Your President, Our Prime Minister." In an article by that name, Michnik proposed that Solidarity be allowed to form its own government in exchange for electing Jaruzelski president. Throughout the remainder of July, the country debated Michnik's proposal while the nation's political future hung in the balance. The prospect of Western financial assistance and debt relief played a crucial role in this national debate. "One of the main arguments for the [Michnik] Plan," the US ambassador reported, ". . . is the rampant expectation that a Solidarity government would be better placed to secure vital economic assistance from the West."[89]

For Solidarity leaders, the heartening prospect of increased Western assistance was balanced by the daunting prospect of taking responsibility for an economy in freefall. At a decisive meeting on August 1, many in the leadership spoke out against Michnik's plan on precisely these grounds. "If the economic diagnosis is bad," Andrzej Stelmachowski said, "it would be folly to take over the government. . . . If we are expecting a deterioration [of the situation], we should not assume responsibility for it." Michnik was of a different mindset. "We have such an international constellation, a historical moment, when we can catch something," he said. He encouraged his comrades to seize it. As for the economics of the situation, Michnik's view was simple. "We are doomed for one [program]," he said, "a sharp, sudden entrance into the market."[90]

• • •

Michnik's plan eventually carried the day. On August 24, Tadeusz Mazowiecki became the first noncommunist prime minister of Poland since the start of the Cold War, and a period of truly extraordinary politics arrived in Warsaw. Balcerowicz, who had been a chief architect of the union's economic platform before martial law in the early 1980s, became finance minister, and he quickly committed the new government to implementing a program of "radical reform."[91] Even before Balcerowicz officially entered office, the Finance Ministry had already composed a four-month plan to impose all the hallmarks of the politics of breaking promises during the Mazowiecki government's early days.[92] Balcerowicz agreed with the ministry that the speed with which the reform was implemented was of the utmost importance. As he wrote in his 1994 article on extraordinary politics, "The brevity of the exceptional period means that a radical economic program, launched as quickly as possible after the breakthrough, has a much greater chance of being accepted that either a delayed radical program or a nonradical alternative that introduces difficult measures (e.g. price increases) in piecemeal fashion. Bitter medicine is easier to take in one dose that in a prolonged series of doses."[93]

The young American economists Jeffrey Sachs and David Lipton very much agreed. After spending the 1980s fighting the fires of the sovereign debt crisis in Latin American, Sachs and Lipton arrived in Poland in the summer of 1989 to advise Solidarity on its economic program. Though they did not use the phrase "extraordinary politics," they knew its logic well, and they urged the Solidarity leadership to seize its moment in the political sun to implement the most unpopular elements of the domestic economic reform program.[94]

Sachs and Lipton also urged Solidarity leaders to think of extraordinary politics in international terms as well. The Mazowiecki government, they maintained, was not just a sign of a new start for Polish citizens domestically;

it was also a sign of the end of the Cold War internationally. Sachs and Lipton urged their Polish counterparts to use this fact to demand debt relief from the nation's Western creditors.[95] On September 14, they sent Balcerowicz "a draft proposal to suggest the kind of document that you could circulate to the Western governments, the IMF, and the World Bank." In the proposal, the new Mazowiecki government would commit to implementing a shock program of breaking promises that would include price increases, subsidy reductions, monetary austerity, trade liberalization, and the privatization of state-owned enterprises based on the model of Thatcher's Britain. In exchange, however, the new government would demand that the IMF apply its conditionality "firmly but also imaginatively" and that Western governments and banks commit to "a definitive reduction of Poland's debt burden."[96] On September 22, Balcerowicz sent Western governments, the IMF, and the World Bank an almost verbatim copy of the Sachs-Lipton document to announce his economic plans. When the IMF received the document, Fund officials concluded that it represented "a good basis for us to work with the authorities."[97]

The Bush administration quickly reached the same conclusion. After almost a decade of waiting, events on the ground in Poland at last aligned with American political and economic conditionality in the fall of 1989. Poland would go through both a democratic revolution and a capitalist perestroika, and Washington was now eager to offer support. On October 3, 1989, Scowcroft wrote to President Bush, "We have said repeatedly, as have our allies, that the West is prepared to assist the Poles when they demonstrate their willingness to accept tough and painful reforms. The Balcerowicz plan suggests that they are ready to do so." The Solidarity leadership, Scowcroft wrote, "has decided that they must institute radical, shock-treatment reforms now, during the Mazowiecki's government's political honeymoon with the Polish population."[98] The administration now stood ready to aid the new government's endeavor. Over the fall of 1989, it rallied Western nations to provide Warsaw with a $1 billion fund to aid Poland's transition to a convertible currency and free trade. In early 1990, Western governments agreed to an unprecedented rescheduling agreement on Poland's debt that stretched out repayment over fourteen years, more than twice its normal repayment schedule.[99] It took longer to reach agreements on debt reduction, but in 1991, Western governments forgave roughly 50 percent of Poland's debt obligations. Commercial banks followed suit with their own debt-reduction package in 1994.[100]

Each of these moves toward international financial relief was tied to Warsaw's implementation of the politics of breaking promises at home. Throughout the fall of 1989, negotiations continued among the Mazowiecki government, the IMF, and Western governments over the shape of the newly titled Balcerowicz Plan. On December 28, the Sejm voted on a package of ten laws intended to fulfill the aims of the Balcerowicz Plan and bring a market economy to Poland. In the years that followed, the politics of breaking promises arrived in full force. Real wages declined by 30 percent and industrial production declined by 25 percent in 1990. Unemployment, which had previously been nonexistent, began an excruciating climb in early 1990 until it reached 13 percent by 1991.[101]

Through it all, Poland's erstwhile communist leaders stood in awe of the economic discipline Mazowiecki and his comrades were able to impose on the Polish people. "If we still had power," Rakowski ruefully wrote in his diary in October 1989, "then there would not be a single peaceful day in the country. . . . One strike would chase another. And today? Although Mazowiecki's government is pursuing a lethal economic policy, there are no strikes."[102] Jaruzelski, who had imposed the most unpopular decision of the postwar period on the Polish people, agreed. The "necessary social support" for economic reform, he eventually concluded, could "be granted only in a system of parliamentary democracy." Only such a system could "carry the burden of unpopular decisions."[103]

CHAPTER 8

The Coercion of Creditworthiness

ON APRIL 10, 1987, the staff of *PlanEcon*, the most authoritative Western publication on the communist economies of the Eastern Bloc, told its readers, "We may sound very cynical, but it is not far from the truth to say that <u>Hungarian economic fortunes in the near future do not depend on anything done in Budapest, but will be determined in Tokyo.</u> We doubt very much that Mr. Kadar yet understands this and the implications of such a situation for Hungarian economic sovereignty." Over the previous two years, the journal noted, Japanese banks flush with surplus capital from the booming Japanese economy had indiscriminately financed the Kádár government's plush domestic economic policy. But time was running out. *PlanEcon* went on, "<u>If and when Western banks finally realize . . . what Hungary is up to, they are likely to bring their lending activities to a screeching halt and cause [a] severe economic crisis in Hungary.</u>"[1]

Almost three years to the day after this stinging analysis, Hungary held its first multiparty democratic elections since the start of the Cold War. The financial pressures described in the dire warnings of a financial trade publication in 1987 were intimately connected to the momentous political changes that shook Hungary, Europe, and ultimately the world in 1989. In the summer of 1987, banks finally realized that Hungary's debt was unsustainable, and the country lost its creditworthiness on global capital markets. To restore its standing in the financial world, the Kádár government was forced to come to terms with the International Monetary Fund (IMF) on an austerity and structural adjustment program. Leading members of Hungary's Communist Party, the Hungarian Socialist Workers' Party (MSZMP), knew such a plan would involve a sharp drop in the living standards of the population, and they consequently feared that the party would lose legitimacy because of the austerity measures. Therefore, in order to build a social consensus around austerity and structural adjustment, the party launched a process to democratize the state.

In their dealings with Budapest, Western actors—particularly Western financial actors—did not intend to democratize Hungary. As in Poland, this would have appeared to be a wildly ambitious goal because there was no reason to think the Soviet Union would let Hungary leave its orbit. Nevertheless, through a process I call "the coercion of creditworthiness," Western actors played a significant role in spurring Hungary's revolution in 1989 by forcing its leadership to confront the politics of breaking promises. Western nations, capitalist banks, and the IMF established a stringent set of economic criteria the Hungarian government needed to meet to maintain access to Western credit markets and receive IMF loans. Because Hungarian officials were dependent on global capital to maintain their domestic social contract, they had little choice but to meet these demands and prepare the country for years of economic hardship. It was this pressure to prepare society for economic adjustment and austerity that ultimately drove Hungarian reformers to embrace political liberalization and multiparty democracy.[2]

◆ ◆ ◆

By the spring of 1984, János Kádár's patience with the austerity of 1979–1983 had worn thin, and he believed the party's restrictions on the domestic economy had become politically dangerous. At the April 17 Central Committee meeting, he told colleagues, "Believe me, comrades, the two main slogans we cite and reference most often 'the international economic environment' and 'to preserve the results achieved in the standard of living' can no longer be retained." He believed that "the deteriorating standard of living" had eroded the support of the people and that a new economic program was needed to restore public confidence. Kádár set the benchmark for the economy's performance at 2.5–3 percent growth in the standard of living, and he told party officials to use whatever means necessary to achieve that goal.[3]

Lucky for Kádár, global economic and financial changes that were completely out of his control brought his thoughts of renewed expansion to fruition. After the collapse of the sovereign lending market in the early 1980s, Western banks were no longer willing to put their own capital on the line to fund loans to sovereign borrowers, so they changed the way they issued debt from loans (issued directly from banks) to bonds, which could be sold to any type or class of investor. For Western banks, one group of customers for these bonds stood above the rest: Japanese investors. Japan was the economic and financial juggernaut of the 1980s, and its investors fueled global capital markets. From their perches at Tokyo investment houses, Japanese bankers invested in anything and everything, most famously in the United States—government bonds and Rockefeller Center. But Japanese companies made so much money exporting their products to the rest of the world that not even the massive United States economy could absorb all their surplus capital. Their banks needed to look beyond the United States for investment opportunities. From 1984 to 1987, Kádár's Hungary became one of the preferred destinations.[4]

János Fekete, the long-standing vice chairman of the National Bank of Hungary (NBH), played Japanese favor for all it was worth. Although investors in New York and London continued to shun Hungarian bonds, Fekete used Tokyo's enthusiasm for Hungarian debt to meet Kádár's policy demands. In 1985, he told the IMF that "he was not concerned about the balance of payments" because "Hungary had at present no difficulty in getting medium and long-term funds."[5]

The communist leadership wasted little time in turning the country's renewed access to capital abroad into new promises at home. When the Thirteenth Party Congress arrived in March 1985, the party endorsed a renewed effort to raise the living standards of the population. NBH governor Mátyás Tímár later explained the dynamics of the congress in terms of the politics of making promises. "As in the West," he said, the elections that took place at the congress were "accompanied by promises. The party congress wanted to paint an optimistic picture and promised more investment and better living standards."[6] As 1985 unfolded, the party released the reins on imports from the West, borrowed Japanese capital to pay for them, and rapidly deteriorated the balance of payments. In the three short years from 1984 to 1987, the country's hard currency debt nearly doubled from $9.4 billion to $18.1 billion.[7]

Despite the leadership's enthusiasm for renewed growth, red flags abounded both within Hungary and across the Atlantic Ocean. Officials at the National Bank of Hungary encouraged the IMF's managing director, Jacques de Larosière, to emphasize in his dealings with Hungarian leaders "that from the external standpoint the economy remained far from a safe harbor."[8] At the IMF annual meetings in the fall of 1985, Fund officials did their best to make clear to Fekete "the risks he [was] running with renewed heavy borrowing."[9] But despite their insistence on "the foolishness of building up a debt exposure," Fekete told them he "felt under no pressure" from global capital markets.[10] The staff at *PlanEcon* judged this mentality acerbically. "In order to please Mr. Kadar," they wrote, "Hungarian bankers are supporting unsustainable economic policies and deliberately bringing the country ever closer to an external payments crisis."[11]

With Fekete whispering in his ear, Kádár remained unconvinced that crisis lay just around the corner. In June 1986, he told the Politburo, "I say, comrades, we cannot change the decision of the Congress, the five-year plan, or the annual plan. . . . Those decisions pointed us in the right direction. . . . The plan must be kept."[12] To the surprise of financial policy makers in both the NBH and the IMF, global markets continued to fund Kádár's unsustainable dreams throughout the summer. L. A. Whittome, a senior official at the Fund, declared himself dumfounded. "It is amazing that the banks are prepared to go on lending at very fine terms to Hungary in this situation."[13]

As summer turned to autumn, however, the country's deteriorating financial position led many leading Hungarian officials to embrace the need for foundational economic and political reform. Károly Grósz, whom many expected to succeed Kádár, signaled a change in his own thinking in an interview with a small Hungarian publication, *Siker*. "Unless we change our present conditions, the economic-technological challenge of the world will impose increasingly heavy burdens on us," he said. Since launching the New Economic Mechanism in 1968, the party had been unable "to modernize the structure of our economy." And these eighteen years of persistent problems had demonstrated that "it is not just a technical problem . . . it is a political problem."

The political problem he had identified was, in essence, the politics of breaking promises. As Grósz said, "If we place greater value on bigger and better performance, then some workers will earn more than others. And if we penalize performances which are below average, then some other workers will get considerably less money than the average worker. In other words, the differences in earnings will increase considerably, a condition which our society still barely tolerates."[14] For Grósz, a man who "publicly expressed admiration for Mrs. Thatcher's achievements in reviving the U.K. economy," this aversion to inequality was born of a misreading of the very socialist doctrine the country professed to follow.[15] Grósz stated, "Marxism has never accepted egalitarianism, but rather the postulate of equal opportunity. This postulate takes into account, in all respects, the possibility of considerable inequality. . . . Equality has never been and cannot be a feature of socialism. Its great advantage consists precisely in its ability to automatically grant greater opportunity to everyone than does capitalism."[16]

It was a view of Marxist doctrine that fit the times, and Grósz was not alone in holding it. At the same moment, Imre Pozsgay, a headstrong cadre who had been banished from the top leadership of the party in 1982 and became leader of the party's umbrella social organization, the Patriotic People's Front (PPF), commissioned a report from a group of fifty economists and social scientists on the causes of the economic crisis and avenues toward reform. The document they collectively produced, "Turnaround and Reform," outlined the leading reformist economic thinking at the time and marked the first step in the Communist Party's strategy to develop social and political pluralism as a means of implementing the politics of breaking promises.

"The 1980s, and particularly the experiences of 1985–86," the report began, "indicate that the Hungarian economy is in a serious situation."[17] The authors believed that the country's reliance on the stilted trading and financing systems of Comecon, the inconvertibility of the forint (the national currency), and significant government restrictions on imports had all unduly sheltered Hungarian industries from the competition of the global economy. If the country was to recover, the party and government would have to close inefficient enterprises, make the forint (Ft) convertible, liberalize imports, cut corporate taxes and subsidies, adopt a restrictive monetary policy, and allow for a greater degree of wage inequality between workers based on their productivity. In short, the authors believed that the country needed to be exposed to the competitive pressures of the world economy and that the state's past promises to its citizens needed to be broken.

This process of structural adjustment—a term the report itself used (*szerkezeti alkalmazkodas*)—would not be quick or popular and would not produce immediate results. "A sincere and realistic reform policy cannot promise rapid economic growth and rising standards of living in the short term," the report concluded. "In fact, it should be openly said that it might even temporarily bring economic losses."[18] Because there would be "victims of the reform policies," the "distribution of burdens" needed to be "made socially acceptable." To do this, the authors believed the economic reforms needed to be accompanied by social and political reforms that would build social support for change. Because the reform program's implementation would depend "on actions embedded in people's behavior," it needed to "be expanded to other areas of social relations, including political relations."[19]

In its vision for reforming the economy, "Turnaround and Reform" sounded as though the IMF itself had written it. Unsurprisingly, then, IMF officials were pleased and impressed when they learned of its economic contents. What did surprise Fund officials, however, were the political, social, and legal changes also called for in the document. One staff economist called it "a remarkable document" that presented "daring solutions" because "the reform process is interpreted as both a government program as well as a social and political movement." Under the reformed political system, "interest groups, as well as individuals, would participate openly and democratically in the debate on, and thus identify with, the reforms."[20]

This image of politics—as a societal forum for interest groups and individuals to express their competing interests and arrive at consensus—defined Imre Pozsgay's vision for Hungarian reform. In a 1987 article titled "Political Institutions and Social Development," Pozsgay sought to diagnose the country's economic woes. He wrote that to develop an answer, "it is necessary to investigate . . . our political system." His own investigation had yielded "the realization that the interest relations cannot be explored, and sound and necessary policy decisions cannot be made, without openly letting interests surface, clash and be represented." This meant that "an essential feature of socialist democracy is . . . the development of a system for the representation of interests." This was not advocacy for a transition to a Western multiparty democracy. That would come later. In Pozsgay's vision of reform, the MSZMP retained its leading role in society. But he argued that the Communist Party could no longer assume or impose social consensus on society. Instead, consensus had to be arrived at through the open recognition and representation of society's competing interests.[21]

While ideas of political reform expanded under the watchful eye of Pozsgay and the PPF, the country's economic deterioration became undeniable to the party leadership in the fall of 1986. In November, the Central Committee held an emergency two-day meeting to discuss paths out of the burgeoning economic crisis. The resolution published after the meeting euphemistically called for "stabilizing" (rather than raising) the standard of living and "selective" (rather than total) industrial development. Behind the evasive language were clear signals that wage differentiation would increase, social subsidies would be cut, and loss-making enterprises would no longer be supported by the state budget. In an interview after the meeting, János Hoos, the chairman of the Planning Commission, said economic reform had "become a life or death issue" whose successful implementation depended on "the existence of a society-wide consensus that supports this type of conflict-ridden economic policy." Therefore, he said, the Central Committee had decided to increase the role of party organs and social organizations in economic life because the party's "main task" in the crisis was to "establish political conditions in which the economic policy can be realized."[22]

As the crisis reached a crescendo in Budapest, Kádár traveled to Moscow in search of Soviet support. In November 1986, he arrived at the meeting of Comecon heads of state at which Gorbachev repealed the Brezhnev Doctrine and told the assembled leaders they now needed to solve their domestic problems on their own. In case Gorbachev's generalities were unclear, the Soviet leader reinforced his message in a private meeting with Kádár. "For now, the USSR cannot really help," Gorbachev told him. Soviet officials were well aware of the onrushing crisis in Hungary. Gorbachev told Kádár that Soviet specialists were giving leaders in Budapest "two years to find a solution" but that he could do little to aid them. Gorbachev offered to buy Hungarian meat and grain with hard currency, which padded Budapest's balance of payments to a small degree, but Kádár returned home to face the burgeoning crisis on his own.[23]

While Kádár headed east in search of economic support, Fekete headed west on the same mission. Throughout the late 1980s, he lectured audiences of capitalists about the injustices of the world economy, particularly the Reagan financial buildup and the IMF's structural adjustment policies. At the IMF Annual Meetings in 1986, Fekete told the assembled financial elite that since the onset of the global debt crisis in the early 1980s, global capital had been flowing in the wrong direction—from the poor to the rich, from the developing world back to the developed. "We are today witnessing a reverse blood transfusion whereby the healthy get blood from the sick," he declared.[24] In a later speech, he cited important and startling numbers: "While during 1972–1982, $147 billion of long-term capital entered the developing countries, the tendency reversed during 1983–1987, when $85 billion flowed out of these countries." What the world needed, he told the West, was more capital, but what it was getting instead was IMF conditionality. "Severe adjustment programs undermine [countries'] potential for future growth," he said, and "the balance of trade surpluses attained by so heavy sacrifices are used to service debts."[25]

As he delivered these lines in December 1986, Fekete must have known his own country was heading in the exact same direction. The buildup of debt from 1984 to 1986 could delay domestic austerity and structural adjustment but not permanently avoid them. Beginning in 1987, markets would start to coerce Fekete, Kádár, and the reluctant bureaucracies of the Hungarian state into imposing domestic discipline. This coercion of creditworthiness would provide reformers in the party with an opportunity to chart a new economic and political course—one that would jettison the political system and ideological foundation that had guided the state for forty years.

◆ ◆ ◆

In what he termed the "24th hour for decision-making in Hungary," Fekete at last took up the reformist cause in February 1987 because markets were losing confidence in his country. After resisting involvement with the IMF throughout the mid-1980s, he now approached the Fund with a request for a three-year financing program to support Budapest's effort at fundamental structural transformation. Fund officials welcomed the government's newfound interest in reform but told Fekete that the conditions Hungary would have to meet for a three-year program would be too severe for the country's current conditions. More appropriate, they thought, would be a one-year standby agreement that would provide the country with some financing but, more importantly, would signal to global financial markets that the government was serious about imposing discipline. Fekete did not like the smaller sum of money that would come with a one-year standby agreement, but he was in no position to make demands. He invited Fund officials to come to Budapest to begin negotiations.[26]

When the Fund team arrived in mid-April, they quickly realized their Hungarian counterparts now shared their same long-term goals but disagreed over how best and how quickly to reach them. The Fund and the Hungarian government served two masters—global capital holders and the Hungarian people—and their negotiations became an extended debate over how best to neutralize popular resistance to austerity in order to produce policies that aligned with the interests of global finance. In his first meeting with the IMF delegation, NBH governor Tímár told the Fund, "There [is] no big difference between the International Monetary Fund and [the] Hungarian leadership as to what should be done, the difference being largely with regard to timing. Political stability in Hungary was a very important issue." Tímár was concerned that although "the population accepted the effects of these measures to a certain degree, one had to guard against overloading." Helen Junz, leader of the IMF delegation, understood his concern but reminded him that he needed to placate global financial markets too. Based on current projections, Hungary would have to borrow $3.5 billion on international credit markets in 1987 and 1988 just to stay financially afloat. "The market," she said, "would only be willing to support such needs if economic policies were perceived to be effectively channeling resources into productive uses."[27]

Promises needed to be broken. Over the course of the Fund's weeklong visit, Hungarian officials informed their visitors of myriad plans to cut subsidies, raise prices, devalue the forint, allow unprofitable enterprises to go bankrupt, and slash the budget and current account deficits. Indeed, their disciplinary campaign had already begun. In March, the government had devalued the forint by 8 percent against a basket of Western currencies, which made Hungarian exports cheaper but increased the price of goods for Hungarian consumers. Further price increases would come from new personal income and value-added taxes that would take effect on January 1, 1988.[28] The leadership was committed to holding the current account deficit for 1987 to $700 million, down from $1.4 billion in 1986, and the state budget deficit to Ft 30 billion, originally projected to be Ft 47 billion.[29] If austerity and adjustment was what the Fund wanted, Hungarian officials believed they were already delivering it, and they assured the Fund that more was on the way.

The IMF was not satisfied. Instead of a deficit of Ft 30 billion, Junz wanted to see a deficit of Ft 20 billion. "The progressive erosion" of capital market access, she warned, "must be counted [as] a clear and present danger."[30] Her Hungarian counterparts did not disagree, but they pleaded for patience while they choreographed the implementation of economic reforms in the domestic political arena. In order to "make the whole process politically more palatable," they planned to "minimize the appearance of outside pressure."[31] First, they said, the Central Committee would approve a reform program by July. Parliament would then give its assent in autumn, and a standby agreement with the Fund could then be signed by December. If all went according to plan, a further three-year "consolidation" (read: austerity) program could then be negotiated and implemented from 1988 on.[32] Fund officials continued to press for more urgent action, but they were willing to defer to their Hungarian counterparts on how best to lay the political groundwork for the discipline to come.[33]

Having coordinated their actions externally with the IMF, Hungarian financial officials turned inward to convince the party leadership of the necessity of taking action. Now fully convinced of the urgency of reform, Fekete told his subordinates at the bank, "The end of May has created a seriously threatening situation, and it is our duty as experts and committed party members to share our opinion. We believe it is essential for the leadership to be aware of [the nation's] financial position." The NBH prepared a bleak report for the Central Committee detailing the troubles on the horizon. "We believe that the [projected] 1987 deficit of more than $1 billion cannot be financed in 1988," the report stated. "There is acute danger, the time to take decisive action is growing short." To escape the crisis, the government "must reach agreement with the IMF in 1987 on an appropriate stand-by credit and create the political and economic conditions" necessary to implement it.[34]

One of those conditions would be ensuring that reformers held the key positions within the Hungarian state. To that end, the thirty-eight-year-old technocrat Miklós Németh was appointed head of the Central Committee's Department of Economic Policy to manage the rapidly expanding reform agenda. Németh later recalled that at the time he took the job, "it was clear to everyone that economic reform steps were not possible without changing the political framework."[35]

Everyone, that is, except the man at the top. Kádár accepted the eventuality of reform but remained reluctant to embrace its urgency. "I do not think that we are close to insolvency status," he told the Central Committee meeting in a June 1987 meeting, "Much of this is a dramatization."[36]

With the general secretary dawdling, the Central Committee could not agree on a package of reform and austerity measures, and Deputy Prime Minister József Marjai told Fund officials that their "old line of warning that the banks would lose confidence and cease to be net lenders no longer had credibility."[37]

To give a jolt to the debates going on in Budapest, IMF officials decided they needed to up the ante. Upon hearing of Marjai's message, they threatened to suspend negotiations on a standby agreement and cancel their next trip to Budapest scheduled for July. Junz wrote to Fekete, "We believe that . . . a visit might not be very productive. In fact, it could be counterproductive. . . . The markets might react negatively if it became known that we had begun talks without any positive outcome."[38] Although the letter was addressed to Fekete, its message surely was meant for the authorities above him wrestling over the fate of the country. Once again, the nebulous but all important "opinion of the market" was being used as a cudgel to steer the course of domestic Hungarian debates.

The IMF's efforts worked. In late June, Károly Grósz formed a new government as prime minister, and the reformers in the NBH and the Ministry of Finance received a mandate to begin disciplining the economy. On July 2, the Central Committee published a new "Program for Stabilization and Evolution" that spoke in weighty tones about the origins and implications of the national economic transformation now required. "In the past decade and a half," the program's statement began, drawing attention back to the oil crisis of 1973, "the world economy has gone through radical changes." But Hungary was "late in adapting to the changed situation." Now, the time for adaption had arrived, and the results would not be pretty. "A period of stabilization is required," the program announced, during which the country would have to take on the "burdens that come with restructuring." Progress would only come by "lowering expenses" and "increasing profitability." The system of "unmanageable subsidies" would need to be broken, and "loss-making activity" could no longer be "financed permanently at the expense of successful companies." Wages would need to be determined according to performance, and there would need to be a "temporary restriction in public and private consumption"—in other words, austerity.[39]

Though none of this would be popular, the reformers knew it nevertheless needed the population's support in order to succeed. Therefore, the Central Committee paired the announcement of economic bad news with hints of political good news. To support the economic reforms, the new program announced that it would be "essential to develop socialist democracy and improve the functioning of the system of political institutions." Through a "comprehensive . . . system of social discussions" with the public, Hungarian citizens would now be asked for their input before "political and economic decisions" were made.[40]

The irony, of course, was that the fundamental decision to put the country on an austere path had already been made, and it had been made to serve the demands of the IMF and global capital holders. On July 21, Fekete tried to sell the Fund on the merits of the new package of reforms by noting it cut state spending by Ft 4 billion. The price of motor oil and gasoline had been increased two forints per liter, and the price of household energy had been raised by an average of 20 percent. The price of tobacco products had gone up 20 percent, and the average price of flour and bakery products had surged 19 percent.[41] Hopefully, the Fund and "the market" would be happy.

When IMF officials returned to Budapest in August, the Hungarians pleaded for a respite from financial pressure to allow their fledgling economic and political reforms to take effect. In the delegation's first meeting, Fekete laid out the authorities' fears of the instability that might accompany moving too quickly. The government "needed to be careful and avoid . . . the limits of social tolerance," he said. If too many loss-making enterprises were liquidated all at once, "there was a risk of a confrontation at the political level."[42] Tímár expected "200,000 layoffs" over the next two years.[43] Miklós Németh agreed with the Fund that further action was necessary, but he maintained that the population still "had to be convinced that there was no other option."[44] As Thatcher, Volcker, Gorbachev, and Jaruzelski had already found, it was no mean feat to convince a country that there was no alternative to broken promises.

Parliament provided its stamp of approval in September, and Deputy Prime Minister Marjai sold the merits of the reform plan to the IMF as "complying with the demands of the foreign markets."[45] Markets were indeed getting demanding. On his way to Budapest in early October, Fund economist Patrick de Fontenay heard in London that Japanese investors' moment of reconsideration had finally arrived. "Hungarian paper was not selling easily in the markets," bankers told him, because "the Japanese were beginning to reconsider their position."[46]

As happened so often during the privatized Cold War, this loss of private market confidence provided public actors with a chance to decisively intervene. On the same day de Fontenay learned of Japanese banks' growing doubts, the West German government of Helmut Kohl announced a new, state-sponsored loan of DM 1 billion to Hungary. Since late 1986, West German officials had watched Budapest's financial deterioration with growing concern for the damage it might do to the cause of Hungarian reform. As 1987 progressed, they resolved to finalize the new *Milliardenkredit* at a moment that would maximize its support for the reformers in Budapest.[47] That moment arrived when Prime Minister Grósz traveled to Bonn to meet with the leaders of West German politics and finance in October 1987. In an unspoken quid pro quo for the loan, Grósz signed a declaration committing his government to respect the rights of the German minority in Hungary and agreed to the opening of a new German cultural center in Budapest. This declaration landed as a "shock" in the Eastern Bloc and a "sensation" in the global financial world because of the growing West German power over Hungary that it portended. Eastern Bloc leaders may not have been pleased, but global capital holders took solace in knowing that the Hungarian government had a new patron in Bonn.[48] For the moment, at least, Hungarian finances were safe under the shield of the Federal Republic.

The relief was brief, however. Despite its largesse, the Kohl government still expected Budapest to soon come to terms with the IMF.[49] So the effort to prepare Hungarian society for further austerity needed to continue. While Hungarian financial officials progressed through their summer of discontent in 1987, Imre Pozsgay was busy building on his vision of democratizing society and the state in the service of economic transformation. On March 15, 1987, he spoke at a rally of nascent opposition groups commemorating the nation's revolution against Austria in 1848—the first opposition rally ever legalized by the authorities.[50]

In September, the PPF published an "action program" aimed at supporting the Program of Stabilization and Evolution making its way through parliament. The preface to the program declared that "as the institution for societal dialogue," the PPF was "prepared to serve as a forum for the broadest possible political activity that is necessary." This broadening of the political role of the PPF was required because "there is a need to establish a consensus."[51] In pursuit of these goals, Pozsgay gave the introductory lecture in the fall of 1987 at a meeting of 150 writers and intellectuals in Lakitelek to discuss ways out of the crisis. This group would go on to become the Hungarian Democratic Forum (MDF), the political party that won the 1990 democratic elections, but in the fall of 1987, it was a group of intellectuals with an inchoate vision of reform and little support among the population. Pozsgay aimed to raise their profile. With his endorsement, the group issued "the Lakitelek proclamation" at the end of the meeting, calling on the government to open a dialogue with society; it was published in one of the country's leading newspapers, *Magyar Nemzet*, in November.

Although the reformers' belief in the power of pluralism to bring about social consensus was sincere, a more cynical strand of thought also underlay their interest in democratization: to compensate for the unpopularity of austerity, the authorities embraced political liberalization as a means of padding their standing among the populace. This is the explanation for liberalization Hungarian officials most often gave to IMF officials in Washington. Miklós Németh, for instance, told IMF officials in 1988 that because "there was no room for any increase in the standard of living for the next three to four years . . . the authorities wanted to compensate [for] the pressure in the economic field by 'increasing freedom of choice in the political field.'"[52] Broken promises were difficult pills for society to swallow, and Hungarian officials hoped the elixir of political liberalization would help them go down more easily.

◆ ◆ ◆

In January 1988, the IMF and the Hungarian government at last came to terms on a standby agreement, but the road had not been easy. Throughout late 1987, Fund officials kept the pressure on their Hungarian counterparts to impose more discipline. The hot-button issue that December was raising the government-determined interest rate on housing loans, which augured political revolt in the minds Hungarian officials. Time and again, Fund officials told their interlocutors the rates needed to be raised, and time and again their Hungarian counterparts agreed in principle but refused a change in practice. "Too politically sensitive" was the common refrain.[53] Prime Minister Grósz feared that the country might "collapse under its burdens." Despite the government's efforts to use the press "to prepare public opinion," he said, "the changes taking place were considerable and the population had not been sufficiently prepared for them."[54]

The key to escaping the gap between creditors' demands for adjustment and the population's resistance to austerity lay in the IMF's bank account. Hungarian officials told the IMF that the larger any potential standby agreement with the Fund was, the easier it would be "for the Hungarian negotiators to justify to the politicians the measures they had agreed to."[55] So more money is precisely what the IMF used to achieve its goals. By increasing the standby amount, the Fund broke Hungarian resistance to the agreement's package of reforms.[56] And quite a list of reforms it was: the freeing of 50 percent of prices, a commitment to reform the wage system and legalize joint stock companies in 1988, limits on domestic credit issued by the NBH, a ceiling on the budget deficit, and quarterly increases on bank deposit interest rates. In addition, Budapest committed to undertaking a 5 percent devaluation of the forint before the IMF Executive Board approved the agreement in May.[57] In return, Hungary received some $350 million in IMF loans and held on to access to international credit markets by its shoestrings.[58]

Strong adjustment ensured difficult politics. Most importantly, it was clear to all in the reformist camp that their cause could not ultimately prevail while Kádár remained at the top of the party and state. So, in early 1988, Grósz and his allies launched a campaign to remove him from office. At an exceptional party conference held May 20–22, 1988, the party sent Kádar into retirement, elected Grósz to take his place, and filled the Politburo with reformers like Németh, Pozsgay, and the original architect of the New Economic Mechanism, Rezső Nyers. At the conclusion of the conference, the party criticized itself for avoiding the challenge of breaking promises. The former leadership had "misjudged the process of change that has taken place in the world economy," party leaders now told the country. They had thought the challenges of "rolling back inefficient production" and "dismantling subsidies" were "avoidable." But in a new lexicon that signaled the momentous change afoot, the party now assured the country it would foster a "socialist market economy" to solve the nation's many challenges and bring about "socialist pluralism based on the leading role of the party" in politics to support the economic reform program's implementation.[59]

What this rhetoric meant in practice remained to be seen. In June, the government passed a new freedom-of-assembly law that was supposed to enhance the ability of social groups to freely congregate and advocate for change. But which groups and what changes went unsaid. Society began to find out when, in late June, thousands of people gathered in Budapest to demonstrate for two very different reasons: to commemorate the anniversary of the execution of Imre Nagy, leader of the country's 1956 uprising, and to protest the Romanian government's treatment of its Hungarian minority. The first cause posed an existential threat to the legitimacy of the ruling party, while the second promised to use Hungarian nationalism to increase the government's popularity. Unsurprisingly, then, security forces violently cracked down on the Nagy commemoration, but they actively encouraged the protest against Romania. This was political pluralism stage-managed for public consumption. As the West German embassy noted, Hungarians had now been given "certain civil liberties," but those liberties were "precisely dosed" to serve the state's purposes.[60]

As with all treatments, it was important to get the dosage of political and economic liberalization just right if communist Hungary was to return to health. But in 1988, this proved a greater challenge than the party's reformers initially envisioned. On the economic front, officials wasted little time in molding the domestic economy on paper to conform to the performance criteria the IMF had tied to the January standby agreement. In July, they devalued the forint yet again, and throughout the summer and fall, they crafted laws liberalizing the wage system and legalizing all forms of ownership. These efforts resulted in a new Law of Associations that began the privatization of the Hungarian economy and opened the country to foreign investment in early 1989.[61] In the fall of 1988, the government also announced plans to eliminate half the state's consumer and producer subsides—some Ft 110 billion—over the next three years. Opening the country to foreign competition through trade liberalization soon followed.[62]

But Hungarian officials ultimately proved better at talking about economic discipline than actually imposing it. As always, the social and political side effects of reform worried policy makers in Budapest. Liberalizing wages meant running the risk of inflation, and liberalizing ownership, cutting subsidies, and opening the country to foreign competition meant inviting mass unemployment. As Grósz told the IMF over the summer of 1988, "If imports were liberalized half of Hungary's industry would collapse." Though he thought this "would not be a major loss" from an economic point of view, it "was not something one could let happen overnight" for political reasons.[63] For this reason, Hungarian officials proved reluctant to see their policies through to their socially disruptive conclusion. Few enterprises were actually forced into bankruptcy, and unemployment remained much lower than the 200,000 people that many officials feared would one day come.[64] This saved Hungarian society from the worst social side effects of economic transformation but also left the IMF unimpressed and did little to alter the economy's basic downward trajectory. Only one point of economic reality changed substantially in 1988: the price level. Inflation rose at an annual rate of 18 percent, while real wages declined by 10 percent, creating deteriorating conditions among the working class that were ripe for political opposition.[65]

By late 1988, a growing list of opposition political parties stood ready to capitalize on the population's discontent. As part of its attempt to build "socialist pluralism," the party legalized the formation of new political parties in November 1988. The opposition's ranks did not take long to fill out. A year after its first meeting at Lakitelek, the Hungarian Democratic Forum became an official party in the fall of 1988. Not long after, liberal opposition leaders formed the Alliance of Free Democrats, and the "historical parties" that had only nominally existed during the period of one-party rule stepped out of the communists' shadow and began to cut an independent figure on the political scene. Last but not least was the League of Young Democrats, known as Fidesz, a band of student radicals led by a young spokesman, Viktor Orbán. Together, these new parties had little interest in playing the role of loyal opposition to the communist state, and they used the population's growing material discontent to build power bases of their own.[66] As an IMF official reported to Washington at the end of 1988, "Political liberalization . . . which was initially aimed at making relative austerity more easily tolerated, has brought to the surface demands by various groups and interests, which the government is finding it difficult to resist as it seeks popular support."[67]

Clearly, for those in the Hungarian leadership who had hoped to use a controlled political liberalization to legitimize austerity, the dosage of economic and political reform administered to Hungarian society in 1988 had not been right. The party had not found the will or the way to impose enough austerity and structural adjustment to fix the domestic economy or resolve the country's debt crisis, and it had let political reform progress far beyond its control. Most importantly, despite the country's meager economic results and increasingly tumultuous politics, the reformers knew that the worst social effects of the economy's restructuring were still to come.[68]

As the horizon of the country's future darkened, Károly Grósz realized his political career would be best served by letting someone else take the fall for the mounting economic hardships. In November 1988, he resigned as prime minister (while retaining his role as party secretary) and handed the post to Miklós Németh. Upon assuming office, the young technocrat believed his cardinal task was crystal clear. "My job," he later recalled, "simply was to save the country from bankruptcy."[69] One of his first decisions was to order the removal of the "Iron Curtain" barbed wire fence that separated Hungary from Austria and prevented Eastern Europeans from escaping to the West. This decision would have a profound effect on the end of the Cold War, but it was not motivated by Cold War considerations in the slightest. Instead, Németh eliminated the fence as part of his broader effort to limit hard currency imports and craft an austerity budget that would conform to the IMF's demands.[70] As 1989 dawned, the pressure to break promises was now directly driving political change in Hungary and across the Cold War.

◆ ◆ ◆

In the history of Hungary's democratic transition, the story of 1989 is well known and widely shared. On January 28, Imre Pozsgay publicly declared the events of 1956 to be a popular uprising rather than a counterrevolution, as the party had long maintained. This immediately threw the party's legitimacy into question, and the leadership soon responded by announcing its openness to holding controlled multiparty elections through which it would still retain a leading role in the country. To pull off such a feat, the party would need to find partners among the opposition, so it immediately began searching for parties that might join it in a ruling coalition. Like Solidarity in Poland, the vast majority of the opposition forces had little interest in being used by the communists to legitimize unpopular policies, so in March they banded together to form the Opposition Roundtable to coordinate their negotiations with the Communist Party. Unable to divide the opposition, the communists were then forced to negotiate with the Opposition Roundtable at the National Roundtable, which opened in June and dragged on until September. All the while, popular protest grew in the streets, as a mass demonstration on March 15 drew 100,000 people to press for political change. The ideological end of communism came on June 16, when over 200,000 people flooded the streets of Budapest to attend the reburial of Imre Nagy. No longer depicted as a traitor to his country, Nagy was now universally recognized, by both the opposition and the reform communists, as a national hero. Nagy's veneration also served as the party's repudiation, a fact made abundantly clear by the communists' implosion as a political force over the remainder of the year. Wrangling over details delayed the elections until the spring of 1990, but when they came, they were fully free and re-sulted in the first noncommunist government in Hungary since the start of the Cold War.[71]

A historical inquiry focused on the coercion of creditworthiness does not contest the importance of the people or events that defined Hunga-ry's 1989. But it does uncover new causes and consequences of the polit-ical transition that took place that year. Just like the Communist Party's political liberalization efforts in late 1986, its halting embrace of multi-party elections in 1989 served the ultimate purposes of legitimizing aus-terity and allowing the party to escape blame for breaking promises. Regardless of the election's outcome, its social, economic, and financial consequences had been determined long before a single vote was cast. No matter who won or lost the election, economic discipline would follow in its wake.

The history of January 28, 1989—the day Pozsgay shook the Hungarian political world with his reevaluation of the events of 1956—serves as an important example of the shift in perspective that comes with focusing on broken promises. At the same time Pozsgay was delivering his explosive statement on Hungarian radio, Károly Grósz was meeting with the IMF's managing director, Michel Camdessus, on the sidelines of the World Eco-nomic Forum in Zurich, Switzerland. If Pozsgay's statement had enormous implications for Hungary's past, Grósz's meeting had equally large impli-cations for the country's future. Grósz had gone to Zurich to meet with the world's financial elite and update Camdessus on his plans for Hungary. Ever since Fekete had raised the possibility of a three-year program with Fund officials in 1987, the Hungarian leadership had remained interested in negotiating one. But a three-year program—titled an Extended Fund Fa-cilities (EFF) in the IMF's vernacular—would come with more stringent structural adjustment and austerity measures attached to it, and IMF offi-cials consistently doubted Budapest could deliver the wrenching domestic changes that would be required. Grósz came to Zurich to tell the managing director that his country would soon be ready. His government "would hope to move to an EFF for the calendar years 1990–92," he said.[72] IMF of-ficials still had their doubts, but if Grósz could deliver enough domestic discipline to comply with the current standby agreement, perhaps a long-term agreement could be worked out.[73]

One week later, Grósz was back in Budapest for the Politburo meeting at which the leadership decided to embrace multiparty democracy. It is clear from the archival record that the country's looming economic hardship weighed heavily on their deliberations. Knowing full well what he had recently discussed with the IMF, Grósz set the terms of the discussion with cold political calculation. "I can picture the transition period in two phases," he began. "The first phase would come to its end . . . at the end of 1990. . . . The second phase would be the period between '90 and '95." He continued, "The first phase . . . is going to be around the elections of 1990. The real test comes after the elections and not before them." Grósz believed it would take some time for the population to weigh the merits of each political party. "The [economic] crisis period would be '92–'93 when everyone is going to be weighed, and put in their places in the political structure, and that is when the MSZMP will be weighed as well—does it have a solution to the crisis, does it have a program to put an end to the crisis, and so on and so forth." Rezső Nyers interjected that the transition "will only change the players in the crisis." "That is it," Grósz replied. "It will not be a solution to the crisis in itself."

Imre Pozsgay accepted the introduction of a multiparty system because the party had "not managed to create pluralism along with the single-party system," as they had envisioned back in May 1988 when they removed Kádár from power. Nyers attributed this inability to the fact that the economic crisis had been more severe than previously thought. "I think in May we had been optimistic concerning the time and the manner of resolving the crisis. It can be seen that [the crisis] is deeper. I agree with comrade Grósz that . . . it will probably be by '95 or the beginning of the '90s that this crisis can be resolved, until then we are going to be a society managing crisis, an economic crisis." For this reason, Nyers believed elections needed to come soon. The political crisis, he said, "must not last as long as the economic crisis, because that would cause a collapse." Building on the idea of Grósz's two phases of transition, Nyers said that after the first phase was complete, "economic crisis management would go on."

At this point, the party leadership's vision for the elections was still not a completely free competition of political parties. Pozsgay argued, "We should aim at a hegemonic position . . . it should be guaranteed in the first round through some kind of . . . compromise and we should face open competition only in the second round."[74] Everyone else agreed on this strategy, and soon the party publicly endorsed multiparty elections.

Clearly, with the Hungarian Democratic Forum winning the 1990 election, this vision of a hegemonic position within a multiparty system was never realized. The opposition's efforts between February 1989 and March 1990 can be understood as a successful struggle to force the communist leadership to move the openly competitive elections up from 1995 to 1990. This was by no means a meaningless difference, but the struggle that transpired during 1989 was over the question of when, not whether, fully free elections would happen. As Grósz told Gorbachev in a meeting in Moscow, "Events in Hungary have lately accelerated. Their direction is according to our intentions, while their pace is somewhat disconcerting."[75]

For financial officials within the NBH, the Ministry of Finance, and the IMF, the importance of the election was of an entirely different order. Who won the election or whether it was fully free was immaterial. As Nyers had said to the Politburo, the vote would merely "change the players in the crisis." Instead, the value of the election lay in the unique opportunity it presented to legitimize the politics of breaking promises and agree to a three-year program with the IMF.

First, however, the country had to actually reach the election without falling into bankruptcy. At the start of 1989, relations between Budapest and the Fund were in the midst of yet another cycle of pressure and accommodation, with Hungary failing to meet a number of performance criteria in their standby agreement and Fund officials attempting to find ways to redefine the criteria so Hungary would not lose the market's confidence. The particular reform measures at issue in 1989 do not need to be recounted here. In November 1989, an IMF official summed the year up nicely for our purposes. "1989 was a bad year for Hungary," he wrote to the managing director. "This is due to the Government's preoccupations with political developments at the expense of the management of the economy."[76] The reason was clear enough: 1989 had become an election year. Ministry of Finance officials told the IMF that Hungary's proliferating political parties "generally agreed that the size of the state's activities . . . should be reduced." But "while Parliament generally endorses this idea in principle, it has failed to provide any specifics . . . . Nor have opposition parties articulated any specifics, given that it would most likely weaken their position in the upcoming election."[77] With these electoral dynamics in play, it was clear to all involved that 1990 would be "a more important year" than 1989 for delivering economic discipline.[78]

In order to get the country to 1990, though, the IMF had to go to dramatic lengths to keep Hungary in the good graces of capital markets throughout 1989. After putting immense pressure on Budapest in 1987 and

1988 to undertake reforms, the Fund changed its tune to one of accommodation in 1989 to ensure the success of the political transition. Everyone knew that one pessimistic sign from the Fund would cause an immediate financing crisis that would lead to the county soon becoming insolvent. Insolvency would harm the hopes of political reform or might dash them altogether, so with the encouragement of Western governments, the Fund bent its rules throughout the year to prevent a deterioration of Hungary's creditworthiness.[79] The most serious Hungarian transgression surfaced in November 1989, and the Fund worked to minimize the damage to the country's creditworthiness. On November 20, Hungarian financial officials informed the IMF they had been continuously underreporting the level of their foreign debt by about 10 percent since the late 1970s. Under normal circumstances this was a serious offense, and Hungary could have faced stiff punitive action from the Fund. But upon learning of the underreporting, Fund officials' immediate concern was to ensure that the news did not rattle the investors in Hungarian debt.[80]

Thus, the IMF's effort to maintain nonmonetary cooperation with Hungary was itself a form of financial assistance from the West. The mere fact of Hungary's unbroken association with the institution kept global capital in Hungary when it was ready to run at the first sign of trouble. This was not a direct form of assistance from Western governments or global financial institutions. But it was the use of Western financial prestige, embodied in the institutional weight of the IMF, to prevent a financial crisis in Hungary during the uncertain months of its political transition.

It was only a temporary reprieve, however. The IMF was only willing to hold the markets' pressure for structural adjustment at bay until the elections were complete. Thus, by the summer of 1989, the attention of both the Fund and Hungarian officials turned to negotiating the reform package the new government—whatever its political stripes—would use its legitimacy to implement. This meant drafting a three-year EFF agreement. During a Fund visit to Budapest in August, Ferenc Bartha, now governor of the NBH, told the IMF that the government had already discussed a medium-term program covering the three years out to 1992. A consensus had been reached, he said, on "reform measures tackling . . . the problems of ownership, budgetary reform, monetary reform and decentralization of the banking system, development of a capital market and the restructuring of trade with the West and CMEA [Comecon] intended to foster the integration of Hungary in the world economy"—in other words, the entire national economy. "It would be desirable," he said, "to reach understandings with the Fund on a medium-term agreement covering these issues which could be implemented by a government which would emerge from the pending elections."[81] In a later meeting, Hungarian officials told the Fund, "The program could only be approved after the pending elections," but "whatever government emerged from the elections had little choice but to implement a program of market oriented reform, with a strict monetary regime and a reduction in the role of government."[82]

This was bad news for Hungary's nascent opposition movements. By the late 1980s, Hungary had a hard currency foreign debt of roughly $19 billion and an annual budget deficit ranging from Ft 30 billion to Ft 60 billion year to year. Until 1987, these figures were considered top secret and were restricted to senior leaders in the Politburo and a narrow section of the financial bureaucracy. Society at large had no understanding of the nation's financial position. An important part of the political liberalization launched in 1987 was informing the country of the nation's real financial state. One newspaper described the population as "shocked" when the numbers were made public.[83] Not one to sugarcoat a situation, Miklós Németh told the country in a 1989 nationally broadcast interview, "The interest burden, to mention only this, last year and this year amounts to $1.2–1.3 billion. . . . This is a burden to the country. And we have to accept this burden in order to maintain our solvency."[84]

This conclusion went virtually unquestioned by all of Hungary's new political parties. Two convictions defined the discussion about the national debt after it became a topic of public conversation in 1987: the debt was part of a global phenomenon, and the debt had to be repaid. In a 1988 article, "The State as Debtor," Istvan Garamvolgi wrote, "This decade we have been witnessing the explosion of debt in most countries of the world . . . mounting national debt is a worldwide phenomenon."[85] János Kis, a prominent member of the opposition Free Democrats, believed that the global nature of the debt problem made the future course of Hungarian development easy to predict. "Let us not forget," he wrote, that "Hungarian crisis processes emanate from Hungary's Western financial dependence. In this respect Western creditors will exert pressure, [and] the International Monetary Fund will offer package plans for the limitation of consumption." The point of comparison for Hungary's future was clear. "In brief: the West will mean to Hungary what the United States means to the masses of less fortunate Latin American countries."[86]

Ironically, Kis's party, the Alliance of Free Democrats, was both the most promarket political party and the only party to even consider asking the international community for debt relief. In an August 1989 article, Tamas Bauer and Marton Tardos, the party's leading economists, wrote, "Hungary may be able to manage its current debt burden for quite some time. It can do so, however, only at the price of further increasing the frightening impoverishment of part of the populace." Bauer and Tardos believed—and had the courage to say—that the Volcker Shock and Reagan financial buildup bore some responsibility for Hungary's debt. It was "an unquestionable fact," they wrote, "that high and unpredictably fluctuating interest rates were caused by budgetary deficits in certain Western countries." Therefore, "the financial pressure choking the Hungarian economy cannot be lifted by granting credit alone." Instead, "a reduction of the accumulated debt service" and "a reduction of interest" were required.[87]

With such views percolating in society, the NBH was not going to leave anything about the opposition's economic and financial views to chance. Bank officials led a coordinated effort to ensure that all political parties viewed Hungary's international debt obligations and plans for structural reform as unbreakable promises. In an August 1989 interview, NBH president Bartha reported that he and his team had recently met with all leading opposition parties. He stated, "We tried to persuade them to include requirements for a strong central bank . . . in their demand, and told them to regard a tight money policy as a measure in the interest of the entire nation. We tried to convince them not to consider the rescheduling of loans and further increases in the indebtedness as passable." The debt represented the accumulated actions of the nation's past, Bartha believed, and the new government could not simply walk away from those actions. "We assume responsibility for the past," he said.[88]

With the opposition's views under control, there was just one problem left by the fall of 1989 for the financial policy makers of the NBH and the IMF: the elections kept getting pushed back due to pesky political quarrels, and the country was running out of money. After having initially been moved up to fall 1989, election day had since been moved back a number of times and was now planned for March 1990. At the end of September, Bartha projected that the country would face a financial crisis in early 1990 unless it received the three-year EFF. But with all the important structural adjustments postponed until a new government took power, the IMF would not grant the EFF until the perpetually deferred election actually took place. Officials projected that the country would need to borrow $1 billion in the first quarter of 1990 and that without an EFF program the NBH likely would not be able to find such funds.

This put in motion the endgame of Hungary's communist period. In late 1989, the European Community provided a $1 billion bridge loan to "tide Hungary over" until the spring election and made the loan contingent on the current communist government coming to terms with the IMF on yet another standby program before the election.[89] When an IMF team arrived in Budapest in December 1989 to negotiate the new standby, Fund officials gave up waiting for the elections and demanded that the current government take a series of steps immediately. The government needed to announce cuts in housing subsidies, increase interest rates, and provide "a list of enterprises against which liquidation procedures had been initiated." Unless it took these measures by January, Fund officials told their Hungarian counterparts, the IMF would not agree to a financing program.[90] With no other option available, Hungarian authorities devalued the forint by 10 percent, increased interest rates, and passed a housing reform program that increased the average rent by 35 percent in December 1989. In January 1990, the authorities cut enough subsidies and freed enough prices to institute a 10 percent increase in the consumer price level while also accelerating the closure of loss-making enterprises.[91] These rounds of brutal austerity caused László Kézdi, the Budapest pensioner we met in this book's opening pages, to write his biting public letter to the Hungarian authorities.

In exchange for these broken promises, the Fund team agreed to submit the standby agreement to the IMF Executive Board before the March election. To ensure that the new government upheld the standby agreement, however, the Fund made each batch of loans beyond the first "subject to a review which would ensure that the new government endorses the program."[92] And so, one week before József Antall and the Hungarian Democratic Forum won the first free election in Hungary since the start of the Cold War, the IMF Executive Board approved an agreement that set the course of the Hungarian economy regardless of the election's outcome.

In May, the managing director visited Hungary and met with Antall, the new prime minister. Antall told Camdessus that "the Government was determined to proceed with reform and that it would be done with appropriate speed but not overnight." To which Camdessus predictably replied, "While the appropriate speed would have to be determined in light of each country's circumstances (including political and historical factors), a minimum critical mass was needed at the outset and there were costs to being too gradual."[93] Clearly, the pressure to break promises had not subsided. Instead, the players had merely changed.

By November 1990, the Antall government had formulated its medium-term reform program, titled the Economic Program of National Renewal. Hungarian officials told the Fund that "strengthening Hungary's credit-worthiness" was one of the primary goals of the program. "To this end," they wrote, "the Government is placing great emphasis on privatization, the reduction of the role of the state in the economy, and the strengthening of market mechanisms."[94] After further rounds of negotiations, the Fund and the Antall government signed an agreement for a three-year EFF in February 1991. Almost four years after *PlanEcon* had published its warning about the financial crisis looming in Hungary, a Hungarian government had agreed to a long-term structural adjustment program aimed at maintaining the market's favor. What *PlanEcon* and the rest of the world did not foresee in 1987 was that the Hungarian government signing the agreement would be the country's first noncommunist government in over forty years.

CHAPTER 9

Exit, Violence, or Austerity

PUBLIC SURPRISES HAVE private histories. The fall of the Berlin Wall shocked the world on November 9, 1989, and people have debated the history of this stunning event ever since. Most often they have searched for its causes in the public histories of the time— the mass protests, mass emigration, ideological crisis, and rhetoric of protest that defined the final months of the German Democratic Republic (GDR). Nothing signifies this focus on public histories more than the widespread use of Albert O. Hirschman's Exit/Voice/Loyalty model to explain the GDR's collapse. Published in 1970, Hirschman's book, *Exit, Voice, and Loyalty: Responses to Decline in Firms, Organizations, and States,* put forth a sociological model for explaining how people respond to declining performance in organizations. Hirschman posited that members of an organization can respond to a decline in performance in three ways: leave the organization (Exit), protest to reverse the organization's decline (Voice), or keep their behavior constant (Loyalty).[1]

In the summer of 1989, Hirschman's model appeared to receive a real-world test in the dramatic dénouement of East Germany. Beginning in May, East German citizens, fed up with the indefatigable deterioration in the performance of their government, sought to express their dissatisfaction and chose Hirschman's methods to do so. By the thousands, they left the GDR and headed for Hungary, where, on account of austerity pressures, Miklós Németh had dismantled the "Iron Curtain" border fence between Hungary and Austria and would soon open the border to East German emigration. As the Exit portion of Hirschman's model suddenly appeared, the Voice component quickly followed. In September, groups of protesters gathered every Monday in Protestant churches in Leipzig and Dresden. At first called "peace meetings," these gatherings soon grew into mass protests throughout the GDR calling for political and economic reform. With the pressures of Exit and Voice mounting as the Wall opened on November 9, it was only natural that observers drew connections between the forces at work in Hirschman's model and the government's ultimate capitulation.[2]

This chapter flips Hirschman's model on its head. Instead of focusing on the public choices available to the East German population, it is structured around the private choices available to the East German government. Exit, Violence, or Austerity: these were the three strategies of governance available to the East German communist party (SED) in 1989. As its citizens fled to the West through Hungary and mounted protests on the streets of East German cities, the SED leadership could either officially sanction their emigration (Exit) or forcefully suppress the protests and restrict travel (Violence). Hanging over each strategy was the looming prospect of national insolvency and a default on the country's debt to its Western creditors. In order to prevent such a development and maintain the country's creditworthiness on international capital markets, the government estimated it would have to cut living standards by 25–30 percent in 1990 (Austerity). The East German leadership accepted Exit and hesitated to use Violence because it viewed Austerity as the worst option and actively tried to avoid it. In choosing Exit, the leadership believed it could extract new loans from West Germany in exchange for opening its borders. In refraining from Violence, the leadership knew that if it cracked down on protesters in the streets, it would lose all access to the Western capital upon which the country heavily depended.

The leading historical accounts of the fall of the Wall and the collapse of the GDR stress the role of accident, contingency, and the power of local actors in bringing these stunning events to fruition.[3] For fear of adding to the triumphalism that accompanied the Cold War's end in the United States, they are also wary of any claim that Western hard power played a significant role in the GDR's demise.[4] While not denying the importance of contingency and local actors, this chapter attempts to recover an understanding of the sources of Western power that influenced the collapse of the GDR without partaking in triumphalism. It focuses on the most important leverage Western political and financial institutions had in the late 1980s—money—and fully recognizes that this leverage more often than not produced consequences Western actors did not foresee or intend. With this leverage in focus, it becomes clear that the United States government indeed played only a minor role in the collapse of East Germany, but other centers of Western political and financial power—namely, the West German government of Helmut Kohl, the International Monetary Fund (IMF), and the global financial system—played critical roles in undermining the GDR's sovereignty, stability, and, ultimately, existence.

♦ ♦ ♦

Through the two billion-mark loans from the West German government in 1983 and 1984, East Germany returned to financial stability by the middle of the decade. To bolster the country's creditworthiness, Alexander Schalck-Golodkowski, leader of the Kommerzielle Koordinierung (KoKo) division, and Günter Mittag, the SED's chief economic official, decided to place the loans on deposit with Western banks instead of using them to pay for new imports. The actions of West German chancellor Helmut Kohl made it clear that the GDR had a new, very rich lender of last resort in place of the Soviet Union, and financial markets responded with enthusiasm. With hard currency in its bank accounts and a new Western financial umbrella to stand under, the GDR regained easy access to Western capital markets in 1984.

But with the financial crisis of the early 1980s fresh in their minds, Mittag and Schalck knew the country's problems were far from solved. Most importantly, the debt level needed to recede if the country was to maintain its independence from the Federal Republic. To foster a sense of urgency in the bureaucratic ranks, Schalck and Deputy Finance Minister Herta König devised a financial model that fudged the nation's finances to make the situation appear worse than it actually was. They hoped that by painting a dire picture, they could spur an increase in economic performance, particularly in the all-important area of exports to the West. Even if the model did not do this, Schalck and König believed that it would still ensure the nation's solvency by holding hard currency secretly in reserve.

This new Schalck/König model relied on one simple trick—altering interest rates. During the GDR's most dire months on the brink of bankruptcy in 1982, it had been forced to borrow money on a short-term basis at a very high rate of interest.[5] After the loans of 1983 and 1984, however, the GDR was once again able to get long-term loans from Western banks at lower interest rates. The Schalck/König trick was simply to pretend that the loans had done nothing to lower the GDR's borrowing costs. Then, when Gerhard Schürer, director of the State Planning Commission, went through his annual process of devising the national economic plan, he would calculate the national debt based on the inflated interest rates provided by Schalck and König. From this one change, two vastly different pictures of the GDR economy emerged: one from Schürer and the other from Schalck and König.[6]

If knowledge is power, then the Schalck/König model significantly concentrated power in the German Democratic Republic. Because the model created a small circle of people with an accurate view of the economic situation—in the mid-1980s, likely only Honecker, Mittag, Schalck, König, and the Stasi head, Erich Mielke—it delegitimized any criticism of the economic situation from outside this small circle. Each year for the rest of the decade, Schürer and the planning commission produced the same wildly optimistic plans for exports and imports in order to make the debt recede on paper. And each year, when the numbers inevitably failed to materialize, Schalck and KoKo would step in with roughly 2 billion valutamarks from the secret KoKo accounts to cover the remaining balance.[7] With no sense of the real economic situation and, for the moment, no real threat of insolvency if performance targets were not met, the East German *nomenklatura* resisted fundamental change, and Honecker refrained from applying pressure for reform.

As it ate away at the internal workings of the East German state, this false sense of security also fueled Honecker's resistance to Gorbachev's perestroika and glasnost in the Soviet Union. The content of Honecker's criticism of Gorbachev's reforms was both practical and ideological. Practically, Honecker believed—and indeed rightly foresaw—that Gorbachev's attempt to modernize the Soviet economy would lead to significant shortages in the domestic supply of food and consumer goods.[8] Ideologically, the implications of the politics of breaking promises that underlay perestroika contradicted everything Honecker had been building under his hallmark initiative, the Unity of Economic and Social Policy, since the early 1970s.

Underlying Honecker's criticism was a confidence grounded in his sense that the East German economy suffered from none of the ills hurting the Soviet Union. In his view, economic problems did not exist in the GDR, and even if they did, any attempt to solve them would incite social unrest and damage the legitimacy of the SED. As long as he had the Schalck/König model's assurances of solvency, he could afford to avoid the political risks associated with the reforms taking place in the Soviet Union, Poland, and Hungary.

◆ ◆ ◆

Although the Schalck/König model's interest rate trickery gave the East German economy a great deal of leeway in meeting its performance targets, it still relied on the achievement of one very hard economic fact: a significant annual export surplus. If the East German economy failed to produce more than it consumed, no amount of accounting deception would save it from eventual insolvency. After the crisis years of 1980–1983, the country's Western trade performance had not met the aggressive targets set by the State Planning Commission, but trade surpluses had comfortably been achieved, going from VM 647 million in 1981 to VM 4.94 billion in 1985.[9]

Then the price of oil collapsed on world markets in the last two months of 1985. By that time, mineral oil refined from subsidized Soviet crude oil was the GDR's most important export to the West, so the collapse in energy prices was particularly damaging to East Berlin. In 1985, the GDR earned VM 2.5 billion from its mineral oil exports to the West, but that number dropped to 1 billion in 1986 and 900 million in 1987.[10]

The oil price collapse quickly changed Schalck's tune regarding the airtight assurances of national solvency he had been presenting in the Schalck/König model. Before the price collapse, in mid-September 1985, he and König presented a confident update of their model to Mittag. The nation, they assured their boss, would still be solvent at the end of the decade.[11] By March 1986, they were far more uncertain. Rather than assuming a VM 4 billion annual trade surplus, as they had the previous year, they were now forced to assume an annual trade surplus of VM 1.2–2 billion. As they wrote, "Compared to projections submitted earlier there is a significant deterioration." Instead of declining by 1990, the national debt would grow by VM 4.4 billion to VM 31.6 billion. Such a development would leave the country open to the volatility of international capital markets, and one external shock from an unforeseen event might cause Western banks to stop lending to the GDR. Therefore, they believed a dramatic change in the country's economic performance was now necessary. If the rise in the debt was to be prevented, it was "essential" that "exports to the West receive a different status in the material distribution of the economy."[12]

Since the early 1970s, Eastern Bloc states had been trying unsuccessfully to produce globally competitive goods by importing Western technology. So far, it had failed in every country in which it had been tried, including the GDR. But with the leadership unwilling to consider cutbacks in East German living standards as a means of balancing the nation's books, growing the economy out of its debt problem was left as the only option. Therefore, in a series of Politburo meetings in May and June 1986, the leadership decided to make another attempt at importing Western technology on credit. The East German microelectronics and computing industry would be one of the biggest recipients of these investments. As Silicon Valley began its ascent in the United States in the 1980s, the GDR leadership—and Mittag, in particular—believed the country could be the Silicon Valley of the socialist world.[13]

It fell to Schalck and Schürer to figure out exactly how to make this happen. Because KoKo maintained large hard currency deposits and good relations with Western banks, Schlack proposed that it take out the loans independently from the East German state. The imports, Schalck wrote the leadership, would "be provided to companies as interest-free credits" and would not "burden the balance of payments from 1986–1990."[14] Of course, KoKo would have to repay the loans at some point in the future, so the East German state would eventually have to pay them off. Under Schalck's plan, the day of reckoning would not come until 1991, giving the technological investments time to generate the hard currency required to pay off the debt. Ghosts of the failure of this strategy during the 1970s in Poland, Hungary, and the GDR itself haunted the proposal, but with nowhere else to turn, Mittag and Honecker authorized the plan. Export growth to the West was now the only way the GDR could survive.

◆　◆　◆

Instead, the trade balance worsened. The export surplus of VM 4.94 billion in 1985 fell back to VM 873 million in 1986 and turned to a VM 1.03 billion trade deficit in 1987.[15] That autumn, as the year-end trade deficit started to come into full view, Schalck and König realized for the first time that they could no longer ensure the solvency of the country over the coming years. Their model had always assumed at least a modest export surplus, and the falling export performance made it clear that this assumption was no longer tenable. They began to sound the alarm internally on impending insolvency. In October, they wrote to Mittag, "The inadequate development of internal economic productivity and efficiency, connected with an insufficient . . . reduction of imports has led to a constant growth in the debt of the GDR." Higher debt meant higher interest payments. They informed Mittag that "five to six billion Valutamarks are necessary just for interest payments" every year. "This is the price that our republic must pay every year for the anticipated national income of future years. At the same time, this means that any trade surplus below 5 billion VM will lead to a further increase in debt." They said they could "guarantee the solvency of the republic in 1990" but only if "the planned trade surplus is actually realized." "For the period after 1990," they noted, "it is a matter of life and death that the improved performance of our economy . . . lead to an export surplus of 5 billion VM." If this was not achieved, they told Mittag, "we see no possibility of securing the solvency of the republic in 1991."[16]

Schalck made his newfound alarm even clearer at a working group of the country's top economists and economic managers taking place the same week in October. "If the GDR does not achieve an export surplus in 1987," he told the group, "the creditworthiness of the country will be critically burdened." Schalck told his colleagues that the GDR's Eastern Bloc allies were already demonstrating in dramatic fashion that global capital markets no longer tolerated long periods of poor economic performance. "The example of Hungary, which for the past two years has not achieved a trade surplus, shows that the country's credit rating has severely deteriorated and it can only receive government-guaranteed loans." Because such loans came with conditions attached, Schalck concluded that "this way is not politically or financially viable for the GDR."[17] If the Hungarian experience showed the perils of trade deficits, the Polish experience showed the catastrophic consequences of insolvency. Schalck later recalled, "[General] Jaruzelski . . . conveyed to me very clearly that a state which is insolvent loses and must lose its political power, and therefore its maneuverability. It can then govern only through bayonets [and] martial law; Jaruzelski . . . did this, but without success."[18]

The KoKo chief's transformation from a beacon of reassurance to a prophet of doom in fall 1987 was an important development. Because he, König, and Mittag had done such a masterful job hiding an accurate picture of the country's finances from both domestic and international audiences, there were very few people, either within the GDR or outside of it, that could issue a credible warning to Erich Honecker about the country's approaching crisis. Schalck was one of the few who could, and after October 1987, he began to regularly warn that the country faced insolvency in the years to come. The illusions of security that his Schalck/König model had provided Mittag and Honecker from 1983 to 1987 were gone. Any continued resistance to beginning a process of economic reform now rested not on confidence in the nation's long-term solvency but instead on fear of the political instability reform would bring.

◆ ◆ ◆

Gerhard Schürer may not have known the country's complete financial picture, but by spring 1988, he could see the writing on the wall. This caused him to break his silence. In preparation for a Politburo meeting in early May, he composed a proposal to fundamentally change the country's economic direction. "Our conclusion must be," he wrote, that "each object, no matter how important it is," must be confronted with "the harsh economic conditions of the world market." The head of the State Planning Commission foresaw no way that his institution would be able to repay Schalck for the recent hard currency loans because he foresaw no way that East German industries would be able to produce globally competitive exports.

Schürer saw only one remaining option to ensure the country's solvency—austerity. Although he believed in the state's mission to provide the working class with a high quality of life, he recognized that "the benefits for the population from the state budget for housing, price supports, fares, education, health, culture, sports and recreation" were far outstripping the country's ability to pay for them. Schürer believed the party could no longer afford to insulate the population from the discipline of the world market.[19] In sending the document directly to Honecker, Schürer later recalled, he wanted to make it clear: "Our republic is going broke."[20]

Schürer's proposal was the most direct challenge to the Unity of Economic and Social Policy—and, by extension, Honecker's leadership—since its implementation in the early 1970s. Honecker forwarded it to Mittag and asked him to formulate a response for discussion in the Politburo. Mittag went straight to the point. Schürer's proposal would "call into question . . . the Unity of Economic and Social Policy," and his "suggestions for price changes" to consumer goods, rents, and energy were connected with issues of "significant mass appeal."[21] With regard to the recent attempt to borrow hard currency to improve the country's computer industry, Mittag held to the position that the only way out of the current impasse was export growth, which required investment in the latest technologies.[22] The choice between Schürer and Mittag boiled down to a difference of belief in the ability of the East German economy to compete on the world market. Schürer believed it could not. Mittag believed it had to. After the Politburo discussed the two positions, Honecker sided with Mittag and directed his comrades to find a way out of the crisis without implementing austerity.

The Politburo meeting began six months of fruitless discussions within the leadership about how to move forward. Despite the threat of looming insolvency, Honecker maintained the strict limits he had set on economic reform. Because the capitalist countries had high unemployment, growing poverty, and deteriorating living conditions for the working class, Honecker believed the generous East German social system was "very advantageous" and needed to be maintained. "We must always keep the improvement of the workplace and living conditions of the workers in mind," he said. It naturally followed that consumer prices should not be increased. The general secretary believed recent events in Poland, where the government's 1988 price increases had spawned widespread strikes, confirmed his point of view. He told his comrades, "Countries where price spirals were set in motion find themselves in a deep crisis. Comrade Jaruzelski told [me] that his decision to increase prices was wrong and that they are now looking at other options."[23]

Thus, by September, Honecker could at once declare that "the decisive issue" was "the problem of ensuring the solvency of the GDR" while also pointing to its neighbors as evidence that price increases and austerity measures were not viable solutions.[24] He concluded, "All countries that have begun the price-wage spiral have then gone bankrupt, see Poland [and] Hungary—in Czechoslovakia, the same thing looms." The GDR could not "go the Romanian way" of imposing draconian austerity, Honecker said, because "the situation with the FRG [Federal Republic of Germany] does not allow for it." As long as West Germany remained an economic and consumerist juggernaut, the GDR could not break its promises to East German citizens.[25] Politburo member Harry Tisch summed up the nature of the country's economic problems with precision: "Our people want social security, safety, job security, and education from us and the department stores of the FRG."[26] Through the end of 1988, the leadership chose not to discipline those desires, and the debt to the West continued to grow.

Schürer sensed that the situation was growing dire. In February 1989, he approached Egon Krenz, heir apparent to Honecker, about over-throwing the general secretary on the grounds that he had run the country into financial ruin. "A reduction in the debt is impossible" with Honecker leading the country, Schürer told him. But not yet feeling a sense of dire urgency, Krenz declined to remove his boss.[27] He too could not contemplate imposing austerity. "For me it is no question whether the Unity of Economic and Social Policy will continue," Krenz said. "It must be continued, because it is socialism in the GDR!"[28]

If the experience of Poland and Hungary demonstrated that price increases and austerity measures were unpopular, it also showed that communist leaders avoided implementing austerity until they had no other choice. With its creditworthiness still intact and its borders still secure through the spring of 1989, the East German leadership still had choices, so it collectively chose short-term stability over long-term solvency. Events along the Hungarian border would soon change these choices, but the priorities of the East German leaders remained unchanged until the end: they would choose any path—including even opening the Berlin Wall—if it allowed them to avoid the implementation of austerity.

◆ ◆ ◆

By the late 1980s, the border fortifications separating Hungary from Austria and the broader West had become dilapidated. The electronic signaling system along the border, meant to alert the guards to any attempted crossing, regularly sounded false alarms due to gusts of wind or wild animals. It needed to be modernized. In the fall of 1987, the head of the border guard wrote a report for the Hungarian Interior Ministry detailing the system's failings and annual cost, as well as estimating the costs of a system renovation. In a country with an annual budget deficit of 30 to 60 billion forints, the report's numbers detailed an unwelcome prospect: the annual cost of the system was 42–50 million forints, and a renovation would cost 1.2 to 1.5 million forints per kilometer along a 366-kilometer border.[29]

As we have seen, when Miklós Németh became Hungarian prime minister in the fall of 1988, dealing with the pressures of IMF-mandated austerity was his first order of business. As Németh went through the country's books line by line, he looked for areas to cut. When he came across the line item detailing the annual cost of the border security system, he "unceremoniously" drew a line through it. Andreas Oplatka has written, "Today, looking back on the success of the border opening, it would no doubt be easy and tempting for Németh to say that he made his decision" as a reform politician "thinking in European dimensions." But "the former prime minister openly and frankly says the opposite. He admits that at the time it was all about cost savings."[30] Németh still needed the rest of the leadership's approval for this decision, so in February 1989, he went to the Politburo with a report detailing the costs of modernizing the border security system. As Oplatka has concluded, this "financial factor was particularly convincing." After hearing of it, "no one opposed the dismantling."[31]

Having gained the assent of the party, Németh moved on to seek the next level of authorization in the Eastern Bloc's chain of command: the Kremlin. On March 3, 1989, he arrived for his first visit with Mikhail Gorbachev. The two leaders touched on many subjects, ranging from the status of Soviet troops in Hungary to the merits of a multiparty democratic system to the challenges of Hungarian economic reform. Eventually, Németh broached the issue of border security: "We have decided to gradually do away with the electronic signaling system between now and January 1, 1991." Gorbachev hesitated and then responded, "I see, frankly, no problem."[32] Surprised at the ease of the acquiescence, Németh returned to Budapest resolute in his decision to move forward with the dismantling of the border fence.

Initially, dismantling the fence drew little public attention. It gained increasing notice, however, after the Hungarian and Austrian foreign ministers, Gyula Horn and Alois Mock, held a symbolic wire-cutting ceremony before TV cameras and newspaper reporters on June 27. Immediately the image of the two foreign ministers was published across Western Europe and thus beamed into East Germany through West German television. East German citizens began to travel to Hungary in the hope they would be allowed to cross the Austrian border.[33] Many holed up in the West German embassy in Budapest (and to a lesser extent in Prague and Warsaw), believing that the West German government would eventually pay the GDR for their release to the West, as it had done many times before for East German political prisoners stuck in East German jails. By July, the Exit had begun.

In August, local civil society groups in the town of Sopron along the Austrian border began organizing what would eventually be billed as the

"Pan-European Picnic." Set for August 19, the picnic would celebrate Hungarians' new freedom of travel by allowing residents to freely cross the border into Austria for three hours during the afternoon. Hearing of the plan and sensing political opportunity, Imre Pozsgay worked with Austrian royal Otto von Hapsburg to raise the plan's profile as an international symbol of European détente. In the run-up to the picnic, Németh nervously endorsed the event as a means of testing how the Soviet Union would react to a complete, if temporary, opening of the border. On the afternoon of August 19, roughly 2,000 people crossed the border under the picnic plan, while around 600 East Germans used the temporary opening to flee across the border. In the days to come, both became global news, a sign of the evaporating barriers between East and West.[34]

Against the backdrop of a worsening economic situation, this event put further pressure on Németh to permanently solve the refugee problem. In retrospect, he concluded that he spent the summer of 1989 consumed with the country's struggle "to remain solvent." Hungary "could not avoid price increases and austerity measures," he remembered. "We had to comply with the tough conditions of the IMF, which we were not able to do despite our best efforts."[35] These pressures forced Németh to view the East German refugee problem through the lens of his own country's economic future.

The flood of East German refugees who followed in the wake of the picnic spurred Németh to a final decision. The choice was between either sending the refugees back or opening the Austrian border for all East Germans to cross freely. The prime minister began by weighing his country's commercial relationship to the two Germanys. He asked his team if there was any economic damage the GDR could inflict on Hungary if he acted against East German interests. They came up with nothing.[36] In contrast, the economic benefits of a good relationship with Bonn were obvious— the Kohl government held the keys to Hungary's fortunes in Western Europe and, along with the United States, determined the country's fate in the IMF. This was enough to convince Németh. On August 22, he confirmed his decision to open the border to Austria with the highest ranks of the leadership and immediately requested an emergency secret meeting with Kohl to inform him.

On August 25, Németh and his closest advisors departed for Bonn under the utmost secrecy. When they landed, they boarded a helicopter to fly to Gymnich Castle outside of Cologne, where Kohl and West German foreign minister Hans-Dietrich Genscher secretly waited. After a discussion of the precarious Hungarian economic situation, Németh announced that the Hungarian government had decided to open its border to Austria for East Germans. Kohl, with "tears in his eyes," thanked the prime minister for his decision and asked what kind of financial compensation he wanted in return. Németh proudly responded, "We do not sell people." This was an allusion to the mercenary Romanian and East German practice of selling the emigration of their dissident, German, and Jewish populations to West Germany in exchange for a substantial amount of hard currency. Németh, at least officially, wanted no part of such a practice. Instead, he asked for Kohl's assistance in bringing Hungary closer to the European Community. Kohl readily agreed and added that the Federal Republic would compensate Hungary for any retaliation carried out by its socialist "brother countries."[37] The meeting concluded with both sides agreeing to work together to coordinate the logistics and timing of the border opening. On September 10, the Hungarian government opened the border to the 7,000 East Germans now waiting to leave for the West.[38] According to one Hungarian estimate, 600,000 East Germans followed suit in the weeks to come.[39]

If there was no quid pro quo in fact, there was certainly one in perception. In the weeks after their meeting, the Kohl government granted the Hungarians a DM 500 million loan in support of "a reform process of pan-European importance" and in recognition of the Hungarian decision "against closed borders, and for the free movement of all citizens."[40] The Hungarians delayed signing the loan until mid-December to perpetuate the appearance of independence, but it fooled nobody. In a meeting on October 7, Honecker and Gorbachev discussed the loan and lamented Hungary's betrayal of socialism in exchange for money. Gorbachev folded the news into a broader explanation of the disintegration of the Socialist Bloc going on around them: "The West promises great gifts of grace [Gnadengeschenke] in exchange for renouncing positions."[41]

Why did the Hungarian government decide to dismantle the Iron Curtain and open its border for East Germans? Among the many reasons is that its leadership had lost the ideological conviction to defend the GDR's repressive brand of socialism. As prime minister, Németh had to think in terms of the Hungarian national interest, and the financial power of the West and the economic weakness of the East significantly shaped his choice. In the broadest sense, Németh and his closest advisors believed the country's future lay in Western Europe. They had been trying to establish ties with the European Community for almost a decade, and they now hoped to gain access to the European Economic Community and the future European Common Market. The West German government would ultimately decide whether and when this happened. Kohl did not even have to mention the retaliatory power he could wield if the Hungarians chose to send the refugees back to East Germany. The fate of the Hungarian economy, and with it the political fortunes of Németh and all the reform communists, depended on the good graces and financial power of Bonn. This broader financial context pushed the Hungarian government to permanently open the Exit option.

◆   ◆   ◆

At the Warsaw Pact's summit in Bucharest, Romania, in early July 1989, Gorbachev publicly renounced the Brezhnev Doctrine.[42] Although this only made public what he had been telling his Eastern Bloc allies in private since 1986, its official enshrinement arrived to the great consternation of Honecker and Krenz. Adding injury to insult, Honecker fell ill at the conference and had to fly home early for medical treatment. Although his condition initially stabilized, the general secretary was forced to have surgery in mid-August and take a leave of absence until the end of September.

Honecker's illness paralyzed the East German leadership's response to its deteriorating domestic and international circumstances. The week after Hungary opened its border, the GDR worked with the Czechoslovak government to end East German travel to Hungary all together. But the Exit movement was now in full bloom, and emigrants continued to leave undeterred. Instead of traveling all the way to Hungary, they now simply stopped in the West German embassy in Prague, where thousands were camped out in miserable conditions by the end of September. As Honecker finally returned to work at the end of the month, he agreed to strike a deal with the West German government. He would "expel" the East Germans in the Prague embassy from the GDR (thus retaining nominal control over who got to leave the country) while also allowing them to travel to the West. From September 30 to October 1, the refugees traveled by night on trains from Prague through the GDR to the Federal Republic. On October 3, Honecker made a last-gasp attempt to shut down the Exit option by completely closing the GDR's borders.

This decision only served to enrage the domestic protest movement now gaining steam. Since the spring of 1989, a small group of dissidents had been using the peace prayer service held in the Nikolai Church in downtown Leipzig every Monday to organize protests against the regime. By September 18, hundreds of Leipzig residents had joined in, and the next week, the protesters began to take to the streets and call for reform. On October 2, roughly 10,000 people set out to march around the city's ring road, and security forces dispersed the crowd with clubs, dogs, and shields. As the trains carrying a last group of refugees from Prague rolled into the Dresden train station on October 4, an estimated 20,000 protestors surrounded the station and blocked the tracks until police forcibly dispersed them. Then, in the days leading up to the SED's celebration of the fortieth anniversary of the GDR on October 7, countless protests in cities throughout the country were put down with force.

The increasing boldness of the protests and the state's harsh response set the stage for the climactic protest in Leipzig on October 9. Since June, when Deng Xiaoping and the Chinese leadership had ordered security forces to shoot protesters in Tiananmen Square, it had been an open question among East German citizens and foreign observers whether Honecker and the SED leadership would do the same in the GDR. Why the East German leadership did not choose Violence owes to a complex interplay among domestic and international factors.

The country's precarious financial position played a key role. Schalck had been keeping Krenz informed about the real state of the country's financial situation for many years before 1989.[43] Honecker had been grooming Krenz since the 1970s to be his successor, and given Honecker's advanced age, it made sense to keep Krenz informed. It is thus very likely that a memo in Schalck's papers dated September 18, 1989, was seen by Krenz as well as Mittag and Mielke.

The document—and the myriad unrecorded and informal conversations Schalck surely had with leading officials at the time—laid out in significant detail the GDR's financial dependence on the capitalist West and suggested how it affected the country's political sovereignty. Schalck stated that in contrast to the previous year's urgent demands for a trade surplus in 1989, the country would, in fact, run a VM 2.5 billion deficit. Despite this horrific economic performance, Schalck and his team had successfully prevented capitalist banks from questioning the GDR's creditworthiness by refusing to publish information on the nation's financial position. But the continued flow of capital, Schalck now wrote, hung by a thread.

The country's solvency now depended on whether the "annual borrowing of 8–10 billion VM can actually be secured," he wrote. "Such a credit volume is an extraordinarily large sum for a country like the GDR, which means we are highly dependent on capitalist banks to maintain our solvency." He continued, "The particularly high risk of dependence lies in the finance credits that are indispensable for us. Maturing principal and interest payments can only be made through finance credits." Like the Hungarians in 1987, Schalck now told the leadership that the country's solvency depended on the continued inflow of Japanese capital. "Currently more than 75 percent of finance credits come from Japanese banks. Should the Japanese government no longer allow the further granting of loans, for example, if the United States blackmails the Japanese government due to its credit boycott policy, there is no way to cover the shortfall in loans through banks in other countries." Beyond American blackmail, Schalck explained that there were other factors that would influence the readiness of capitalist banks to keep lending money to the GDR. These included "the impact of political factors on the lending willingness of capitalist banks, and the position of the governments of countries such as Japan and the FRG, which has a signaling effect on banks in other countries."[44]

It is impossible to know precisely how this memo affected the leadership (which, at this point, was still without Honecker due to his leave of absence), but it is clear that discussion of the financial situation continued as the protests grew in the streets. Ten days after Schalck's memo, on September 28, all the leading economic state officials—Schalck, Schürer, König, Minister of Foreign Trade Gerhard Beil, and President of the State Bank Werner Polze—composed another extended memo examining the nation's financial position. Sounding the alarm, they noted that "we already are significantly dependent on capitalist banks to meet our payment obligations of principal and interest as well as to implement our yearly import plan." The "extraordinarily high sum" of VM 8–10 billion needed to "be mobilized annually from approximately 400 banks at any one time." This mobilization was growing increasingly difficult because "capitalist banks set country limits for their credit orientation toward socialist countries, just as they do for developing countries. Due to the already high debt, banks are not willing to significantly increase this limit for the GDR." The GDR's access to credit markets in the years to come, the authors warned, was "largely dependent" on "the impact of political factors on the lending willingness of capitalist banks and the positions of the governments of countries such as Japan and the FRG, which are among the most important creditors of the GDR." Even if the country managed to keep the markets' favor, it would still need to double its exports in the next five years while holding imports constant. Such export growth would have been unprecedented in the history of the GDR.

Nevertheless, any deviation from these surpluses would certainly lead the country into insolvency, the authors warned, which would have dire consequences. "Assuring the solvency of the Republic without conditions is the crucial prerequisite for the political stability of the GDR and further economic development." This was because "failure to meet upcoming repayment obligations on loans or untimely payment of interest would lead to the total cessation of credit granted by capitalist banks. With this, no more loans would be available for the GDR's imports." Just as Schalck had drawn lessons from Hungary's example two years earlier, the economists now urged the leadership to look to Poland to see the disastrous results of failing to maintain solvency. "Poland," they wrote, "has received no new loans from capitalist banks since its cession of payments in 1981." The Polish example showed that the world of finance had become more demanding of debtors. Debt rescheduling agreements with few or no conditions attached "no longer exist," the economists wrote. "For years now, debt rescheduling agreements with capitalist banks have only been concluded with the involvement of the IMF."

East German leaders saw the IMF as an organization hell-bent on dismantling socialism. The economists believed the history of socialist countries' relationship with the IMF in the 1980s only provided new, disturbing evidence to support their conviction. They wrote, "The prerequisite for a possible debt restructuring is the fulfillment of conditions that have been issued by the IMF." From the experience of other socialist countries, it was clear these conditions would include: "the renunciation of the state's right to intervene in the economy (example of Poland); the reduction of subsidies with the intention to abolish them (examples Poland, Yugoslavia, and Hungary); [and] the liberalization of imports from Western countries, that is, the renunciation of the state's ability to determine its import policy." In other words, dealing with the IMF would mean the forced repeal of socialism. This led the group to one overarching conclusion: "Therefore, the issue of assuring the solvency of the Republic is to be granted the highest political and economic priority."

Here, just as in Hungary and Poland, the coercion of creditworthiness was at work. The economists proposed the government adopt unpopular domestic policies that would invite social unrest in order to maintain the country's international creditworthiness. The current financial situation made the following policies "necessary," they wrote: "a systematic change in the basic proportions between accumulation and consumption . . . ; a reduction of societal consumption—and if that is not enough—also individual consumption; and the development of industrial export sectors, including the redistribution of labor for the benefit of . . . export-critical branches within industries."[45] Put simply, maintaining solvency would require the hallmarks of the politics of breaking promises—price increases, cutbacks in social benefits, and labor mobility—as well as the continued support of the country's Western creditors.

Schalck reiterated this last point in a memo to Krenz four days after the October 9 protest in Leipzig. Although the memo was written after that fateful day, it almost certainly put ideas already floating through the two men's minds on paper rather than proposed something completely new. "The attitude of the FRG government and the business circles of [the] Federal Republic influence the attitude of the other states and Japan toward the GDR to a large degree," Schalck wrote. We must take "the political and economic influence of the FRG, especially in the European Community and also in relation to financial circles and credit markets outside Europe very much into account."[46] Thus, if it was not written plainly on a document to be found in the archives, it was certainly plain for Egon Krenz to see that if he chose to use violence against protesters in Leipzig or elsewhere, the country would soon be insolvent. Insolvency clearly meant one thing: a repeat of the Polish experience in the 1980s, a prospect no one in the leadership, particularly Krenz, welcomed.

What Krenz, rather than Honecker, believed in the early days of October is important because by October 9 the overthrow of Honecker had been set in motion. Honecker held on to power long enough to celebrate his country's fortieth birthday on October 7. But by the next day, the plot to bring him down had finally begun to take shape.[47] Honecker issued orders to all local leaders and security forces to prepare "measures" to prevent future "riots" "from the outset."[48] But when decision time came the following day in Leipzig to put down the protest or let it go on, the party's acting leader there, Helmut Hackenberg, called Krenz, not Honecker, because he had already heard that Krenz had begun planning Honecker's overthrow.[49]

Neither the country's financial weakness nor Krenz's scheming against Honecker were known to the East Germans who gathered that day. To them, the East German state remained a mass of repressive instruments that could be and would be used against citizens who spoke out in dissent. This did not stop roughly 70,000 of them from gathering outside Nikolai Church after the Monday peace prayers and bravely circling the ring road that surrounded the city center. The ring road had become the weekly battleground between protesters and the security forces. As the protesters began to make their way around, Hackenberg made his call to Krenz to report that the protest was far larger than anyone had predicted and ask what he should do. Krenz told him he would call him back. According to accounts of personnel at the scene, it took him a half hour or forty-five minutes to call back, by which time Hackenberg had individually decided not to disperse the protesters without a firm order from East Berlin—and Krenz, in particular. The next morning, the consequences of the previous evening were clear: the protest immediately became a symbol of the growing power of the people in the GDR, who had lost their fear of the state's power of repression.[50]

In taking so long to call back, Krenz ultimately did not decide how events unfolded that night, but a more decisive leader would have. The reasons for his hesitance in calling back are unclear, but the reasons for his hesitance to use violence were manifold. He has always claimed to have had a deep personal conviction to not use force, and Gerhard Schürer confirms this conviction in his memoirs.[51] In addition, by the fall of 1989, Gorbachev had made his support for nonviolence well known and had officially renounced any Soviet willingness to intervene in allied countries to defend socialism.[52] The country's international financial position added yet another reason for restraint. If the leadership had implemented a "Chinese solution," they well understood that national insolvency, the politics of breaking promises, and the Polish experience would follow. They stopped short of Violence, then, because they feared Austerity.

❖ ❖ ❖

Krenz's official move against Honecker came at the Politburo meeting on October 17.[53] The next day, at a meeting of the broader SED Central Committee, Honecker announced his resignation due to "health reasons" and asked the committee to elect Krenz as the new general secretary. Upon his official election, Krenz gave a speech defining the direction

he intended for the country. He announced what he called "the Turn"—
die Wende. As he launched his *Wende*, Krenz clearly felt constrained
by the nation's economic and financial circumstances. On the day the
Berlin Wall opened, he told the Central Committee, "The balance of
payments . . . puts limits on us; it prevents us from making political decisions that would be necessary." He continued, "Every day new facts become
apparent that affect our economic situation. And without the economy
nothing else works."[54]

To solve the country's economic problems, Krenz turned to the problem
of Exit. Even before he had officially overthrown Honecker, Krenz had
developed a draft of new travel regulations to allow East Germans to travel
to the West and asked Schalck to review it for its financial implications.
Schalck responded on October 13 with a proposal to essentially trade the
controlled opening of the Berlin Wall for hard currency. "The decisions
and principles laid out in the draft are of seminal importance in order to
continue socialist development in the GDR and improve the attractive-
ness of our society. At the present time, we see no other solutions," Schalck
noted. Furthermore, he told Krenz, the government should expect "a significant pent-up demand in East German travel to the West, particularly
to the FRG but especially also to West Berlin." Schalck assumed at least
five million East German citizens would want to travel to West Germany
in the first year and a further five million would want to travel to West
Berlin. All of this would cost the East German state money it did not
have—DM 300 million in the first year, according to Schalck's calculations. "Immediately after a decision on and before the publication of the
regulations, I think it would be absolutely appropriate to obtain through
informal talks a reasonable financial contribution from the FRG government to enable this policy, which the FRG has sought for a long time," he
wrote. Schalck envisioned a lump-sum contribution of DM 300–500 million from the FRG to fund East German travel. He believed this would
solve the immediate travel problem; the government could then return to
the travel issue in the mid-1990s, presumably after solving its looming
debt problems. He concluded, "At a later date (possibly the middle of the
1990s) we should examine to what extent opportunities exist to provide
GDR citizens an amount in foreign currency every three years . . . for traveling abroad in the West."[55] Krenz held a meeting with the rest of the leadership on October 16 to discuss the travel question, and the group adopted
Schalck's strategy.

In pursuit of this objective, Krenz sent Schalck to Bonn on October 24 to open "informal discussions" with the FRG about new forms of cooperation. Schalck later wrote, "For the past two to three years, it was clear to me that the GDR was headed toward an economic confederation with the FRG. Only with West German financial power could the GDR be preserved. I certainly knew better than most of my comrades that the economic and financial support would come at the price of significant political changes." As he left for Bonn, he wrote, "I still hoped that the price would not be self-sacrifice."[56] He described his orders from Krenz for the negotiations: "I should explore the possibility of closer economic cooperation, while upholding [the GDR's] socialist system. Meanwhile, it was clear that travel would be unlimited—it was only a matter of time. I thought pragmatically of the costs associated with this for the GDR. New border crossings and an expansion of transit routes [would] increase the need for hard currency. I knew that we did not have the money for this. One had to get the Federal Republic to pay, through a packaged deal if necessary: money in exchange for expanded travel."[57]

Schalck's first meeting took place with Rudolf Seiters and Wolfgang Schäuble, senior ministers in the Kohl government. Schalck attempted to stand by his orders to increase cooperation while also upholding the GDR's socialist system. He told Seiters and Schäuble that it was "the firm intention" of the party leadership to implement "extensive renewals and reforms" through "a comprehensive dialogue with all levels of society." But, he maintained, "the socialist system of the GDR is not up for debate" and "the SED will continue to play the leading role . . . in the process of renewal." He then informed Seiters and Schäuble that the GDR would be implementing a new travel law that would dramatically expand the foreign travel of East German citizens, particularly to West Germany. In view of the "clear additional economic burdens" such a law would impose on the GDR, Schalck told Seiters that the two sides should find "shared solutions" to the problem. In sum, he said that the SED leadership foresaw the possibility of raising inter-German relations to "a new level" as long as it was based on "the principles of equality, regard for sovereignty, and non-intervention" in each other's internal affairs.

Seiters and Schäuble responded with questions and concerns of their own. First and foremost, they told Schalck that officials in the Federal Republic "observed with great attention and also with concern the economic development of the GDR in recent years." They were concerned "particularly about the effectiveness of the GDR economy and the growth in debt." Because any new forms of cooperation between the two states would require West German money, they would only be justifiable "from the standpoint of the Federal Republic if the GDR thought through important questions in its economic policy" and took decisions that increased "the efficiency in the economy." To the Kohl government, "it would be necessary, for example, to cut subsidies and take steps to ensure the international competitiveness of East German companies." Lastly, because they anticipated that East German travel laws would stress the capacities of West Berlin, both sides should explore "in what ways the interests of West Berlin" could be addressed "in other areas."[58] With the first hints of conditionality lingering in the air, the two sides parted ways to consult with their respective governments.

Krenz was furious upon reading Schalck's detailed report. To him, the intentions of the Kohl government were now obvious. As he wrote in his memoirs, "It is not about their 'brothers' and sisters'' freedom of movement at all. Bonn is not interested in whether or not East Germans can travel. Bonn wants everything; Bonn wants the GDR."[59]

Two days later, on October 26, Kohl and Krenz spoke for the first time by phone. After an exchange of greetings, Kohl said he had high hopes for Krenz's announced *Wende*. In particular, he told the general secretary that he believed resolving three issues was "especially important": a new law on the freedom to travel, an amnesty for political prisoners arrested during the recent demonstrations, and "a positive solution" to the question of refugees. "If one can connect your name with a generous step," Kohl said, "it will not only have a very considerable effect here [in the FRG], but also in the GDR." This was politely veiled conditionality, and Krenz saw it for was it was. He replied, "A turn [*Wende*] does not mean upheaval [*Umbruch*]." He informed Kohl that the SED leadership had made the decision "under the complete sovereignty of our country" to implement a new travel law. However, the law would bring "considerable additional economic burdens" with it for the GDR, which he hoped the FRG could cover. He pressed Kohl for the earliest possible agreement on financing the law, but the chancellor refused to discuss any specifics or make a clear declaration of financial support. Instead, he played for time and committed to making Seiters and Schäuble available for further discussions.[60]

Schalck, who sat next to Krenz during his conversation with Kohl, wrote in his memoirs that "something decisive happened during this phone call." He wrote, "Up to that point, the Federal Republic had simply followed the events in the GDR attentively, [but] now Kohl presented demands for the first time"—new rules for the freedom of travel in East Germany, an amnesty for political prisoners, and a positive resolution to the embassy refugee crisis.[61] "That, and not November 9 [when the Wall fell], was for me the key situation. That was the *Wende*. On the same day we came up with a package of measures to implement the points raised by Kohl. From that moment on, the Federal Republic ruled the GDR."[62] In the days that followed, the Interior Ministry and the Stasi began drafting the new travel law.[63]

A key component of Krenz's *Wende* was to make the real economic situation of the country clear to the full Politburo and Central Committee. In late October he tasked Schürer, Schalck, and the other economic leaders with writing a comprehensive report on the economy for discussion at the Politburo meeting on October 31. The report, "An Analysis of the Economic Situation of the GDR with Conclusions," served as a stinging indictment of Honecker's Unity of Economic and Social Policy and an urgent call for change. "The debt to the West has grown since the 8th Party Congress [when the Unity policy had been announced] to such a level that it calls into question the solvency of the GDR." Higher domestic consumption than domestic production had caused "debt to the West to grow from 2 billion VM in 1970 to 49 billion VM in 1989."[64]

The economists made plain that the debt now left the country completely dependent on Western capital. In their words, "1989's planned hard currency income can only cover about 35% of the hard currency payments. . . . 65% of the payments must be financed through bank credits and other sources." For a country like the GDR, this was unusual and precarious. They continued, "In the analysis of a country's creditworthiness it is internationally assumed that the debt service ratio . . . should not be more than 25%. 75% of [the money received from] exports should be available to pay for imports and other expenses. Based on its hard currency exports, the GDR has a debt service ratio of 150%." They outlined the implications of this position for the domestic economy. "If we are to prevent the debt from rising in 1990, . . . [it] would require a reduction in consumption by 25–30%." An export surplus of VM 2 billion would have to be achieved in 1990, and this number would have to grow to VM 11.3 billion in 1995 merely to keep the debt level stable.[65]

If this did not happen, the economists told the Politburo, the penalties would be stiff. "The consequences of imminent insolvency would be a moratorium (debt restructuring), in which the International Monetary Fund would determine what must happen in the GDR," they concluded. The IMF would "demand that the state renounce its right to intervene in the economy, the re-privatization of companies, the restriction of subsidies with the aim of abolishing them entirely, [and] the renunciation of the state['s right] to determine import policy. It is necessary to do everything to avoid going down this path."[66]

What did they propose for the years ahead? "The basic task of the new economic policy lies in bringing output and consumption back into agreement." The country could "only consume domestically what is available after the deduction of the necessary export surpluses." Furthermore, wage increases would need to be connected to higher performance, prices would need to be raised and subsidies would need to be cut, and the planning and administrative mechanisms of the state would need to be reduced at all levels. The politics of breaking promises lay ahead.[67]

To soften the burden of breaking promises, they proposed the government look for ways to expand cooperation with as many Western countries and companies as possible: "It is essential for the assurance of solvency in 1991 to negotiate with the government of the FRG at the appropriate time about 2–3 billion VM in finance credits above current credit lines." They ruled out "any idea of reunification with the Federal Republic or the creation of a confederation." But they also recommended that the SED make clear to the FRG that "conditions could be created" in the years to come that would make "the currently existing form of borders between both German states superfluous."[68] This last line was struck from the version published after the Politburo meeting because of its political sensitivity, but its erasure did not eliminate the fact that leading state officials were now considering ransoming the opening of the Berlin Wall for loans from West Germany in order to extend the GDR's existence.[69]

Krenz recalled his reaction to the document: "The biggest problem of the analysis for me is the debt to capitalist countries." He noted the particular challenge this posed to the GDR: "Is that state bankruptcy? Not at all. A state does not go bankrupt if it has debts. Otherwise the majority of the countries in the world would have to perish or would have perished long ago. Our problem is that we have debts to a political adversary who is working towards the liquidation of the GDR. This is the real danger." The looming 25–30 percent reduction in consumption convinced him of the proposal's urgency. He stated, "With their warning about the 'un-governability of the GDR', the authors of the document emphasize just how existentially necessary it is for the GDR [to implement] a fundamental change in its economic policies." The SED needed to implement this transformation because the authors made clear that it was necessary "to exclude the dictates of the International Monetary Fund from the GDR." He also noted that the economic analysis was "connected with far-reaching political conclusions," most importantly the suggestion that the current borders between the two German states could be slowly dismantled. Such a change would clearly require the consent of the Soviet Union, Krenz wrote, but he nevertheless believed the "Analysis" should be put to the Politburo unaltered on October 31 for discussion.[70]

In times of crisis, it had been a forty-year tradition for the leader of the GDR to seek refuge in Moscow's protection. Krenz was no different, and so, on November 1, he flew to the Soviet capital for his first meeting with Gorbachev. He believed Soviet economic, rather than military, support was the key to his country's survival. "If we are unable to raise the necessary economic cooperation with the Soviet Union to a higher level, the renewal of our society will remain a dream," he wrote. Packing Schalck's and Schürer's "Analysis" in his briefcase, he knew it would "be a crucial point of [his] talks in Moscow."[71]

Gorbachev had long been urging the SED, and particularly Honecker, to undertake political and economic reforms, but with Krenz now in power, the merits of reform were a settled issue. Instead, the issue at the heart of the November 1 meeting was resources, specifically whether the Soviet Union could increase its economic support to its most important ally in its time of greatest need. Krenz quickly steered the conversation to his first priority—the economy. It was, for him, "the decisive problem."[72] He told Gorbachev that by the end of 1989, East Germany's debt would reach $26.5 billion, or VM 49 billion; he also said that the country would have $5.9 billion in income in 1989 with which to pay $18 billion for debt service and imports. This would leave the GDR with a $12.1 billion shortfall, which meant the GDR would have to take out new loans from Western banks and governments.[73] Krenz said, "Our job is to maintain solvency. If the International Monetary Fund gets a say in [our affairs], it will be bad for us."[74] Through a variety of sources, Gorbachev was well briefed on the state of the GDR economy. Nevertheless, he was "astonished" to learn of these numbers and asked whether they were precise because "he had not imagined the situation to be so precarious." Krenz confirmed that they were and told Gorbachev that if the standard of living was based "exclusively on the country's own production," it would have to be lowered "by 30% immediately." This, he said, "was not politically feasible."[75]

For Gorbachev, this was now a familiar refrain; he had heard variations of it from Hungarian and Polish officials in recent years. He told his East German counterpart that he had to come clean with the population and confront them with the nation's economic reality. The SED leadership, he told Krenz, "had to find a way to tell the population that it had lived beyond its means in the last few years."[76] The Soviet Union would do its best to meet the raw material deliveries it had already committed to in the 1986–1990 Five-Year Plan, but it could provide nothing above and beyond this.[77]

To fix the GDR's economy, Gorbachev therefore told Krenz to look to the West. This, he said, was what Hungary and Poland had done. "They, after all, had no choice in this matter," Gorbachev said. "It was often asked what the USSR would do in this situation. But it could do very little in economic terms. It was an absurdity to think that the Soviet Union could support 40 million Poles." In Hungary, "Comrade Kádár was given an ultimatum by the IMF in 1987; in case of non-compliance with the numerous demands, a suspension of the loans was threatened."[78] These two statements appear to have sent a clear and lasting message to Krenz. In his memoirs, he quoted these words exactly and then wrote, "I understand Gorbachev as follows: You cannot expect additional economic assistance from the Soviet Union, but don't let it come to joining the International Monetary Fund under any circumstances. Help yourself, as best you can!"[79] After four hours of conversation and a comradely lunch replete with vodka toasts to the future of socialism, Krenz boarded his plane for the GDR with the weight of such thoughts on his shoulders.

He returned to a country in free fall. Under the threat of strikes from workers, the government decided on November 1 to repeal its earlier decision to close its borders to the Eastern Bloc. Immediately, the refugee problem resurfaced, as 4,000 East Germans filled the West German embassy in Prague once more. Fearing a spillover destabilization, the Czechoslovak leadership pressured East Berlin to fix its travel regulations quickly. To make matters worse, the Federal Republic's permanent representative to the GDR informed the SED that the West German mission in East Berlin would soon reopen, two months after closing for "renovations" (in fact, it had closed to prevent refugees from filling it as they had the embassies in Prague and Warsaw). Its reopening would surely mean a massive refugee crisis in the heart of the GDR. As pressure from east and west mounted, it also surged on the streets of the capital. On November 4, an estimated half a million people flooded Alexanderplatz in East Berlin to demand reform.[80] Continuing the chant first used in Leipzig weeks earlier, "Wir sind das Volk!" (We are the people!), they dared their leaders to take their slogans about democracy seriously and demanded a say in their country's future.

Amid the public upheaval, Schalck quietly traveled again to Bonn for another conversation with Seiters and Schäuble. This time he arrived with the more concrete offer that the GDR was "prepared to implement generous regulations for travel between the capital of the GDR and West Berlin via newly opened border crossings" as long as the Federal Republic was prepared to cover the "significant financial and material costs." Additionally, he informed his interlocutors that the GDR was seeking "long-term loans up to ten billion VE [accounting units, most likely DM]" over the next two years that would be "paid back over a period of at least ten years" to support new forms of cooperation, such as "joint ventures and equity investments" from West German companies. On top of the DM 10 billion, Schalck said his government "saw the necessity of discussing additional lines of credit in hard currencies that could begin in 1991 and total DM 2–3 billion annually." This would be required "to meet the demands" of new levels of cooperation. The KoKo chief made it clear, in short, that if the Wall was going to be bought and sold, its price was going to be extremely high.

But while Schalck's price had increased, so too had the Federal Republic's. Schäuble told Schalck that much depended on Krenz's upcoming speech to the East German Central Committee on November 8. Krenz would have to make clear "the credibility of the *Wende* course" and would need to appoint "credible and new people" to implement the announced reforms. "A fundamental problem in this context," Schäuble said, "was Article 1 of the GDR constitution, which guaranteed the leading role of the Marxist-Leninist party." Schäuble "strongly advised" that the SED make it clear that it was willing to allow a "peaceful transition supported by all political, social and religious organizations" and to constitutionally change "the leading role of the SED into a constructive, consensus-building cooperation with all democratic forces in the interests of socialism and the GDR." He also told Schalck that the "state border with West Berlin" should be made "more permeable" and that the West German government continued to assume the GDR would "decisively dismantle its subsidies" to the economy. In closing, Schäuble suggested "urgently once again, that General Secretary Krenz take up the ideas expressed [in this meeting] in his speech. Otherwise Chancellor Kohl would not be able to justify in the Bundestag financial assistance from West German taxpayers."[81]

Schalck went straight to Krenz upon returning to East Berlin. In his memoir, Krenz termed the demands made at their meeting "blackmail."[82] Schalck expanded further, "Diplomatically it was an outrage [*Ungeheuerlichkeit*]—an interference in the internal affairs of the GDR. Historically, it was consistent. For the West German government, there were no internal affairs of the GDR anymore. Due to the political upheavals and the desperate economic situation of the GDR—I brought to the conversation a demand for credit in the amount of 10 billion Deutsche Marks—the internal affairs of the GDR had become intra-German."[83]

While Schalck met with Seiters and Schäuble, East German newspapers published a preliminary draft of the new travel law in hopes of appeasing the population's demand to leave the country. It failed spectacularly. Most importantly, the law still required East Germans to obtain a visa before being allowed to exit, which could be denied at the state's discretion. Even if a citizen received a visa, the law provided no commitment on behalf of the state to finance foreign travel with hard currency. Because Schalck had not yet secured from the FRG a means of paying for East Germans' foreign travel, the government still had no way to pay for all the travel that was to come. Clearly, this was no sign of progress, and more than half a million people jammed the streets of Leipzig the same day in protest.[84]

That evening, after learning of the Leipzig protest and receiving a report from Seiters and Schäuble about their conversation with Schalck, West German policy makers met to discuss their next move. The document prepared for the discussion noted that the conversation with Schalck showed that "the new government [in the GDR] seeks a fundamental restructuring of the economy . . . but would like to avoid fundamental reforms of the political structure." In particular, the GDR leadership did not appear "open to a restriction of the SED's monopoly on power and to concessions in the direction of pluralism." Instead, "they expect massive financial and material support from us for their restructuring efforts and simultaneously our renunciation of efforts to work towards a change in the political system." However, the enormous scale of Schalck's financial request also made clear that "the GDR—at least in the short and medium term—does not expect to obtain the necessary amounts of economic assistance from anyone other than us. The alternative would, in fact, be a policy of austerity."[85] This left the FRG in a powerful negotiating position, and the Kohl government knew it. After being briefed by Seiters and Schäuble on their meeting, Kohl decided the time had come to set firm preconditions for his government's financial support.

The next day, Seiters called Schalck to transmit a message directly from Kohl for Krenz. The chancellor told Krenz he needed to "declare publicly that the GDR is prepared to guarantee that opposition groups will be permitted and affirm that free elections will be held within a period to be announced if the GDR wants to receive material and financial assistance from the FRG. This applies also to the financial arrangements regarding travel." The message continued, "It should be noted that this path is only possible if the SED relinquishes its claim to absolute power." The party "should be prepared to work on equal terms, and in consensus, with all societal forces, churches and religious communities to discuss a true renewal, with the goal of achieving democratic socialism." Seiters told Schalck that if these conditions were met, "the Chancellor thinks a great deal can be achieved and every option can be explored."[86] Krenz again called this "blackmail" and "a crude attempt to interfere in the internal affairs of the GDR." But he saw no alternative. "Once again it is clear how constrained my political freedom of movement is," he wrote. "Ultimately, everything depends on the economy."[87] The next day, Kohl further increased the pressure by publicly announcing these conditions during his "State of the Nation" address.[88]

With their first attempt at publishing a new travel law proving to be a disaster, the Politburo reconvened on November 7 to work out a new policy. Because their Czechoslovak comrades were now threatening to close their border with the GDR if the government did nothing to stop the flow of emigrants, the leadership decided to immediately put into effect the portion of the travel law allowing East German citizens to permanently emigrate. As they moved on to preparations for the upcoming meeting of the Central Committee, the Politburo handed responsibility for drafting the revised law to the Interior Ministry and the Stasi.

At this point, it is worth reflecting on where the GDR was headed on November 8, the day before the Wall opened in dramatic and accidental fashion. The country's financial position and the Soviet Union's inability to provide extra economic support had driven the leadership to embrace four policy positions. First, financial dependence on the West was not the only factor restraining the leadership from using violence, but it was an important one. Second, Krenz and the Politburo had not endorsed an uncontrolled opening of the Berlin Wall, but they had endorsed a strategy of trading opening the Wall in return for hard currency. Third, this strategic choice and the anticipated financial shortfall of the early 1990s had led the leadership to negotiate with the Federal Republic as a means of avoiding insolvency and negotiations with the IMF. The leadership's choice to negotiate with the FRG was therefore a strategic decision based on its belief that the FRG's demand for the freer movement of people posed a smaller risk to the GDR than the IMF's demand for austerity and structural adjustment. Exit was safer than Austerity. Finally, the protests in the GDR drove the Kohl government to expand its conditionality in the early days of November beyond the freer movement of people to include demands for a complete reform of the East German economy and a renunciation of the SED's one-party state. As part of his *Wende,* Krenz had shown a vague inclination to couple political liberalization with economic reform, but by November 7, the Federal Republic's conditionality left him with no choice but to implement this strategy.

In other words, even before the Berlin Wall fell, the GDR's circumstances were already pointing the country down the path recently taken by Poland and Hungary. The opening of the Wall may have been accidental, but the collapse of the country was not. By the afternoon of November 9, that collapse was a historical certainty, one that derived from the potent combination of emigration, demonstration, and Western financial leverage. What remained to be determined—and what the opening of the Wall decisively influenced—was *how* and *how fast* the GDR collapsed.

* * *

On the morning of November 9, officials from the Interior Ministry and the Stasi met to draft a revised travel law. Their orders from the Politburo were to immediately authorize permanent emigration from the GDR to the FRG and—crucially—West Berlin as well. After seeing the reaction to the first draft law, Gerhard Lauter, the senior Interior Ministry official at the meeting, felt that allowing permanent emigration but not temporary travel would only stoke popular resentment, so he rewrote the law to immediately authorize both permanent and temporary travel. All historical evidence suggests that he received no direction from his superiors to make this change, and it certainly did not conform to Krenz's and

Schalck's strategy of leveraging freer travel to gain more hard currency. Thus, it stands as a decisive moment of contingency in which a local actor altered the trajectory of his nation. Nevertheless, as Lauter himself would later say, it was a change in how fast policy would be implemented, not a change in policy itself. In explaining his mindset that morning, he said, "We still had the task ahead of us to put forth a draft of the travel law in 1989 that would bring about the freedom to travel. In principle, November 9 could also have been December 21, and then it would have happened legally and not been surprising. We had all of this in the back of our minds."[89] Lauter's group sent the new law up the bureaucratic chain of command, where it reached Krenz by noon on November 9.

Since he had overthrown Honecker in mid-October, Krenz had placed all his hopes for the renewal of the SED and the launch of an economic reform program on the Tenth Meeting of the Central Committee, set to take place November 8–10. The first day and a half had not gone according to plan, as the meeting had gotten bogged down in endless debates about the reorganization of the party leadership. In midafternoon on November 9, Krenz interrupted the meeting to gain approval of the revised travel law. "Comrades! . . . You are aware that there is a problem that wears on us all: the question of exit [from the GDR]," he said.[90] The general secretary read the full draft of the new law to the committee, and eager to get back to what they considered bigger issues, the members had only minor tweaks to suggest. The draft was quickly approved, and Krenz gave it to Günter Schabowski to announce at a press conference to be broadcast live on East German television and covered by international news outlets that evening.

As the press conference came to a close, Schabowski announced the travel law revision almost as an afterthought. Haltingly, he told the world, "We have decided today (um) to implement a regulation that allows every citizen of the German Democratic Republic (um) to (um) leave the GDR through any of the border crossings." After a barrage of questions burst forth, Schabowski decided it would probably be a good idea to read the precise law. "Applications for travel abroad by private individuals can now be made without the previously existing requirements. . . . The travel authorizations will be issued within a short time. . . . Permanent exit is possible via all GDR border crossings to the FRG." Asked when the regulation would come into effect, Schabowski looked down at his papers and found the word "immediately." He answered, "That comes into effect, according to my information, immediately, without delay." And what about West

Berlin? "Does this also apply for West Berlin?" someone asked. Skimming the document again, he found the words, "Permanent exit can take place via all border crossings from the GDR to the FRG and West Berlin, respectively." Well, then, what about the Berlin Wall? "What is going to happen to the Berlin Wall now?" someone asked. Here, at the logical but unresolved end point of the past four weeks of negotiations over trading the freer movement of people for hard currency, Schabowski realized he had no answer and quickly ended the press conference.[91]

As word spread that the government's new law allowed *all* citizens to travel or emigrate *immediately* through *any* border crossing, East Berliners took to the streets to test out the new reality. They began showing up in droves at crossings in the Wall demanding to be let through. Because the travel law was, in fact, not supposed to go into effect until the next day (despite its talk of "immediately"), the border guards were caught completely unprepared. For five and a half hours after the press conference, tension and confusion reigned while the guards tried to seek clarification. Receiving none by 11:30 p.m., Harold Jäger, the officer on duty at the Bornholmer Street crossing, accelerated the course of his country's history and ordered his subordinates to open the gates to the thousands of East German citizens pressing to get across. Within an hour, the Berlin Wall had fallen.[92]

◆ ◆ ◆

Five days after the Berlin Wall opened, Schalck and König wrote to Schürer to tell him they had been lying to him about the debt for the past eight years. "The debt is actually 12.6 billion VM lower than you previously thought," they wrote. Detailing the secret accounts KoKo and the Ministry of Finance had maintained since the 1970s to store extra hard currency, they told Schürer the actual debt at the end of 1989 would be roughly VM 38 billion, or $20.6 billion. Despite the difference, they maintained that the billions of deutsche marks stored in their accounts were still "not enough to solve the liquidity problems arising in 1991/92."[93]

Nine years later, the German Bundesbank was not so sure. In 1998, the bank went back to examine the GDR's balance of payments situation in the 1970s and 1980s. It discovered that even Schalck—keeper of the country's financial secrets—did not accurately understand his country's financial position. Rather than $20.6 billion in debt, the Bundesbank found that the GDR in fact only had $10.8 billion in debt at the end of 1989.

East German leaders believed they confronted a financial reality in 1989 that threatened the existence of their regime, but it was in many ways a false reality. In retrospect, all the numbers cited in this chapter turned out to be inaccurate. The GDR's financial position in 1989 was so threatening only because its leaders believed it was. The real financial picture, although not without problems, was much less foreboding. The Exit/Violence/Austerity dynamics derived their power from a socially constructed reality built on faulty foundations, but they were no less powerful for it. Social constructions derive their power precisely from their ability to determine what is real and what is not.

CHAPTER 10

Discipline or Retreat

IN THE DAYS after the Berlin Wall fell, West German chancellor Helmut Kohl did everything in his power to temper his dreams of German unity. The scenes of East Germans crossing into West Berlin and West Germans standing atop the Wall were joyous signs that a better, freer life for all Germans might take shape. But a politician of Kohl's stature and experience needed no reminder that his nation's fate did not ultimately lie in German hands. Since the defeat of Hitler's armies in 1945, it had been the victorious powers of the Second World War—the United States, Soviet Union, Great Britain, and France—that held legal jurisdiction over German lands, and it had been the world's two super-powers that held ultimate control over the so-called German question. The Cold War had begun in the late 1940s because neither the Soviet Union nor the United States was willing to let the totality of German power fall into the other's hands, and over four dangerous decades, both sides had threatened the world with nuclear annihilation to prevent the delicate balance of power in the heart of the European continent from changing.

Jubilant though it was, the fall of the Berlin Wall had not altered this well-worn reality. The Soviet Union still maintained 380,000 troops on East German territory. Under any theory of politics, narrative of history, or tenet of ideology, the Kremlin had no reason to retreat from German soil, at least not without extracting significant concessions from the West. Moscow's right to determine Germany's fate was both the ultimate prize for its victory over Nazism and its ultimate security guarantee against future Western aggression. Kohl, therefore, tried to be realistic about the prospects for change. "It would take five or ten years to achieve unity," he told his close aide Horst Teltschik. "Even if unity was not achieved until the end of this century, it would still be a historic stroke of luck."[1]

He need not have been so modest. Eleven short months later, on October 3, 1990, the chancellor stood in front of the Brandenburg Gate in Berlin surrounded by throngs of citizens to celebrate the unification of their country. Rather than being a long and tortured affair, the process of unification had been surprisingly quick and easy. And rather than making concessions to facilitate the Kremlin's agreement, Kohl and his allies in the Bush administration had gotten everything they desired: quick and peaceful unification, the promised removal of all Soviet armed forces from German territory, and the accession of the newly unified Germany to the North Atlantic Treaty Organization (NATO). Their victory had been complete, and the global balance of power had peacefully and fundamentally shifted in the West's favor.

How could this process unfold with such speed and amity after decades of rancor and danger? History tells us that changes in the balance of power are usually violent and destructive occurrences, so the reunification of Germany stands out as an anomaly. In accounting for the stunning turn of events, scholars and former policy makers have largely focused on the agency of diplomatic elites and the contingency of the diplomatic processes that led to German unity. If not for men like George H. W. Bush and Helmut Kohl, and their deputies James Baker and Horst Teltschik, these authors claim, German unification may not have happened at all or may not have unfolded on Western terms.[2]

This chapter takes a different view. The actions of Western diplomatic elites and processes of international statecraft were indeed important factors in German unification, particularly in consolidating Western governments behind the goals of perpetuating NATO and keeping a united Germany fully integrated into the alliance. But the ultimate causes of the peaceful shift in the balance of power did not lie in the West. They lay, instead, in two aspects of Eastern political economy: the collapse of the East German state and economy after the fall of the Berlin Wall and

Mikhail Gorbachev's unwillingness to implement the politics of breaking promises in the Soviet Union.[3] These were the causes propelled unification forward with such shocking speed, and these were the sources of the Kremlin's precipitous turn to pliability on the German question after decades of intransigence.

Consider the view from Gorbachev's Kremlin. Given that neither he nor any other leading Soviet official wanted to use violence in Central Europe, Gorbachev would have needed to implement two policies with significant economic consequences to resist German unity.[4] First, he would have had to divert substantial resources from the Soviet economy to prevent the collapse of the German Democratic Republic (GDR). The fall of the Berlin Wall transformed German unification from an intractable geopolitical impasse into an immediate economic challenge. The unrelenting march of hundreds of thousands of East German citizens westward created a sieve in the East German economy and society. Only governments that could slow this exodus and arrest the economic collapse had the power to determine the speed and direction of events. The West German government obviously held such power; if the Soviets had wanted to resist the rush to German unity, they would have needed to exert such power too.

Second, Gorbachev would have had to impose the politics of breaking promises in the Soviet Union. Because of the collapse in world energy prices and Gorbachev's failure to impose economic discipline in the first five years of perestroika, by early 1990 Western banks would only lend to Moscow with the support of their governments. This meant that the Kremlin's access to hard currency depended on the political opinion prevailing in Western capitals. If Gorbachev had meaningfully resisted German unity on Western terms, Western goodwill would have quickly evaporated, and Moscow would have lost all access to global capital markets. Out of pure financial necessity, the politics of breaking promises would no doubt soon have followed.

Gorbachev, therefore, faced a choice between supporting the Soviet social contract at home and securing the Soviet empire abroad. To save the empire abroad, the Soviet leader would need to impose economic discipline at home; and to avoid imposing economic discipline at home, he would need to give up the empire abroad. He would either need to discipline or retreat. Throughout the process of German unification, Gorbachev consistently chose to retreat from abroad to minimize economic discipline at home. As long as he did so, Western policy makers were pushing against an open Soviet door in Central Europe in late 1989 and 1990. Unless the Soviet leader was willing to break promises at home, there was no *plausible* alternative to Washington's and Bonn's most ardent desires: a peaceful Soviet retreat from the European continent and a united Germany in NATO. Without economic discipline in the Soviet Union, German reunification on Western terms was inevitable.

Dealt the winning hand by history, West German and American policy makers played it skillfully. Alone among Western leaders, George H. W. Bush fully supported Kohl's drive for German unity as long as the West German chancellor promised to keep Germany in NATO and American troops in Germany. Kohl was happy to make this deal, and the Americans' support steeled his conviction as he aggressively used the tools of the privatized Cold War to seal German unity. Kohl well understood the leverage hard currency and credit market access gave him in East Germany and the Soviet Union, and he used it to great effect. To win the hearts and minds of the East German population, he offered them unlimited access to the scarcest good the GDR had known: the deutsche mark. And to secure Soviet acquiescence, he offered Gorbachev over DM 20 billion in grants and loans to facilitate the Soviet Army's departure from German soil and the Kremlin's acceptance of a united Germany in NATO. On October 3, 1990, Germans united and the Cold War ended—not with a bang, but with a checkbook.

◆ ◆ ◆

"History left us with good cards," Kohl told Bush after the Berlin Wall fell. "I hope with the cooperation of our American friends we can play them well."[5] Kohl and Bush had plenty of reasons to like their hand. The capitalist perestroika that had unfolded in the West since the Volcker Shock at the turn of the 1980s had left the Western world in a resurgent economic position, and Western governments maintained a stability and self-confidence born of renewed material prosperity. The biggest beneficiary of this renewal was the Federal Republic of Germany (FRG). Perhaps Bush summarized Bonn's economic position best when he told Kohl simply, "You've got deep pockets."[6]

Mikhail Gorbachev's Soviet Union, by contrast, found itself by the autumn of 1989 in economic free fall. Four years into Gorbachev's tenure in the Kremlin, his unwillingness to impose economic and financial discipline on Soviet society had left the country mired in socioeconomic crisis. Short-ages of basic goods were mounting, and the population's patience with re-form was waning. Worst of all—and as was true with all instances of the politics of breaking promises—the solution to the country's economic prob-lems appeared to be politically impossible. "What is the solution?" Soviet premier Nikolai Ryzhkov rhetorically asked the Politburo in February 1989. "Price increases? But this means social tension that threatens perestroika."[7]

Even without price increases, social tension in an economy of profound shortage was not long in coming. In July 1989, a wave of strikes involving over 170,000 miners broke out across the country. The miners walked off the job in protest over declining living and working conditions and only returned to work after the Kremlin partook in a new round of promises to improve housing, work environments, and the supply of food. How these promises could possibly be kept given the prevailing economic crisis was anyone's guess, but the strikes served as a warning of the resistance that would greet any attempt to impose economic discipline.[8] Gorbachev, like Ryzhkov, was at a loss for what to do but urgently aware that something must be done. "We have a year, maximum two" to fix the economy, he told the Politburo at the end of June. "Otherwise, we'll have to resign."[9]

If prices were left untouched, only the world market could fill the yawning void between supply and demand in the economy. By the start of 1989, however, this too was becoming problematic. A burgeoning hard currency crisis had begun to compound the domestic economy's litany of foibles. This was a novel development for the Kremlin. Though its allies had dealt with severe sovereign debt problems throughout the 1970s and 1980s, the Soviet Union's vast natural resources had allowed it to avoid any significant dependence on Western capital. But the oil price collapse of 1985–1986 and the economic reforms of the early years of perestroika had not been kind to Moscow's balance of payments (see Figure 10.1 for the decline in Soviet hard currency energy export earnings). By early 1989, serious questions had emerged on global capital markets about the Soviet Union's creditworthiness. In March, Yuri Moskovskii, president of Vneshekonombank, the Soviet foreign trade bank, wrote to Ryzhkov, "The growing debt of the Soviet Union is increasingly becoming the object of close attention and speculation in the Western press." As a result, he con-cluded, banks had recently "shown a more cautious attitude towards pro-viding untied loans [i.e., loans not connected to a specific trade or investment project] to the Soviet Union."[10]

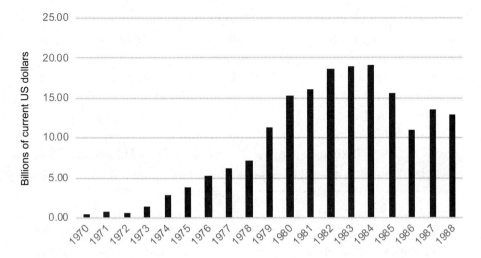

Figure 10.1 **Soviet hard currency energy export earnings.**
Data source: Central Intelligence Agency, *Soviet Energy Data Resource Book*, May 1990, CIA Online Reading Room, accessed February 20, 2020, https://www.cia.gov/library/readingroom/docs/DOC_0000292332.pdf, 7.

The problem was not the absolute level of Soviet debt but rather the dramatic rate of its increase. Soviet net hard currency debt increased 150 percent from $16 billion to $40 billion between 1985 and 1989.[11] To the gatekeepers of the world's capital, this appeared to signal that the Kremlin had lost all control of its own balance of payments. One Western banker likened Soviet enterprises' explosive demand for imports to "children on a shopping spree."[12]

By the summer of 1989, the sound of Moskovskii's alarm had risen to a fever pitch. On August 12, he again wrote Ryzhkov, this time with a much more urgent warning. Global capital holders, he warned, had begun to adopt a "wait and see policy" in their lending to the Soviet Union because the "the USSR's credit risk is already considered to be increased." He assured Ryzhkov that the bank was doing everything in its power to raise more funds on global capital markets, but problems were beginning to mount. Global capital holders' doubts were "already adversely affecting practical results."[13]

Against this backdrop Gorbachev traveled to Bonn in June 1989 for his first visit to West Germany. From his earliest days in the Kremlin, Gorbachev had hoped to build a strong relationship with the Federal Republic, and he had always seen economics as the foundation of that relationship. Speaking to the Politburo in July 1986, he had declared that economic relations were "the most important part" of the Soviet–West German relationship, and he encouraged his comrades to explore joint ventures, economic cooperation, and loans with West German firms.[14] Over the next three years, the two sides further developed their economic relationship, including a DM 3 billion loan from Deutsche Bank to the Soviet state in 1988.[15] As the Soviet Union's domestic crises became acute, Gorbachev's desire to tap the wellspring of West German economic power grew in equal measure.[16] Kohl and the West German business community stood ready to oblige. In their first bilateral meeting, Kohl told Gorbachev, "The Federal Republic is aware of its role as your country's largest Western economic partner. We are ready to expand our cooperation."[17]

Gorbachev returned home to a country where cooperation was ever more elusive. The political reforms of glasnost and perestroika had opened the way for the Soviet Union's many peoples to rekindle their national identity, and by 1989, nationalist movements from the Baltics to the Caucasus were pushing for independence. Gorbachev attempted to craft a response to the nationalists' challenge at a special Central Committee Plenum on Nationalities in September. But even as he tried to forge a new political foundation for Soviet unity, he remained committed to the belief that the economy would ultimately determine perestroika's fate. "If we could take the tension out of the consumer market, a lot would clear up," he told former West German chancellor Willy Brandt in October. "If social tension continues to grow and living conditions continue to deteriorate, then any match can suffice. That is why the fate of perestroika depends on how we manage to untie these knots: the market and finances."[18]

As the crisis in East Germany reached its crescendo in early November, the trials of the outer empire and the travails of the domestic social contract converged on the crowded agenda of the Soviet Politburo. On November 1, Egon Krenz shocked Gorbachev with the news that the GDR was $26 billion in debt to the West (even if it actually wasn't). Two days later, the Politburo learned it would have to import an additional thirty-six million tons of grain from abroad just to make it through the rest of 1989. Ryzhkov gave voice to the widespread dismay in the chamber. "Why can't we feed ourselves? From year to year we buy more and more abroad, and the situation is getting worse!" At the same meeting, they addressed the deteriorating situation in the GDR. Gorbachev admitted that the Soviet Union's resource constraints left no choice but to cooperate with the Federal Republic on German issues. The Soviet domestic crisis was too severe to even contemplate saving East Germany on their own.[19]

A week later, on the same day the Berlin Wall fell, the overlapping economic and nationality crises within the Soviet Union dominated the Politburo agenda. Everyone agreed that improving the economy was the only way to save perestroika and the union, but they tiptoed around the issues that stood the best chance of delivering improvement: price reform and the introduction of free markets. "We can't let go of prices," Gorbachev repeated yet again. As for the market, it would eventually be necessary, but "if we immediately 'introduce' it today, all the people will go out and sweep away the government." Ryzhkov agreed, noting that the introduction of a free market between the union's republics "would mean chaos" that threatened the very core of the union itself. In other words, breaking promises was the quickest route to the failure of perestroika and the collapse of the union, and therefore, it could not be done. Instead, Gorbachev declared that "emergency measures" should be taken to "reduce the severity of the financial situation and reduce social tension."[20]

Reducing social tension would no doubt require access to global capital markets, which was hanging by a thread. By November, the Soviet banking system lacked enough hard currency to pay the country's entire import bill, and soon Soviet bankers were informing the leadership that the country had amassed 2 billion rubles in arrears to foreign companies.[21]

The country's domestic social contract and international creditworthiness had now become fully intertwined. If the Kremlin's credibility on global capital markets faltered any further, its standing with the Soviet people would swiftly falter too, and the union itself would be in grave danger. As the fall of the Wall removed all constraints from the movement of East German citizens, the precarious yet powerful relationship between the world's capital and the Soviet people imposed new constraints on Gorbachev's every move.

◆ ◆ ◆

The fall of the Berlin Wall unleashed the full power of Eastern Bloc peoples to determine their own destiny. In the weeks following November 9, the dominos of Communist Party rule fell in quick succession in Czechoslovakia, Bulgaria, and Romania. On the same night the Wall fell, leading members of the Bulgarian Communist Party removed the country's long-time leader, Todor Zhivkov, in a palace coup. His replacement, Petar Mladenov, hoped to stabilize communist rule by charting a path of one-party reform, but the Bulgarian people had other ideas. Mass protests began in Sofia in mid-November, and in mid-December, Mlad-enov announced that the Communist Party would abandon one-party rule.

Events moved even more quickly in Czechoslovakia. When riot police violently suppressed a student demonstration in Prague on November 17, hundreds of thousands of Czechoslovaks took to the streets in the days that followed to demand the Communist Party's ouster. A mere seven days later, General Secretary Miloš Jakeš resigned, and his successors tried in vain to chart a reformed communist path. Here, too, the people showed little patience for the authorities' plans and continued to demand radical political change. Without a turn to Soviet-sponsored violence, their efforts could not be stopped, and the regime soon collapsed. In mid-December, the first noncommunist government since the 1940s took its seat in Prague, and on December 29, the great Czech playwright and dissident Václav Havel was elected president of the country.

History's course took a more violent, but no less speedy, path in Romania. On December 16, the country's Hungarian minority in the town of Timișoara began protesting the eviction of a dissident pastor, László Tőkés. Their efforts were met with violent repression, and over the coming days, many answered this violence with rioting in the streets. On December 21, Nicolae Ceaușescu tried to reestablish his preeminence over the nation with a speech to adoring masses in Bucharest, but few Romanians still adored him. The crowd unexpectedly interrupted the dictatorial ruler with boos and jeers, and protests quickly spread throughout the capital. Elements of the army soon began supporting the protesters, leading to violent clashes with those who still supported the regime. Ceaușescu and his wife fled the capital early on December 22 but were quickly caught and arrested. On Christmas Day, 1989, they met a grisly end, as a hastily convened tribunal tried and convicted them of numerous crimes and had them summarily executed by firing squad.

As the dominos of the Soviet empire fell around them, East Germans did not wait passively for history to come to them. They too realized the power that now lay in their hands, and they set about using their voices and feet to alter the trajectory of their nation. The opening of the Wall turned the previous stream of East Germans heading westward into a veritable flood. In November alone, 130,000 East German citizens decided to permanently emigrate to the FRG.[22] Those who stayed behind were no less decisive for their immobility. Protesters continued to turn out by the hundreds of thousands, and a mere four days after the fall of the Wall, they quickly added a call for unification, "Wir sind ein Volk" (We are one people), to their persistent demand for democratic recognition, "Wir sind das Volk" (We are the people).[23] Collectively, those who left and those who stayed spurred the precipitous collapse of the East German economy and state, which, in turn, became the driving force behind the rush to unification. As such, they—more than any diplomat or world leader—constituted the most potent force in the Cold War during late 1989 and early 1990.[24] If any government, East or West, also wanted to play a role in deciding the future of the GDR, it would now have to win the East German people's hearts, capture their minds, and control their feet.

This inconvenient truth applied with greatest force to the East German communist government itself. Party leader Egon Krenz did not last long in a country of open borders and free assembly. His best efforts to distance himself from the cruelties and corruptions of the Honecker era fooled no one, and in early December, the party forced him to resign as part of a rushed attempt to gain legitimacy in the eyes of the population.

This left the creaking ship of state in the hands of Hans Modrow, the Dresden party chief. Unlike Krenz, Modrow came by his reformist sympathies sincerely, and he fully understood the scale and nature of the challenge he faced: to impose the politics of breaking promises in a system losing its legitimacy and workforce with astounding speed. As Modrow wrote in his memoirs, he had long campaigned from his seat in Dresden to revise the GDR's ruinous price subsidies and build a socialist economy that prioritized "companies' profitability" and individuals' "personal responsibility."[25] Once in office in Berlin, he believed that the "true fate of the GDR" lay in revising its "price and subsidy system."[26] But like every politician in both East and West who had tried to break promises, he found that "the more we dealt with it [the issue of subsidies] in government, the clearer the challenge associated with it became."[27] To successfully meet that challenge, the new East German leader concluded he would need time, popular support, and external financing, three things in frightfully short supply after the fall of the Wall.

Modrow knew better than to begin his search for external support in Moscow. Since the oil cutbacks of 1981, East German officials had experienced little more than a decade of disappointment in their economic dealings with the Kremlin. So, like the emigrants he aimed to stop, Modrow turned west. On November 17, he called for a "treaty community between two sovereign states" to formalize the West Germans' support for the GDR. His was a vision very similar to the one Krenz had tried to project in his secret negotiations with Bonn before the fall of the Wall—willing to take the Federal Republic's money, but highly resistant to accepting any conditions that might infringe on East German sovereignty. Even in the early days after the fall of the Wall, East German sovereignty was already a flimsy foundation on which to resist the financial power of the Federal Republic. But until the West Germans called the question on East German statehood and publicly projected a path to unity, the fiction of airtight East German sovereignty could persist.

Providing such a path was the purpose of Helmut Kohl's famous Ten-Point Plan. Speaking to the Bundestag on November 28, the chancellor declared that his government would henceforth aim to "develop confederative structures" between the two German states with the eventual aim of "creating a federation." He provided no timeline for the creation of these structures but rather conditioned them on the existence of "a democratically legitimized government in the GDR." In the meantime, future economic aid to the GDR would only come if the country "opens itself up to Western investment, if it creates conditions for a market economy and enables private economic activity." Conscious of the leverage implicit in his words, the chancellor hastened to add that these stipulations were "not preconditions" but rather "plainly and simply the objective requirement if assistance is to have any chance of taking hold." And conscious of the provocation to the bipolar Cold War order implicit in his proposal, Kohl made it clear that any move toward a united Germany would happen in conjunction with efforts to deepen European integration, overcome the division of Europe, and build—in Gorbachev's phrase—a "common European house."[28]

The world was none too soothed. To prevent the ten points from being leaked by his ministers or watered down by his allies, Kohl did not inform anyone except the Bush administration of his plans.[29] This made his Bundestag speech an unwelcome surprise for leaders on a continent with dark memories of powerful German leaders launching unilateral initiatives to unite the German people. For Margaret Thatcher in London and François Mitterrand in Paris, Kohl's actions raised the prospect that a united Germany might make a habit of not consulting with its allies and neighbors. Given Germany's expansionist history, who knew where that could lead. Would a united Germany pay anything more than lip service to the project of European integration? Would it remain committed to

NATO? Would it accept the postwar borders that had given roughly 20 percent of its territory in the east to a rebuilt Poland? Thatcher and Mitterrand were eager to find out, and until they had answers, they committed themselves to resisting Kohl's unilateral rush to unity.

Only the Americans appeared to be untarnished by the scars of history. Alone among world leaders, George H. W. Bush welcomed the prospect of a unified German nation.[30] He steadfastly believed that the fount of European security during the Cold War had been the presence of American forces in Germany under the institutional umbrella of NATO. As long as Kohl was willing to support the perpetuation of those foundational security structures in the emerging post–Cold War world, he would have the American president's full support. The chancellor gave these assurances in a phone call with Bush the day after his announcement of the ten points, and the two leaders were off and running.[31]

Under the cover of American diplomatic support and the East German people's unrelenting destruction of their own state through demonstration and emigration, Kohl stymied the fledgling French and British attempt to slow or resist German unity. London and Paris could not hope to match Bonn's financial power to control the collapse of the GDR, so they were powerless to alter the root cause of the drive to unity. And without the Americans on their side, they could not mount a meaningful diplomatic challenge to Kohl's plans. Mitterrand was quicker to see this stubborn reality than Thatcher, but eventually both fell in line.[32]

Responsibility for resisting German unity therefore returned to the same place it had always been: the Kremlin. Like every other world leader not in Washington, Gorbachev had been forced to learn of Kohl's "objective" requirements for aid and "stabilizing" plans for confederative structures from the news. He saw them as anything but disinterested statements of self-evident facts. "These are ultimatums that have been put to an independent and sovereign state," he thundered to West German foreign minister Hans-Dietrich Genscher. A cascade of questions followed to signal the fundamental issues at stake. "A confederation presupposes unified defense and foreign policy," Gorbachev fumed. "Where will the FRG be then? In NATO? In the Warsaw Pact? Or will it perhaps become neutral? And what does NATO mean without the FRG? Have you thought everything through?"[33]

No, the West Germans had not. But given the Soviets' situation, Kohl and his government had guessed they did not need to. Their preponderance of power to determine the broad course of unification was coming clearly into view. They knew, for instance, that the supply situation in the Soviet Union was "very critical" and that Gorbachev was "critically reliant on external support." And they concluded, as did Gorbachev, that the general secretary's popularity was "diminishing among the [Soviet] population due to a lack of material results." The relevant consideration, therefore, was not what the Soviet Union might do to stop unification but rather what the nations of the West should do economically to help Gorbachev remain in power.[34] In such a situation, Gorbachev would no doubt noisily protest the pace of change in East Germany, but he was unlikely to take drastic measures to stop it. "Recourse to the armed forces would be inconceivable," the West German permanent representative to East Berlin wrote in early December, because "the GDR cannot expect outside help."[35]

The only outside help the East Germans could expect—and, indeed, would absolutely need—was that of global capital markets. As the full scale of reforming the East German economy became clear, policy makers in Bonn quickly realized that even the deep coffers of the Federal Republic could only cover a small sliver of what would be required to reform the GDR. To have any chance of successfully reforming, the GDR would need *private* capital, and lots of it. "Economic cooperation with the GDR . . . is essentially concerned with the <u>question of how billions of deutsche marks worth of capital can flow from the Federal Republic to the GDR</u>," an internal West German strategy document noted in early December. Relying on private capital made breaking promises within the GDR an absolute necessity. The memo noted that a number of "requirements for private capital" would need to be included in any East German economic reform: a credible announcement of market-based reforms and monetary discipline, legal conditions for the participation of private capital in East German companies, and an investment protection agreement that would guarantee the right to transfer profits out of the country. These would all be needed because "<u>by far the largest part of the GDR's capital needs would have to be provided by private western investors.</u>"[36]

But breaking promises was best done in an environment of political legitimacy, and events in the GDR continued to confirm that Modrow's government had none. In the weeks after Kohl's ten-points announcement, East Germans on the ground continued to set the pace of change. Every day, some 2,000 people left for the West, and every week, protests in Leipzig, Dresden, and East Berlin drew over 100,000 calls for German unity. In response, the communists attempted to save themselves through great feats of political cannibalism. In early December, the entire Politburo and Central Committee resigned, the party jettisoned the name Sozialistiche Einheitspartei Deutschland (SED) in favor of "the Party of Democratic Socialism," and Modrow's government arrested every leader of the old guard it could get its hands on.[37] The tumult reached such a roaring pitch that outside observers began to doubt that *any* government could have a significant influence over the course of events. "The pace and direction of the revolution in the GDR will be dictated by the people of the GDR," the British ambassador wrote on December 6, and "influenced, if at all, by the FRG."[38]

Kohl reached a similar conclusion when he landed in Dresden for a meeting with Modrow on December 19. Officially, he had come to Dresden to talk about money. Modrow wanted a lot of it—DM 15 billion in 1990 alone to cover the government's bills and support the flagging economy. As always, Kohl came ready with conditions that would need to be implemented before aid of this magnitude would follow. Specifically, the cornerstones of democratic governance and neoliberal economics—a law ensuring free elections and a legal framework to allow and protect foreign investment in the GDR—were prerequisites for aid. These remained bogged down in the GDR's tumultuous politics, so the chancellor maintained that he could not provide the substantial aid Modrow wanted until conditions on the ground reflected his demands.[39] The two sides agreed to continue negotiations, and Kohl departed to address an adoring crowd of 100,000 East Germans in central Dresden about the promise of German unity.[40]

Here, again, the West's power of omission was at work. In order for events to continue going his way, the West German chancellor did not need to provide any aid. After all, the people crossing the inter-German border were headed in *his* direction, and the thousands that gathered in central Dresden were chanting to join *his* country. Like Western creditors before him, Kohl could wait for conditions on the ground to conform to his demands before releasing the purse strings.

◆　◆　◆

Gorbachev had no such luxury. If he wanted to influence the course of events in Germany, he would have to intervene quickly and massively to prevent the collapse of the GDR. After Gorbachev's piqued reaction to Kohl's ten points, Soviet leaders continued to send menacing signals about their potential for action in Germany. In December, Foreign Minister Shevardnadze reminded the international community that the Four Powers had "at their disposal a considerable contingent of armed forces equipped with nuclear weapons on the territory of the GDR and the FRG."[41] The implicit threat was lost on no one. However, as the Soviet leadership had already concluded in Poland in 1981 and experienced in Afghanistan throughout the decade, military intervention carried its own enormous material costs—costs they had been unwilling to bear for many years. The fall of the Berlin Wall had not altered this basic unwillingness.[42]

Therefore, if Soviet leaders had wanted to mount an *actual* threat to Kohl's plans for unity, they would have had to do so through economic means. They would have had to reinforce their empire's basic purpose in Eastern Europe since the oil crisis of 1973: to insulate socialist states from the pressure of breaking promises. Such reinforcements would have reversed more than a decade of Soviet foreign policy that had sought to lessen the material burden of empire, but desperate times called for desperate measures. In the context of late 1989 and early 1990, insulating the GDR from the pressure to break promises would have required the adoption of three economic policies: the imposition of economic discipline within the Soviet Union to lessen the country's import dependence and divert resources to the GDR, the willingness to forgo all Western economic aid to the Soviet Union to maximize Soviet diplomatic leverage and maneuverability on the German question, and the delivery of increased and subsidized amounts of energy, hard currency, and other goods to the GDR. Saving the GDR from the politics of broken promises, in short, would have required imposing that same politics within the Soviet Union.

Gorbachev wanted no part of such a strategy. Rather than implementing these three policies, he pursued their exact opposite to preserve his foremost priority, perestroika. Since his first days in office, Gorbachev had always viewed his foreign policy as a means to the domestic end of transforming and strengthening the Soviet Union. Though his circumstances had significantly deteriorated by the end of 1989, this guiding light had not. "To be or not to be—1990 will be decisive for perestroika," he told the Politburo on January 2, 1990. "First of all, we need to take care of stabilizing the economy."[43]

The economy, as ever, needed discipline. Government economists told the leadership that incomes across the country had risen 40 percent faster than consumption in 1989, a sure sign Soviet citizens were caught in an inflationary spiral shackled to fixed prices that were too low.[44] In 1989, the military had remained stubbornly resistant to budget cuts, total price subsidies had reached a ruinous record of 93 billion rubles, and the budget deficit had remained dangerously high at 8.5 percent of GDP.[45] To return the economy to health, advisers recommended balancing the budget and generally implementing "measures to strengthen discipline in the economy."[46]

Gorbachev—reacting to the perennial challenge of imposing discipline with his perennial political instinct to avoid it—recognized the need for reform but saw no political path to pursue it. Separatist emergencies in Lithuania and Azerbaijan, mass protests on the streets of Moscow, and bitter feuding between reformers and hard-liners in the leadership dominated Soviet politics in the early months of 1990. Amid the tumult, Gorbachev could not find the personal will or political consensus to take immediate action in the economy. Instead, he delegated the task of developing a comprehensive economic reform plan to Ryzhkov and focused his attention on the perpetually changing vectors of the Soviet political scene.[47] This left the country's plummeting economic trajectory unchanged and left no resources available for the tasks of imperial maintenance. "We have no grain and we have no foreign currency," Ryzhkov concluded in February. "The situation is hopeless."[48]

If there was hope, it was in the West. Rather than pivoting toward austerity to resolve the Soviet Union's economic crisis, Gorbachev pivoted westward. Even as he was trying to resist the West Germans' rush to unity, he confirmed West German projections of his internal weakness by requesting emergency food aid. Kohl and his team sensed an opportunity to improve "the climate of relations" with Moscow. They snapped into action to find Gorbachev as much food aid as possible. Later that night in a conversation with his close advisors, Kohl concluded that gestures like food aid contributed "more to security in Europe than new weapon systems." In light of the gesture's evident power, he vowed to "help Gorbachev comprehensively."[49]

The same Soviet circumstances that drove Kohl to help Gorbachev comprehensively also prevented Gorbachev from helping Modrow even modestly. The continued flow of subsidized oil to the GDR would have been the sine qua non of any serious Soviet defense of East Germany. Instead, at the final meeting of Comecon on January 9–10, 1990, the Kremlin not only failed to support the GDR, but it pulled the plug on the entire economic edifice of its empire. Ryzhkov, who headed the Soviet delegation, at last resolved the tension between allied stability and Soviet national interest by demanding full payment for Soviet raw materials in hard currency. After almost two decades of internal debate over the merits and demerits of subsidizing their empire, the Soviet government had finally and definitively chosen to cut the empire free. For Modrow, who headed the East German delegation, the implications were plain to see. "What had previously looked like an alliance could not be maintained," he later wrote. "My conclusion was . . . that only an orientation towards the Federal Republic was a real alternative for us."[50]

Paying for Soviet oil in hard currency would make survival in East Berlin difficult enough, but not receiving Soviet oil at all would make it simply impossible. This soon became the GDR's fate. By the end of 1989, Soviet oil production had stagnated so much that the Kremlin struggled to meet its delivery commitments to its few remaining allies. In January 1990 alone, the GDR received 508,000 fewer tons of oil than had been agreed to with the Soviets. This put the country on pace for a roughly 30 percent drop in Soviet oil deliveries in 1990, a development that would, Modrow plaintively concluded, have "huge negative consequences" for all facets of economic and political life in the GDR. "Can we count on help [with oil]?" he asked Gorbachev and Ryzhkov directly in a meeting at the Kremlin at the end of the month. "This is a very difficult problem for us," Ryzhkov replied. "Oil production has dropped by 17 million tons. We are in a difficult position." Modrow returned to East Berlin empty-handed, with only his thoughts of a westward orientation to keep him company.[51]

The Soviet choice between the empire abroad and the social contract at home was therefore desperate but real. Saving the empire—or even slowing its dissolution—would have required significant economic discipline at home, while avoiding discipline at home required relinquishing the empire abroad. For Gorbachev and the rest of the Soviet leadership, the choice was clear. Rather than impose discipline domestically, refrain from accepting Western aid internationally, and increase material support for the GDR in its hour of need, they did the exact opposite in the hope of preserving perestroika. This choice—to prioritize the domestic Soviet economy and the well-being of the Soviet people over the maintenance of the empire—was not a radical departure from recent Soviet priorities but rather a continuation of them. By 1990, the circumstances had changed, but the principle remained the same.

It is little wonder, then, that when Gorbachev finally convened a key group of Soviet leaders on January 26 to discuss policy on German unity, no one even mentioned the idea of saving the GDR. "The SED's days are numbered," KGB chairman Vladimir Kriuchkov said. "We have to start getting our people used to a reunification of Germany." The process was "unstoppable," Ryzhkov seconded. "We cannot maintain the GDR. All barriers have already been torn down. Their economy is destroying them. . . . Preserving the GDR is unrealistic." On this, everyone agreed.

Where opinions differed was on how best to accomplish what Gorbachev called "the most important thing": to prevent a united Germany from remaining in NATO. The exchange of views went round and round for four hours, and a number of priorities emerged. First, it was important to "drag the process out" as long as possible, Gorbachev said, to provide time for domestic and international adjustment to the new state of affairs. Second, it was important for the Soviet military to begin to plan their retreat from German territory. There were over 300,000 troops in the GDR, 100,000 of them officers with families. This made the impending retreat as much a challenge to the Soviet economy as it was to the country's international prestige. "We have to put them somewhere!" Gorbachev's aide Anatolii Cherniaev exclaimed to his diary. In the meantime, however, "nobody should expect a united Germany to join NATO," Gorbachev said. "The presence of our armed forces will not allow that. And we can withdraw them if the Americans also withdraw their armed forces."[52]

Gorbachev's line of thinking had formed the backbone of the Cold War balance of power: the Soviets and Americans both had troops in the two Germanies, and neither side would retreat unless the other did as well. For over four decades, this line of thinking had perpetuated peace among the great powers but also precluded progress. And even at this late hour in the Cold War, this line of thinking evidently still held sway over the minds of men in the Kremlin and remained the circle the Western leaders had not yet been able to square. How could they get the Soviets to go home while allowing the Americans to stay right where they were? The Cold War could not come to a definitive end without an answer, so Western policy makers turned their attention to this question in February 1990. Their answer—a two-pronged approach that involved making reforms to NATO to give the alliance a nonmilitary visage and paying the Soviets to leave

Europe and accept Germany in NATO—proved to be a strikingly successful final act in the privatized Cold War. Its success depended on an unprecedented state of Soviet affairs: bankruptcy.

♦ ♦ ♦

The first act of paying the Soviets to leave was not directed at the Soviets at all. It was, instead, directed at those East Germans on the street who continued to set the pace of change. The dawn of a new year had done nothing to slay the twin-headed hydra of emigration and demonstration destroying the GDR from within. Indeed, the pace of change had only quickened. Emigration, which had shown signs of plateauing at the end of 1989, picked up in early 1990 as 1,500 people left permanently for the West every day.[53] Calls for political reform grew in strength and urgency, and the socialist economy began to lose all purchase on the minds of East Germans. After transitioning their calls for democratic recognition to demands for German unity, protesters now simply demanded a currency worth something. "If the DM doesn't come to us," they began to warn, "we'll go to it."[54]

Realizing he could no longer even pretend to govern without the support of the people, Modrow moved up the date for the country's first free elections from May to March and asked the country's nascent opposition roundtable to form a "Government of National Responsibility" with him in the interim. As the state's authority collapsed around him, the East German leader took to hoping the GDR could simply make it to the March elections without descending into complete chaos. In talks with West German officials in early February, Modrow began to darkly warn that "he could not exclude collapse and chaos within two weeks."[55]

It fell to Bonn to prevent the worst from happening. Modrow continued to plead for DM 15 billion to stabilize the country until the election, but Kohl remained skeptical that more deutsche marks in the hands of communists would solve the GDR's problems.[56] Instead, he and his ministers began to heed the calls of the East German people and contemplate putting the deutsche mark directly in their hands.[57] Since the fall of the Wall, policy makers had always viewed an economic and monetary union between the two German states in which the deutsche mark would become the official currency of both countries as an eventual step on the road to unity. But like everything else, this idea took on new urgency as the collapse of the GDR accelerated and East German elections moved ever closer. By early February, Kohl was ready, as he recalled in his memoirs, "to provide an unusual, even revolutionary response to unusual, even revolutionary events in the GDR," and on February 6, he announced his intention to begin negotiations on a currency union immediately.[58]

It was a decision of monumental importance. West German politics, East German politics, and the waning international politics of the Cold War would never again be the same. First, much like his announcement of the ten points in November, Kohl's announcement of the currency union bolstered the chancellor's bona fides as the preeminent West Germany politician fighting for unification. As he jostled with his political rivals in Bonn for position in the national elections approaching at the end of 1990, this reinforcement of his image as the chancellor of unity paid enormous political dividends.[59]

Large though it was, this boost in Kohl's political fortunes was nothing compared to the gains his allies made within the GDR. The day before the currency union announcement, Kohl had launched a coalition of East German political parties—the Alliance for Germany—to stand in the elections now set for March 18. The conventional wisdom held that Kohl's left-leaning rivals, the Social Democratic Party (SDP), would hold a natural electoral advantage in the socialist GDR. But the commitment to currency union immediately gave Kohl's Alliance an unmatched calling card—a new politics of making promises—to run on in the approaching election. The Alliance's election platform called for exchanging East German marks into deutsche marks at a one-to-one ratio for at least some of each East German's savings. The exact arrangement would not be decided until after the election, but the one-to-one offer began to paint a rosy picture of economic life in a united Germany.

During a month of campaigning across the GDR, Kohl finished the picture off with the glossy veneer of the Federal Republic's welfare state. In a newly united Germany, he told swelling crowds across the country, pensions would be protected, the social safety net would soften the shocks of adjustment to the market, and living standards would soon reach the levels of the FRG. To make this vision a reality as quickly as possible, the chancellor and his East German allies also committed to uniting the two countries through Article 23 of the Federal Republic's constitution. Rather than spend tedious time forging a whole new German state and constitution, Article 23 would allow the FRG to simply take over the GDR.[60] Many observers decried this as a new Anschluss in the Hitlerite tradition, but

East Germans liked what they heard, and on March 18, they delivered Kohl a surprising and resounding victory. The Alliance won 48 percent of the vote, and the head of the East German Christian Democratic Union (CDU), Lothar de Maizière, became the GDR's new prime minister. The mandate for change within the two German states was now undeniable.

But there were still those 380,000 Soviet troops, as well as the prickly matter of Germany's relationship to NATO. Here, too, Kohl's announcement of the deutsche mark's impending extension to the GDR proved to be of enormous consequence. The reason was subtler than the public politicking of political campaigns but no less fundamental. As Gorbachev had told the Soviet leadership in January, the troops were supposed to be the Kremlin's ultimate trump card in the negotiations over a united Germany's military status. But in order to station troops in East Germany, the Soviet Union had to pay them, and in order to pay them in a GDR run on the deutsche mark, the Kremlin would need mountains of hard currency it increasingly did not have. Unless Kohl was willing to pay the Soviets' bills—he was, but only if they were leaving—the military anchor of the Soviet empire would turn into an albatross on the Soviet budget as soon as the currency union was implemented. In one fell swoop, Kohl had accomplished with deutsche marks what four decades of Western military policy had not: he had made the Soviet military position in Central Europe untenable.[61]

The Americans did not want this opportunity to go to waste. As the process of unification accelerated in early 1990, so too did American efforts to secure their own position in Europe through NATO. "This is a rare period in which we can seek to achieve a fundamental shift in the strategic balance, particularly in Europe," National Security Advisor Brent Scowcroft wrote to President Bush at the start of the year.[62] This shift would be for naught, however, if the administration did not find a way to perpetuate its own power on the continent. "We are entering the end-game of the Cold War," Scowcroft continued a month later, and "when the end-game is over, the North Atlantic Alliance and the U.S. position in Europe [must] remain the vital instruments of peace and stability that we inherited from our predecessors."[63] Germany was the anchor of the American presence in Europe, so bringing a unified German state into the alliance was of paramount importance. But it would not be enough. The times were changing, and if NATO was to survive, it would have to change with them—or at least *appear* to do so. And this meant giving its military structure a new semblence of political purpose. "European security is increasingly being seen as more a political problem than a military one," American officials concluded. "Accordingly, NATO must respond by enhancing its political role."[64]

This was the message US secretary of state James Baker brought to Moscow in early February. Important details of the Western powers' position on Germany's membership in NATO remained in flux. Baker, for instance, assured Gorbachev that the alliance's jurisdiction would not expand to cover East German territory, only to later backtrack on this commitment.[65] But his overriding message for the Soviet leader was a clear and tough sell: American forces should remain on the continent because they were a "force of stability," a united Germany should join NATO because it would be less dangerous as an ally of Washington than as an independent power in the heart of Europe, and the alliance itself would no longer threaten the Soviet Union because it would become "far less of [a] military organization" and "much more of a political one." This was, in so many words, a request that the Soviets forget the Cold War and trust the Americans. "Neither the president nor I intend to extract any unilateral advantages from this process," Baker assured his hosts.[66]

Gorbachev, to say the least, remained unconvinced. Hollow assurances of benign intent—particularly when they were obviously contradicted by the very proposals he was supposed to accept—did nothing to change his thinking. But he figured that a long path of diplomatic maneuvering lay ahead, so it was not worth fighting Baker on the details (something for which he would later be criticized). During Baker's visit, both sides agreed to establish a "two-plus-four" forum composed of the two German states and the Four Powers to work through the diplomatic and security aspects of German unification. This would be the forum, Gorbachev thought, for the Kremlin to state its views and exert its leverage. For now, therefore, it was only worth stating what appeared to be obvious. "It goes without saying," Gorbachev told Baker, "that a broadening of the NATO zone is not acceptable."[67]

Of more immediate concern was the prospect of German monetary union. Gorbachev had the opportunity to discuss Kohl's new proposal when the chancellor arrived in Moscow on Baker's heels. Gorbachev wanted to know when would it happen. "I cannot answer this question," Kohl replied. "If I had been asked about it at the end of December, I would have replied that such a transition would take several years. . . . But now I'm not being asked. People decide everything with their feet." As a result, Kohl said, it could probably begin "in a few weeks, perhaps in a few months."

Neither openly acknowledged the significance of this prospect, but Gorbachev allowed himself to gesture at it obliquely. Unification raised an extensive "catalog of questions," he said as their conversation came to a close. "You are planning to introduce the deutsche mark in the GDR. But we have our armed forces there, and their pay is tied to the other mark. Here we have something to think about." Kohl answered with the same veil of ambiguity. "We will not shy away from any questions," he assured Gorbachev.[68]

This was not a throwaway line for the West German chancellor. He and his team had thought seriously about how they could and should use their economic leverage to shape the Kremlin's decision-making. On the eve of his travels to Moscow, Kohl received a memo from his foreign policy aide, Teltschik, laying out the geopolitical rationale for economic support for Moscow. "Fundamentally, it is important to make clear to the SU [Soviet Union] that . . . a united, economically strong . . . Germany is a more interesting partner than the GDR in decline." Only through economic integration with the West, Teltschik projected, would the Kremlin "support comprehensive security structures."[69] Among friends, Kohl put the point more bluntly. Germany's NATO membership "may end up being a matter of cash," he told President Bush and Secretary of State Baker when he met them at Camp David in late February. "They [the Soviets] need money."[70]

They did indeed. But this was not a perennial condition of Soviet affairs. Throughout the Cold War, the Kremlin had not conducted a mercenary foreign policy, and its two decades of generous energy subsidies to Eastern Europe was proof enough that Soviet leaders did not usually think of their national security interests as simple "matters of cash." The Soviet drive for money was instead a condition unique to the spring of 1990 and a product of the Kremlin's loss of creditworthiness on global capital markets. Private capital holders had shut the door on the Kremlin, and this gave Western governments power to shape Soviet decision-making in ways they previously could not. Germany's NATO membership became a "matter of cash" because, quite simply, the Kremlin had nowhere else to get it.

Soviet bankers had done their level best to keep Moscow's lines of credit open as long as possible. While the Wall was falling and the Cold War order was collapsing throughout Eastern Europe, the Kremlin's money men had traveled the world to hunt vigilantly for new sources of capital. From November 1989 to April 1990, they took fifty-four trips to the beating hearts of global finance. In the boardrooms of Goldman Sachs and Chase Manhattan in New York, Morgan Grenfell and National Westminster

Bank in London, Deutsche Bank and Commerzbank in Frankfurt, Dai-Ichi Kangyo Bank and Fuji Bank in Tokyo, and the sovereign wealth fund of Kuwait, Soviet bankers attempted to breathe new life into capitalists' souring image of perestroika's communist renaissance. Time and again, the banks turned them away. Moskovskii, president of the foreign trade bank, reported in April 1990 that his officials could no longer issue bonds or take out syndicated loans because there had been a "constant strengthening of foreign creditors' negative attitude toward the provision of funds . . . to the Soviet Union." Soviet officials had partially compensated for this drop in foreign confidence by increasing borrowing on a short-term basis, and 50 percent of the new money flowing into the Soviet Union came in the form of short-term interbank deposits. But these could be withdrawn at a moment's notice, leaving the country "dangerously dependent" on the whims of far-flung, foreign, and fickle financial institutions.[71]

Soviet officials well understood that the danger in dependency lay in the Western political conditionality that would surely accompany a loss of market access. In late February 1990, the Soviet leadership asked Gosbank officials to study the government's options as it confronted global capital's dwindling confidence. Officials reported back in April that the prospects were not pretty. Rescheduling the country's debt was not a palatable choice because it would inevitably lead the Kremlin into the hands of the International Monetary Fund (IMF). Officials wrote, "As the experience of countries forced to take this path in the eighties (Mexico, Brazil, a number of Latin American countries, as well as Poland and Yugoslavia)" shows, . . . the postponement of paying off external debt has adverse economic and political consequences." Therefore, in the opinion of the bank, rescheduling the country's debt was "an unacceptable measure that could inflict economic and political damage on an unpredictable scale." Borrowing directly from Western governments was little better. "External borrowing at the intergovernmental level [is] fraught with great material and political damage to our country," they wrote. As a general rule, they continued, borrowing from other governments "significantly limits the sovereignty of the borrowing country." Soviet borrowing from Western countries was bound to be even worse because the attachment of "tough political conditionality" to the loans would be "inevitable." Such borrowing should "only be used as a last resort when no other sources of foreign currency are available."[72]

By April, the time for financial last resorts arrived at the very moment the question of Germany's membership in NATO was coming to a head.

On the domestic front, Soviet officials reported that the country was now behind on its payments for imports of everything from bread to medicine.[73] Foreign companies were withholding deliveries until payment arrived, so the foundations of the Soviet social contract were now under severe threat. Foreign banks left no doubt about what they would need before extending any further credit. "Private capital will not risk coming here in any form," a Deutsche Bank representative told Politburo member Alexander Yakovlev on April 4, "without guarantees and support from . . . governments."[74] Therefore, banks recommended that the Kremlin appeal directly to European governments. In another meeting with Deutsche Bank on April 27, the bankers told their Soviet counterparts that if the Soviet request came from a leading official like Ryzhkov, Shevardnadze, or Gorbachev himself, Western governments would likely be supportive. Desperate for money and unable to find it, Soviet bankers sent word of this idea up the bureaucratic ladder to the highest levels of the leadership.[75]

At the same time, hard-line members of the party and foreign policy elite pressed Gorbachev to maintain a firm line on what remained of the German question. In early April, the prevailing Politburo opinion was one of obstinate resistance to any inclusion of Germany in NATO. "It is illusory [for the US] to believe that under pressure the USSR would put up with an effective Anschluss of the GDR, with the breakdown of the military political balance in the centre of Europe," the group said in its guidance for Shevardnadze's ongoing negotiations with the Americans. "The President [Bush] should be told clearly that we cannot agree to see the united Germany in NATO."[76] On April 18, the leading Soviet expert on German affairs, Valentin Falin, wrote to Gorbachev urging that the West Germans not be spared from a more pugnacious approach. Washington and Bonn knew that Moscow's "freedom of maneuver" was "currently extremely limited" and therefore believed they could press their "long-standing claims to the maximum without the risk of a serious confrontation." They were angling to present the Soviet Union with a "fait accompli" on Germany's military status that it would not be able to resist or refuse. Falin encouraged Gorbachev to disabuse them of these dangerous notions. "You have to use every effort to show the Europeans and especially the Germans that their hopes can be betrayed once more," he wrote. The "prerequisite for success," he told Gorbachev, was "firmness."[77]

One of the conditions to which Moscow would adhere most firmly was its economic relationship with the GDR. Soviet officials feared the harm that would befall their economy if a unified Germany chose not to trade with the Soviet Union at the same level as the GDR. The day after Falin's memo to Gorbachev, the Kremlin demanded in a memorandum to Bonn that the Federal Republic assume the GDR's economic obligations to the Soviet Union.[78] This played right into Kohl's strategy for shaping Soviet decision-making through economics. At a meeting with the Soviet ambassador to Bonn on April 23, the chancellor not only agreed to cover the GDR's economic obligations to Moscow but also expressed interest in signing a new treaty with the Kremlin that would place the two countries' economic cooperation on a "comprehensive and long-term basis" after unification was complete.[79] The ambassador dutifully reported Kohl's vision back to Moscow.[80]

By late April, then, the choice between discipline at home and retreat from abroad had arrived on Gorbachev's desk in the form of two different piles of memos laying out two widely divergent policies. In one pile, Soviet bankers warned him that the country was on the verge of losing all access to hard currency unless he made a direct appeal to Western governments for state-sponsored loans. Soviet diplomats in Bonn reported that Kohl had all but confirmed his willingness to support such loans. Soviet financial officials knew this appeal would invite Kohl and the broader Western coalition to attach political conditions to the loans, but it was a risk they felt the country had to take. Without hard currency, the government would not be able to import the food and medicine that comprised the foundation of the Soviet social contract, and economic discipline would soon follow.

In the other pile, party hard-liners and foreign policy officials urged Gorbachev to stand firm in resisting Germany's inclusion in NATO. They warned him that the country's security and prestige were on the line. Unless he disrupted Western governments' machinations on the German question, the Soviet Union would be presented with a fait accompli and forced to accept a united Germany in the Atlantic alliance. The balance of power would irrevocably shift in the West's favor, and the Soviet Union's 380,000 troops would retreat under a cloud of humiliating geopolitical defeat. If he chose, instead, to stand his ground, he would lose the goodwill of Western governments and be forced to impose austerity domestically, but at least he would salvage the nation's pride and security on the international stage. It was now up to Gorbachev to choose between these two dreadful options.

In early May, he chose retreat over discipline. In the Politburo on May 3, to appease the hard-liners, he still blustered about stonewalling German membership at all costs. "Do not let Germany into NATO and that's that!" he roared.[81] But the next day he sent Shevardnadze to Bonn for the first foreign ministers' meeting of the "two-plus-four" with a secret request for massive new West German loans. In a meeting with Kohl, Shevardnadze reaffirmed his government's resistance to German membership in the alliance, but he "did not rule out that a compromise could be found." As a discreet signal of the Kremlin's growing flexibility, Shevardnadze encouraged Kohl to meet with Gorbachev in Moscow in July, after the upcoming Communist Party congress. He did not broach the topic of loans until the very end of their meeting, and the issue was so sensitive that it was not recorded in the official minutes. Shevardnadze made it clear that the request came directly from Gorbachev himself, and he did his best to put the patina of pride on his supplication. "Because the Soviet Union is a rich country, there is no risk with such loans," he said. But the Federal Republic's willingness to grant the loans was nevertheless "important." Recognizing the sensitivity of the request, Kohl agreed to address the issue himself as soon as he possibly could.[82]

Few officials in either Bonn or Moscow knew of Shevardnadze's request, but those who did understood its political importance. The Soviet ambassador to Bonn, Yuli Kvitsinskii, recalled feeling "very displeased." Sending the foreign minister to Bonn "and having him beg for money," Kvitsinskii later wrote, "meant that, whether we wanted it or not, we indicated a connection between the solution of the German question and the granting of credit."[83] For precisely this reason, Kohl's aide Teltschik was elated. "Quick help for the Soviet Union," he wrote, "the second time this year after the food aid in January, could improve the climate and also be helpful in solving major political problems."[84]

The Soviets soon followed Shevardnadze's meeting with a formal request for DM 20 billion in loan guarantees, and Kohl met with leading West German bankers on May 8 to discuss it. Collectively, they concluded they could not provide DM 20 billion in guarantees, but they could fund DM 5 billion and work to get other countries to contribute as well. So as not to embarrass Gorbachev, Kohl believed this needed to be discussed with the Soviet leadership in private, so he sent Teltschik and the bankers on a top-secret mission to Moscow.[85]

On May 14, the entire Soviet leadership stood ready to discuss the dire state of the Soviet economy with their West German guests. In morning

meetings with Ryzhkov, Shevardnadze, Moskovskii, and Kvitsinskii, Teltschik and the bankers heard about the Kremlin's economic and financial
problems in "great detail."[86] Ryzhkov confided that it was not the union's
many past and present economic problems that concerned him, but rather
its coming hardships. Over the previous few months, he had been hard at
work evaluating plans for the country's transition to a market economy,
and under any reform scenario, economic hardship for the Soviet population was inevitable. This hardship would only increase if Moscow could
not access global capital markets, so Western governments' loan guarantees could play the vital role of softening the blow of the market transition.
The country had "to go through a very complicated stage," he told the West
Germans. "It was during this time that the USSR needed help to keep the
situation stable." The transition to the market could be done without "outside help," but then the government would "have to lower the standard of
living of the population and restrict imports." They wanted to do this
"under no circumstances" because "it could destroy all the hope that people
place in perestroika."[87] The more access to hard currency the government
had, the fewer promises it would need to break, and Ryzhkov was intent on
breaking as few as possible.

Teltschik lent a sympathetic ear, but he had come to Moscow for a very
particular purpose: to tie the granting of West German loans to a satisfactory resolution to the German question. In his memoir, Teltschik recalled
making clear to Ryzhkov and Shevardnadze that the West German government saw its financial support "as part of the overall package, which
should help to solve the German question."[88] The Soviets received the
message loud and clear. Kvitsinskii remembered that the West Germans'
attempt to link their financial support to the German question "was not to
be overlooked."[89]

After lunch, Gorbachev tried in vain to keep the two issues separate.
Perhaps sensing the leverage the meeting implied, he began his conversation with a distinction he hoped would hold up under pressure. "It would
not be acceptable for the Soviet Union to be dependent, especially politically," he said. "On the other hand, everyone in this world is interdepen-
dent." The Soviet Union had abundant resources with which to repay its
debts, he assured his guests. All it needed was "oxygen in order to survive
two or three years." He was particularly concerned that "the financial situation" did not allow the government "to fully develop social programs."
If he could use Western government-sponsored loans to improve the

social situation, that would "open up great prospects for not letting market prices out of control." He did not launch into an extended critique of Germany's potential membership in NATO, but he nevertheless maintained that a solution should be found to Europe's many security issues in which "nobody's security interests are diminished." Perhaps the best solution, he speculated, would be for both alliances to dissolve.[90]

Kohl saw things differently. After Teltschik returned to Bonn, Kohl told his advisers, "The message to Gorbachev must be that the federal government would help if it had been made clear beforehand that the two-plus-four talks would be successfully concluded." He "could not vouch for loans on such a scale, if no consideration was linked to that."[91] On May 22, he made this message explicit in a letter to Gorbachev announcing his willingness to issue DM 5 billion in loan guarantees. Such an amount was "a considerable political effort on the part of the Federal Government," he wrote. Therefore, "I link it with the expectation that your government, will do everything in the same spirit as part of the two-plus-four process to bring about the necessary decisions that will enable the issues at stake to be resolved constructively." He asked Gorbachev to confirm that this arrangement would work for him and committed himself to work on the Soviets' behalf to campaign for loan guarantees from other Western governments.[92]

News that Gorbachev was now looking for Western governments to sponsor loans quickly made its way to Washington. When Baker arrived in Moscow in mid-May, the Soviet leader gave him the same basic pitch about needing oxygen that he gave Teltschik and the West German bankers.[93] The secretary of state reported to Bush that Gorbachev would "hit you up" for credits when the two leaders met in Washington at the end of the month.[94] The administration therefore spent the last week of May debating what the National Security Council called "the $20 billion question": should the United States essentially pay for a peaceful change in the global balance of power? Should it pay Gorbachev to leave Central Europe?[95] Scowcroft was crystal clear about the historic stakes in a memo to the president on May 29:

> This is—and you should view it as such—a strategic choice about whether economic assistance is a direct and expeditious means by which to secure the victory of the West in the Cold War by obtaining the unification of Germany in NATO and the withdrawal of the Soviet military from Central and Eastern Europe. . . .

When one thinks of the extraordinary amount of money that we have spent in forty-five years to contain Soviet communism, $20 billion to secure its final demise in Europe is less daunting. If—and it is a big if—Gorbachev were willing to take these terms, financial assistance could in effect seal the armistice in the Cold War on our terms.[96]

Amazingly, the rest of the administration had no interest. Even the prospect of *winning the Cold War*—the organizing principle of all US foreign policy since the 1940s—was not a big enough development to justify opening the American checkbook. For a US government that had grown accustomed to imposing stringent conditionality on all manner of debtor countries in the 1980s, it appeared there were still many more political conditions for the Kremlin to meet. There were the ongoing problems with Lithuania. Leaders in Vilnius had declared independence from the Soviet Union in March, and Gorbachev had responded with an oil and gas embargo meant to coerce them back to the negotiating table. Add to that the Soviet Union's continued support for the eternal bugaboo of America's Cold War politics—Fidel Castro's Cuba—and the administration saw no geopolitical way or reason to justify aiding the Soviet leader.[97]

Beyond politics, there was still the dismal state of the Soviet economy. Gorbachev had been unable or unwilling to impose the kind of discipline that market reform required, and the US Treasury was not in the habit of supporting half-hearted socialism. "The Soviets seem to lack any sense of the true magnitude of reforms that are required," Treasury secretary Nicolas Brady wrote Bush on May 24.[98] The United States would expect something "along the lines of an IMF austerity program" in exchange for any aid, and Gorbachev had given no sign this was something he could deliver.[99] Only once the socialist perestroika really started to resemble a capitalist perestroika would US economic conditionality be met. So, for reasons of both politics and economics, the Bush administration had little more than a "purely symbolic" trade deal to offer Gorbachev when he arrived in Washington.[100]

Lucky for the Americans, Gorbachev was not conditioning the withdrawal of Soviet troops and his acceptance of Germany in NATO on a precise amount in Western loans. The circumstances did not give him that luxury. His gambit was instead one that sought to extract as much economic gain as possible from decisions he believed he would eventually have to make anyway.[101] In his secret meeting with Teltschik and the bankers, Gorbachev discussed his determination to carry out domestic economic reform as follows: "If you ask whether or not we [will] go the path we have chosen without Western support, there is only one answer: we will, and no one will stop us." But without the support of the West, he added, his domestic political opponents could "sabotage" perestroika by "increasing tensions in society and discontent among the working people."[102] Whether it was DM 5 billion or $20 billion, Western financial support would only aid this campaign to ward off perestroika's many saboteurs.

So too would cutting costs in East Germany. By mid-May, German monetary union had been set for July 1, which meant that the burden of stationing Soviet forces there was about to skyrocket. The East German government put the cost at DM 1.25 billion just for the remainder of 1990 when they presented Soviet officials with a bill for that amount in mid-June. The Kremlin knew sums this large were nowhere to be found, so at the end of the month, the Politburo instructed all organs of the Soviet government to prepare for negotiations with both German states on financial and economic issues. Their goal should be "reducing to the minimum Soviet expenditures in foreign currency to pay for the stay of the Soviet group of forces on the territory of Eastern Germany in 1991."[103] It was time to cut losses and make for the exits.

Of course, Western leaders did not know this yet, and the West Germans were not about to take any chances. On June 9, Gorbachev responded with vague affirmation to Kohl's letter linking the DM 5 billion in loans to cooperation on the German question. His letter was light on specifics, but it reaffirmed his interest in meeting with Kohl in July, which gave West German officials confidence that they could "expect something in return" for the loans.[104] In the meantime, they thought it wise to continue to up their offer. In June, they signed an agreement with Moscow to cover the DM 1.25 billion cost of stationing Soviet troops in the GDR through the end of 1990 and allowed Soviet troops stationed in the GDR to exchange their savings from East German marks to deutsche marks at the favorable rate of two to one.[105] At the end of the month, they finalized DM 5 billion in loan guarantees to keep Moscow financially afloat. The route of retreat back to Moscow would be a difficult one for the pride of the Soviet Army, but at least it would be gilded in hard currency.

The Americans would not partake in the gilding, but they were happy to lead the second half of the Western strategy to keep the United States in

Europe: NATO reform. Since Baker had first attempted in February to convince Gorbachev there was nothing to fear from an alliance that would become a "political" organization, American officials had rounded out the picture with a series of policy proposals meant to make the West's burgeoning military superiority appear less threatening. When Baker visited Gorbachev in May, he presented him with a list of nine reforms to that effect. Beyond reforming NATO into a political organization, they ranged from limiting the size of the German armed forces to establishing a formal transition period after unification that would allow Soviet forces to withdraw from eastern Germany before NATO moved in.[106] In June, Shevardnadze strongly hinted that a reformed NATO would be an easier sell to the Soviet people, so all eyes turned to an alliance summit in London scheduled for early July.[107]

Washington and Bonn left nothing to chance. When the allies converged on the British capital, they were presented with a communiqué crafted by the two governments with the Soviet public in mind. It stated that NATO and the Warsaw Pact were no longer adversaries and promised that NATO would never "be the first to use force." It committed to replacing the risky Cold War military doctrine of "flexible response," which had sought to deter a Soviet conventional attack through the prospect of nuclear escalation, with a policy that made nuclear weapons "truly into weapons of last resort." Conventional forces in both East and West would be dramatically reduced through the ongoing Conventional Forces in Europe (CFE) process, and the NATO troops that remained on the continent would be reorganized into multinational units. As the Warsaw Pact changed (and soon melted away), the nations that comprised it, including the Soviet Union, would be welcome to send diplomatic representation to NATO headquarters in Brussels. The alliance would not budge on its foundational goals—keeping the United States' military in Europe and bringing a united Germany into NATO—but it aimed to make these bedrocks appear less menacing.[108]

◆ ◆ ◆

For Gorbachev, these changes were enough, or at least the best to be hoped for, as he pursued his primary goal of transforming the Soviet Union. When the party congress opened in Moscow, he and Shevardnadze parried attacks on their foreign policy with the crutch of a reformed NATO. The new-look Atlantic alliance had paved the way for "a safe future for the entire European continent," they told the Soviet press.[109] Many of their comrades stridently disagreed, but with Boris Yeltsin rising in Russia as a nationalist challenger to the union's core, party members saw Gorbachev as the best hope for holding the country together and dutifully reelected him general secretary.[110]

Gorbachev was now free to pursue the two most politically difficult tasks on his agenda: discipline and retreat. As the German question came to a head in the summer of 1990, so too did the Soviet domestic debate over how to transition to a market economy. Policy makers and the public alike were well aware that the move to a market economy would imply economic discipline of many kinds, making it an extremely difficult political issue for the Soviet leadership. Ryzhkov's mere mention in May 1990 of a planned increase in the price of bread had set off a wave of panic buying among consumers and a chorus of derision among politicians. The prime minister had hastily retracted his proposals for further study, and he and Gorbachev had publicly committed to providing a new plan for the country's market transition by September. Thus, when Helmut Kohl arrived in Moscow on July 14 with hopes of resolving the German question once and for all, the search was on inside the Kremlin for the most politically feasible way to achieve the politically impossible task of transitioning to the market.

Both Soviet and West German policy makers knew that German money could be decisive in meeting this challenge. As Kohl and his team departed Bonn on July 14, Finance Minister Theo Waigel informed the chancellor that the Soviets had already burned through the DM 5 billion in guaranteed loans. This gave them hope that their continued financial assistance could finally seal the deal on a German settlement.[111]

Gorbachev did not make them wait long for a breakthrough. At Kohl and Gorbachev's first meeting on July 15, the chancellor proposed the terms of their debate: he needed a plan for Soviet troop withdrawal from Germany and Gorbachev's assent to Germany's membership in NATO, and, in return, he would be willing to limit the size of Germany's armed forces and offer further economic support for Moscow. Gorbachev, in turn, wanted to ensure that Germany would accept its border with Poland and forswear the development of biological, chemical, and nuclear weapons. Kohl had already affirmed both these positions and had no problem affirming them once again.

Then the diplomatic and legal ballet began. Gorbachev granted that a united Germany could join NATO but stipulated that "NATO's structures" should not extend to East German territory while Soviet troops were still there. The troops' presence, in turn, would be extended for three or four years on the legal basis of their current rights of occupation. Kohl saw both promise and problem in this proposal. He had gained the long-sought Soviet recognition of Germany's right to join NATO, but he could not consider Germany fully sovereign while Soviet troops continued to occupy the country. More to the point, he could not ask the German people to fund their own occupation by a foreign power. Far better, he thought, if Moscow renounced its Four Power rights at the moment of unification, along with the other Western countries, and the two sides negotiated a separate agreement to address the Soviet troops' presence. If the Soviets granted Germany complete sovereignty, Kohl told Gorbachev that he looked forward to providing funding for the withdrawal and resettlement of the Soviet Army and signing a broad treaty of cooperation. With little leverage of his own, Gorbachev gave way to the chancellor's vision.[112]

As a sign of the two parties' growing goodwill, Gorbachev had invited Kohl to travel with him to his hometown of Stavropol in the Russian Caucasus. So, on the afternoon of July 15, the two leaders and their senior advisors headed south. In the mountain village of Archys outside the city, the diplomatic ballet continued as the two sides wound their way toward final agreement. Gorbachev and Shevardnadze tried in vain to get the West Germans to agree that NATO's military structures would never extend to the GDR. Kohl was willing to prohibit NATO's nuclear weapons and foreign troops from ever being stationed on East German territory, and he offered to cap the German army at 370,000 soldiers, but he demanded that NATO's full structures extend to the former GDR once the Soviets left. Gorbachev once again gave way.[113]

If this was as good as the diplomatic deal was going to get for the Soviets, Gorbachev thought it was time to talk money. His deputy, Stepan Sitarian, laid bare how German monetary union had destroyed the Soviet position in East Germany. He did so through the only Soviet product as valuable around the world as the deutsche mark—oil. He stated, "The maintenance of Soviet armed forces in the GDR currently costs the equivalent of 6 million tons of oil. If no changes are made, the stationing of the Soviet troops in the future will cost the equivalent of 17 million tons in DM." This was as much as the Kremlin had annually supplied to the entire GDR, he said, so clearly some significant form of compensation would be required. Kohl offered to sign a "transfer agreement" to cover the Soviets' additional costs associated with the introduction of the deutsche mark and the challenge of resettling troops in the Soviet Union. Financial officials from both sides could surely work out the details, he thought. The two leaders could instead focus on the big picture—a comprehensive treaty that would give Soviet-German relations "a new quality" and make unification "profitable for both sides." With assurances of future financial compensation, Gorbachev agreed, and the two leaders went out to tell the world of their accord.[114]

Soviet leaders did what they could to dilute the optics of selling their empire for hard currency, but the reality proved difficult to avoid. Since June, Cherniaev had been warning Gorbachev to avoid the appearance that "the German[s] quickly won him over with loans," and after the July summit, he maintained that "it is not the bait (loans) but the fact that it is pointless to resist" that caused Gorbachev to give in. Others in the Soviet leadership recognized that the futility of opposition and the allure of loans were not opposing, but rather mutually reinforcing, forces. "We cannot stop the unification," Shevardnadze told his aide when asked on the plane ride back from Stavropol why Gorbachev had quickly given in to Kohl. "In addition, our economic situation and nationalities situation are catastrophic. . . . It is either: return to the cold war, or: peace in Europe." If the Kremlin gave Europe peace by granting the Germans unity, then perhaps the Germans would continue to keep the Soviet economy afloat. "Five billion marks from [the] Germans are saving us from bankruptcy," Shevardnadze continued. "Ryzhkov warned that in half a year we would be bankrupt."[115]

The West Germans had saved the Soviet Union from financial catastrophe, and now Soviet leaders hoped they would also ease the country's transition to the market. While the West Germans celebrated Kohl's breakthrough and rushed to finish unification by autumn, the debate within the Soviet leadership over the speed and scope of transitioning to the market reached a fever pitch. In late July, Gorbachev formed a team of academic economists and government policy makers to build a consensus on the shape of market reform. No one doubted that the move to the market would require that promises be broken and discipline imposed. But *how many* promises and *how much* discipline remained open questions whose answers depended in part on whether the Soviet Union maintained access to global capital markets. Under various reform scenarios, officials projected consumer price increases of 50–150 percent, unemployment numbers ranging from twenty-five to seventy million people, declines in real wages of 10 percent over five years, and a fall in output of 12–15 percent in 1991. Economic growth would not return until 1994 or 1995.[116] Losing access to hard currency would only sharpen the severity of the blows to the Soviet economy and society. "A binding external constraint," Gosplan officials concluded, "would reduce the availability of imported inputs, and so reduces output further still."[117] As Gorbachev and Ryzhkov had recognized since the spring, access to hard currency was not required to carry out market reforms, but it was required if they wanted to smooth the treacherous politics of reform by lessening the coming blow to Soviet living standards.

The riches of retreat from Germany were just the lifeline they needed. Against the backdrop of the market reform debate, Soviet policy makers began calculating just how many deutsche marks the transfer agreement with Bonn should include. When the two sides reconvened for negotiations in late August, the Soviets demanded close to DM 20 billion to cover the stationing, transport, and resettlement of their troops. The West Germans had come to the meeting with the meek sum of DM 5–6 billion in mind, which left a gaping hole between the two sides that only Kohl and Gorbachev could close.[118]

For the two leaders, talking about money proved to be much more contentious than talking about NATO. On September 7, Kohl called Gorbachev to increase the West German offer to DM 8 billion. Gorbachev told him emphatically that such an offer was a "dead end." As a warning shot across the German bow, he mentioned the upcoming final round of the "two-plus-four" negotiations, where Bonn would still need Moscow's formal approval before Kohl's dreams of unity could be realized. Given the paltry West German offer, he wondered aloud if he should tell Shevardnadze to withhold Soviet approval. Kohl got the message, and he told Gorbachev he would call him back after "think[ing] things over again."[119]

After a desperate search of every last inch of the state's coffers, he called back on September 10 with an offer of DM 12 billion. The tension of unmet expectations hung on the phone line. Gorbachev dropped all pretense that the money would be used to pay for the troop transition and appealed to the coming challenges of transitioning to the market. "You know that the situation in our country is very difficult," he told Kohl. "We need to decisively correct the economic situation. . . . I am in a very difficult position and cannot bargain. . . . I think 15–16 billion [deutsche] marks will still be found." Kohl was also at the end of his leash. "I don't want to haggle. My proposal is reasonable and realistic," he responded. "The new stage" in Soviet-German relations that would come after German unity was completed, he assured Gorbachev, would be full of material benefits for the Soviet Union. Right now, however, all he could offer was DM 12 billion.

Gorbachev had built the entirety of perestroika's foreign policy on a foundation of trust between East and West, but now, in the breach, he could show none toward Kohl's rosy vision of the future. "I don't know what to tell you," he told the chancellor heavily. "Maybe we have to think about going back to the beginning or extending the deadlines." He absolutely could not budge; the challenge of breaking promises awaited him at home. "We are now compiling a list of stabilization measures" for the economy, he said. "Among other things, tough measures are planned with regard to internal processes. I am in a difficult position and you have to see it." After five years of concessions to Western interests, Gorbachev was now making a final stand in the hope of softening the coming blow of discipline at home.

Kohl realized the contest of wills was his to lose, and he reached for a loan to bridge the gap between his means and Gorbachev's ends. What if he added an interest-free loan of DM 3 billion? he asked Gorbachev. That would bring the Kremlin's total access to hard currency from the deal to DM 15 billion. Gorbachev, at last, had gotten what he needed. "I shake your hand, Mr. Chancellor," he said, and the deal was done.[120]

The final steps of German unification and the end of the Cold War were not long in coming. On September 12, the foreign ministers of the six "two-plus-four" countries signed a final agreement in Moscow, and the four victorious powers of the Second World War gave up their rights to determine Germany's destiny. On October 3, Kohl celebrated with throngs of German citizens in front of the Brandenburg Gate as the Federal Republic absorbed the GDR and a united Germany took its place among nations. A month later, on the one-year anniversary of the fall of the Berlin Wall, Gorbachev and Kohl signed bilateral treaties regulating the removal of Soviet troops from Germany by 1994 and inaugurating a hopeful new era of bilateral cooperation. A week after that, the signing of the Treaty on Conventional Armed Forces in Europe on November 17 in Paris enshrined the Soviet military retreat from the European continent and the end of the Cold War conventional arms race.[121] The problem that had inaugurated the Cold War as a geopolitical conflict—the United States' and Soviet Union's militarized disagreement over the postwar fate of German power—had been definitively resolved.

All the while, the challenge of breaking promises in the Soviet Union went unmet. After months of deliberation, Gorbachev delayed the transition to the market yet again in the fall of 1990 until the eternally elusive political consensus could be built around the necessity of reforms. Cherniaev wrote in his diary in mid-September 1990 that Gorbachev continued "asking everyone for money and loans" so that he could defer the challenge of economic discipline to yet another day.[122]

The Cold War might end in defeat. The balance of power might shift to the east. And the Soviet Army might retreat back to Moscow. But for the man inside the Kremlin, the political costs of those historically unprecedented developments were nothing compared to the herculean task of breaking promises to the Soviet people.

Conclusion

The Triumph of Broken Promises

"IT IS POLITICS that follows economics and not vice versa," Gorbachev told the Lithuanian Communist Party in January 1990 during an abortive bid to keep the nation from leaving the Soviet Union.[1] Evidently, the general secretary retained the foundational causal precept of Marxism, even as he jettisoned innumerable legacies of Marxism-Leninism. There was no way the Lithuanians would leave the union, he thought. It made no economic sense. The tiny Baltic state imported most of its energy from the rest of the Soviet Union, and all its economic links ran through Moscow. Nationalist pride might momentarily surge, but eventually politics would follow economics.[2]

It did not take long for the Lithuanians to prove him wrong. When they declared their independence three months later, they did so for a range of historical, ethnic, and nationalist reasons that belied pure economic motivation. They took only a moment's pause when Gorbachev changed their economic calculus by imposing an oil and gas embargo in April 1990, and they persevered through violent intimidation in 1991 to achieve the independence forcibly denied them ever since the Red Army beat back Hitler's eastward march and reoccupied the Baltic states in 1944.

Lithuania's drive to independence is only the most proximate of countless episodes in the historical record that make a mockery of the breezy simplicity of Gorbachev's dictum. There is, of course, no universal and ironclad relationship between economic causes and political effects, so it is incumbent upon anyone who would propose a relationship between a particular set of economic causes and a particular set of political effects to justify the reasons for doing so and specify the exact nature of the causal relation.

This book has been one such attempt at justification and specificity. It has argued that the economic forces unleashed by the 1973 oil crisis ultimately brought the Cold War to a peaceful end and gave rise to the neoliberal global economy of the late twentieth century. Those economic forces—oil, finance, and economic discipline—exerted such a profound effect because they fundamentally altered the nature of the competition between democratic capitalism and state socialism. The Cold War began as a competition between democratic capitalist and state socialist governments to harness the forces of industrial modernity to improve the economic security and well-being of their people. The two sides raced to make promises to their people and expand the social contracts that prevailed in their societies.

The economic crises of the 1970s made this politics of making promises untenable. The oil crisis of 1973 produced both the pressure to break promises and the means of avoiding that pressure. Over the long term, the industrialized economies of both East and West had to learn to produce more economic output with fewer inputs, a wrenching process of breaking promises whose true magnitude remains hidden behind the economist's prosaic phrase "intensive growth." But in the short term, they could avoid this challenge by seeking refuge in the global economy's two new vast pools of wealth—global capital markets and energy resources—which vastly expanded in value after the oil crisis. As long as nation-states maintained access to either capital markets or energy resources, they could continue making promises at home and fighting the Cold War abroad. If, however, they lost access to one or both, they would have to turn to the politics of breaking promises and implement policies of economic discipline at home.

As we have seen, these moments of economic discipline abounded in the last two decades of the Cold War and ultimately decided its outcome. Though the Cold War began as a race to make promises, it ended as a race to break promises, and democratic capitalism prevailed over state socialism because it proved capable of breaking promises and imposing discipline. Neoliberalism rose as the Cold War ended because it provided ideological justification for acts of breaking promises; it made a virtue out of economic discipline. Combined with electoral democracy, it gave democratic capitalist states a political and ideological tool kit to meet the challenge of breaking promises. Lacking these tools, the states of the Eastern Bloc democratized their political systems and reformed their ideology in the 1980s as a means of imposing economic discipline. It is this process of political change and ideological reform that we now call the collapse of communism and the end of the Cold War.

Historians have traditionally identified a series of people and forces as the principle causes of the end of the Cold War: Gorbachev's launch of glasnost and perestroika, his bold superpower diplomacy with Ronald Reagan and George H. W. Bush, the "people power" of Eastern Europeans in the streets, and the lucky confluence of a series of contingent events, like the opening of the Berlin Wall, that no one foresaw or intended. The account offered in this book does not deny the importance of any of these traditional markers of the end of the Cold War. Instead, it places these markers in a new light—one that was not ignited in the present and shone back onto the past, but rather one that once burned bright in the past and grew dim over time.

It was not the present study, after all, that first identified the connection between the oil crisis, Eastern Bloc sovereign debt, and policies of economic discipline. It was instead the East German Central Committee that obsessed over this connection on November 9, 1989, just hours before the Berlin Wall opened. "In 1973 there was a very large worldwide price explosion," financial expert Günter Ehrensperger told his comrades on that fateful day. "Because of this price explosion, the procurement of oil and other raw materials for the GDR [German Democratic Republic] became much more expensive." Rather than adjust the domestic economy to meet this new reality, Ehrensperger said, the GDR had delayed its fate by borrowing money from the capitalist world. "If you want to characterize in one sentence why we are in this situation today," he said in reference to the debt, "then you have to say objectively that since at least 1973 we have fooled ourselves and lived beyond our means year after year. Debts were paid with new debts." Economic discipline was the only logical response. "If we want to get out of this situation," Ehrensperger concluded, "we have to work hard and consume less than we produce for at least 15 years."[3] Far from drawing connections that contemporaries in the Cold War did not see, this book has merely elaborated on the dynamics that concerned the highest levels of the East German leadership on the day the foundation of their regime came crashing down.

Nor was it an interpretive invention of this book to describe the dilemmas of Soviet imperial governance and the sources of Soviet imperial collapse in primarily economic terms. It was, instead, Mikhail Gorbachev, who, when discussing the fate of Poland in the 1970s and 1980s, rhetorically asked the Politburo in March 1988, "What was it all based on? On credits from the West and on our cheap fuel. The same goes for Hungary. . . . We cannot remain a provider of cheap resources for them forever."[4] And it was Yuli Kvitsinskii, the Soviet expert on Germany, who confided to a colleague in November 1990 that "the Deutschmark decided everything" about the process of German unification and the precipitous Soviet retreat that followed.[5] This book has been unable to match Gorbachev's and Kvitsinskii's parsimony, but it has taken inspiration from, rather than imputed motivations to, their descriptions of the reasons for the Soviet imperial collapse.

Even this book's two most adventurous claims—that electoral democracy made governments in the West more adept at breaking promises than the authoritarian governments of the East and that the economic problems and solutions of the West and East were fundamentally similar— are not retrospective insights of the present imposed on the past but rather past observations brought forth into the present. It was a tired and defeated Mieczysław Rakowski who first noticed, in the fall of 1989, the decisive role that democratic legitimacy played in the imposition of economic discipline in Poland. As he watched Solidarity's prime minister, Tadeusz Mazowiecki, take his first steps toward shock therapy, he committed to his diary that "in principle . . . he says the same thing that I do." But, he lamented, if "any PZPR [Polish communist party] government implemented the policies that the Mazowiecki government does, we'd already have a civil war. Our society patiently bears constant price increases and hyperinflation because this is 'our government.'"[6] The present study has expanded the scope of Rakowski's observation across time and beyond Poland, but it has merely followed him in arguing for the importance of democratic legitimacy to processes of breaking promises.

Similarly, though it sounds bold in retrospect to declare a fundamental similarity between the quintessential project of neoliberal reform, Thatcherism, and the seminal project of socialist renewal, perestroika, we have seen that such a conclusion was commonplace at the time. Whether it was Rakowski in Poland, Károly Grósz in Hungary, or Gorbachev in the Soviet Union, the sense among socialist reformers that they shared many of the Iron Lady's ends and envied the effectiveness of her means lurked as an uncomfortable tenet in their thinking.

The reader can be sure, then, as this book comes to a close, that it is not so much a work of historical revision as it is a work of historical recovery. The people to whom its story would have made the most intuitive sense—indeed, the people who likely would have found this entire narrative unsurprising—were the communist leaders themselves. They knew how important subsidized Soviet oil and Western finance were to the viability of their nation-states; they understood both the economic necessity and political impossibility of revising their social contracts; and they fully believed that their governing challenge was analogous to, rather than distinct from, the one faced by the industrial nation-states of the West. But they were also the Cold War's losers, and thus it is hardly surprising that their perspective received short shrift after the Cold War's end. This book looks to them, the communists who lost, to justify its focus on the connection between a particular set of economic causes—oil, finance, and economic discipline—and a particular set of political effects—the collapse of communism, the end of the Cold War, and the rise of neoliberalism. To title this causal process the triumph of broken promises is, in this way, to tell its history from the losers' point of view.

If that serves to explain the book's subject, what then of its specific findings? How *exactly* does conceptualizing the end of the Cold War as a race to break promises explain its discrete events? How *exactly* does the race to break promises explain the broad global shift in governing ideologies in the late twentieth century that constitutes the rise of neoliberalism?

Here, again, we need not conceive of an answer in the present and project it onto the past. The past already holds the answer, and we need only bring it forward. Recall Margaret Thatcher's chief strategist, John Hoskyns. On June 12, 1979, one month after Thatcher became prime minister, he laid out the coming challenge of transforming Britain's economy in an internal memo. In this document, we can see the origins, challenges, and consequences of the politics of breaking promises. "We can represent the whole process as follows," he wrote, before taping a graph to the memo (Figure C.1).

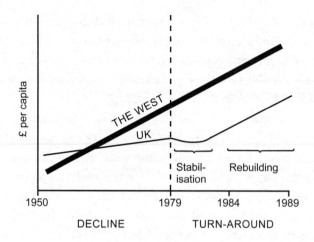

Figure c.1 **John Hoskyns's vision of the politics of breaking promises.**
Reformatted from John Hoskyns, "Government Strategy," June 12, 1979, PREM 19/24 f11, Margaret Thatcher Foundation, Thatcher MSS (digital collection), accessed December 14, 2017, https://www.margaretthatcher .org/document/115016.

What, exactly, do we have here? We have a country in stagnant decline relative to "the West," which is itself defined as a relentlessly upward sloping line of increasing individual wealth and well-being that proceeds without setback infinitely into the future. To reverse its fall behind the West, this country's government must confront a seeming paradox and explain it to its people: as a means of reversing its decline vis-à-vis "the West," the government must first implement a period of "stabilisation" in which living standards would decline and the country would fall further behind the West for years on end. "Stabilisation is the difficult bit," Hoskyns wrote, unknowingly summarizing the entirety of this book in one short sentence. "There is likely to be a noticeable J-curve effect over the first 2 or 3 years, when economic deterioration, as judged by the traditional indicators—growth, unemployment, inflation—will all look worse than they did in 1978/9." This would make the politics of implementing stabilization treacherous, but if the country wanted to remain a significant force in the world, it could not be avoided. "The alternative," he concluded, "is to continue to drop slowly out of the Western world in political, social, and military terms."[7]

This was the politics of breaking promises in a single graph, and now that we have reached the end of this study, we can see that its dynamics were hardly confined to Thatcherite Britain. We need only change the years along Hoskyns's x-axis, the currency along his y-axis, and the country of his concern to describe the central dilemmas of many governments in the late Cold War. This was the situation Paul Volcker faced when he put millions of Americans out of work and caused thousands of bankruptcies in a bid to revive the US economy and renew the United States' preeminent position in the world. This was the situation Edward Gierek faced in 1980 when his attempted price increases spurred the formation of Solidarity. And this was the situation Polish and Hungarian leaders faced in 1987 and 1988 when they decided to liberalize their political systems as a means of gaining their societies' acceptance of austerity.

Most of all, this was the situation Mikhail Gorbachev faced when he walked into the Kremlin on March 11, 1985, as the new general secretary of the Communist Party of the Soviet Union. What was perestroika if not an economic reform program that aimed to reverse the Soviet Union's relative decline vis-à-vis "the West" in order to avoid the alternative of continuing "to drop slowly out of [or, in Gorbachev's case, behind] the Western world in political, social, and military terms"? Gorbachev did not need to attempt reform in the Soviet Union. As many historians have stressed, the country could have gone on for many years persisting in stagnation. But once he did initiate reforms, Gorbachev's ultimate failure—and the source of the Soviet Union's economic and geopolitical collapse—lay precisely in the fact that he was never willing to tolerate a J curve in the Soviet Union's fortunes. First for reasons of ideology and domestic politics, he was unable to carry out the politics of breaking promises at home and instead lost control of the Soviet economy. Then, by 1990, when he recognized that a substantial J curve was unavoidable, he surrendered the Soviet Union's military position on German soil to save hard currency, gain access to Western capital, and soften the domestic blow of the J curve to come.

Indeed, in Gorbachev's story, we can see that the pressure to break promises drove political and ideological change in the late Cold War in two distinct ways. First, a series of political and diplomatic events that were vital developments in the end of the Cold War were by-products of communist leaders' desire to *lessen* the severity of breaking promises at home or *avoid* breaking promises altogether.

The changes in Soviet foreign policy that contributed to the end of the Cold War should be understood in these terms. The Kremlin's desire after the oil crisis to lessen the material burden of its empire and its growing desire to lessen the burden of the arms race were both born of this inclination and reached their zenith under Gorbachev. His bold nuclear arms diplomacy and repeal of the Brezhnev Doctrine in 1986, his willingness to accept the highly asymmetric Intermediate-Range Nuclear Forces (INF) Treaty in 1987, his announcement of a unilateral withdrawal of Soviet forces from Eastern Europe at the United Nations in 1988, his acceptance of noncommunist governments in Eastern Europe in 1989, and his agreement to German unification on Western terms in 1990 were all attempts to cut back Soviet guns (and subsidized energy deliveries) to give the Soviet people more butter. Gorbachev thought that if he could free the Soviet Union from the burden of arms and allies, perhaps he would not have to break promises to his people. His success in breaking free from these burdens was at best partial (as one would expect in the face of the formidable entrenched interests confronting him), but it was the desire to break free of the material burden of arms and allies that motivated the signature developments in Soviet foreign policy on the road to the end of the Cold War.

The political side effects of efforts to avoid broken promises were hardly confined to the Kremlin. The desire to avoid or lessen economic discipline also contributed, in fundamental ways, to the shape of events in Eastern Europe. Most fundamentally, of course, Eastern European leaders' steadfast determination to avoid breaking promises was the original source of the bloc's financial dependence on Western governments and global capital markets after the 1973 oil crisis. We have seen how this dependence produced specific and decisive political changes during the Cold War's endgame. It was Wojciech Jaruzelski's desire to regain access to hard currency that contributed to his decision to declare a general amnesty and set Solidarity's leadership free in September 1986. It was Miklós Németh's desire in late 1988 to find cuts in the Hungarian budget that would not harm living standards that drove him to order the removal of the "Iron Curtain" fence separating Hungary from Austria. It was Egon Krenz's desire to avoid domestic austerity that contributed to his reluctance to use violence against the East German people and drove his attempt to exchange the opening of the Berlin Wall for West German hard currency. And it was Gorbachev's desire to lessen the hardship of the Soviet Union's coming transition to a market economy that drove him to accede to German unification on Western terms and ask for billions of dollars and deutsche marks in return. Thus, out of a fear of implementing Hoskyns's J curve or a desire to lessen the dip of the J, communist leaders of the Eastern Bloc slowly relinquished their coercive hold on the populations of Eastern Europe and, bit by bit, set the stage for the stunning events of 1989 and 1990.

Second, if attempts to *avoid* the politics of breaking promises drove important political and diplomatic change in the late Cold War, attempts to *confront* the politics of breaking promises drove political and ideological change of an even greater magnitude. Confronting the challenge of breaking promises meant actually revising the postwar social contract, and such revisions needed to be justified in ideological terms to domestic political constituencies. Breaking promises therefore required ideological and domestic political change. As Hoskyns wrote to Thatcher, "We are dealing with social systems, not mechanical ones. . . . Government therefore has to persuade people to think and feel differently, before the behavior of the system can change."[8] Gorbachev would have agreed with that sentence verbatim (with perhaps, in his early years as general secretary, the single change of "government" to "the party"), and he expressed much the same sentiment in regard to perestroika on numerous occasions. Paul Volcker also would have agreed that Hoskyns's sentiment precisely described the nature of his quest to use monetarism to defeat Americans' inflationary expectations, and Ronald Reagan would have concurred that it summarized quite nicely the goals of his bid to revive American economic growth through supply-side economics and launch a revolution in Americans' views of the role of government. Finally, Wojciech Jaruzelski would have agreed that "changing the behavior of the system" was precisely his goal when he launched the Polish roundtable. All these efforts were attempts to change a prevailing political or ideological system in order to justify and rationalize broken promises. Therefore, even as important political change emerged from attempts to *avoid* the politics of breaking promises, the most fundamental and lasting changes in the political and ideological currents of democratic capitalism and state socialism emerged from attempts to *confront* it.

Hoskyns's *J* curve also allows us to specify the exact ways three very important groups of actors—Western governments and international institutions, global capital holders, and the people of the Eastern Bloc—influenced the end of the Cold War. This book made clear at its outset that the last two decades of the Cold War really operated as a *privatized* Cold War in which both state and nonstate actors controlled nation-states' access to energy and finance. Over the subsequent pages, we saw that Western governments and international institutions like the International Monetary Fund (IMF) had no influence over communist countries as long as global capital holders maintained confidence in those countries. Only when communist governments faced the imminent threat of losing access to private capital, or had already lost it completely, were Western governments and international institutions able to wield power and influence.

This is what made the capitalist perestroika so important. Throughout the 1970s, global capital holders were willing, indeed eager, to provide virtually limitless amounts of capital to the Eastern Bloc, leaving Western governments and international institutions with little power in the region. Only the potent combination of the Volcker Shock, the Reagan financial buildup, and the Polish Crisis caused global capital holders to question their lending to sovereign borrowers in general and to the communist world in particular. And after Western policy makers unwound the East-West interdependence of the 1970s, the potential for Western leverage over the Eastern Bloc emerged. The communist world did not permanently lose access to global capital markets after the early 1980s, but never again did it receive the unquestioning allegiance of global capital holders. This made future losses of market confidence, and thus future moments of leverage for Western governments and international institutions, inevitable.

The same forces that weakened the Communist Bloc's standing on global capital markets renewed the United States' preeminent position in the international system. Paul Volcker's choice to impose Hoskyns's *J* curve on the American population was *the* key act of renewal for the structural power of the United States in the international system in the postwar period. Volcker's willingness to impose unprecedented economic discipline on the American people showed global capital holders that American policy makers could and would ultimately protect the interests of capital over the interests of labor. In return, they rewarded American policy makers and citizens with a deluge of capital inflows that erased the United States' choice between guns and butter, renewed American prosperity, worsened inequality, and underwrote the projection of American power abroad. The two facts that have allowed the United States to remain hegemonic in the international system since 1980—the US dollar's undiminished role as the world's reserve currency and the United States' ability to run virtually continuous budget and current account deficits for forty years—are both results of the confidence Volcker gave global capital holders that their money was safe in American hands.

Ronald Reagan was the inaugural beneficiary of this new and unforeseen configuration of American global power. The combination of Volcker and Reagan's policies had enormously detrimental consequences for many groups both within the United States and abroad, most significantly American workers and the nations of the Global South. But they served three constituencies in the United States enormously well: consumers, the wealthy, and the government. The financial buildup that began under Reagan's tenure funded both the largest tax cuts and the largest peacetime military buildup in the nation's history. Given the complex interplay of economic, political, and ideological forces discussed in this book, it would be both absurd and highly simplistic to suggest, as some popular lore has it, that the Reagan military buildup ended the Cold War by bankrupting the Soviet Union. But we can also see that Reagan's renewal of American military power in the 1980s produced its intended effect: to make clear to Soviet leaders that they could not match the bountiful material resources at Washington's disposal for pursuit of the arms race and would be better off seeking its end.

The fact that the immense resources at Reagan's disposal were not, as he liked to conclude, the product of a newly entrepreneurial *American* capitalism reinvigorated by supply-side incentives, but were instead the result of an increasingly *globalized* capitalism supercharged by the free flow of capital around the world, took nothing away from their potency. Indeed, by getting Japanese, West German, and Arab investors to pay for the development of the next generation of American military power indirectly through debt markets, Volcker and Reagan unwittingly accomplished a feat Soviet leaders were never able to achieve: getting their empire to pay for itself. After 1980, the American empire became an enormous material asset to Washington, while the Soviet empire remained an enormous material burden on Moscow. This disparity created a gaping imbalance of power between Washington and Moscow that was not just a matter of scale but also of form. Washington not only had more hard economic and military power than Moscow, but it also had allies that were materially integral to sustaining the projection of that power. A great deal about the subsequent collapse of the Soviet empire and the persistence of the American empire stems from this foundational difference in imperial form.

For a time, communist countries also benefited from the free flow of surplus capital around the world in the 1980s. The unexpected connection unearthed in these pages between the goulash of János Kádár's communism in Hungary and the yen of Japanese investment houses in Tokyo bears witness to this fact. But communist states eventually lost access to global capital markets, and in these moments, Western governments and international institutions gained the power to influence their fate. This power came in two forms. First, through what I have called "the power of omission," Western governments and international institutions *withheld* money from communist governments to force them to undertake domestic economic or political reforms. This was the essence of the power of the US government and the IMF in Poland and Hungary beginning in 1986 and 1987, the nature of the West German government's power over the GDR beginning in October 1989, and the motivation behind the US government's refusal to grant the Soviet Union large-scale financial aid in the spring and summer of 1990. By withholding communist states' access to both public and private capital, Western governments and the IMF forced them to confront Hoskyns's *J* curve and the treacherous political and ideological questions that came with that confrontation.

Second, through a form of power that is something closer to rewarding good behavior, Western governments *granted* communist governments money that allowed them to avoid or soften the blow of breaking promises in return for political and diplomatic concessions. This was, in fact, a tool that only the West Germans used on two important occasions. First, in August 1989 they granted Miklós Németh a DM 500 million loan and gave him broader assurances of economic support in return for his decision to let East German refugees amassed in Hungary leave for the West through Austria, striking a fatal blow to the viability of the GDR. And second, they offered Gorbachev a DM 5 billion loan and broader economic assurances in 1990 in return for his cooperation on German unification and accession to NATO, sealing the fate of German unity on Western terms. The evidence suggests that both Németh and Gorbachev made their decisions before reaching out to the West Germans. But it also makes clear that both governments stood on the precipice of losing access to global capital markets. Each man's primary concern was softening the coming blow of Hoskyns's *J* curve on their own population, and they knew that West German financial support could play a crucial role. Bonn, in turn, recognized the decisiveness of its financial support and was happy to help both leaders ease their domestic troubles if they granted significant political concessions in return.

In sum, we can see that a broad array of Western actors—governments, international institutions, and global capital holders—had a profound causal influence on the end of the Cold War. Scholars have long been reluctant to identify *any* significant Western role in bringing about the collapse of communism and the Cold War's end, usually because those who did claim a decisive Western role used that version of history to pernicious ends in the post–Cold War world. But identifying instances of decisive Western power need not equal endorsement of that power's use. Indeed, the most strident critiques of American, Western, or capitalist power are built on an understanding that Americans, Westerners, and capitalists are all *too* capable of producing results in foreign countries, not that they are more impotent than commonly thought. In addition to enhancing our empirical understanding of how the Cold War actually ended, this book allows us to make such an analytical move. We can identify the full scale, scope, and nature of American, Western, and capitalist power in the international system during this period without automatically endorsing it.

It should also be made clear, however, that there were no straight lines of influence from the halls of Western power to events in the Eastern Bloc. This book is emphatically not a story of how a quiet cabal of Wall Street financiers, secretive international institutions, and Western finance ministries magically and purposefully brought communism to its knees, nor is it a recommendation that financial coercion works at all times and in all places. Like the idea that the Reagan military buildup single-handedly ended the Cold War, we can see that the complex interplay of economic, political, and ideological forces at play in both the East and the West would make such claims highly simplistic and absurd. But this is a story of how a conjuncture of pressures—sometimes purposeful, sometimes not; sometimes coordinated, sometimes not—emanated from Western governments, international institutions, and global capital holders to slowly winnow the choices available to Eastern Bloc leaders. And through their incomplete patchwork of intentions, purposes, and coordination, Western actors played a substantial part in ending the Cold War.

But only a part. Western actors could force communist leaders to confront the politics of breaking promises, but only the people of the Eastern Bloc could make that confrontation a torturous, and ultimately fatal, political process for them. If the Soviet, Polish, Hungarian, and East German people had accepted economic discipline as passively (relatively speaking) as the American or British people did, there would be no collapse of communism and end of the Cold War to speak of. Once again, Hoskyns's J curve helps us pinpoint exactly when and why popular resistance proved decisive. Hoskyns wrote in his memo that implementing his period of stabilization would depend on the population having "confidence about the future" so they would be willing "to make present sacrifices for future benefits."[9]

This confidence—not just in the future but also in their government—was precisely what was lacking among the populations of the Eastern Bloc. It is why their moments of mass activism began exactly when their governments asked them to "make present sacrifices" in return for "future benefits." The Polish working class, of course, set the standard for the whole bloc, and its revolts against austerity in 1970, 1976, 1980, and 1988 were the principal reason communist governments were never able to successfully implement the politics of broken promises. Solidarity's bold emergence and brave persistence sent a message far beyond Poland's borders about the political consequences of economic discipline. Working-class resistance was not as strident in other Eastern Bloc countries, but it did not need to be. Communist leaders in other countries feared that their own version of the Polish Crisis lurked behind any attempt to impose austerity at home.

Ultimately, Eastern Bloc peoples would not accept economic discipline unless it came from "their" government, as Rakowski concluded in 1989, and both the people and the communist leaders knew that whatever bond they might once have shared had long since been lost. Reestablishing that bond so that the state could implement the politics of breaking promises was the reason communist governments democratized themselves in the late 1980s. Thus, we can conclude that the peoples of the bloc played an essential and—given the formidable forces of violent repression arrayed against them—heroic role in creating their own future.

That conclusion coexists uneasily, however, with another one we must draw. It was common, in the euphoric moments of 1989 and its immediate afterglow, to think that the fall of communism and the birth of electoral democracy in the former Eastern Bloc signaled the dawn of a new era of popular sovereignty and self-determination for the peoples of the region. Rakowski's diary entry about the Polish people's feeling that at last they had "their" government in Warsaw attests to this sentiment. But this book has shown in detail that the government the Polish people thought was theirs was not theirs alone. It was, instead, a servant of two masters: the people and the market, or, if you like, capital and labor. From the preceding pages, we can see that one of the central contradictions—perhaps *the* central contradiction—of the collapse of communism was that the seat of government was returned to the people only so that their power to resist the government could be transcended. The end of the Cold War, we must conclude, was the moment in which the people's power peaked and the moment in which it was overcome.

This contradiction was hardly confined to the collapsing states of the Eastern Bloc. *Every* government that lived on credit after the oil crisis—which, as we have seen, was most of them—was beholden to the twin masters of global capital and their own people, and this set distinct limits on the domestic policies they could pursue. Britain's IMF crisis in 1976, the Federal Reserve's fight to save the US dollar from 1978 onward, Mitterrand's U-turn in France in 1982, and the countless structural adjustment programs imposed on the debtor countries of the Global South throughout the 1980s testify to these limits.

At its foundation, this book offers a structural explanation for the growing dependence of governments across the Global North on finance after the oil crisis of 1973: even though the world economy stopped growing at its exceptional postwar rate around 1970, people's expectations of social and material progress did not. The politics of making promises remained far more popular and easy than the politics of breaking them, and governments found in finance capital a lifeline that made making promises still possible. The impulse to continue making promises was a perfectly natural, even noble, inclination on the part of governments, but it inevitably added a new counterparty—global capital holders—to the social contract between citizens and their states. As the relationship between citizen and state increasingly became mediated by borrowed capital, it is hardly surprising that it also morphed over time into a relationship between debtors and creditors, with the state—democratic or otherwise—mediating the relationship between the two. Nor is it surprising that the state slowly dropped its commitments to protecting the interests of labor and replaced them with commitments to protect the interests of capital. Neoliberalism—the governing ideology of capital, if nothing else—rose in the late twentieth century because nation-states' dependence on finance capital to fulfill their social contracts rose as well.

It would be a mistake, however, to leave our explanation of the rise of neoliberalism there, as a story of capitalists accumulating more capital on account of the oil crisis and using that capital to impose their interests on the rest of the world. This book has also shown that neoliberalism rose because it proposed a relatively attractive ideological vision that promised to meet the governing challenge posed to both East and West by the oil crisis: how to justify in political terms and achieve in economic terms the transition from industrial stagnation to postindustrial modernity.

What was that vision? Hoskyns, again, put it right down on his page in words that shock our retrospective eyes. "Everyone knows that the UK economic problem is one of structural fatigue," he wrote. "What is really needed is 10 years of vulgarly pro-business and pro-industry policies." Those policies would include "zero, or near-zero inflation," "reductions in Government's % of GNP," "the restoration of personal incentives," "freeing up the labour market," and, perhaps most importantly, "a profound cultural change" in attitudes toward wealth. "Fashion follows money," he told the cabinet. "As the American academic said at the end of his lecture, 'Don't clap. Throw dollars!'" Previous governments, Hoskyns maintained, had been "constrained by union power in industry and the prevailing egalitarian mood." Only if the government broke the unions' grip and made the private sector "a better way of accumulating personal capital" would the country's economic fortunes turn around. He hoped such a change in cultural sentiments could happen quickly but admitted that "it probably won't happen until managers [in the private sector] are so prosperous and so lightly taxed that they begin to attract the attention of other parts of the population." Changing the public's negative perceptions of vast wealth and high inequality was the key. Once the country overcame its "traditional British hang up—the lurking fear that a few individuals might make a lot of money," Hoskyns assured the cabinet, "a lot of good things will start happening."[10]

The reason we know that the global spread of this vision—as neoliberal as any ever put to paper in a practical governing document—was not only the result of capitalists' pressure on societies is that similar sentiments were soon being expressed on the other side of the Iron Curtain. Until the late 1980s, the Soviet Union had no significant dependency on Western capital and remained the bastion of Marxist-Leninist resistance to capitalist exploitation. And yet, as this book has shown, Soviet officials often lamented the "structural fatigue" of their industrial economy and the "egalitarian mood" of their population. They too wrestled with how to restore personal incentives to work, reduce the state's role in the economy, free up the labor market, and close down unprofitable enterprises. They too settled on a form of "Don't clap. Throw rubles!" as their motto and increasing inequality as their method. And they were not alone. It was the Hungarian communist leader Károly Grósz, an admirer of Thatcher, who put the prevailing view most bluntly. "Marxism has never accepted egalitarianism, but rather the postulate of equal opportunity," he said in 1986. "This postulate takes into account, in all respects, the possibility of considerable inequality. . . . Equality has never been and cannot be a feature of socialism."[11]

This turned the race to make promises that started the Cold War on its head. Far from debating how much economic equality and security would produce the most social progress, the countries of the East and West now found themselves debating how much economic *in*equality and *in*security would launch a new golden era. Just as in the race to make promises, their differences of degree were substantial, but they were not differences in kind. Far from racing to make promises, the two sides were now racing to break them.

Communism, however, made no sense in an era of breaking promises. The party could claim no special right to rule if it was just going to be any empty vessel for the allocation of the market's punishments and rewards. Neoliberalism suffered from no such quandary. Not only did it seek to turn the state into as much of an empty vessel as possible for the market's provision of luxury and anguish, but it went further. As Hoskyns's words make clear, neoliberals sought to use the state to actively *advance* the interests of the wealthy few, all while justifying this pursuit in a lexicon of political and economic freedom. The collapse of communism and the rise of neoliberalism were thus two sides of the same ideological coin, the coin that governments use to justify the role they choose in mediating the relationship between their citizens and the economy.

We can close this book with one final observation about the legacy of broken promises for the world we currently inhabit. It comes in the form of yet another comment on Hoskyns's graph. A keen observer will have noticed that the countries that go through his *J* curve of broken promises do not actually catch back up to the skyrocketing trajectory set by the postwar West. Their wealth and well-being slowly increase, but they forever remain in the shadow of that postwar Western line, which sprints off inexorably into a future of ever-increasing material and social progress.

That disparity is an apt indication of both the exceptional nature of the postwar period through the early 1970s and the mounting challenges of political and economic life in our own time. There is, in the end, no actual place called "the West." It is, instead, the term used to signify expectations of eternal progress. The uniqueness of the postwar period until 1973—indeed, the uniqueness of the race between democratic capitalism and state socialism to make promises in the first half of the Cold War—was that for a brief moment in both East and West, there was no disparity between their line on Hoskyns's graph and the Western one, no daylight between many of their citizens' expectations and lived experience. At the significant price of racial and gender hierarchy in the West and authoritarian rule in the East, governments were able to promise at least their white men a better life and deliver on that promise almost as fast as those men could imagine what a better life was.

The economic turmoil of the 1970s swept away that neat alignment between promises and expectations, and we now live in a world forever in its shadow. In the wake of the wave of broken promises that swept the world in the late twentieth century, economic growth continues. But it is accompanied by vast wealth inequality that destabilizes our politics and environmental exploitation that destroys our planet. How we can achieve a world in which states sustainably keep their promises to *all* their citizens is the vital question that arises after broken promises have triumphed. It is the question that defines our time.

NOTES

Introduction

1   "In Today's Mail," *Magyar Nemzet,* December 15, 1989, 6, translated in Joint Publications Research Service, Eastern Europe (JPRS-EER), JPRS-EER-90-005, 28–29.

2   "In Today's Mail," 29.

3   Although I refer throughout this book to "the Cold War" and "the end of the Cold War" writ large for narrative purposes, I am confining my analysis to the Cold War in what is now called the Global North, formerly referred to as the First and Second Worlds or the Eastern and Western Blocs. In the interest of narrative, I also use terms such as "democratic capitalism" and "state socialism," "industrialized nations of the West" and "state socialist countries of the East," "Western Bloc" and "Eastern Bloc," and "Western welfare states" and "state socialist states" throughout the text. I do so with the recognition that there was a great deal of variation within "the West" and "the East" and that any term such as "welfare state," "democratic capitalist," or "state socialist" presupposes certain characteristics about nation-states within each bloc that were present in highly varying degrees in each state. This book, however, is primarily interested in comparing the experience of the two blocs—i.e., the Global North—in the world economy of the 1970s and 1980s, so terms that signify what united the two blocs or distinguished the two blocs from each other will have to be used.

4   Kenneth Rogoff, *The Curse of Cash* (Princeton, NJ: Princeton University Press, 2016), 119.

5   Paul Volcker and Toyoo Gyohten, *Changing Fortunes: The World's Money and the Threat to American Leadership* (New York: Times Books, 1992), 166.

6   Within the voluminous literature on neoliberalism, some of the most important works are David Harvey, *A Brief History of Neoliberalism* (Oxford; New York: Oxford University Press, 2005); Quinn Slobodian, *The Globalists: The End of Empire and the Birth of Neoliberalism* (Cambridge, MA: Harvard University Press, 2018); Philip Mirowski and

Dieter Plehwe, eds., *The Road from Mont Pèlerin: The Making of the Neoliberal Thought Collective* (Cambridge, MA: Harvard University Press, 2009); Johanna Bockman, *Markets in the Name of Socialism: The Left-Wing Origins of Neoliberalism* (Stanford, CA: Stanford University Press, 2011); Daniel Rodgers, *Age of Fracture* (Cambridge, MA: Harvard University Press, 2011); Angus Burgin, *The Great Persuasion: Reinventing Free Markets since the Depression* (Cambridge, MA: Harvard University Press, 2012); Daniel Stedman Jones, *Masters of the Universe: Hayek, Friedman, and the Birth of Neoliberalism* (Princeton, NJ: Princeton University Press, 2012); Wendy Brown, *Undoing the Demos: Neoliberalism's Stealth Revolution* (Cambridge, MA: Harvard University Press, 2015); Wolfgang Streeck, *Buying Time: The Delayed Crisis of Democratic Capitalism,* 2nd ed., trans. Patrick Camiller and David Fernbach (London: Verso, 2017); Leo Panitch and Sam Gindin, *The Making of Global Capitalism: The Political Economy of American Empire* (London: Verso, 2012); Julian Germann, *Unwitting Architect: German Primacy and the Origins of Neoliberalism* (Stanford, CA: Stanford University Press, 2021); and Thomas Piketty, *Capital in the Twenty-First Century* (Cambridge, MA: The Belknap Press of Harvard University Press, 2014).

7   Two notable exceptions to this are Charles Maier and Stephen Kotkin. This book is highly indebted to their numerous calls over the past three decades to see capitalism and communism in comparative perspective. Among many examples, see Charles S. Maier, "The Collapse of Communism: Approaches for a Future History," *History Workshop,* no. 31 (Spring 1991), 34–59, and Stephen Kotkin, "The Kiss of Debt," in *The Shock of the Global: The 1970s in Perspective,* ed. Niall Ferguson et al. (Cambridge, MA: Harvard University Press, 2010), 80–96. See also Odd Arne Westad, *The Cold War: A World History* (New York: Basic Books, 2017), and Giovanni Arrighi, "The World Economy and the Cold War, 1970–1990," in *The Cambridge History of the Cold War,* vol. 3, ed. Odd Arne Westad and Melvyn Leffler (Cambridge: Cambridge University Press, 2010), 23–44. Other scholars have also ably investigated the economic history of Eastern European socialist states. See Angela Romano and Federico Romero, eds., *European Socialist Regimes' Fateful Engagement with the West: National Strategies in the Long 1970s* (New York: Routledge, 2021); Randall Stone, *Satellites and Commissars: Strategy and Conflict in the Politics of Soviet-Bloc Trade* (Princeton: Princeton University Press, 1996); Ivan Berend, *From the Soviet Bloc to the European Union: The Social and Economic Transformation of Central and Eastern Europe since 1973* (Cambridge: Cambridge University Press, 2009); Kazimierz Poznanski, *Poland's Protracted Transition: Institutional Change and Economic Growth* (Cambridge: Cambridge University Press, 1996); André Steiner, *The Plans That Failed: An Economic History of the GDR* (New York: Berghahn Books, 2010); Jonathan Zatlin, *The Currency of Socialism: Money and Political Culture in East Germany* (Cambridge: Cambridge University Press, 2007); and Attila Mong, *Kádár Hitele* (Budapest: Libri Kiadó, 2012).

8   Important studies of the global history of energy and finance in the late twentieth century include Eric Helleiner, *States and the Reemergence of Global Finance: From Bretton Woods to the 1990s* (Ithaca, NY: Cornell University Press, 1994); Daniel Yergin, *The Prize: The Epic Quest for Oil, Money, and Power* (New York: Free Press, 2003); David Spiro,

The Hidden Hand of American Hegemony: Petrodollar Recycling and International Markets (Ithaca, NY: Cornell University Press, 1999); Rawi Abdelal, *Capital Rules: The Construction of Global Finance* (Cambridge, MA: Harvard University Press, 2007); Daniel Sargent, *A Superpower Transformed* (Oxford: Oxford University Press, 2014); and Giuliano Garavini, *The Rise and Fall of OPEC in the Twentieth Century* (Oxford: Oxford University Press, 2019).

9   For discussion of this phenomenon, including its limits in the United States, see Samuel Moyn, *Not Enough: Human Rights in an Unequal World* (Cambridge: Harvard University Press, 2018). See also, Melvyn Leffler, "Victory: The 'State,' The 'West,' and the Cold War," in *Safeguarding Democratic Capitalism: U.S. Foreign Policy and National Security, 1920–2015* (Princeton, NJ: Princeton University Press, 2017), 221–242.

10   See Kristy Ironside, *A Full-Value Ruble: The Promise of Prosperity in the Postwar Soviet Union* (Cambridge, MA: Harvard University Press, 2021), and William Taubman, *Khrushchev: The Man and His Era* (New York: Norton, 2003), chap. 18.

11   Important works that address the end of the Cold War as a whole include Hal Brands, *Making the Unipolar Moment: US Foreign Policy and the Rise of the Post-Cold War Order* (Ithaca, NY: Cornell University Press, 2016); Robert Service, *The End of the Cold War, 1985–1991* (New York: Public Affairs, 2015); and Jeffrey Engel, *When the World Seemed New: George H. W. Bush and the End of the Cold War* (New York: Houghton Mifflin Harcourt, 2017). The so-called Reagan Victory School can be found in Peter Schweizer, *Victory: The Reagan Administration's Secret Strategy That Hastened the Collapse of the Soviet Union* (New York: Atlantic Monthly Press, 1994). Some of the most important work on the end of the Cold War has been done through edited volumes. Among the most important are Thomas Blanton, Svetlana Savranskaya, and Vladislav Zubok, eds., *Masterpieces of History: The Peaceful End of the Cold War in Europe, 1989* (New York: Central European University Press, 2010); Silvio Pons and Federico Romero, eds., *Reinterpreting the End of the Cold War: Issues, Interpretations, Periodizations* (New York: Frank Cass, 2005); and Wolfgang Mueller, Michael Gehler, and Arnold Suppan, eds., *The Revolutions of 1989: A Handbook* (Vienna: OAW, 2015).

12   Some may be inclined to include a fifth process, the breakup of the Soviet Union, in the end of the Cold War. But while the *collapse* of the USSR as a communist state from 1985 to 1990 was an integral part of the end of the Cold War, the *breakup* of the Soviet Union in 1991 was not. As a geopolitical conflict, the Cold War had started over the Soviet-American contest to determine the fate of postwar Germany. Thus, it ended on October 3, 1990, when the German Democratic Republic was dissolved and the newly reunited Germany emerged on fully Western terms.

13   Among many works, see Melvyn Leffler, *For the Soul of Mankind: The United States, the Soviet Union, and the Cold War* (New York: Hill and Wang, 2007); Simon Miles, *Engaging the Evil Empire: Washington, Moscow, and the Beginning of the End of the Cold War* (Ithaca: Cornell University Press, 2020); James Graham Wilson, *The Triumph of Improvisation: Gorbachev's Adaptability, Reagan's Engagement, and the End of the Cold War* (Ithaca: Cornell University Press, 2014); Raymond Garthoff, *The Great Transition: American-Soviet Relations*

and the End of the Cold War (Washington, DC: Brookings, 1994); Frances FitzGerald, *Way Out There in the Blue: Reagan, Star Wars, and the End of the Cold War* (New York: Simon & Schuster, 2000); and Matthew Evangelista, *Unarmed Forces: The Transnational Movement to End the Cold War* (Ithaca: Cornell University Press, 2002).

14   Robert English, *Russia and the Idea of the West: Gorbachev, Intellectuals and the End of the Cold War* (New York: Columbia University Press, 2000) and "Power, Ideas, and New Evidence on the Cold War's End: A Reply to Brooks and Wohlforth," *International Security* 26, no. 4 (Spring 2002); and Evangelista, *Unarmed Forces*. Much of the most important work on the end of the ideological competition has been done by scholars taking Mikhail Gorbachev or human rights as their subjects. On Gorbachev, see William Taubman, *Gorbachev: His Life and Times* (New York: W.W. Norton, 2017); Andrei Grachev, *Gorbachev's Gamble: Soviet Foreign Policy and the End of the Cold War* (Cambridge: Cambridge University Press, 2008); and Archie Brown, *Seven Years that Changed the World: Perestroika in Perspective* (New York: Oxford University Press, 2007). On human rights, see Sarah Snyder, *Human Rights Activism and the End of the Cold War: A Transnational History of the Helsinki Network* (Cambridge: Cambridge University Press, 2011).

15   The classic account of the 1989 revolutions is Timothy Garton Ash, *Magic Lantern: The Revolution of '89 Witnessed in Warsaw, Budapest, Berlin, and Prague* (New York: Random House, 1990). A highly revisionist account is Stephen Kotkin and Jan Gross, *Uncivil Society: 1989 and the Implosion of the Communist Establishment* (New York: Modern Library, 2009). See also Mark Kramer, "The Demise of the Soviet Bloc," *Journal of Modern History* 83, no. 4 (December 2011): 788–854. Other monographs explaining change across Eastern Europe in 1989 include Jacque Lévesque, *The Enigma of 1989: The USSR and the Liberation of Eastern Europe* (Berkeley: University of California Press, 1997), and Padraic Kenney, *Carnival of Revolution: Central Europe 1989* (Princeton: Princeton University Press, 2002). Recent scholarly monographs on the collapse of various communist states include Gregory Domber, *Empowering Revolution: America, Poland, and the End of the Cold War* (Chapel Hill: University of North Carolina Press, 2014); Andrzej Paczkowski, *Revolution and Counterrevolution in Poland, 1980–1989*, trans. Christina Manetti (Rochester, NY: University of Rochester Press, 2015); Lazlo Borhi, *Dealing with Dictators: The United States, Hungary, and East Central Europe, 1942–1989* (Bloomington, IN: Indiana University Press, 2016); Mary Sarotte, *Collapse: The Accidental Opening of the Berlin Wall* (New York: Basic Books, 2014); and Hans-Hermann Hertle, *Der Fall der Mauer: Die unbeabsichtigte Selbstauflösung des SED-Staates* (Opladen: VS Verlag für Sozialwissenschaften, 1996). On the collapse of the Soviet state, see R. G. Pihoia and A. K. Sokolov, *Istoriia sovremennoi Rossii: krizis kommunisticheskoi vlasti v SSSR i rozhdenie novoi Rossii. Konets 1970-kh - 1991 gg* (Moscow: Rosspen, 2008); Stephen Kotkin, *Armageddon Averted: The Soviet Collapse 1970–2000* (Oxford: Oxford University Press, 2008); Christopher Miller, *The Struggle to Save the Soviet Economy: Mikhail Gorbachev and the Collapse of the USSR* (Chapel Hill: University of North Carolina Press, 2016); and Yegor Gaidar, *The Collapse of an Empire: Lessons for Modern Russia*, trans. Antonina Bouis (Washington, DC: Brookings Institution Press, 2007).

16   While recognizing the important historical difference between titling this process "uni-fication" versus "reunification," this book uses the terms interchangeably in the interest of nar-rative. Works that have dealt with the history of German reunification include Kristina Spohr, *Post Wall, Post Square: How Bush, Gorbachev, Kohl and Deng Shaped the World after 1989* (New Haven, CT: Yale University Press, 2020); Philip Zelikow and Condoleezza Rice, *To Build a Bet-ter World: Choices to End the Cold War and Create a Global Commonwealth* (New York: Twelve, 2019) and their earlier *Germany Unified and Europe Transformed: A Study in Statecraft* (Cam-bridge, MA: Harvard University Press, 1995); Mary Sarotte, *1989: The Struggle to Create Postwar Europe* (Princeton, NJ: Princeton University Press, 2014); Andreas Rödder, *Deutschland einig Vaterland: Die Geschichte der Wiedervereinigung* (Bonn: Bpb, 2010); and the four volumes of the *Geschichte der Deutschen Einheit* (Stuttgart: Deutsche Verlags-Anstalt, 1998).

17   John Lewis Gaddis, *The Long Peace: Inquiries into the History of the Cold War* (New York: Oxford University Press, 1987).

18   This is not to deny, of course, that Eastern and Western governments, particularly the United States and the Soviet Union, were keenly aware from the beginning of the Cold War that access to plentiful oil was extremely significant. The Soviet Union spent the first two decades of the postwar period building up its own oil extraction and refining capabilities, and the United States sought to secure oil's flow from the Middle East long before 1973. See Daniel Yergin's *The Prize: The Epic Quest for Oil, Money, and Power* (New York: Free Press, 1991) and David Painter, "Oil and the American Century," *Journal of American History* 99, no. 1 (June 2012): 24–39, among others.

19   Thane Gustafson, *Crisis Amid Plenty: The Politics of Soviet Energy Under Brezhnev and Gorbachev* (Princeton: Princeton University Press, 1989), 23.

20   Marc Levinson, *An Extraordinary Time: The End of the Postwar Boom and the Return of the Ordinary Economy* (New York: Basic Books, 2016).

21   Eric Hobsbawm, *The Age of Extremes: A History of the World, 1914–1991* (New York: Vin-tage Books, 1996), part 2. Barry Eichengreen, *The European Economy since 1945: Coordinated Capitalism and Beyond* (Princeton, NJ: Princeton University Press, 2007), chaps. 4 and 7.

22   Angus Maddison, *The World Economy,* vol. 1, *A Millennial Perspective* (Paris: OECD, 2006), 265, appendix B, table B-22.

23   "The Kitchen Debate—Transcript," July 24, 1959, CIA Online Reading Room, ac-cessed April 28, 2017, https://www.cia.gov/library/readingroom/docs/1959-07-24.pdf.

24   Among many, see Ferenc Jánossy, *The End of the Economic Miracle* (White Plains, NY: International Arts and Sciences Press, 1971); Phillip Armstrong, Andrew Glyn, and John Harrison, *Capitalism since 1945* (Oxford: Oxford University Press, 1991); and Robert Gordon, *The Rise and Fall of American Growth* (Princeton, NJ: Princeton University Press, 2016).

25   Armstrong, Glyn, Harrison, *Capitalism since 1945,* chap. 14; Gordon, introduction to *Rise and Fall.*

26   From 1974 to 1982, per capita growth in the industrialized West averaged 1.4 percent per year, while it averaged 1.3 percent in Eastern Europe and 1.2 percent in the Soviet Union. "Selected Macroeconomic Indicators, 1951–1988," table 18 in *World Economic Outlook: A Survey by the Staff of the International Monetary Fund* (Washington, DC: International Monetary Fund, 1990), 65.

27   Anatolii Cherniaev, ed., *V Politbiuro TsK KPSS: Po zapisiam Anatoliia Cherniaeva, Vadima Medvedeva, Georgiia Shakhnazarova* (Moscow: Gorbachev-Fond, 2006), 180.

28   Document 18, "Record of Negotiations between Gorbachev and Margaret Thatcher, London," April 6, 1989, in Csaba Békés and Malcolm Byrne, eds., *Political Transition in Hungary, 1989–1990: A Compendium of Declassified Documents and Chronology of Events* (Washington, DC: National Security Archive, 1999).

29   "Urban Population (% of Total Population)—China," World Bank, World Development Indicators, Urban Population Statistics, https://data.worldbank.org/indicator/SP .URB.TOTL.IN.ZS?locations=CN.

30   On the importance of these differences for China and the Soviet Union, see Miller, *Struggle to Save the Soviet Economy,* particularly the conclusion.

31   On China's price reform debates in the 1980s, see Isabella Weber, *How China Escaped Shock Therapy* (New York: Routledge, 2021). See also, Barry Naughton, *Growing out of the Plan: Chinese Economic Reform, 1978–1993* (New York: Cambridge University Press, 1995).

32   I thank Max Krahé for our many conversations on these issues and for making this particular point clear to me. See his "TINA and the Market Turn: Why Deindustrialization Proceeded under Democratic Capitalism but Not State Socialism," *Critical Historical Studies* 8, no. 2 (Fall 2021).

33   For two important examples, see Michel Crozier, Samuel Huntington, and Joji Watanuki, *The Crisis of Democracy: Report on the Governability of Democracies to the Trilateral Commission* (New York: New York University Press, 1975), and Paul McCracken et al., *Toward Full Employment and Price Stability: A Report to OECD by a Group of Independent Experts* (Paris: OECD, 1977).

1   The Oil Shock to the Cold War

1   "Niederschrift über die Verhandlungen zwischen dem Vorsitzenden des Ministerrates der DDR, Genossen Willi Stoph und dem Vorsitzenden des Ministerrates der UdSSR, Genossen A.N. Kossygin, am 10.12.1976," December 12, 1976, DE/1/58569, Bundesarchiv Berlin-Lichterfelde (BArch Lichterfelde).

2   Conversation reconstructed from two documents that recorded the same events. Willi Stoph, "Information über die Beratung mit Genossen Kossygin am 10.12.1976 in Moskau," and "Niederschrift über die Verhandlungen," both in DE/1/58569, BArch Lichterfelde.

3   Except for Romania, which imported most of its oil from the world market. This freed the country from dependence on Soviet oil but dramatically increased its dependence on Western capital.

4   Daniel Yergin, *The Prize: The Epic Quest for Oil, Money, and Power* (New York: Free Press, 1991), chap. 29.

5   Daniel Sargent, *A Superpower Transformed* (Oxford: Oxford University Press, 2014), 132, 135.

6   Robert Brenner, *The Economics of Global Turbulence* (New York: Verso, 2006), chap. 9.

7   "Inflation (CPI)," OECD, accessed March 19, 2017, https://doi.org/10.1787/eee82e6e-en.

8   Harold James, *International Monetary Cooperation since Bretton Woods* (New York: Oxford University Press, 1996), 264.

9   Charles S. Maier, "Inflation and Stagnation as Politics and History," in *The Politics of Inflation and Economic Stagnation: Theoretical Approaches and International Case Studies,* ed. Leon N. Lindberg and Charles S. Maier (Washington, DC: Brookings Institution, 1985), 17.

10   "Inflation (CPI)," OECD.

11   Quoted in Robert J. Samuelson, *The Great Inflation and Its Aftermath* (New York: Random House, 2008), 55.

12   Charles S. Maier, "'Fictitious Bonds . . . of Wealth and Law': On the Theory and Practice of Interest Representation," in *In Search of Stability: Explorations in Historical Political Economy* (Cambridge: Cambridge University Press, 1987), 251.

13   See Maier and Lindberg, ed., *Politics of Inflation,* especially Albert O. Hirschman, "Reflections on the Latin American Experience," 53–77.

14   *Business Week* and Samuelson quoted in Jefferson Cowie, *Stayin' Alive: The 1970s and the Last Days of the Working Class* (New York: New Press, 2010), 223.

15   Fritz Stern, "The End of the Postwar Era," *Commentary* 57, no. 4 (April 1974): 27.

16   Cowie, *Stayin' Alive,* 72.

17   Andrei S. Markovits, Appendix 10, "Wages and Productivity per Person," in *The Politics of the West German Trade Unions: Strategies of Class and Interest Representation in Growth and Crisis* (Cambridge: Cambridge University Press, 1986), 459.

18   Kevin Hickson, *The IMF Crisis of 1976 and British Politics* (London: I. B. Tauris, 2005), 53.

19   James, *International Monetary Cooperation,* 283.

20   T. J. Pempel, "Japanese Foreign Economic Policy: The Domestic Bases for International Behavior," in *Between Power and Plenty,* ed. Peter J. Katzenstein (Madison: University of Wisconsin Press, 1978), 184.

21   Richard P. Mattione, *OPEC's Investments and the International Financial System* (Washington, DC: Brookings Institution, 1985), 23.

22   William Withrell for Assistant Secretary Parsky, "World Capital Markets Study," August 14, 1974, Folder "1974," Box 1, Office of Assistant Secretary for International Affairs, Chronological Files of the Office of Financial Resources and Energy Finance, 1974–1977 (OASIA), National Archives and Records Administration (NARA), College Park, Maryland.

23   Department of State to OECD Capitals, "OECD Committee on Financial Markets Meeting, November 21–22, 1974," Folder "1974," Box 1, OASIA, NARA.

24   Charles Stabler, "Jitters on the Euromarkets," *Wall Street Journal,* June 28, 1974, 14.

25   "Remarks by William Witherell, Director of the Office of Financial Resources, U.S. Department of the Treasury," June 17, 1975, Folder "June 1975," Box 1, OASIA, NARA, 12.

26   Jeffrey A. Frieden, *Global Capitalism: Its Fall and Rise in the Twentieth Century* (New York: W. W. Norton, 2006), 368–369.

27   Judith Stein, *Pivotal Decade: How the United States Traded Factories for Finance in the Seventies* (New Haven, CT: Yale University Press, 2010), 112–115.

28   Markovits, *Politics of West German Trade Unions,* 126–132, quote at 126.

29   Fred Hirsch, *The Social Limits to Growth* (Cambridge, MA: Harvard University Press, 1976), 11, 170, 190.

30   Calculated based on oil and currency values in "Preise für den Import von Erdöl und Erdgas aus der UdSSR seit 1972 Gegenüberstellung dieser Preise zu den kapitalistischen Weltmarktpreisen und Ausweis des Vorteils für die DDR," undated but 1985, DE/1/58747, BArch Lichterfelde.

31   Gerhard Schürer, "Information über ein Gespräch zwischen Genossen Schürer und Genossen Baibakow am 9.12.1974," December 9, 1974, DE/1/58586, BArch Lichterfelde. Soviet officials expressed the same sentiments in their meetings with Hungarian officials. See, "Zapis' Besedy—nachal'nika Upravleniia torgovli s sochialisticheskimi stranami Uvropy t. Loshakova M.G. s nachal'nikom upravleniia Ministerstva vneshnei torgovli VNR t. A Federerom," July 10, 1974, Russian State Archive of the Economy (RGAE), f. 413, o. 31, d. 6631, l. 22.

32   "Standpunkt der DDR zur Gestaltung der RGW-Preise 1976–1980," May 30, 1974, DE/1/58577, BArch Lichterfelde.

33   Attila Mong, *Kádár Hitele* (Budapest: Libri Publishing House, 2012), 150.

34   "Standpunkt der DDR," BArch Lichterfelde.

35   Underlining in the original. Horst Sölle, "Niederschrift über eine Zusammenkunft des Ministers für Außenhandel der DDR, Genossen Sölle, mit dem Minister für Außenhandel der UdSSR, Genossen Patolitschew, anläßlich der Übergabe des Aid-mémoires zur

Bildung der Vertragspreise im RGW 1976–1980 und 1975," October 3, 1974, DE/1/58588, BArch Lichterfelde.

36   Sölle, "Niederschrift über eine Zusammenkunft," BArch Lichterfelde.

37   Letter from Erich Honecker to Leonid Brezhnev, December 9, 1974, DE/1/58586, BArch Lichterfelde.

38   Gerhard Schürer, "Information über ein Gespräch zwischen Genossen Schürer und Genossen Baibakow am 9.12.1974," December 9, 1974, DE/1/58586, BArch Lichterfelde.

39   Patolichev quoted in, "Niederschrift über die Beratung zwischen Genossen Erich Honecker und Genossen Baibakow am 21.12.1974," December 21, 1974, DE/1/58586, BArch Lichterfelde.

40   Klopfer, "Persönliche Niederschrift über eine Beratung beim 1. Sekretär des Zentralkomitees der SED am 9.8.1974," August 9, 1974, DE/1/58586, BArch Lichterfelde.

41   Klopfer, "Persönliche Niederschrift über eine Beratung beim 1. Sekretär des Zentralkomitees der SED am 9.8.1974," August 9, 1974, DE/1/58586, BArch Lichterfelde.

42   Gerhard Schürer, "Vermerk," January 31, 1975, DE/1/58746, BArch Lichterfelde.

43   Quoted in Mong, *Kádár Hitele*, 151.

44   Mong, *Kádár Hitele*, 150–151.

45   Gerhard Schürer, *Gewagt und Verloren: Eine deutsche Biographie* (Frankfurt/Oder : Frankfurter Oder Editionen), 75.

46   Günter Mittag, *Um Jeden Preis: Im Spannungsfeld zweier Systeme* (Berlin: Weimar Aufbau-Verlag, 1991), 61–63.

47   At this time, a valuta mark was valued at a rate of 2.5 VM to 1 US dollar, so this total represented about $3.5 billion.

48   Günter Ehrensperger and another author whose signature is illegible, "Probleme und Konsequenzen aus der Arbeit am Volkswirtschaftsplan 1974 auf dem Gebiet der Zahlungsbilanz gegenüber dem nichtsozialistischen Wirtschaftsgebiet bis 1980," November 6, 1973, DY/30/25761, BArch Lichterfelde.

49   See James, *International Monetary Cooperation*, 320 for this context.

50   Grünheid, "Information für Genossen Schürer über die Planberatung mit dem Minister für Außenhandel, Genossen Sölle, zum Stand der Ausarbeitung der Staatlichen Aufgaben für 1975 und zur Konzeption für den Zeitraum 1976 bis 1980," March 28, 1974, DE/1/58580, BArch Lichterfelde.

51   "Die Auswirkungen der krisenhaften Situation auf dem Eurogeldmarkt auf die Lösung der Finanzierungsaufgaben der Außenhandelsbank im Rahmen der Zahlungsbilanz

1975 und für die weiteren Jahre," attachment to "Tagesordnung für die Sitzung der Arbeits-gruppe Zahlungsbilanz am 27. September 1974, 8.30 Uhr, Zimmer 441," September 27, 1974, DY 3023/963, BArch Lichterfelde.

52   William Witherell, "Policy Issues in International Finance," June 17, 1975, Folder "June 1975," Box 1, OASIA, NARA.

53   This figure only counted *publicized* Eurocurrency loans and so likely substantially understates the total flow of capital into the region. A much-greater, but also untraceable, percentage of the debt was built up through short-term deposits that Western banks placed in Eastern Bloc central and foreign trade banks. See "How the East Bloc Tapped the Euro-markets," *Euromoney*, January 1977, 24.

54   Charles Schmidt, "Comecon's Borrowing Requirements in 1976," *Euromoney*, January 1976, 12.

55   Schmidt, "Comecon's Borrowing," 14.

56   "The Debt That Overhangs East-West Dealings," *Business Week*, May 3, 1976, 118–119.

57   Bernard Nossiter, "U.S. Urges Wariness in East Trade," *Washington Post*, June 22, 1976.

58   "Information über Aspekte und Beziehungen SW/NSW Nr. 8," February 2, 1976, DN/11/6431, BArch Lichterfelde.

59   "Debt That Overhangs," *Business Week*.

60   Richard Ensor and Francis Ghiles, "CMEA Debts May Be $45 Billion, but the Loans Have Kept Flowing," *Euromoney*, January 1977, 23.

61   Ensor and Ghiles, "CMEA Debts," 23.

62   "Debt and Transition (1981–1989)," International Monetary Fund, Money Matters: An IMF Exhibit—The Importance of Global Cooperation, accessed October 17, 2021, https://www.imf.org/external/np/exr/center/mm/eng/mm_dt_01.htm

63   Schmidt, "Comecon's Borrowing," 12.

64   Gabriel Eichler, "Country Risk "Country Risk Analysis and Bank Lending to Eastern Europe," in *Eastern European Economic Assessment: Part 2–Regional Assessments*, (Washington, DC: Government Printing Office, 1981), 759–775, quote at 767.

65   Padraic Fallon, "Hungary's Marxist Economist and Central Banker, János Fekete," *Euromoney*, January 1977, 14–17.

66   Description of Wołoszyn in Padraic Fallon, "Roman Malesa. Bank Handlowy's President and Negotiator," *Euromoney*, January 1977, 31.

67   Nicholas Cumming-Bruce, "Jan Wołoszyn's Struggle for Poland," *Euromoney*, October 1980, 60–62.

68   The best historical monograph on Schalck and KoKo is Matthias Judt, *KoKo: Mythos und Realität: Das Imperium des Schalck-Golodkowski* (Berlin: Ed. Berolina, 2015). A stimulating and comprehensive overview of West German *Ostpolitik* and its attendant financial transfers remains Timothy Garton Ash, *In Europe's Name: Germany and the Divided Continent* (New York: Knopf, 1993).

69   Edward C. Keefer and Peter Kraemer, eds., *Foreign Relations of the United States, 1969–1976*, vol. E-15, part 1, *Documents on Eastern Europe, 1973–1976* (Washington, DC: United States Government Printing Office, 2008).

70   See Michael Kieninger, Mchthild Lindemann, and Daniela Taschler, eds., *Akten zur Auswärtigen Politik der Bundesrepublik Deutschland 1975* (Munich: R. Oldenbourg Verlag München, 2006).

71   Fallon, "Hungary's Marxist Economist," 17.

72   Author's calculations based on tables 8 and 9 of Jan Vanous, "Soviet and Eastern European Trade in the 1970's: A Quantitative Assessment," in *Eastern European Economic Assessment,* part 2, *Regional Assessments*, 696.

73   János Fekete, *Back to the Realities: Reflections of a Hungarian Banker* (Budapest: Akademiai Kiado, 1982), 12.

2   Years of Illusion and Reckoning

1   Figures given in Joan Parpart Zoeter, "Eastern Europe: The Hard Currency Debt," in *Eastern European Economic Assessment, part 2, Regional Assessments* (Washington, DC: Government Printing Office, 1981), 716–731, figures at 720.

2   Andrzej Paczkowski, *The Spring Will Be Ours,* trans. Jane Cave (University Park: Pennsylvania State University Press, 2003), 357–358. Timothy Garton Ash, *The Polish Revolution* (London: Penguin, 1999), 19.

3   For a characteristic interpretation, see Garton Ash, *Polish Revolution*.

4   Harold James, *International Monetary Cooperation since Bretton Woods* (New York: Oxford University Press, 1996), 279–282.

5   Original italics. Samuel Brittan, *Economic Consequences of Democracy* (London, UK: Temple Smith, 1977), xi, 255, 267.

6   Quote from James, *International Monetary Cooperation,* 279–282, quote at 282. On the decline of the British Left, see Kevin Hickson, *The IMF Crisis of 1976 and British Politics* (London: I. B. Tauris, 2005).

7   The communists did not formally join the government, but the ruling coalition relied on the communists' abstention from voting to pass legislation.

8   See Robert Flanagan, David Soskice, and Lloyd Ulman, *Unionism, Economic Stabilization, and Incomes Policies* (Washington, DC: Brookings Institution, 1983), 546–556. Also James, *International Monetary Cooperation*, 283–285.

9   "Niederschrift über eine Beratung zum Entwurf des Fünfjahrplanes 1976–1980 unter Leitung des Generalsekretärs des ZK der SED, Genossen Erich Honecker, am 5.11.1076," November 5, 1976, DE/1/58633, BArch Lichterfelde.

10   Attila Mong, *Kádár Hitele* (Budapest: Libri Publishing House, 2012), 157, 160.

11   Włodzimierz Brus, "Aims, Methods, and Political Determinants of the Economic Policy of Poland, 1970–1980," in *The East European Economies in the 1970s*, ed. Alec Nove, Hans-Hermann Hohmann, and Gertraud Seidenstecher (London: Butterworth-Heinemann, 1982), 108–139.

12   "Wpływ Bilansu Płatniczego y Krajami Kapitalistycznymi na Społeczno-Gospodarczy Rozwoj Polski w Latach 1977–1980," March 11, 1977, PZPR-KC XI A-510, Archiwiwum Akt Nowych, Warsaw. I would like to thank Lukas Dovern for sharing this document with me.

13   Quoted in Hans-Hermann Hertle, *Der Fall der Mauer: Die unbeabsichtige Selbstauflösung des SED-Staates* (Opladen, Germany: Westdeutscher Verlag, 1999), 37.

14   Hertle, *Der Fall der Mauer*, 38.

15   "Notizen zu einer Beratung des Generalsekretärs mit den 1.Sekretären der Bezirkleitung der SED im Anschluß an die 6. Tagung des Zentralkomitees am 24.6.1977," July 1, 1977, DE/1/58618, BArch Lichterfelde.

16   Quoted in Hertle, *Der Fall der Mauer*, 38.

17   Richard Ensor and Francis Ghiles, "CMEA Debts May Be $45 Billion, but the Loans Have Kept Flowing," *Euromoney*, January 1977, 23.

18   Central Intelligence Agency, Intelligence Memorandum, The Impending Soviet Oil Crisis, March 1977, CIA Online Reading Room, accessed March 22, 2017, https://www.cia.gov/library/readingroom/docs/DOC_0000498607.pdf.

19   Central Intelligence Agency, Intelligence Memorandum, *The Impending Soviet Oil Crisis*, March 1977, CIA Online Reading Room, accessed March 22, 2017, https://www.cia.gov/library/readingroom/docs/DOC_0000498607.pdf.

20   Thane Gustafson, *Crisis Amid Plenty: The Politics of Soviet Energy under Brezhnev and Gorbachev* (Princeton, NJ: Princeton University Press, 1989), particularly 27–29.

21   Abteilung UdSSR, "Arbeitsniederschrift über das Gespräch zwischen Genossen Grünheld und Genossen Worow am 12.2.1978 in Berlin," February 12, 1978, DE/1/58564, BArch Lichterfelde.

22   "Rede des Leiters der Delegation der UdSSR auf der XXXI. Tagung des RGW, Genossen A.N. Kossygin," June 15, 1977, DE/1/55847, BArch Lichterfelde. On how the

oil-production problems began to affect the Soviets' bilateral relations with bloc countries, see, for example, "Zapis' besedy Predsedatelia Gosplana SSSR t Baibokova s zamestitelem Predsedatelia Soveta Ministrov NRB tov A Lukanovym," November 11, 1977, Russian State Archive of the Economy (RGAE), f. 4372, o. 66, d. 819, l. 19–25.

23   Underlining in the original. Staatliche Plankommission, "Information zu einigen Problemen der Außenhandelsbeziehungen der DDR," May 21, 1975, DE/1/58558, BArch Lichterfelde.

24   "Zur langfristigen ökonomischen Zusammenarbeit zwischen der DDR und der UdSSR und Arbeit an den Zielprogrammen," November 30 and December 1, 1976, DE/1/58569, BArch Lichterfelde.

25   Staatliche Plankomission Abt. Energiewirtschaft, "Problemmaterial zur energetisch-en Sicherung der Entwicklung der Volkswirtschaft 1981–1985 unter Berucksichtigung vom Prämissen aus den Verhandlungen mit der UdSSR über Rohstoff- und Energieträgerliefer-mögichkeiten," undated but likely from 1978 or 1979, DE/1/58657, BArch Lichterfelde.

26   "Zur Frage der Aufwendungen der DDR in freikonvertierbaren Währung im Zeitraum 1971/76," July 10, 1977, DE/1/58554, BArch Lichterfelde.

27   Abteilung UdSSR, "Arbeitsniederschrift über das Gespräch zwischen . . .," BArch Lichterfelde.

28   Karl Grünheid, "Information über Gespräche mit Vertretern des Gosplan der UdSSR auf Expertenebene zu den Fragen der Rohstofflieferungen im Zeitraum 1981 bis 1985," October 29, 1978, DE/1/58665, BArch Lichterfelde.

29   "Überschlagsrechnung zur Auswirkung der bisherigen Mitteilungen über Rohstof-flieferungen der UdSSR 1981/85 gegenüber der volkswirtschaftlichen Konzeption," October 30, 1978, DE1/58665, BArch Lichterfelde.

30   "Information über die Beratung mit Genossen Kossygin im Moskau am 8. Dezember 1978," December 8, 1978, DE/1/58666, BArch Lichterfelde.

31   "Stenografische Niederschrift der Beratung des Vorsitzenden des Minterrates der DDR Genossen Willi Stoph, mit dem Vorsitzenden des Ministerrates der UdSSR Genossen Alexei Kossygin," December 8, 1978, DE/1/58666, BArch Lichterfelde.

32   The amount of $3.2 billion is the author's calculation from the numbers given in the document using an exchange rate of 2.5 valutamarks to 1 US dollar. Staatliche Plankomis-sion Abt. Energiewirtschaft, "Problemmaterial zur energetischen Sicherung der Entwick-lung der Volkswirtschaft 1981–1985," BArch Lichterfelde.

33   Werner Polze, "Bericht über eine Dienstreise nach den USA und Kanada in der Zeit von 8. bis 19.5.1978," May 23, 1978, DN/10/447, BArch Lichterfelde.

34   The front-page article is Christopher Bobinski and Anthony Robinson, "Poland Seeking Long-term $500m Euro-loan" Financial Times, November 30, 1978, 1. Quotes from

Christopher Bobinksi, "Poland to Open Its Books for $500m Loan," *Financial Times*, November 30, 1978, 2.

35   Werner Polze, "Bericht über eine Dienstreise des Präsidenten der Deutschen Außenhandelsbank nach Großbritannien in der Zeit vom 25.10.–2.11.1978," November 3, 1978, DN/10/447, BArch Lichterfelde.

36   Underlining in the original. State Planning Commission, "Information und Vorschläge zur Ausarbeitung des Planansates 1980," June 7, 1979, DE/1/58657, BArch Lichterfelde.

37   "Stenographische Niederschrift der Zusammenkunft des Generalsekretärs des ZK der SED und Vorsitzenden des Staatsrates der DDR, Genossen Erich Honecker, sowie der weiteren Mitglieder und Kandidaten des Politbüros des ZK der SED mit dem Generalsekretär des ZK der KPdSU und Vorsitzenden des Präsidiums des Obersten Sowjets der UdSSR, Genossen Leonid Iljitsch Breschnew," October 4, 1979, DY 30/2378, Stiftung Archiv der Parteien und Massenorganisationen der DDR im Bundesarchiv, Berlin (SAPMO), 91. Brezhnev pounding his fist during this meeting comes from Hertle, *Der Fall der Mauer*, 42.

38   Quoted in William Greider, *Secrets of the Temple: How the Federal Reserve Runs the Country* (New York: Simon & Schuster, 1987), 58.

39   "The Polish Problem," *Euromoney*, April 1979, 5.

40   Quoted in Theodore H. White, *America in Search of Itself: The Making of the Presidents 1956–1980* (New York: Harper and Row, 1982), 149.

41   "Historic Inflation United States—CPI Inflation," inflation.eu, Worldwide Inflation Data, accessed March 26, 2017, http://www.inflation.eu/inflation-rates/united-states/historic-inflation/cpi-inflation-united-states.aspx.

42   James, *International Monetary Cooperation*, 303–306.

43   Daniel Yergin, *The Prize: The Epic Quest for Oil, Money, and Power* (New York: Free Press, 1991), chap. 33. Judith Stein, *Pivotal Decade: How the United States Traded Factories for Finance in the Seventies* (New Haven, CT: Yale University Press, 2010), 211–215.

44   Underlining in the original. W. Michael Blumenthal, Memorandum for the President, May 25, 1979, Folder "Venice Summit 1980," Box 90, Staff Office—Council of Economic Advisors, Jimmy Carter Presidential Library (JCPL), Atlanta, GA.

45   Jimmy Carter, "Energy and National Goals: Address to the Nation," July 15, 1979, Jimmy Carter Library, accessed March 27, 2016, https://www.jimmycarterlibrary.gov/documents/speeches/energy-crisis.phtml.

46   Jefferson Cowie, *Stayin' Alive: The 1970s and the Last Days of the Working Class* (New York: New Press, 2010), 300–301.

47   See Greider, *Secrets*, 47. See also W. Carl Biven, *Jimmy Carter's Economy: Policy in the Age of Limits* (Chapel Hill, NC: University of North Carolina Press 2002), 238–239.

48   Arthur Burns, "The Anguish of Central Banking," in *The 1979 Per Jacobsson Lecture,* September 30, 1979, accessed March 27, 2017, http://www.perjacobsson.org/lectures/1979.pdf.

49   Quoted in William L. Silber, *Volcker: The Triumph of Persistence* (New York: Bloomsbury 2012), 197.

50   Greider, *Secrets,* 121.

51   Greider, *Secrets,* 83–86, Schulz quote at 86.

52   Coldwell quoted in Greider, *Secrets,* 123.

53   "Transcript of Press Conference with Paul A. Volcker, Chairman, Board of Governors of the Federal Reserve System, October 6, 1979," accessed October 18, 2021, https://fraser.stlouisfed.org/title/statements-speeches-paul-a-volcker-451/transcript-press-conference-held-board-room-federal-reserve-building-washington-dc-8201.

54   The $200 million figure is calculated from the VM 520 million figure given in the document at an exchange rate of 2.5 VM to 1 US dollar. Letter and Attachment from Horst Kaminsky to Günter Mittag, October 25, 1979, DY 3023/1093, SAMPO, 129–131.

55   Benjamin Cohen, *In Whose Interest? International Banking and US Foreign Policy* (New Haven, CT: Yale University Press, 1986), chap. 6.

56   Horst Kaminsky and Werner Polze, "Analyse der Lage auf den internationalen Geld- und Kreditmärkten, besonders des US-Dollar als Leit- und Reservewährung und Massnahmen zur Erhöhung des Aufkommens an relative stabilen Wahrungen sowie Sofortmassnahmen fur die Arbeit auf der Leipziger Frühjahrsmesse 1980," February 6, 1980, DY 3023/1094, SAPMO.

57   "Notatka w sprawie aktualnej oceny warunków realizacji Narodowego Planu Społeczno-Gospodarczego na rok 1980 i wniosków wynikających z tej oceny," May 31, 1980, in *Tajne Dokumenty Biura Politycznego* (London: Aneks, 1992), 7–13.

58   Fred Hirsch, *The Social Limits to Growth* (Cambridge, MA: Harvard University Press, 1976), 175.

59   Greider, *Secrets,* 107.

3   A Tale of Two Crises

1   On Thatcher and Thatcherism, see John Campbell, *The Grocer's Daughter* (London: Jonathan Cape, 2000) and *The Iron Lady* (London: Jonathan Cape, 2003); Charles Moore's three volume biography, *Margaret Thatcher: From Grantham to the Falklands* (New York: Knopf, 2013); *Margaret Thatcher: At Her Zenith* (New York: Knopf, 2016); *Margaret Thatcher: Herself Alone* (New York: Knopf, 2019); Robert Skidelsky, ed., *Thatcherism* (London: Chatto & Windus, 1988); and Andrew Gamble, *The Free Economy and the Strong State: The Politics of Thatcherism,* 2nd ed. (London: Macmillan, 1994). On 1980s Britain, see Graham

Stewart, *Bang! A History of Britain in the 1980s* (London: Atlantic Books, 2013) and Alwyn W. Turner, *Rejoice, Rejoice! Britain in the 1980s* (London: Aurum, 2010). On the Polish Crisis, the most important titles in English are Timothy Garton Ash, *Solidarity: The Polish Revolution* (London: Granta Books, 1991); Andrzej Paczkowski and Malcolm Byrne, eds., *From Solidarity to Martial Law: The Polish Crisis of 1980–1981* (Budapest: Central European University Press, 2007); David Ost, *Solidarity and the Politics of Anti-Politics: Opposition and Reform in Poland Since 1968* (Philadelphia, PA: Temple University Press, 1990); and Gregory Domber, *Empowering Revolution: America, Poland, and the End of the Cold War* (Chapel Hill: University of North Carolina Press, 2014).

2   For Thatcher's thoughts on Hoskyns, see Margaret Thatcher, *The Downing Street Years* (New York: HarperCollins, 1993), 30. For Jaruzelski's thoughts on Rakowski, see Wojciech Jaruzelski, *Mein Leben für Polen: Erinnerungen* (Munich: Zürich Piper, 1993), 243.

3   Thatcher, *Downing Street Years*, 377.

4   Letter from John Hoskyns to Keith Joseph, quoted in John Hoskyns, *Just in Time: Inside the Thatcher Revolution* (London: Aurum Press, 2000), 26.

5   Hoskyns's journal, quoted in Hoskyns, *Just in Time*, 28.

6   Hoskyns's journal, quoted in Hoskyns, *Just in Time*, 40.

7   Hoskyns's journal, quoted in Hoskyns, *Just in Time*, 63.

8   Hoskyns's journal, quoted in Hoskyns, *Just in Time*, 40.

9   John Hoskyns and Norman Strauss, "Stepping Stones," November 14, 1977, original in Margaret Thatcher Papers, Churchill Archives Centre, Cambridge University, (THCR), File THCR 2/6/1/248. Accessed via Margaret Thatcher Foundation Digital Collection (MTFDC), accessed December 19. 2017, https://www.margaretthatcher.org/document/111771, S-1 and S-2.

10   Hoskyns and Strauss, "Stepping Stones," 22, 24, 25, 27.

11   Hoskyns and Strauss, "Stepping Stones," Appendix, "The Union Problem," A-1, A-2.

12   Hoskyns, *Just in Time*, 79.

13   Quoted in Hoskyns, *Just in Time*, 80. See also Stewart, *Bang!*, 23.

14   Quoted in Hoskyns, *Just in Time*, 85.

15   Rakowski, *Rzeczpospolita na progu lat osiemdziesiątych* (Warsaw: Państwowy Instytut Wydawniczy, 1981), 69.

16   Rakowski, *Rzeczpospolita na progu lat osiemdziesiątych*, 56, 31.

17   Rakowski, *Rzeczpospolita na progu lat osiemdziesiątych*, 32–33.

18   Rakowski, *Rzeczpospolita na progu lat osiemdziesiątych*, 33, 183, 177, 188, 189, 190.

19   Only after the Polish Crisis began and Rakowski's views became mainstream was the book published in 1981.

20   Ost, *Solidarity*, 99–121.

21   Quoted in Rakowski, *Dzienniki polityczne 1979–1981* (Warsaw: ISKRY, 2004), 278.

22   Jaruzelski, *Mein Leben für Polen*, 242–243.

23   Stewart, *Bang!*, 56.

24   Stewart, *Bang!*, 57–59.

25   Hoskyns, *Just in Time*, 118, "moral and intellectual bankruptcy" from 125.

26   See introduction in Paczkowski and Byrne, *From Solidarity*, for further analysis of public opinion during the crisis.

27   In March 1980, the governor of the Bank of England conveyed his "serious misgivings about the whole exercise" to Thatcher in a meeting of senior advisors. A. J. Wiggins to John Hoskyns, March 10, 1980, MTFDC, https://www.margaretthatcher.org/document/113049.

28   Nigel Lawson, *The View from No. 11: Memoirs of a Tory Radical* (London: Corgi, 1993), 67.

29   John Hoskyns, "Economic Strategy," June 13, 1980, PREM19/172 f129, Margaret Thatcher Foundation, Thatcher digital archive (MSS), accessed December 29, 2017, https://www.margaretthatcher.org/document/115536.

30   Italics in the original. Hoskyns to the Prime Minister, "Public Sector Pay," July 18, 1980, PREM19/182 f134, Margaret Thatcher Foundation, Thatcher digital archive (MSS), accessed December 20, 2017, https://www.margaretthatcher.org/document/115669.

31   Hoskyns to Thatcher, "Policy Options," November 11, 1980, PREM19/174 f222, Margaret Thatcher Foundation, Thatcher digital archive (MSS), accessed December 20, 2017, https://www.margaretthatcher.org/document/115566.

32   Hoskyns to Thatcher, November 20, 1980, PREM19/174 f196, MTFDC, accessed December 29, 2017, https://www.margaretthatcher.org/document/115568.

33   Hoskyns to Thatcher, "Government Strategy," December 22, 1980, PREM19/174 f11, MTFDC, accessed December 29, 2017, https://www.margaretthatcher.org/document/115579.

34   Margaret Thatcher, "Speech to Conservative Party Conference," October 10, 1980, CCOPR 735/80, MTFDC, accessed June 15, 2021, https://www.margaretthatcher.org/document/104431.

35   Thatcher, "Speech to Conservative Party Conference."

36   Hoskyns's diary, quoted in Hoskyns, *Just in Time*, 260.

37   Thatcher, *Downing Street Years,* 132.

38   Capitalization and italicization in the original. Memorandum from Alan Walters, David Wolfson, and John Hoskyns to Thatcher, "Budget Strategy," February 20, 1981, PREM19/439 f200, MTFDC, accessed December 29, 2017, https://www.margaretthatcher.org/document/114016.

39   Quoted in Stewart, *Bang!,* 59–60.

40   See, for example, the debate on British policy in Michael Bordo and Athanasios Orphanides, eds., *The Great Inflation: The Rebirth of Modern Central Banking* (Washington, DC: National Bureau of Economic Research Conference Report, 2013) and Skidelsky, ed., *Thatcherism,* chaps. 5 and 6.

41   Lawson, *View from No. 11.*

42   Stewart, *Bang!,* 85–99.

43   Quoted in Garton Ash, *Solidarity: The Polish Revolution,* 153.

44   Rakowski, *Dzienniki polityczne 1979–1981,* 336.

45   Rakowski, *Dzienniki polityczne 1979–1981,* 355–356.

46   Rakowski, *Dzienniki polityczne 1979–1981,* 360.

47   For the intricate details and primary sources of this Soviet pressure, see Paczkowski and Byrne, *From Solidarity to Martial Law.* For further details on the domestic aspects of the Bydgoszcz crisis, see Ost, *Solidarity,* 125.

48   Mark Kramer estimates total Soviet financial assistance during the crisis reached almost $3 billion. See Mark Kramer, ed., "Soviet Deliberations in the Polish Crisis," Special Working Paper No. 1, April 2000, Cold War International History Project, 135n216.

49   Paczkowski and Byrne, "The Polish Crisis: Internal and International Dimensions," in *From Solidarity to Martial Law,* 22.

50   Mario Nuti, cited in Garton Ash, *Solidarity: The Polish Revolution,* 202.

51   Garton Ash, *Solidarity: The Polish Revolution,* 115.

52   Paczkowski and Byrne, *From Solidarity to Martial Law,* xl.

53   Rakowski, *Dzienniki polityczne 1981–1983,* 9.

54   Rakowski, *Dzienniki polityczne 1981–1983,* 18–19.

55   Rakowski, *Dzienniki polityczne 1981–1983,* 12.

56   Official report of the meeting, quoted in Garton Ash, *Solidarity: The Polish Revolution,* 205. Also Ost, *Solidarity,* 128.

57   Accounts of the August negotiations are notoriously contradictory on the issue of who was ultimately responsible for the breakdown in the talks. This account is based on Rakowski, *Dzienniki polityczne 1981–1983*, 18–22; Garton Ash, *Solidarity: The Polish Revolution*, 204–206; Ost, *Solidarity*, 128; and Władysław Baka, *Zmagania o Reformę: z dziennika politycznego 1980-1990* (Warsaw: Wydawn, 2007), 40–41.

58   Rakowski, *Dzienniki polityczne 1981–1983*, 23.

59   Ost, *Solidarity*, 132.

60   "The Solidarity Program," in *The Solidarity Sourcebook*, ed. Stan Persky and Henry Flam (Vancouver, Canada: New Star Books, 1982), 211.

61   Ost, *Solidarity*, 136; "The Solidarity Program," 211; and Garton Ash, *Solidarity: The Polish Revolution*, 221.

62   Rakowski, *Dzienniki polityczne 1981–1983*, 64, 71, 72.

63   Rakowski, *Dzienniki polityczne 1981–1983*, 77, 80.

64   Rakowski, *Dzienniki polityczne 1981–1983*, 89.

65   Document 73, "Protokół nr 14 z posiedzenia Biura Politycznego KC PZPR 10 listopada 1981 r." in Zbigniew Wlodek, ed., *Tajne Dokumenty Biura Politycznego: PZPR a "Solidarność," 1980–81* (London, UK: Aneks, 1992), 516–527.

66   Rakowski, *Dzienniki polityczne 1981–1983*, 112–119. Ost, *Solidarity*, 144.

67   Rakowski, *Dzienniki polityczne 1981–1983*, 120.

68   Document 77, "Protokół nr 18 z posiedzenia Biura Politycznego KC PZPR 5 grudnia 1981 r.," in Wlodek, ed., *Tajne Dokumenty Biura Politycznego*, 549–550.

69   Document 77, "Protokół nr 18 z posiedzenia Biura Politycznego," 562.

70   Rakowski, *Dzienniki polityczne 1981–1983*, 125.

71   Rakowski, *Dzienniki polityczne 1981–1983*, 126.

72   Quoted in Andrzej Paczkowski, *Revolution and Counterrevolution in Poland, 1980–1989*, trans. Christina Manetti (Rochester, NY: University of Rochester Press, 2015), 97.

73   Garton Ash, *Solidarity: The Polish Revolution*, 274.

74   Polish Ministry of Foreign Affairs, "The Polish Economic Reform: Major Prerequisites, Model Provisions, and State of Implementation," undated but spring of 1982, Box 58, File 1, EUR Country Files, International Monetary Fund (IMF) Archives, Washington, DC.

75   David Mason, *Public Opinion and Political Change in Poland, 1980–1982* (Cambridge: Cambridge University Press, 1985), 231.

76   Moore, *Margaret Thatcher: From Grantham to the Falklands*, 643.

77   Peter Walker to the Prime Minister, "Memorandum on a Conservative Strategy for the Next Two Years," February 16, 1982, THCR 1/15/6 f3, MTFDC, accessed December 29, 2017, https://www.margaretthatcher.org/document/122920.

78   Moore, *Margaret Thatcher: From Grantham to the Falklands,* 752.

79   Moore, *Margaret Thatcher: From Grantham to the Falklands,* chaps. 23 and 24 provide a thorough history of the Falklands War.

80   Quoted in Moore, *Margaret Thatcher: From Grantham to the Falklands,* 755.

81   Figure 2.1 in David Butler and Dennis Kavanagh, *The British General Election of 1983* (London: Macmillan, 1984), 15.

82   Thatcher to Hayek, February 17, 1982, Margaret Thatcher Foundation, Hayek MSS (Hoover Institution), Box 101, MTFDC, accessed December 29, 2017, https://www.margaretthatcher.org/document/117179.

83   John Vereker to Alan Walters, December 24, 1982, PREM19/1092 f155, MTFDC, accessed December 29, 2017, https://www.margaretthatcher.org/document/138788.

84   Nigel Lawson to Margaret Thatcher, January 21, 1983, PREM19/1092 f134, accessed December 29, 2017, https://www.margaretthatcher.org/document/138768.

85   Hoskyns to Thatcher, March 27, 1981, PREM19/540 f186, MTFDC, accessed January 4, 2018, https://www.margaretthatcher.org/document/126057.

86   Hoskyns wrote this in a memo about a possible Civil Service strike, but as his "general rule" phrase suggests, he believed it equally held for all areas of the economy. Hoskyns to Thatcher, April 8, 1981, PREM19/400 f64, MTFDC, accessed January 4, 2018, https://www.margaretthatcher.org/document/125602.

87   Lawson to Thatcher, January 21, 1983, PREM19/1092 f134, MTFDC, accessed January 4, 2018, https://www.margaretthatcher.org/document/138768.

88   Figures from Butler and Kavanagh, *The British General Election of 1983,* 280.

89   Peter Gregson to Thatcher, September 14, 1983, PREM19/1329 f244, MTFDC, accessed January 5, 2018, https://www.margaretthatcher.org/document/133119.

90   "Record of a Meeting Held at No. 10 Downing Street," September 15, 1983, PREM19/1329 f243, MTFDC, accessed January 5, 2018, https://www.margaretthatcher.org/document/133121.

91   David Pascall to Andrew Turnbull, March 7, 1984, PREM19/1329 f140, MTFDC, accessed January 5, 2018, https://www.margaretthatcher.org/document/133140.

92   Quoted in Thatcher, *Downing Street Years,* 350.

93   David Pascall, "The Coal Dispute—Public Opinion," June 14, 1984, PREM19-1331 f225, MTFDC, accessed June 21, 2021, https://www.margaretthatcher.org/document/133376.

94   Moore, *Margaret Thatcher: At Her Zenith,* 155.

95   Moore, *Margaret Thatcher: At Her Zenith*, 162.

96   "The Miners and the TUC Conference," August 31, 1984, PREM19-1332 f10, MTFDC, accessed June 21, 2021, https://www.margaretthatcher.org/document/133497.

97   Pascall, "The Coal Dispute—Public Opinion," June 14, 1984.

98   Moore, *Margaret Thatcher: At Her Zenith* , 156.

99   Police approval rating in Pascall, "The Coal Dispute—Public Opinion," June 14, 1984; Thatcher approval rating in "Public Opinion Background Note," July 4, 1984, THCR 2-6-3-87 f262, MTFDC, accessed June 21, 2021, https://www.margaretthatcher.org/document/137582.

100   Marc Levinson, *An Extraordinary Time: The End of the Postwar Boom and the Return of the Ordinary Economy* (New York: Basic Books, 2016), 192, 194.

4   The Capitalist Perestroika

1   The most straightforward English translation of the word *perestroika* is "restructuring." For a holistic definition, see Abel Aganbegyan, *The Economic Challenge of Perestroika,* trans. Pauline M. Tiffen (Bloomington, IN: Indiana University Press, 1988). Note that this book was published using the transliteration "Aganbegyan," and thus I have retained that spelling when referring to this book in the notes.

2   Gosbank memorandum, "Mezhdunarodnyi valiutnyi fond i sotsialisticheskie strany," November 11, 1983, Russian State Archive of the Economy (RGAE), f. 2324, o. 33, d. 406.

3   "Usloviia kreditovaniia zapadom razvivaiushchikhsia stran progressivnoi orientatsii," March 20, 1987, RGAE, f. 2324 o. 33 d. 640.

4   Anatolii Cherniaev, ed., *V Politbiuro TsK KPSS:Po zapisiam Anatoliia Cherniaeva, Vadima Medvedeva, Georgiia Shakhnazarova* (Moscow: Alpina, 2006), 180.

5   V. B. Benevolenskii, "Ekonomicheskaia vzaimozavisimost' i vneshniaia politika SShA," January 21, 1989, Archive of the Russian Academy of Sciences (ARAN), f. 2021 d. 2 o. 70, l. 266.

6   Jonathan Levy, *Ages of American Capitalism: A History of the United States* (New York: Random House, 2021), 605.

7   Kevin Kruse and Julian Zelizer, *Fault Lines: A History of the United States since 1974* (New York: W. W. Norton, 2019), 105.

8   Paul Volcker, "A Rare Opportunity," Speech at the Tax Foundation, December 3, 1980, Folder "Federal Reserve Board Paul Volcker (1 of 7)," Box 15, Subject File, Martin Anderson Files, Ronald Reagan Presidential Library (RRPL), Simi Valley, CA.

9   Statement by Paul A. Volcker, Chairman, Board of Governors of the Federal Reserve System before the Committee on Banking, Housing and Urban Affairs, United States

Senate, January 7, 1981, Folder "Federal Reserve Board Paul Volcker (1 of 7)," Box 15, Subject File, Martin Anderson Files, RRPL.

10   This refers to the bank prime loan rate. See Federal Reserve data at "Bank Prime Loan Rate," Federal Reserve Bank of St. Louis, accessed June 5, 2021, https://fred.stlouisfed.org/series/MPRIME,.

11   Figure 2.2 in Andrew Glyn, *Capitalism Unleashed: Finance, Globalization, and Welfare* (New York: Oxford University Press, 2006), 26.

12   Levy, *Ages of American Capitalism,* 603.

13   Michael Mussa, "U.S. Monetary Policy in the 1980s," in *American Economic Policy in the 1980s,* ed. Martin Feldstein (Chicago: University of Chicago Press, 1994), 104.

14   Steven Greenhouse, *The Big Squeeze: Tough Times for the American Worker* (New York: Knopf, 2008), 80–83.

15   "First Inaugural Address of Ronald Reagan," January 20, 1981, Yale Law School, Lillian Goldman Law Library, The Avalon Project, accessed June 5, 2021, https://avalon.law.yale.edu/20th_century/reagan1.asp,.

16   Levy, *Ages of American Capitalism,* 379.

17   Calculated from the constant dollar data set for Figure 9.1 in Thomas Piketty, *Capital in the Twenty-First Century* (Cambridge, MA: Harvard University Press, 2014), 309. Data set available at http://piketty.pse.ens.fr/files/capital21c/en/xls/, accessed June 15, 2021.

18   Herbert Meyer, "The Decline of Strikes," *Fortune,* November 2, 1981, 66.

19   Quoted in Jefferson Cowie, *Stayin' Alive: The 1970s and the Last Days of the Working Class* (New York: New Press, 2010), 363.

20   Levy, *Ages of American Capitalism,* 605.

21   Meyer, "Decline of Strikes," 70.

22   Stephen Hayward, *The Age of Reagan,* vol. 2, *The Conservative Counterrevolution, 1980–1989* (New York: Three Rivers Press, 2009), 173.

23   Greenhouse, *Big Squeeze,* 80.

24   Barry T. Hirsch and David A. Macpherson, Union Membership and Coverage Database, "Union Membership, Coverage, Density and Employment, 1973–2020, Private Sector Historical Table," accessed July 2, 2021, http://unionstats.com.

25   Robert Brenner, *The Economics of Global Turbulence* (New York: Verso, 2006), 196.

26   For more detailed discussion of this broad conclusion, see Brenner, *The Economics of Global Turbulence,* 209–210.

27   "Business Conditions: How High the Rate?," July 26, 1981, *New York Times*, sec. 3, 18.

28   Figure 9.3 in Barry Eichengreen, *The European Economy since 1945* (Princeton, NJ: Princeton University Press, 2007), 265.

29   Glyn, *Capitalism Unleashed*, 116.

30   Brenner, *Economics of Global Turbulence*, 230.

31   Tony Judt, *Postwar: A History of Europe since 1945* (New York: Penguin, 2005), 555.

32   Marc Levinson, *An Extraordinary Time: The End of the Postwar Boom and the Return of the Ordinary Economy* (New York: Basic Books, 2016), 215; Laura Cabeza Garcia and Silvia Gomes Anson, "The Spanish Privitsation Process: Implications on the Performance of Divested Firms," *International Review of Financial Analysis* 16 (2007): 390–409.

33   Cherniaev, ed., *V Politbiuro TsK KPSS*, 180. Levinson, *An Extraordinary Time*, 217.

34   OECD social spending data set at "Social Spending," OECD, accessed July 8, 2021, https://data.oecd.org/socialexp/social-spending.htm#indicator-chart.

35   Thomas Rodney Chistofferson, *The French Socialists in Power, 1981–1986: From Autogestion to Cohabitation* (Newark: University of Delaware Press, 1991), chap. 2.

36   Levinson, *Extraordinary Time*, 204–208; Judt, *Postwar*, 551–554.

37   Judt, *Postwar*, 554.

38   Rawi Abdelal, *Capital Rules: The Construction of Global Finance* (Cambridge, MA: Harvard University Press, 2007), particularly chap. 4.

39   Levinson, *Extraordinary Time*, 196.

40   Judt, *Postwar*, 558.

41   David A. Stockman, *The Triumph of Politics: How the Reagan Revolution Failed* (New York: Harper & Row, 1986), 8.

42   Stockman, *Triumph of Politics*, 265.

43   Stockman, *Triumph of Politics*, 67.

44   Stockman, *Triumph of Politics*, 60.

45   "First Inaugural Address of Ronald Reagan," January 20, 1981, Yale Law School, Lillian Goldman Law Library, The Avalon Project, accessed June 5, 2021, https://avalon.law.yale.edu/20th_century/reagan1.asp.

46   The ERTA favored debt investment over equity investment much more than the law's authors initially intended. The 50 percent estimation is from *1989 Economic Report of the President* (Washington, DC: United States Government Printing Office, 1989), 87.

47   Calculation based on current dollar figures provided in table 4.5 in James Poterba, "Federal Budget Policy in the 1980s," in ed. Feldstein, *American Economic Policy in the 1980s*, 248.

48   Emphasis in the original. Stockman, *Triumph of Politics*, 343.

49   Reagan, October 17, 1981, in Douglas Brinkley, ed., *The Reagan Diaries* (New York: HarperCollins, 2007), 44.

50   Brinkley, *Reagan Diaries*, 53.

51   Statement by Paul Volcker, Chairman, Board of Governors of the Federal Reserve System before the Committee on the Budget, United States Senate, September 16, 1981, Folder "Federal Reserve Board Paul Volcker (4 of 7)," Box 15, Subject File, Martin Anderson Files, RRPL.

52   Lawrence Kudlow, Memorandum for the Council on Economic Affairs, "Financial and Economic Update (Executive Summary)," January 21, 1982, Box 19, WHORM Subject File, Federal Government Organization, Cabinet Councils, RRPL.

53   Memorandum for Secretary of the Treasury et al., "The Cabinet Council on Economic Affairs Working Group on International Investment," June 17, 1981, Folder "Cabinet Council on Economic Affairs June 1981," Box OA7424, James Burnham Files, RRPL.

54   Murray Weidenbaum, "The United States and the World Economy," September 16, 1981, Folder "Cabinet Council on Economic Affairs September 1981," Box OA7424, James Burnham Files, RRPL.

55   Henry Kaufman and Paul Volcker being two of the most prominent doubters. See Paul Volcker's "The Twin Deficits," *Challenge* 26 (March/April 1984): 4–9, and Henry Kaufman, *Interest Rates, Markets, and the New Financial World* (New York: Times, 1986).

56   William A. Niskanen, *Reaganomics: An Insider's Account of the Policies and the People* (New York: Oxford University Press, 1988), 110.

57   The 1984 Deficit Reduction Act and the Tax Reform Act of 1986 also followed. "Piecemeal" is James Poterba's characterization in "Federal Budget Policy in the 1980s," 250.

58   From July 1980 to March 1985, the dollar appreciated 18.1 percent against the Japanese yen, 94.5 percent against the deutsche mark, and 122.6 percent against the British pound. Harold James, *International Monetary Cooperation since Bretton Woods* (New York: Oxford University Press, 1996), 419.

59   Martin Feldstein, Memorandum for the Cabinet Council on Economic Affairs, "Is the Dollar Overvalued?," April 8, 1983, OA10700, William Poole Papers, RRPL.

60   Roger B. Porter, "Economic Policy Study Number 9: Economic Impact of International Trade," June 30, 1983, Folder "Cabinet Council on Economic Affairs, July 1984 (1)," Box OA10700, William Poole Papers, RRPL.

61   Robert Dederick, Memorandum for the Cabinet Council on Economic Affairs, "Report of the CCEA Working Group on the Economic Impact of International Trade," September 26, 1983, Folder "Cabinet Council on Economic Affairs, October 1983 (1)," Box OA10700, William Poole Papers, RRPL.

62   William Greider, *Secrets of the Temple: How the Federal Reserve Runs the Country* (New York: Simon & Schuster, 1987), 561.

63   Greider, *Secrets,* 561.

64   Greta R. Krippner, *Capitalizing on Crisis: The Political Origins of the Rise of Finance* (Cambridge, MA: Harvard University Press, 2011), 189n34.

65   Robert G. Dederick, "Report of the CCEA Working Group on the Economic Impact of International Trade," September 26, 1983, Folder "Cabinet Council on Economic Affairs, October 1983 (1)," Box OA10700, William Poole Papers, RRPL.

66   Sidney Jones, "Report of the CCEA Working Group on the Economic Impact of International Trade: Macro Economic Policy Options," January 24, 1984, OA10700, William Poole Papers, RRPL.

67   Stuart Auerbach, "U.S. Becomes World's No. 1 Debtor Nation," *Washington Post,* June 25, 1986, G01.

68   Calculated from data series in table S8.2, "Top Income and Wage Shares in the US, 1900–2010," in Piketty, *Capital in the Twenty-First Century,* available in "Chapter9TablesandFigures.aspx" at http://piketty.pse.ens.fr/files/capital21c/en/xls/.

69   Doubling of consumer credit statistic from Louis Hyman, *Debtor Nation: The History of America in Red Ink* (Princeton, NJ: Princeton University Press, 2011), 223, fig 7.3. Two-thirds of American households with credit cards from Louis Hyman, *Borrow: A History of America in Red Ink* (New York: Vintage, 2012), 226.

70   Giovanni Arrighi, "The World Economy and the Cold War, 1970–1990," in *The Cambridge History of the Cold War,* vol. 3, ed. Melvyn P. Leffler and Odd Arne Westad (Cambridge: Cambridge University Press, 2010), 23–44.

71   Peter Field, "The Shunning of the Sovereign Borrower," *Euromoney,* May 1982, 27, 30.

72   National Intelligence Council Memorandum, "Implications of the LDC Debt Problem," October 1982, CREST, CIA Online Reading Room, accessed November 5, 2018, https://www.cia.gov/library/readingroom/document/cia-rdp85m00363r001302940047-6.

73   William Clark, Memorandum for the White House Summit Group, "Give-and-Take Session with the President," April 21, 1983, Folder "Economic Summit Meeting Notes," Box OA9811, Martin Feldstein Papers, RRPL.

74   Roger W. Robinson to Norman A. Bailey, "Comments Related to Federal Reserve Staff Paper on IMF date 4/5/82 for Meeting of International Monetary Group on 4/20/82,"

Folder "International Finance 4/20/1982—11/16/82," RAC Box 3, Roger Robinson Papers, RRPL.

75   James, *International Monetary Cooperation,* chap. 12 recounts the Latin American debt crisis in great detail. Very similar packages of IMF aid, commercial bank and government financing, and domestic structural adjustment were signed with Argentina and Brazil in fall 1982.

76   See the summary of the US debt strategy provided in Christopher Hicks, "IG-IEP on International Debt," August 15, 1984, Folder "Interagency Group on International Economic Policy (IG-IEP) on International Debt," Box OA10699, William Poole Papers, RRPL.

77   "Reagan Thanks Democrats," *New York Times,* October 25, 1983, D1.

78   Minutes of National Security Council Meeting, November 23, 1982, NSC00067, NSC Executive Secretariat Meeting Files, RRPL.

79   Hal Brands, *Latin America's Cold War* (Cambridge, MA: Harvard University Press, 2010), 233.

80   Brands, *Latin America's Cold War,* 224. See also James, *International Monetary Cooperation,* 386; Barbara Stallings and Robert Kaufman, eds., *Debt and Democracy in Latin America* (Boulder, CO: Westview Press, 1989); Samuel Huntington, *The Third Wave: Democratization in the Late Twentieth Century* (Norman: University of Oklahoma Press, 1991); and Peter H. Smith, *Democracy in Latin America: Political Change in Comparative Perspective* (New York: Oxford University Press, 2011).

5   The Economic Cold War

1   Padraic Fallon and David Sheriff, "The Betrayal of Eastern Europe," *Euromoney,* September 1982, 21.

2   Fallon and Sheriff, "Betrayal," 22.

3   L. A. Whittome to the Managing Director, December 21, 1981, File 3, Box 29, European Department Immediate Files (EDIF), International Monetary Fund (IMF) Archives, Washington, DC.

4   Fallon and Sherriff, "Betrayal," 19.

5   These numbers are drawn from the Central Intelligence Agency's *Handbook of Economic Statistics, 1983* (Washington, DC.: Central Intelligence Agency, 1983), 68, table 47.

6   See Thane Gustafson, *Crisis Amid Plenty: The Politics of Soviet Energy under Brezhnev and Gorbachev* (Princeton, NJ: Princeton University Press, 1989), chap. 3.

7   Yakov Feygin, "Reforming the Cold War State: Economic Thought, Internationalization, and the Politics of Soviet Reform, 1955–1985" (Publicly Accessible Penn Dissertations, 2017), 308.

8   Memorandum for the Record, "The Dollar Costs of Soviet Military Involvement in Afghanistan," June 12, 1981, CIA Online Reading Room, accessed March 14, 2019, https://www.cia.gov/library/readingroom/docs/CIA-RDP96R01136R003100080030-5.pdf.

9   Document 3, "Session of the CPSU CC Politburo," October 31, 1980, in Mark Kramer, ed., "Soviet Deliberations during the Polish Crisis, 1980–1981," Special Working Paper No. 1, Cold War International History Project, 57.

10   The precise level is difficult to evaluate, but $4 billion is the figure mentioned by Brezhnev in his meeting with Kania and Jaruzelski in August 1981. See Document 16, "Information about Cde. L. I. Brezhnev's Meeting with Cdes. S. Kania and W. Jaruzelski," August 22, 1981, in Kramer, "Soviet Deliberations," 135.

11   Document 2, "Session of the CPSU CC Politburo," October 29, 1980, in Kramer, "Soviet Deliberations," 52–53.

12   Document 38, "Transcript of CPSU CC Politburo Meeting," March 26, 1981, in *From Solidarity to Martial Law: The Polish Crisis of 1980–1981,* ed. Andrzej Paczkowski and Malcolm Byrne (Budapest: Central European University Press, 2007), 234–235.

13   "Niederschrift über das Treffen zwischen Genossen L. I. Breshnew und Genossen E. Honecker am 3. August 1981 auf der Krim," DY 30/11853, SAPMO.

14   Breznhev to Honecker, August 31, 1981, DE/1/58682, BArch Lichterfelde.

15   Quoted in Hans-Hermann Hertle, *Der Fall der Mauer: Die unbeabsichtige Selbstauflösung des SED-Staates* (Opladen, Germany: Westdeutscher Verlag, 1999), 47.

16   "Niederschrift über das Gespräch des Generalsekretärs des ZK der SED, Genossen Erich Honecker, mit dem Sekretär des ZK der KPdSU, Genossen Konstantin Vikorowisch Russakow, am 21. Oktober 1981," DY 30/23379, SAPMO, 80.

17   "Niederschrift über das Gespräch des Generalsekretärs," 82.

18   "Niederschrift über das Gespräch des Generalsekretärs," 67.

19   Matthew J. Ouimet, *The Rise and Fall of the Brezhnev Doctrine in Soviet Foreign Policy* (Chapel Hill: University of North Carolina Press, 2003), 182–183.

20   Document 43, "Transcript of CPSU CC Politburo Meeting," April 9, 1981, in Paczkowski and Byrne, *From Solidarity to Martial Law,* 259–264.

21   Quoted in Ouimet, *Rise and Fall of the Brezhnev Doctrine,* 202. Vojtech Mastny provides slightly different timing for this decision, placing it in April 1981, in his "The Soviet Non-Invasion of Poland in 1980/81 and the End of the Cold War," Working Paper No. 23, September 1998, Cold War International History Project.

22   Ouimet, *Rise and Fall of the Brezhnev Doctrine,* chap. 6.

23   Quote from Document 56, "Report to HSWP CC Politburo with Verbatim Transcript of July 21 Telephone Conversation between Kania and Brezhnev," in Paczkowski and Byrne, *From Solidarity to Martial Law,* 317. For other references to similar Soviet messages, see Kramer, "Soviet Deliberations," 18–20.

24   For evidence of debt affecting internal actions toward Solidarity, see Document 26, "Protocol of Meeting of Leading *Aktiv* Members of Ministry of Internal Affairs," in Paczkowski and Byrne, *From Solidarity to Martial Law,* 171. For discussions with Soviet officials, see Document 60, "Information on Brezhnev Meeting with Kania and Jaruzelski on August 14, 1981, August 22, 1981," in Paczkowski and Byrne, *From Solidarity to Martial Law,* 342.

25   See my own "Fugitive Leverage: Commercial Banks, Sovereign Debt, and Cold War Crisis in Poland, 1980–1982," *Enterprise & Society* 18, no. 1 (March 2017): 72–107.

26   Wojciech Jaruzelski, *Mein Leben für Polen: Erinnerungen* (Munich: Piper, 1993), 426.

27   Document 81, "Transcript of CPSU CC Politburo Meeting," December 10, 1981, in Paczkowski and Byrne, *From Solidarity to Martial Law,* 449.

28   Paczkowski and Byrne, *From Solidarity to Martial Law,* 450.

29   Ouimet, *The Rise and Fall of the Brezhnev Doctrine,* particularly chaps. 6, 7, and conclusion.

30   Douglas Brinkley, ed., *The Reagan Diaries* (New York: HarperCollins, 2007), 55.

31   Constant dollar figure cited in Hal Brands, *Making the Unipolar Moment: U.S. Foreign Policy and the Rise of the Post-Cold War Order* (Ithaca, NY: Cornell University Press, 2016), 76.

32   Special Intelligence Estimate, "Dependence of Soviet Military Power on Economic Relations with the West," November 17, 1981, in *Foreign Relations of the United States (FRUS) 1981–1988,* vol. 3 (Washington, DC: United States Government Publishing Office), 352.

33   Quoted in Brands, *Making the Unipolar Moment,* 75.

34   Quoted in Brands, *Making the Unipolar Moment,* 87.

35   Quoted in Brands, *Making the Unipolar Moment,* 78.

36   Robert Service, *The End of the Cold War: 1985–1991* (London: Macmillan, 2015), 45.

37   National Security Planning Group Meeting, December 5, 1984, NSPG 0101, Ronald Reagan Presidential Library (RRPL).

38   Memorandum from Allen to Reagan, "Economic/Financial Situation of the Soviet Union and Eastern Europe Countries," November 18, 1981, in *FRUS 1981–1988,* vol. 3, 362.

39   "The State of the Soviet Economy and the Role of East-West Trade," October 26, 1981, in *FRUS 1981–1988,* vol. 3, 342.

40   "The Impact of Credit Restrictions on Soviet Trade and the Soviet Economy," April 21, 1982, Folder "Buckley Mission Apr 1982–Present [1983] [6 of 10]," RAC Box 5, Norman Bailey Papers, RRPL.

41   Special National Intelligence Estimate, "The Soviet Gas Pipeline in Perspective," September 21, 1982, in *FRUS 1981–1988*, vol. 3, 706.

42   Intelligence Assessment Prepared by the Central Intelligence Agency, "Can the Soviets Stand Down Militarily?," July 1982, in *FRUS 1981–1988*, vol. 3, 652. A similar, albeit more tentative, conclusion is reached in "The Impact of Credit Restrictions," RRPL, 48–49.

43   Minutes of a National Security Council Meeting, October 16, 1981, in *FRUS 1981–1988*, vol. 3, 322.

44   The internal administration debate over a formal policy for engaging the Soviet Union extended through January 1983, when Reagan endorsed National Security Decision Directive 75, a foundational strategy document for his administration. For the text of the directive, see *FRUS 1981–1988*, vol. 3, 861.

45   Stephan Kieninger, *The Diplomacy of Détente: Cooperative Security Policies from Helmut Schmidt to George Schultz* (London: Routledge, 2018), 109, and "Energy and Economic Evaluation of the Soviet-West European Natural Gas Pipeline Project," October 7, 1982, Box 28, Folder "October–December 1982," Soviet Flashpoints Collection, National Security Archive, Washington, DC.

46   Minutes of a National Security Council Meeting, February 4, 1982, in *FRUS 1981–1988*, vol. 3, 482.

47   "Response to NSSD 11–82: U.S. Relations with the USSR," December 6, 1982, in *FRUS 1981–1988*, vol. 3, 820.

48   The key NSC meetings on this issue took place on February 4 and February 26, 1982. See *FRUS 1981–1988*, vol. 3, 481–484, 490–495.

49   Memorandum of Conversation, "Debrief of Under Secretary Buckley's Trip to Europe," March 25, 1982, in *FRUS 1981–1988*, vol. 3, 505.

50   Quotes from Kieninger, *Diplomacy of Détente*, 113, and paragraph based on chap. 3.

51   Memorandum of Conversation, "Debrief of Under Secretary Buckley," 506.

52   Minutes of National Security Council Meeting, May 24, 1982, in *FRUS 1981–1988*, vol. 3, 563.

53   Quoted in editor's note, *FRUS 1981–1988*, vol. 3, 572–573.

54   National Security Directive 66, November 29, 1982, in *FRUS 1981–1988*, vol. 3, 812.

55   Author's calculations from appendix table C.10 in *Economic Survey of Europe in 1990–1991* (Geneva, SZ: United Nations, 1991), 249.

56   See the essays in Duccio Basosi, Giuliano Garavini, and Massimiliano Trentin, eds., *Counter-Shock: The Oil Counterrevolution of the 1980s* (London: I. B. Tauris, 2018).

57   Schlack to Mittag, December 1, 1981, DY 3023/981, SAPMO, 322–324.

58   L. A. Whittome to the Managing Director and the Deputy Managing Director, December 21, 1981, Box 29, File 3, EDIF, Country Files (CF), IMF.

59   Gerhard Schmitz, "Information zu Meinungen sowjetische Genossen über die Frage der Verschuldung sozialistischer Länder in konvertierbaren Devisen," March 3, 1982, DY 3023/982, SAPMO, 32.

60   Schalck to Honecker, March 5, 1982, DY 3023/982, SAPMO, 33.

61   Horst Kaminsky to Günter Mittag, April 8, 1982, DY 3023/982, SAPMO, 84.

62   L. A. Whittome to the Acting Managing Director, November 2, 1981, Box 57, File 3, EUR Country Files, IMF.

63   Blair A. Ruble, "Summary: Discussion of Polish Economic Situation and Prospects for Economic Reform," September 15, 1981, Box 57, File 3, EUR Country Files, IMF.

64   Underlining in the original. "Zur Entwicklung der Zahlungsbilanz im 1. Halbjahr 1982," attached to Schalck to Mittag, March 4, 1982, DY 3023/982, SAPMO, 19–21.

65   Gerhard Schmitz, "Information zu Meinungen sowjetische Genossen über die Frage der Verschuldung sozialistischer Länder in konvertierbaren Devisen," March 3, 1982, DY 3023/982, SAPMO, 28–31.

66   Kaminsky to Mittag, April 8, 1982, DY 3023/982, SAPMO, 90.

67   W. J. E. Charles, "The International Banking System: The Effect of an Eastern Bloc Default," January 21, 1980, 3A143/1, Bank of England (BoE) Archives, London, United Kingdom.

68   I have not found an instance of a communist official even raising the idea of collective default as a remote possibility to be considered.

69   P. J. Bull, "June EDC Paper: Poland," June 5, 1980, 3A143/2, BoE Archives. For the broader debate among Western central banks over the dangers and likelihood of a communist default, either as individual countries or as a bloc, see the other files in 3A143/1–3A143/7 at the BoE Archives.

70   For exemplary statements of this view from the Soviet perspective, see "Mezhdunarodnyi valiutnyi fond i sotsialisticheskie strany," November 11, 1983, Russian State Archive of the Economy (RGAE), f. 2324, o. 33, d. 406, and "Usloviia kreditovaniia zapadom razvivaiushchikhsia stran progressivnoi orientatsii," March 20, 1987, RGAE, f. 2324, o. 33, d. 640.

71   See the files in Box 29, File 2, European Department Immediate Files, Country Files, IMF.

72   Poland became a member in 1946 but withdrew from membership in 1950 under pressure from the Soviet Union.

73   Roger Gough, *A Good Comrade: János Kádár, Communism and Hungary* (London: I. B. Tauris, 2006), 214. Also "Information über den Beitritt der UVR zum Internationalen Währungsfonds und zur Internationalen Bank für Wiederaufbau und Entwicklung," November 11, 1982, DE/1/58682, BArch Lichterfelde.

74   Kaminsky to Mittag, April 8, 1982, DY3023/982, SAPMO, 89.

75   L. A. Whittome to the Managing Director, June 2, 1982, Box 29, File 3, EDIF, CF, IMF.

76   "IMF Executive Board Meeting," December 8, 1982, EBM/82/157–12/8/82, accessed April 18, 2019, https://archivescatalog.imf.org/Details/ArchiveExecutive/125000218.

77   See "Press Release: Hungary Stand-By Agreement," January 13, 1984, accessed April 24, 2019, https://archivescatalog.imf.org/Details/ArchiveExecutive/125073812.

78   Author's calculations from World Bank project history database, accessed April 29, 2019, http://projects.worldbank.org/search?lang=en&searchTerm=&countrycode_exact=HU.

79   "Hungary—Membership Mission, Minutes of Meeting No. 1," November 25, 1981, Box 30, File 1, EDIF, CF, IMF.

80   P. de Fontenay, Memorandum for Files, "Meeting on September 28 with Mr. Marjai," September 29, 1982, Box 29, File 4, EDIF, CF, IMF.

81   H. B. Junz to the Managing Director, May 16, 1983, Box 30, File 3, EDIF, CF, IMF.

82   "Briefing Paper—1984 Mid-Term Review and Possible Use of Fund Resources," March 30, 1984, Box 31, File 4, EDIF, CF, IMF.

83   "Hungary—Staff Visit, Minutes of Meeting," September 11, 1984, Box 31, File 4, EDIF, CF, IMF.

84   Quoted in Attila Mong, *Kádár Hitele* (Budapest: Libri Publishing House, 2012), 238.

85   L. G. Manison, "Recovery of Lending to Eastern Europe," July 13, 1984, Box 21, File 2, EUR Department Fonds, Country/Country Desk Files, IMF.

86   Alexander Schalck-Golodkowski, *Deutsche-Deutsche Erinnerungen* (Reinbek, Germany: Rowohlt, 2000), 285.

87   The East German government imposed very limited austerity in the early 1980s, essentially holding living standards constant in 1982 and 1983. See Matthias Judt, *Das Bereich Kommerzielle Koordinierung: Das DDR-Wirtschaftsimperium des Alexander Schalck-Golodkowski—Mythos und Realität* (Berlin: Ch. Links Verlag, 2013), 166–171.

88   A. Schalck, "Niederschrift über das am 25.05.1983 zwischen dem Vorsitzenden der CSU, F.J. Strauß, und Genossen Schalck in Spöck/Chiemsee geführten Gespräches," May 26, 1983, DL/226/1137, BArch Lichterfelde.

89   Matthias Judt, *KoKo: Mythos und Realität: Das Imperium des Alexander Schalck-Golodkowski* (Berlin: Ed. Berolina, 2015), 158.

90   Stephan Kieninger, "Freer Movement in Return for Cash: Franz Josef Strauß, Alexander Schalck-Golodkowski, and the *Milliardenkredite* for the GDR, 1983–1984," in *New Perspectives on the End of the Cold War: Unexpected Transformations?*, ed. Bernhard Blumenau, Jussi Hanhimäki, and Barbara Zanchetta (London: Routledge, 2018).

91   Judt, *KoKo,* 164.

92   The Soviets were not completely unwilling or unable to help the GDR. In early 1982, Schalck devised an arbitrage scheme to buy extra oil from Moscow using hard currency with a ninety-day payment period, resell it on the world market, and use the funds to service the GDR's debts during the ninety-day lag. See Judt, *KoKo,* chap. 2.2.

93   "Niederschrift über das Treffen zwischen Genossen Erich Honecker und Genossen Konstantin Ustinowitsch Tschernenko am 17. August 1984," August 17, 1984, DY30/2380, SAPMO, 107.

94   "Zasedanie politbiuro TsK KPSS 23 maya 1984 goda," May 23, 1984, f. 89, o. 42, Hoover Archives.

95   William Taubman, *Gorbachev: His Life and Times* (New York: Simon & Schuster, 2017), 209.

6   The Socialist Perestroika

1   Robert English, *Russia and the Idea of the West: Gorbachev, Intellectuals, and the End of the Cold War* (New York: Columbia University Press, 2000).

2   Abel Aganbegyan, *Moving the Mountain: Inside the Perestroika Revolution* (London: Bantam Press, 1989), 65–66.

3   Linda J. Cook, *The Soviet Social Contract and Why It Failed: Welfare Policy and Workers' Politics from Brezhnev to Yeltsin* (Cambridge, MA: Harvard University Press, 1993).

4   Chris Miller makes this point particularly well in his *The Struggle to Save the Soviet Economy: Mikhail Gorbachev and the Collapse of the USSR* (Chapel Hill: University of North Carolina Press, 2016).

5   Stephen Kotkin, *Armageddon Averted: The Soviet Collapse, 1970–2000* (Oxford: Oxford University Press, 2001), chap. 1.

6   Aganbegyan, *Moving the Mountain,* 68.

7   This paragraph discusses capitalist economies in their ideal type. Capitalist economies do not and did not live up to this ideal type, as oligopolistic behavior pervaded capitalist economies and continues to do so. See János Kornai, "'Hard' and 'Soft' Budget Constraint," *Acta Oeconomica* 25, no. 3/4 (1980): 231–245.

8 Nikolai Ryzhkov, *Desiat' let velikikh potriasenii* (Moscow: Assotsiatsiia "Kniga Prosveshchenie Miloserdie," 1995), 42.

9 Working Memorandum, "Soveshchanie sekretarei TsK KPSS," January 18, 1983, Container 25, Reel 17, Dmitry Volkogonov Papers (DVP), Hoover Institution Archives (HIA), Stanford, CA. See also Robert Service, *The End of the Cold War, 1985–1991* (New York: Public Affairs, 2015), chap. 5.

10 Ryzhkov, *Desiat' let,* 42–47.

11 For two slightly different accounts of this price-increase episode, see Mikhail Gorbachev, *Zhizn' I reformy,* Vol. 1 (Moscow: Novosti, 1995), 234–235, and Valentin Pavlov, *Upushchen li shans? Finansovi kliuch k rynku* (Moscow: Terra, 1995), 69–72.

12 "Ekonomicheskaia strategiia partii," July 14, 1983, Gorbachev Foundation Archive (GFA), Moscow, Russia, f. 14574, o. 5, d. 1.

13 E. I. Kapustin, "Problemy ratsional'nogo ispol'zovaniia trudovykh resursov," August 13, 1984, GFA, f. 5, o. 1, d. 15011.

14 V. N. Kirichenko, "O nekotoryx predposylkakh obespecheniia dinamichnogo razvitiia ekonomiki strany i dal'neishego sotsial'nogo progressa," January 30, 1984, GFA, f. 5, o. 1, d. 14912.

15 Kirichenko, "O nekotoryx predposylkakh obespecheniia."

16 Ryzhkov, *Desiat' let,* 59. English, *Russia and the Idea of the West,* chap. 5.

17 Service, *End of the Cold War,* 111.

18 S. F. Akhromeev and G. M. Kornienko, *Glazami marshala i diplomata* (Moscow: Mezhdunarodnye Otnosheniia, 1992), 35.

19 Anatoly Chernyaev, trans. Robert English and Elizabeth Tucker, *My Six Years with Gorbachev* (University Park: Pennsylvania State University Press, 2000), 22. Note that this book was published using the transliteration "Anatoly Chernyaev" so that spelling has been retained in the notes for this book.

20 Anders Aslund, *Gorbachev's Struggle for Economic Reform: The Soviet Reform Process, 1985–1988* (Ithaca: Cornell University Press, 1991), 68.

21 Aslund, *Gorbachev's Struggle,* chap. 3.

22 Aslund, *Gorbachev's Struggle,* 78.

23 Anatolii Cherniaev, ed., *V Politbiuro TsK KPSS: Po zapisiam Anatoliia Cherniaeva, Vadima Medvedeva, Georgiia Shakhnazarova* (Moscow: Alpina, 2006), 66.

24 Table H.1 in International Monetary Fund, *A Study of the Soviet Economy,* vol. 1 (Washington, DC: International Monetary Fund, 1991), 109.

25 Cherniaev, ed., *V Politburo TsK KPSS,* 50.

26   All preceding quotes from Cherniaev, ed., *V Politburo TsK KPSS*, 102–105.

27   Mikhail Gorbachev, *Memoirs* (New York: Doubleday, 1996), 401.

28   See Anatoly Dobrynin, *In Confidence: Moscow's Ambassador to Six Cold War Presidents* (Seattle: University of Washington Press, 2015), 570. Akhromeev and Kornienko, *Glazami marshala i diplomata*, 36. Pavel Palazchenkel, *My Years with Gorbachev and Shevardnadze: The Memoirs of a Soviet Interpreter* (University Park: Pennsylvania State University Press, 1997), 81.

29   A. A. Kokoshin, "Finansirovanie voennykh prigotovlenii SShA v 1986–1992 gg.," May 27, 1987, Achive of the Russian Academy of Sciences (ARAN), f. 2021, o. 2, d. 40, l. 117–125.

30   See, for example, James Graham Wilson, *The Triumph of Improvisation: Gorbachev's Adaptability, Reagan's Engagement, and the End of the Cold War* (Ithaca: Cornell University Press, 2014).

31   Quoted in Vladislav M. Zubok, *A Failed Empire: The Soviet Union in the Cold War from Stalin to Gorbachev* (Chapel Hill: University of North Carolina Press, 2009), 307.

32   Cherniaev, ed., *V Politbiuro TsK KPSS*, 86–87.

33   For a summary, see Service, *End of the Cold War*, chap. 14.

34   Service, *End of the Cold War*, chaps. 17 and 18.

35   Quoted in Chernyaev, *My Six Years*, 84.

36   Cherniaev, ed., *V Politbiuro TsK KPSS*, 86.

37   See Service, *End of the Cold War*, chap. 20.

38   Cherniaev, ed., *V Politbiuro TsK KPSS*, 103.

39   Cherniaev, ed., *V Politbiuro TsK KPSS*, 77.

40   "Document No. 9: Notes of CC CPSU Politburo Session, January 29, 1987," in Thomas Blanton, Svetlana Savranskaya, and Vladislav Zubok, eds., *Masterpieces of History: The Peaceful End of the Cold War in Europe, 1989* (New York: Central European University Press, 2010), 241–243.

41   "Niederschrift über das Treffen der Generalsekretäre und Ersten Sekretäre der Zentralkomitees der Bruderparteien der Teilnehmerstaaten des Warschauer Vertrages am 23. October 1985 in Sofia," DY 30/2352, SAPMO, 103–109.

42   Calculations and quote from "Soviet Energy Trade During 1986–87," *PlanEcon* 4, no 28 (July 15, 1988): 5.

43   Cherniaev, ed., *V Politbiuro TsK KPSS*, 77.

44   Cherniaev, ed., *V Politbiuro TsK KPSS*, 69.

45   Cherniaev, ed., *V Politbiuro TsK KPSS,* 93.

46   "Document No. 7: Notes of CC CPSU Politburo Session," July 3, 1986, in *Masterpieces of History,* 234–235.

47   "Niederschrift über das Treffen der führenden Repräsentanten der Bruderparteien sozialistischer Länder des RGW am 10. Und 11. November 1986 in Moskau," November 10–11, 1986, DY 30/2358, SAPMO, 5–6.

48   "Rede des Genossen Mikhail Gorbatschow," November 10, 1986, DY 30/2359, SAPMO, 8–46, at 14.

49   "Niederschrift über das Treffen der führenden Repräsentanten der Bruderparteien sozialistischer Länder des RGW am 10. Und 11. November 1986 in Moskau," November 10–11, 1986, DY 30/2358, SAPMO, 18–20.

50   "Niederschrift über das Treffen," SAPMO, 11.

51   "Document 8: Transcript of CC CPSU Politburo Session, November 13, 1986," in *Masterpieces of History,* 236–240.

52   "Document No. 9: Notes of CC CPSU Politburo Session, January 29, 1987," in *Masterpieces of History,* 241–243.

53   See, for example, Jacques Lévesque, "The East European Revolutions of 1989," in *The Cambridge History of the Cold War,* vol. 3, ed. Melvyn P. Leffler and Odd Arne Westad (Cambridge: Cambridge University Press, 2010), and Zubok, *A Failed Empire,* chap. 10.

54   Even the leading conservative Yegor Ligachev said in reference to the decision to let Eastern Europe go free, "We made that decision in 1985, 1986. . . . We already had the example of Afghanistan before us." David Remnick, *Lenin's Tomb: The Last Days of the Soviet Union* (New York: Random House, 1993), 234.

55   See influential accounts in Archie Brown, *The Gorbachev Factor* (Oxford: Oxford University Press, 1997) and Lévesque, "East European Revolutions."

56   Quotes from Cherniaev, ed., *V Politbiuro TsK KPSS,* 59. See also Service, *End of the Cold War,* 105, 150, 330–331. The war continued for two more years as the Kremlin sought a negotiated exit from the conflict. The last Soviet troops left Afghanistan in February 1989.

57   IMF, *A Study of the Soviet Economy,* 22.

58   Cherniaev, ed., *V Politbiuro TsK KPSS,* 169.

59   Chernyaev, *My Six Years,* 108–109. IMF, *A Study of the Soviet Economy,* vol. 2, 14.

60   Chernyaev, *My Six Years,* 109.

61   Cherniaev, ed., *V Politbiuro TsK KPSS,* 169.

62   Ryzhkov, *Desyat' let,* 80.

63   "Gorbachev Speech to June Central Committee Plenum," in Foreign Broadcast Information Service, Soviet and Central Asia (FBIS-SOV), FBIS-SOV-87-123, June 26, 1987, R28.

64   Abel Aganbegyan, "People and Economics," *Ogonyok*, July and August 1987, in *Gorbachev and Glasnost: Viewpoints from the Soviet Press*, ed. Isaac J. Tarasulo (Lanham, MD: Rowman & Littlefield, 1989), 94.

65   Nikolai Shmelev, "Advances and Debts," *Novy Mir*, no. 6 (1987), in *Gorbachev and Glasnost*, 83.

66   Shmelev, "New Worries," *Novy Mir*, no. 4 (April 1988), in *Gorbachev and Glasnost*, 124.

67   Ryzhkov speech to the Supreme Soviet, "On the Restructuring of the Management of the National Economy at the Present Stage of the Country's Economic Development," *Pravda*, June 30, 1987, translated in FBIS-SOV-87-126, R6 and R10.

68   Gorbachev speech, June Plenum, in FBIS-SOV-87-123, June 26, 1987, R33.

69   Yakovlev, "Text of Presentation at the CC CPSU Politburo Session," September 28, 1987, in "Perestroika in the Soviet Union 30 Years On," National Security Archive Electronic Briefing Book No. 504, March 11, 2015, accessed December 4, 2016, http://nsarchive.gwu .edu/NSAEBB/NSAEBB504/, 1.

70   Cherniaev, ed., *V Politbiuro TsK KPSS*, 198.

71   Gorbachev, *Memoirs*, 315.

72   *Daily Report*, January 28, 1987, in FBIS-SOV-87-018, R20.

73   Author's calculations from lines 4 and 5 of table D.6 in IMF, *A Study of the Soviet Economy*, 99.

74   The 1989 numbers are estimates collected by the IMF from Soviet officials in 1991. Table II.2.3 in IMF, *A Study of the Soviet Economy*, 55.

75   Aganbegyan, *Moving the Mountain*, 70.

76   Cherniaev, ed., *V Politbiuro TsK KPSS*, 187.

77   Cherniaev, ed., *V Politbiuro TsK KPSS*, 180.

78   Cherniaev, ed., *V Politbiuro TsK KPSS*, 184–185.

79   Gorbachev, *Memoirs*, 235.

80   Cherniaev, ed., *V Politbiuro TsK KPSS*, 187.

81   "Basic Provisions for Radical Restructuring of Economic Management," *Pravda*, June 27, 1987, translated in FBIS-SOV-87-125, R11–12.

82   "Plenum Theses," June 29, 1987, FBIS-SOV-87-125, R10.

83   Memorandum of Conversation, Robert Gates and V. I. Kryuchkov, February 9, 1990, folder "Gorbachev (Dobrynin) Sensitive July–December 1990 [1]," OA/ID 91128-001, Special Separate USSR Notes Files, Gorbachev Files, Brent Scowcroft Collection, George H.W. Bush Presidential Library.

84   "USSR: Financial Assets of Enterprises, 1980–1990," table K7 in IMF, *A Study of the Soviet Economy*, 131.

85   IMF, *A Study of the Soviet Economy*, 98, table D5.

86   IMF, *A Study of the Soviet Economy*, 96, table D3.

87   Chernyaev, *My Six Years*, 192.

88   "Document No. 12: Notes of CC CPSU Politburo Session," April 16, 1987, in *Masterpieces of History*, 249–252, quote at 251.

89   Service, *End of the Cold War*, 246–247.

90   "Postanovlenie TsK KPSS, O nashei dal'neishei takticheskoi linii v otnoshenii peregovorov s SShA po voprosam iadernykh i kosmicheskikh vooruzhenii," February 20, 1987, Vitalii Leonidovich Kataev Papers, Box 5, Folder 24, HIA. Cherniaev, ed., *V Politbiuro TsK KPSS*, 151–152.

91   See, for example, Wilson, *Triumph of Improvisation*, 123–124, and Andrei Grachev, *Gorbachev's Gamble: Soviet Foreign Policy and the End of the Cold War* (Cambridge: Cambridge University Press, 2008), 93–100.

92   These internal Soviet dynamics on the decision to decouple the arms control package are best discussed in Service, *End of the Cold War*, chap. 22.

93   Cherniaev, ed., *V Politbiuro TsK KPSS*, 169.

94   "Memorandum of Conversation between M.S. Gorbachev and US Secretary of State George Schultz," April 14, 1987, in Svetlana Savranskaya and Thomas Blanton, eds., "The INF Treaty and the Washington Summit: Twenty Years Later," National Security Archive Electronic Briefing Book No. 238, accessed December 15, 2016, https://nsarchive2.gwu.edu/NSAEBB/NSAEBB238/index.htm.

95   Cherniaev, ed., *V Politbiuro TsK KPSS*, 160.

96   Cherniaev, ed., *V Politbiuro TsK KPSS*, 161.

97   Quoted in Milan Svec, "The Prague Spring: 20 Years Later," *Foreign Affairs* 66, no. 4 (Spring 1988): 990.

98   Cherniaev, ed., *V Politbiuro TsK KPSS*, 166.

99   Cherniaev, ed., *V Politbiuro TsK KPSS*, 274.

100   Cherniaev, ed., *V Politbiuro TsK KPSS*, 275.

101   Cherniaev, ed., *V Politbiuro TsK KPSS*, 242.

102   Cherniaev, ed., *V Politbiuro TsK KPSS*, 230.

103   Service, *End of the Cold War*, 277–289.

104   Service, *End of the Cold War*, 287, 291.

105   Andrei Grachev, "Gorbachev and the 'New Political Thinking,'" in *The Revolutions of 1989: A Handbook*, ed. Wolfgang Mueller et al. (Vienna: Verlag der Osterreichischen Akademie der Wissenshaften, 2015), 41n14.

106   "Address by Mikhail Gorbachev at the UN General Assembly Session (Excerpts)," December 07, 1988, History and Public Policy Program Digital Archive, CWIHP Archive, accessed October 30, 2021, http://digitalarchive.wilsoncenter.org/document/116224.

107   "Document No. 26: Notes of CC CPSU Politburo Session," June 20, 1988, in *Masterpieces of History*, 286–287.

108   Chernyaev, *My Six Years*, 194–195.

109   All words in brackets were added by the translator in "Document No. 35: Transcript of CC CPSU Politburo Session," December 27–28, 1988, in *Masterpieces of History*, 332–340.

110   "Document No. 19: Notes of CC CPSU Politburo Session," March 10, 1988, in *Masterpieces of History*, 265–267.

111   Y. V. Ponomarev, "O valyutno-finansovom polozhenii sotsialisticheskikh stran," November 24, 1988, Russian State Archive of the Economy (RGAE), f. 2324, o. 33, d. 696.

112   "Document 1: Georgy Shakhnazarov's Preparatory Notes for Mikhail Gorbachev for the Meeting of the Politburo," October 6, 1988, in *The End of the Cold War*, Cold War International History Project Bulletin, Issue 12/13 (Fall/Winter 2001), 15.

113   "Document No. 39: Report from Mikhail Gorbachev to the CC CPSU Politburo regarding His Meeting with the Trilateral Commission," January 21, 1989, in *Masterpieces of History*, 349–351.

114   Emphasis in original. Document No. 41: Memorandum from CC CPSU International Department, "On a Strategy for Relations with the European Socialist Countries," February 1989, in *Masterpieces of History*, 353–364.

115   "Document 42: Memorandum from the Bogomolov Institute, 'Changes in Eastern Europe and Their Impact on the USSR,'" February 1989, in *Masterpieces of History*, 365–381.

116   "Document No. 51: Notes of Mikhail Gorbachev's Meeting with Soviet Ambassadors to Socialist Countries," March 3, 1989, in *Masterpieces of History*, 414–417.

117   E. Shevardnadze, D. Yazov, and V. Kamenstev, "Tovarishu Gorbachevu M.S.," March 25, 1989, Kataev Papers, Box 13, Folder 14, HIA.

118   "'Europe as a Common Home' Address Given by Mikhail Gorbachev to the Council of Europe (Strasbourg, 6 July 1989)," Making the History of 1989, Roy Rosenzweig Center for History and New Media, accessed December 10, 2016, https://chnm.gmu.edu/1989 /archive/files/gorbachev-speech-7-6-89_e3ccb87237.pdf.

7   A Period of Extraordinary Politics

1   Leszek Balcerowicz, "Understanding Postcommunist Transitions," *Journal of Democracy* 5, no. 4 (October 1994): 75–89, quotes at 84–85.

2   Two examples are Timothy Garton Ash, "The Year of Truth," in *The Revolutions of 1989,* ed. Vladimir Tismaneanu (London: Routledge, 1999) and Gregory F. Domber, *Empowering Revolution: America, Poland, and the End of the Cold War* (Chapel Hill: University of North Carolina Press, 2014).

3   Quoted in Domber, *Empowering Revolution,* 136.

4   Quote and figures in Domber, *Empowering Revolution,* 136, 139.

5   W. Allen Holmes to the Secretary of State, "Poland: Effectiveness of Economic Sanctions," May 28, 1982, Folder May–June 1982, Box 27, Soviet Flashpoints Collection (SFC), National Security Archive (NSA), Washington, DC.

6   For an example of such an exchange, see "Zasedanie Politbiuro TsK KPSS," April 26, 1984, Container 25, Reel 17, Dmitrii Volkogonov Papers, Hoover Institution, Stanford, CA.

7   L. A. Whittome, Memorandum for Files, "Poland," March 25, 1985, Box 36, File "Poland 330—Meetings with Banks 1981–1989," Country/Country Desk Files, Country Files (CF), International Monetary Fund (IMF) Archives, Washington, DC.

8   Paul McCarthy, "Poland: The Long Road Back to Creditworthiness," July 21, 1986, Poland—corresp. and memos 1986 (Jan.–Sept), Box 60, EUR Country Files, IMF Archives.

9   "Poland—Debt Restructuring," undated, Box 60, File "Poland—corresp. and memos 1986 (Jan.–Sept)," EUR Country Files, IMF Archives.

10   "Take out" from Jim Prust to Mr. Hole, "Poland—Debt Servicing Prospects," January 6, 1987, File 1, Box 24, EUR Division Country Correspondence Files, IMF Archives.

11   Domber, *Empowering Revolution,* 40–41.

12   National Security Decision Directive 54, "United States Policy toward Eastern Europe," September 2, 1982, Ronald Reagan Presidential Library (RRPL), accessed April 20, 2018. https://www.reaganlibrary.gov/sites/default/files/archives/reference/scanned-nsdds/ nsdd54.pdf.

13   Walt Raymond to Paula Dobriansky, April 16, 1983, File "Poland—Strategy EE," RAC Box 4, Paula Dobriansky Files, RRPL.

14   William Clark to George Schultz, "Poland: Next Steps," undated but late March or early April 1983, File "Poland—Strategy EE," RAC Box 4, Paula Dobriansky Files, RRPL.

15   "Poland: Implications of IMF Membership," intelligence memorandum with no author, August 24, 1984, File "Poland—IMF (1)," RAC Box 3, Paula Dobriansky Files, RRPL, 10–11.

16   Domber, *Empowering Revolution,* 74–80.

17   Quoted in Domber, *Empowering Revolution,* 75.

18   Polish emissary Adam Schaff quoted in Domber, *Empowering Revolution,* 123.

19   Domber, *Empowering Revolution,* 123–127.

20   Jan Vanous quoted in Stanislaw Gomulka, "Polish Economy in the 1980s and the International Monetary Fund's Reform and Policy Options," September 15, 1985, Box 59, File 3, EUR Country Files, IMF Archives.

21   Schmitt to Whittome, "Poland—Negotiating a Program," June 25, 1986, Box 60, File "Poland—corresp. and memos 1986 (Jan.–Sept)," EUR Country Files, IMF Archives.

22   Memorandum from the Economic Commission of the Parisian Collective—Solidarite avec Solidarnosc—to Peter Hall and A. Whittome," September 17, 1985, Folder "Polish Trade Union 'Solidarnosc,'" Box 1, Country Files, Central Files, IMF Archives.

23   Memorandum from SecState to AmEmbassy Warsaw, May 23, 1989, Box 35, File "May 16–30, 1989," SFC, NSA.

24   Memorandum from the Economic Commission of the Parisian Collective, September 17, 1985, IMF Archives.

25   Andrzej Olechowki and Jan Woroniecki, "Notatka w sprawie korzystania przez Polskę ze środków MFW i Banku Swiatowego (strategia, procedury, instyucje)," April 10, 1986, Kolekcja Miedzeszyn M10—Sprawy gospodarcze i referendum 1987, Box 6, KC PZPR Files, Hoover Institution.

26   Paul McCarthy, "Poland: The Long Road Back to Creditworthiness," July 21, 1986, Poland—corresp. and memos 1986 (Jan.–Sept), Box 60, EUR Country Files, IMF Archives.

27   Memorandum for Files, "Poland—Managing Director's Lunch with Professor Baka," February 26, 1987, Box 24, File 1, EUR Division Country Correspondence Files, IMF Archives.

28   Domber, *Empowering Revolution,* 155–156.

29   Prust to Whittome, "Poland—Your Meeting and Lunch with Mr. Krowacki and Colleagues," April 28, 1987, Box 24, File 1, EUR Division Country Correspondence Files (EUR DCCF), IMF Archives.

30   Memorandum for Files, "Poland—Meeting with Polish Delegation to Annual Meetings," October 2, 1986, Box 24, File 1, EUR DCCF, IMF Archives.

31   Document 1, "Propozycje w sprawie rozszerzenia zakresu stosowania ustawy z dnia 17 lipca 1986 r. o szczególnym postępowaniu wobec sprawców niektórych przestępstw," in *Polska 1986–1989: Koniec Systemu, vol. III, Dokumenty*, ed. Antoni Dudek and Andrzej Friszke (Warsaw: Trio/ISP PAN, 2002), 14–15.

32   Document 4, "Pro memoria dla abp. Bronisława Dąbrowskiego z rozmowy Andrzeja Święcickiego, Jerzego Turowicza i Andrzeja Wielowieyskiego z Kazimierzem Barcikowskim, Stanisławem Cioskiem i Kazimierzem Secomskim w Belwederze 18 października 1986 r.," in Dudek and Friske, *Polska 1986–1989*, 25–26.

33   Quoted in Andrzej Paczkowski, *The Spring Will Be Ours: Poland and the Poles*, trans. Jane Cave (University Park: Pennsylvania State University Press, 2003), 486.

34   Document 8, "Zapis stenograficzny rozmowy Ericha Honeckera z Wojciechem Jaruzelskim 16 września 1987 r. (fragmenty)," September 16, 1987, in Dudek and Friszke, *Polska 1986–1989*, 48.

35   Anatolii Chernaiev quoted in "Dialogue, The Musgrove Conference, May 1–3, 1998," in *Masterpieces of History: The Peaceful End of the Cold War in Europe, 1989*, ed. Svetlana Savranskaya, Thomas Blanton, and Vladislav Zubok (Budapest: Central European University Press, 2010), 134.

36   Karen Elliott House, Robert Keatley, and Barry Newman, "Jaruzelski Seeks Major Economic Reform," *Wall Street Journal*, July 30, 1987, 18.

37   Jim Prust to Mr. Russo, "Poland," July 31, 1987, Box 24, File 1, EUR DCCF, IMF Archives.

38   Document 8, "Zapis stenograficzny rozmowy," in Dudek and Friszke, *Polska 1986–1989*, 52–53.

39   "A Synthesis of the Domestic Situation and the West's Activity," August 28, 1987, in "The End of the Cold War," *Cold War International History Project Bulletin*, no. 12/13 (Fall/Winter 2001), 98–99.

40   Domber, *Empowering Revolution*, 203–204.

41   "Poland: Options for U.S. Policy if the Roundtable is Successful," Condoleezza Rice 1989–1990 Subject Files, Folder "Poland—Roundtable," George H. W. Bush Presidential Library (GHWBL), College Station, TX.

42   Quoted in Michał Sieziako, "Kulisy referendum z 29 listopada 1987 r.," *Polityka*, November 28, 2017, accessed October 1, 2019, https://www.polityka.pl/tygodnikpolityka/historia/1728812,1,kulisy-referendum-z-29-listopada-1987-r.read.

43   "Jaruzelski Says Reforms 'A Necessity' in Poland," December 16, 1987, Box 38, File "Poland 914—Economic reform 1987 and onwards," Country/Country Desk Files, Central Files, IMF Archives.

44   Antoni Dudek, *Reglamentowana rewolucja: Rozkład dyktatury komunistycznej w Polsce 1988-1990* (Krakow, Poland: Wydawn. Arcana, 2004), 124.

45   Document 10, "Informacja o stanie nastrojów społecznych i działalności przeciwnika w pierwszym okresie n etapu reform," March 2, 1988, in Dudek and Friszke, *Polska 1986-1989*, 78-79.

46   Dudek, *Reglamentowana rewolucja*, 121-122.

47   Quoted in Dudek, *Reglamentowana rewolucja*, 127-128.

48   Quoted in Dudek, *Reglamentowana rewolucja*, 127.

49   Tellingly, the advisors proposed no similar consultations with their Soviet comrades in Moscow. Dudek, *Reglamentowana rewolucja*, 129-130.

50   Document 12, "Uwagi ekspertów o sytuacji w kraju i wynikających z niej wniosków," May 6, 1988, in Dudek and Friszke, *Polska 1986-1989*, 86-87.

51   Massimo Russo to Mr. Whittome, "Poland," June 24, 1988, Box 24, File 3, EUR DCCF, IMF Archives.

52   Document 12, "Uwagi zespołu ekspertów KC PZPR o sytuacji kraju i wynikających z niej wnioskach przesłane członkom kierownictwa PZPR 6 maja 1988 r.," in Dudek and Friszke, *Polska 1986-1989*, 89.

53   Dudek and Friszke, *Polska, 1986-1989*, 85.

54   Memorandum for Files, "Poland: MD's Lunch with Mr. Sadowski," June 27, 1988, Box 61, File "Poland—corresp + memos June—Sept 1988," EUR Country Files, IMF Archives.

55   Wojciech Jaruzelski, *Erinnerungen: Mein Leben für Polen* (Munich: Piper, 1993), 323.

56   Dudek, *Reglamentowana rewolucja*, 132, 165.

57   Document 12, "Uwagi zespołu ekspertów KC PZPR o sytuacji kraju i wynikających z niej wnioskach przesłane członkom kierownictwa PZPR 6 maja 1988 r.," in *Polska 1986-1989*, 89.

58   Dudek, *Reglamentowana rewolucja*, 147-148.

59   Dudek, *Reglamentowana rewolucja*, 166.

60   Mieczysław Rakowski, *Dzienniki polityczne, 1987-1990* (Warsaw: Iskry, 2005), 213.

61   Dudek, *Reglamentowana rewolucja*, 162.

62   "Spotkanie Robocze w Magdalence, 16 września 1988 r., godz. 15.15-19:00," in *Magdalenka, Transakcja epoki: Notaki z poufnych spotkań Kiszczak-Wałęsa*, ed. Krzysztof Dubiński (Warsaw: Sylwa, 1990), 19-20.

63   Paczkowski, *The Spring Will Be Ours*, 492-493.

64   Rakowski, *Dzienniki polityczne, 1987–1990*, 218–219.

65   "Informacja z roboczej wizyty w Moskwie Członka Biura Politycznego KC PZPR Prezesa Rady Ministrów Mieczysława F. Rakowskiego (20–21.10.1988 r.)," Folder "NR 2/49 (2/2)," Box 49, Mieczysław Rakowski Papers, Hoover Institution. In his memoirs, Rakowski describes many journalists drawing parallels between him and Thatcher, parallels that he ultimately dismissed. See Mieczysław Rakowski, *Es begann in Polen: Der Anfang vom Ende des Ostblocks*, trans. Maria Janssen (Hamburg, Germany: Hoffman und Campe, 1995), 217–219.

66   "Excerpts from "Debate Between Lech Walesa and Alfred Miodowicz, 30 November 1988," *Making the History of 1989*, The Roy Rosenzweig Center for History and New Media, George Mason University, accessed November 20, 2019, http://chnm.gmu.edu/1989/archive/files/walesa-miodowicz-debate_019f3357aa.pdf.

67   Dudek, *Reglamentowana rewolucja*, 218–219.

68   Dudek, *Reglamentowana rewolucja*, 221–224.

69   Dudek, *Reglamentowana rewolucja*, 231.

70   Underlining original to the document. Jim Prust to Massimo Russo, "Poland—Missions and Visits," February 2, 1989, Box 61, EUR Country Files, IMF Archives.

71   J. Prust to the Managing Director and the Deputy Managing Director, "Poland-Back-to-Office Report on Staff Visit," November 10, 1988, Folder "Poland—corresp. + memos Oct–Dec. 1988," Box 61, EUR CF, IMF Archives.

72   "Poland—Staff Visit, Minutes of Meeting No. 7," October 28, 1988, Folder "Poland—corresp. + memos Oct–Dec. 1988," Box 61, EUR CF, IMF Archives.

73   Jim Prust to Mr. Russo, "Poland: ETR's Comments on Draft Briefing Paper," March 6, 1989, Folder "Poland—corresp. + memos Jan.–May 1989," Box 61, EUR CF, IMF Archives.

74   Memorandum AmEmbassy Warsaw to SecState, January 30, 1989, Box 35, File "January 1989," SFC, NSA.

75   Memorandum AmEmbassy Warsaw to SecState, January 30, 1989, Folder "January 1989," Box 35, SFC, NSA.

76   Memorandum from AmEmbassy to SecState, February 9, 1989, Folder "Feb. 1–17 1989," Box 35, SFC, NSA.

77   Memorandum from AmEmbassy to SecState, February 15, 1989, Folder "February 1–17 1989," Box 35, SFC, NSA.

78   Memorandum from AmEmbassy to SecState, February 15, 1989, Folder "February 1–17 1989," Box 35, SFC, NSA.

79   Memorandum from AmEmbassy Warsaw to SecState, February 17, 1989, Folder "February 17–28 1989," Box 35, SFC, NSA.

80   Memorandum AmEmbassy Warsaw to SecState, February 21, 1989, Folder "February 17–28 1989," Box 35, SFC, NSA.

81   Memorandum from AmEmbassy Warsaw to SecState, March 3, 1989, Box 35, Folder "March 1 -15, 1989," SFC, NSA.

82   Memorandum from AmEmbassy Warsaw to Sec State, March 1, 1989, Box 35, Folder "March 1–15, 1989," SFC, NSA.

83   SecState to AmEmbassy Warsaw, "Department Meeting with Solidarity Advisor Jacek Kuroń," May 3, 1989, Box 35, File "May 1–15, 1989," SFC, NSA.

84   Underlining in the original. Condoleezza Rice to Robert Gates, "DC Meeting on U.S. Policy Options if the Polish Roundtable Succeeds," March 29, 1989, OA/ID CF00716-014, Condoleezza Rice 1989–1990 Subject Files, GHWBL.

85   Brent Scowcroft, "Meeting with the National Security Council," April 4, 1989, OA/ID 90000-009, NSC Meeting Files, GHWBL.

86   Robert Hutchings to Brent Scowcroft, "National Security Council Meeting on Western Europe and Eastern Europe," April 3, 1989, NSC0008a, NSC Meeting Files, GHWBL.

87   Rice to Gates, "DC Meeting on U.S. Policy Options if the Polish Roundtable Succeeds," March 29, 1989, OA/ID CF00716-014, Condoleezza Rice 1989–1990 Subject Files, GHWBL.

88   SecState to AmEmbassy Warsaw, April 17, 1989, Box 35, Folder "April 16–30," SFC, NSA.

89   AmEmbassy Warsaw to SecState, "Continuing Controversy on the 'Michnik Plan,'" July 6, 1989, Box 34, File "Poland Cables January–September 1989," SFC, NSA.

90   "Minutes of the Meeting of the Presidium of the Citizens' Parliamentary Club," August 1, 1989, in "The End of the Cold War," *Cold War International History Project Bulletin*, no. 12/13 (Fall/Winter 2001): 120–121.

91   Jeffrey Sachs, *Poland's Jump to the Market Economy* (Cambridge, MA: MIT Press, 1993), 32.

92   Document 171, "Projekt harmonogramu działań Rządu na najbliższe miesiące," undated but late August 1989, in *Stanisław Gomułka i transformacja polska : dokumenty i analizy 1968–1989*, ed. Stanisław Gomułka and Tadeusz Kowalik (Warsaw: Wydawn. Nauk. Scholar, 2010), 493–495.

93   Balcerowicz, "Understanding Postcommunist Transitions," 84–85.

94   Sachs, *Poland's Jump*, 33.

95   Jeffrey Sachs, *The End of Poverty: Economic Possibilities for Our Time* (New York: Penguin, 2005), 120.

96   Jeffrey Sachs and David Lipton to Leszek Balcerowicz, "Preparation of a Document for International Circulation," September 14, 1989, Box 62, File "Poland—corresp. + memos August–Sept 1989," EUR Country Files, IMF Archives.

97   Massimo Russo to the Managing Director and the Deputy Managing Director, "Poland," September 25, 1989, Box 62, File "Poland—corresp. + memos August–Sept 1989," EUR Country Files, IMF Archives.

98   Brent Scowcroft to the President, "NSC Meeting on New Assistance for Poland," October 3, 1989, OA/ID CF00716-011, Condoleezza Rice 1989–1990 Subject Files, GHWBL.

99   Steve Greenhouse, "Poland's Foreign Lenders Accept Unusual Extension of Payments," *New York Times,* February 17, 1990, 1.

100   Letter to Michel Camdessus, August 27, 1993, Box 1, File "Fund Relations with Commercial Banks," Country Files, Central Files, IMF Archives. Letter to Michel Camdessus, March 25, 1994, Box 1, File "Fund Relations with Commercial Banks," Country Files, Central Files, IMF Archives.

101   Sachs, *Poland's Jump,* 39–40, 48.

102   Rakowski, *Dzienniki polityczne, 1987–1990,* 555.

103   Jaruzelski quoted in Wiktor Osiatynski, "The Roundtable Talks in Poland," in *The Roundtable Talks and the Breakdown of Communism,* ed. Jon Ester (Chicago: University of Chicago Press, 1996), 62–63n7.

8   The Coercion of Creditworthiness

1   Underlining in the original. *PlanEcon Report* 3, no. 14–15 (April 10, 1987): 3, 5.

2   Scholars have long recognized the "negotiated" nature of Hungary's revolution in 1989, but they have not drawn a significant connection between this reform process and the country's international financial position. For leading accounts, see Lazlo Borhi, *Dealing with Dictators: The United States, Hungary, and East Central Europe, 1942–1989* (Bloomington: Indiana University Press, 2016) and Rudolf Tőkés, *Hungary's Negotiated Revolution: Economic Reform, Social Change, and Political Succession, 1957–1990* (Cambridge: Cambridge University Press, 1996). This chapter is highly indebted to Attila Mong's outstanding book, *Kádár Hitele* (Budapest: Libri Publishing House, 2012), for perspectives on Hungarian debt.

3   Quoted in Mong, *Kádár Hitele,* 238.

4   Memorandum for Files, "Hungary," September 23, 1986, Box 159, File 1, European Department Immediate Files, Country Files (EURAI CF), International Monetary Fund (IMF) Archives, Washington, DC.

5   Memorandum for Files, "Meeting with Mr. J. Fekete, Senior Vice President, National Bank of Hungary," March 27, 1985, Box 32, File 2, EURAI CF, IMF Archives.

6   Minutes of Meeting, "Meeting with the President of the NBH," August 17, 1987, Box 32, File 3, EURAI CF, IMF Archives.

7   United Nations, Economic Commission for Europe, *Economic Survey of Europe, 1991* (Geneva: United Nations, 1991), 250, appendix table C.11.

8   Memorandum for Files, "Hungary," April 26, 1985, Box 32, File 2, EURAI CF, IMF Archives.

9   L. A. Whittome to the Managing Director, "Hungary," October 9, 1985, Box 32, File 2, EURAI CF, IMF Archives.

10   Memorandum for Files, "Hungary," October 10, 1986, Box 32, File 2, EURAI CF, IMF Archives.

11   *PlanEcon Report* 3, no. 14–15 (April 10, 1987): 4.

12   Quotes in Mong, *Kádár Hitele,* 258.

13   L. A. Whittome to the Managing Director, April 8, 1986, Box 32, File 3, EURAI CF, IMF Archives.

14   "Our Problems and Possibilities: An Interview with Karoly Grósz," translated and added to Memorandum for Files, "Hungary—Interview with Mr. Karoly Grosz," December 4, 1986, Box 159, File 1, EURAI CF, IMF Archives.

15   "Hungary: Brief for the Managing Director's Visit to the United Kingdom," May 5, 1988, File 1, Box 172, EUR Country Files, IMF Archives.

16   "Our Problems and Possibilities: An Interview with Karoly Grósz," translated and added to Memorandum for Files, "Hungary—Interview with Mr. Karoly Grosz," December 4, 1986, Box 159, File 1, EURAI CF, IMF Archives.

17   Quoted in Tibor Kovácsy, "Politikai reformtervek Magyarországon—FORDULAT ÉS REFORM," in *Magyar Füzetek 18, Válság és reform,* accessed June 28, 2021, https://epa .oszk.hu/02200/02201/00016/pdf/, 91–103, quote at 92.

18   Quoted in Kovácsy, "Politikai reformtervek Magyarországon," 100.

19   Quoted in Kovácsy, "Politikai reformtervek Magyarországon," 94.

20   George Kopits, Memorandum for Files, "Hungary—Overview of Change and Reform," March 26, 1987, Box 32, File 3, EURAI CF, IMF Archives.

21   Imre Pozsgay, "Political Institutions and Social Development," *Tarsadalmi Szemle,* no 3 (1987), translated in Joint Publications Research Service—Eastern Europe (JPRS-EER), JPRS-EER-87-060, 41–49.

22   "After the Resolution: Interview with Janos Hoos," *Otlet,* December 4, 1986, translated in JPRS-EEC-87-024, 20–26.

23   Document 8, "Transcript of CC CPSU Politburo Session," in *Masterpieces of History: The Peaceful End of the Cold War in Europe, 1989,* ed. Svetlana Savranskaya, Thomas Blanton, and Vladislav Zubok (Budapest: Central European University Press, 2010), 239.

24   Unknown financial periodical article, "Bad Blood," November 1986, in Box 159, File 1, EURAI CF, IMF Archives.

25   János Fekete, "Proposal for the Solution of the Debt Crisis: A Program for World Economic Recovery," December 4–5, 1986, Box 159, File 1, EURAI CF, IMF Archives.

26   Memorandum for Files, "Hungary- Meeting with Mr. J. Fekete," March 3, 1987, Box 32, File 3, EURAI CF, IMF Archives.

27   Minutes of Meeting No. 2, "Hungary—Staff Visit," April 13, 1987, Box 32, File 3, EURAI CF, IMF Archives.

28   "Interview with Bela Szikszay, State Secretary and President of the Office of Material and Price Control," *Figyelő,* July 2, 1987, translated in JPRS-EER-87-145, 69.

29   Minutes of Meeting No. 17, "Hungary- Staff Visit," April 18, 1987, Box 32, File 3, EURAI CF, IMF Archives. The 1986 current account deficit and initial budget deficit projection is from "Briefing Paper- Use of Fund Resources," November 20, 1987, Box 33, File 1, EURAI CF, IMF Archives.

30   Helen Junz to Mr. J. Marjai and Mr. J. Fekete, "Staff Visit to Hungary, April 12–18, 1987," April 17, 1987, Box 32, File 3, EURAI CF, IMF Archives.

31   Helen Junz to the Managing Director and the Deputy Managing Director, "Hungary-Back-to-Office Report—April 12–18, 1987," April 28, 1987, Box 32, File 3, EURAI CF, IMF Archives.

32   Minutes of Meeting No. 17, Mr. Fekete and Mr. Németh, April 18, 1987, Box 32, File 3, EURAI CF, IMF Archives.

33   Helen Junz to the Managing Director and the Deputy Managing Director, "Hungary-Back-to-Office Report."

34   Quoted in Mong, *Kádár Hitele,* 269.

35   Quoted in András Oplatka, *Nêmeth Miklós: Mert ez az ország érdeke* (Budapest: Helikon, 2014), 138.

36   Quoted in Mong, *Kádár Hitele,* 267.

37   L. A. Whittome to Mr. Rose, "Hungary," June 8, 1987, Box 32, File 3, EURAI CF, IMF Archives.

38   Helen Junz to János Fekete, June 12, 1987, Box 32, File 3, EURAI CF, IMF Archives.

39   Dokumente 1, "Stellungnahme des Zentralkomitees der Ungarischen Sozialistischen Arbeitspartei bezüglich des Programms der wirtschaftlich-gesellschaftlichen Entfaltung

vom 2. Juli 1987," in *Die politisch-diplomatischen Beziehungen in der Wendezeit, 1987–1990,* ed. Andreas Schmidt-Schweizer (Berlin: De Gruyter Oldenbourg, 2018), 215–227.

40   Dokumente 1, "Stellungnahme des Zentralkomitees," in *Die politisch-diplomatischen Beziehungen,* 226.

41   János Fekete to Massimo Russo, Patrick de Fontenay, and Helen Junz, July 21, 1987, Box 32, File 3, EURAI CF, IMF Archives.

42   Minutes of Meeting No. 1, "Hungary—Staff Visit," August 17, 1987, Box 32, File 3, EURAI CF, IMF Archives.

43   Minutes of Meeting No. 2, "Hungary—Staff Visit," August 17, 1987, Box 32, File 3, EURAI CF, IMF Archives.

44   Minutes of Meeting No. 10, "Hungary—Staff Visit," August 19, 1987, Box 32, File 3, EURAI CF, IMF Archives.

45   József Marjai to Michel Camdessus, September 24, 1987, Box 32, File 3, EURAI CF, IMF Archives.

46   P. de Fontenay, Memorandum for Files, "Hungary," October 9, 1987, Box 32, File 3, EURAI CF, IMF Archives.

47   István Horváth, *Die Sonne ging in Ungarn auf* (Munich: Universitas, 2000), 230.

48   Horváth, *Die Sonne ging,* 252.

49   Dokument 6 in Schmidt-Schweizer, *Die politisch-diplomatischen Beziehungen,* 249–250.

50   "Our Wishes Can Be Realized on the Basis of National Consensus," *Magyar Nemzet,* March 16, 1987, translated in JPRS-EER-87-077, 33–34.

51   "Taking a Stance," *Magyar Nemzet,* September 26, 1987, translated in JPRS-EER-87-151, quotes on 1–2.

52   Memorandum for Files, "Hungary—Meetings with Mr. Németh, Secretary of the MSZMP Central Committee," June 17, 1988, File 2, Box 33, EURAI Country Files, IMF Archives.

53   Memorandum for Files, "Reform of Housing and Housing Finance," December 28, 1987, Box 33, File 1, EURAI CF, IMF Archives.

54   Memorandum for Files, "Hungary—Meeting with the Prime Minister, Mr. Grosz," January 11, 1988, Box 33, File, 1 EURAI CF, IMF Archives.

55   Memorandum for Files, "Hungary- Meeting State Development Institution and Interest Rate Trigger," January 12, 1988, Box 33, File, 1 EURAI CF, IMF Archives.

56   P. de Fontenay to the Acting Managing Director, "Hungary- Stand-By Arrangement," January 25, 1988, Box 33, File, 1 EURAI CF, IMF Archives.

57   P. de Fontenay to Mr. Boorman, "Hungary-Stand-by Arrangement," February 11, 1988, Box 33, File, 1 EURAI CF, IMF Archives.

58   Mong, *Kadar Hitele,* 272.

59   Dokumente 11, "Stellungnahme der Landeskonferenz der Ungarishen Sozialistichen Arbeiterpartei . . . ," May 22, 1988, in Schmidt-Schweizer, *Die politisch-diplomatischen Bezie-hungen,* 290–305.

60   Dokumente 13, "Bericht der bundesdeutschen Botschaft in Budapest . . . ," July 6, 1988, in Schmidt-Schweizer, *Die politisch-diplomatischen Beziehungen,* 316–317.

61   "Hungary—1988 Stand By Review," July 1, 1988, Box 33, File, 1 EURAI CF, IMF Archives.

62   G. Belanger to the Managing Director, "Hungary—Staff Visit," September 13, 1988, Box 33, File, 1 EURAI CF, IMF Archives.

63   P. de Fontenay to Mr. Whittome, "Hungary- Briefing Paper for the Review Mission," June 29, 1988, Box 33, File 1, EURAI CF, IMF Archives.

64   "Hungary—1989 Use of Fund Resources, Meeting No. 2," August 29, 1989, Box 34, File 2, EURAI CF, IMF Archives.

65   G. Belanger to the Managing Director, "Hungary—First Mid-Term Review," July 13, 1988, Box 33, File 1, EURAI CF, IMF Archives. Hans Schmitt to Mr. Russo, "Hungary—SBA Review," August 8, 1988, Box 33, File 1, EURAI CF, IMF Archives.

66   Tökés, *Hungary's Negotiated Revolution,* 305–314.

67   P. de Fontenay to the Acting Managing Director, "Hungary- Staff Visit," December 15, 1988, Box 11, File "Hungary 1988," Country Files, Office of the Managing Director Fonds Michel Camdessus Sous-Fonds, IMF Archives.

68   See Németh's comment on December 13, 1988, about the economy returning to health in four more years in "Chronology," in *Political Transition in Hungary, 1989–1990: A Compendium of Declassified Documents and Chronology of Events,* National Security Archive and Cold War International History Project, accessed June 29, 2021, https://www .wilsoncenter.org/publication/political-transition-hungary-1989-1990.

69   Quoted in film *1989: A Statesman Opens Up,* dir. Anders Ostergaard and Erzsebet Racz (New York: Icarus Films, 2014).

70   Németh has offered this explanation on a number of occasions. For statements in English, see film *1989.* He has not explicitly linked the decision to IMF pressure, but it is clear from the documentary record that the 1989 budget was crafted under significant pres-sure from the IMF. See Memorandum for Files, "Hungary: Minutes of the Opening Meeting held at the National Bank of Hungary on February 16, 1989," March 2, 1989, Box 34, File 1, EURAI CF, IMF Archives.

71   For a succinct summary and analysis of these events, see Andreas Oplatka, "Hungary 1989: Reunification of Power and Power-Sharing," in *The Revolutions of 1989: A Handbook,* ed. Wolfgang Mueller et al. (Vienna: Verlag der Osterreichischen Akademie der Wissenschaften, 2015), 77–91.

72   Memorandum for Files, "Hungary," January 30, 1989, Box 34, File 1, EURAI CF, IMF Archives.

73   Massimo Russo to the Managing Director, January 18, 1989, Box 34, File 1, EURAI CF, IMF Archives.

74   All the previous quotes from the February 7, 1989, meeting come from Document 9, "Meeting of the MSZMP Political Committee. Verbatim Record of Minutes," February 7, 1989, in *Political Transition in Hungary*, 63–94.

75   Document 16, "Memorandum of Conversation between M.S. Gorbachev and Károly Grósz," March 23–24, 1989, in *Political Transition in Hungary*, 133–134.

76   Massimo Russo to the Managing Director and the Deputy Managing Director, "Brief for President Delors' Visit to Hungary and Poland," November 14, 1989, Box 34, File 1, EURAI CF, IMF Archives.

77   Minutes of Meeting No. 7, "Hungary—1989 Use of Fund Resources," November 16, 1989, Box 34, File 2, EURAI CF, IMF Archives.

78   Minutes of Meeting No. 14, "Hungary—1989 Use of Fund Resources," September 5, 1989, Box 34, File 2, EURAI CF, IMF Archives.

79   Gérard Bélanger to the Acting Managing Director, "Hungary—Staff Visit and Request for Follow-Up," June 1, 1989, Box 34, File 2, EURAI CF, IMF Archives.

80   "Mr. Camdessus' Telephone Conversation with Mr. Bartha on Monday," November 20, 1989, Box 34, File 1, EURAI CF, IMF Archives.

81   Minutes of Meeting No. 1, "Hungary—Use of Fund Resources," August 28, 1989, Box 34, File 2, EURAI CF, IMF Archives.

82   Minutes of Meeting No. 6, "Hungary- 1989 Use of Fund Resources," August 31, 1989, Box 34, File 2, EURAI CF, IMF Archives.

83   "The Plundering of Resources Did Not Begin with Foreign Indebtedness," *Heti Vilaggazdasag,* March 18, 1989, translated in JPRS-EER-89-050, 42–44.

84   Németh interview with "The Week," translated in Foreign Broadcasting Information Service—Eastern Europe (FBIS-EEU), FBIS-EEU-89-072.

85   Istvan Garamvolgyi, "The State as Debtor," *Magyarorszag,* December 3, 1988, translated in JPRS-EER-89-012, 35–36.

86   János Kis in "Reform and Hungary, Szazadveg's Questionarre Concerning Reform," *Szazadveg,* no. 4–5 (1987), translated in JPRS-EER-88-042, 15.

87   Tamas Bauer et al., "Capitalist Support for Hungary: Target Premium," *Heti Vilaggazdasag,* August 5, 1989, translated in JPRS-EER-89-103, 41–42.

88   "The Hungarian National Bank President and the Hungarian Democratic Forum: He's Bluffing," *Heti Vilaggazdasag,* August 19, 1989, translated in JPRS-EER-89-104, 5.

89   Eva Kaluzynska, "Delors Suggest Bridging Loan for Hungary," November 17, 1989, Box 34, File 1, EURAI CF, IMF Archives.

90   Minutes of Meeting No. 24, "Hungary—1989 Use of Fund Resources," December 6, 1989, Box 34, File 2, EURAI CF, IMF Archives.

91   G. Bélanger to the Managing Director and the Deputy Managing Director, January 31, 1990, Box 159, File 2, EURAI CF, IMF Archives.

92   Massimo Russo to the Managing Director and the Deputy Managing Director, "Hungary- Follow-up Mission for the Use of Fund Resources," January 10, 1990, Box 159, File 2, EURAI CF, IMF Archives.

93   G. Bélanger to Mr. de Fontenay, "Mr. Szapary's Report on the Managing Director's Visit to Budapest," May 16, 1990, Box 159, File 4, EURAI CF, IMF Archives.

94   Imre Tarafás and Ferenc Rabár to Michel Camdessus, November 13, 1990, Box 160, File 2, EURAI CF, IMF Archives.

9   Exit, Violence, or Austerity

1   Albert Hirschman, *Exit, Voice, and Loyalty: Responses to Decline in Firms, Organizations, and States* (Cambridge: Harvard University Press, 1970).

2   The *Frankfurter Allgemeine Zeitung,* the leading newspaper in West Germany, published an article six days after the fall of the Wall titled "Abwandern, Widersprechen: Zur aktuellen Bedeutung einer Theorie von A.O. Hirschman." Hirschman discusses the use of his theory in the GDR in Albert Hirschman, "Exit, Voice, and the Fate of the German Democratic Republic," *World Politics* 45, no. 2 (January 1993): 173–202. See also, Stephen Pfaff, *Exit-Voice Dynamics and the Collapse of East Germany* (Chapel Hill, NC: Duke University Press, 2006).

3   See Hans-Hermann Hertle, *Der Fall der Mauer: Die Unbeabsichtige Selbstauflösung des SED-Staates* (Opladen: VS Verlag für Sozialwissenschaften, 1996) and *Das Ende der SED: Die Letzten Tage des Zentralkomitees* (Berlin: Links, 2014); Charles S. Maier, *Dissolution: The Crisis of Communism and the End of East Germany* (Princeton, NJ: Princeton University Press, 1997); and M. E. Sarotte, *The Collapse: The Accidental Opening of the Berlin Wall* (New York: Basic Books, 2014).

4   See, in particular, Sarotte, *Collapse*.

5   Schalck and König, "Information zur Kostenentwicklung," May 14, 1986, DL/226/1145, BArch Lichterfelde, 4–7.

6   Untitled, Schalck and König to Mittag, January 29, 1985, DL/226/1145, BArch Lichterfelde, 178–185.

7   Schalck and König, "Standpunkt zum vorgelegten Material der Staatlichen Plankomission 'Grundlinien der Zahlungsbilanz für den Fünfjahrplanzeitraum 1986–1990," March 19, 1985, DL/226/1146, BArch Lichterfelde, 144–147.

8   Egon Krenz, *Herbst '89* (Berlin: Neues Leben, 1999), 214.

9   Numbers cited from Matthias Judt, *Das Bereich Kommerzielle Koordinierung: Das DDR-Wirtschaftsimperium des Alexander Schalck-Golodkowski—Mythos und Realität* (Berlin: Ch. Links Verlag, 2013), 232, table 45.

10   Export values cited in André Steiner, *The Plans That Failed: An Economic History of the GDR* (New York: Berghahn, 2010), 175.

11   Untitled Letter, Schalck and König to Mittag, September 16, 1985, DL/226/1249, BArch Lichterfelde, 213–214.

12   Untitled Letter, Schalck and König to Mittag, March 6, 1986, DL/226/1249, BArch Lichterfelde, 296–298.

13   Hertle, *Der Fall der Mauer*, 63.

14   Schalck to Mittag, August 5, 1986, DL/226/1249, BArch Lichterfelde, 180–181.

15   Matthias Judt, *KoKo: Mythos und Realität: Das Imperium des Schalck-Golodkowski* (Berlin: Ed. Berolina, 2015), 232, table 45.

16   All underlining original throughout the chapter. Schalck and König, "Standpunkt zur voraussichtlichen Entwicklung der Zahlungsbilanz NSW 1988 -1990 und der NSW-Verschuldung," October 16, 1987, DL/266/1143, BArch Lichterfelde, 47–52.

17   Schalck quoted in Gerhard Schürer, "Information über die Beratung der Ständigen Arbeitsgruppe zur operativen Leitung und Kontrolle der Durchführung der Zahlungsbilanz der DDR mit dem nichtsozialistischen Writschaftengebiet vom 15.10.1987," October 15, 1987, DL/266/1143, BArch Lichterfelde, 100–103.

18   Schalck interview in Theo Pirker et al., eds., *Plan als Befehl und Fiktion: Wirtschaftsführung der DDR* (Opladen : Westdeutscher Verlag, 1995), 148.

19   Schürer, "Überlegungen zur weiteren Arbeit am Volkswirtschaftsplan 1989 und darüber hinaus," April 26, 1988, DE/1/58736, BArch Lichterfelde, 318–330. Quotes at 320, 325, and 326–327.

20   Quoted in Hertle, *Der Fall der Mauer*, 69.

21   Günter Mittag, "Zur Prüfung des Materials des Vorsitzenden der Staatlichen Plankomission, Genossen Gerhard Schürer . . . ," undated but May 1988, DE/1/58736, BArch Lichterfelde.

22   Quoted in Hertle, *Der Fall der Mauer*, 69.

23   Heinz Klopfer, "Persönliche Notizen über die Beratung im Politbüro des ZK der SED am 28.6.1988," June 28, 1988, DE/1/58736, BArch Lichterfelde.

24   "Arbeitsniederschrift über eine Beratung beim Generalsektretär des ZK der SED, Genossen Erich Honecker, zu den Materialen des Entwurfs der staatlichen Aufgaben 1989," September 6, 1988, DE/1/58738, BArch Lichterfelde.

25   Quoted in Hertle, *Der Fall der Mauer*, 71.

26   "Arbeitsniederschrift über eine Beratung," DE/1/58738, BArch Lichterfelde.

27   Quote in Krenz, *Herbst '89*, 120; Also see Gerhard Schürer, *Gewagt und Verloren: Eine deutsche Biographie* (Frankfurt Oder: Frankfurter Oder Editionen, 1996), 158.

28   Quoted in Hertle, *Der Fall der Mauer*, 73.

29   Andreas Oplatka, *Der Erste Riß in der Mauer: September 1989—Ungarn öffnet die Grenze* (Vienna: Paul Zsolnay Verlag, 2009), 25.

30   Oplatka, *Erste Riß*, 36.

31   Oplatka, *Erste Riß*, 46.

32   Oplatka, *Erste Riß*, 67.

33   Sarotte, *Collapse*, loc. 815 of 8079, Kindle.

34   Oplatka, *Erste Riß*, 154–164.

35   Andreas Oplatka, *Németh Miklós: Mert ez az ország érdeke* (Budapest: Helikon, 2014), 224.

36   Oplatka, *Erste Riß*, 178.

37   Oplatka, *Erste Riß*, 194–197.

38   Serge Schmemann, "Hungary Allows 7,000 East Germans to Emigrate West," September 11, 1989, *New York Times*, accessed June 27, 2016, http://www.nytimes.com/1989/09/11/world/hungary-allows-7000-east-germans-to-emigrate-west.html?pagewanted=all.

39   Sarotte, *Collapse*, loc. 889 of 8079, Kindle.

40   Document 57, "Schreiben des Bundeskanzlers Kohl an Ministerpräsident Németh," October 4, 1989, in Hanns Jürgen Küsters and Daniel Hofmann, eds. *Deutsche Einheit: Sonderedition aus den Akten des Bundeskanzleramt 1989/90* (Munich: R. Oldenbourg, 1998), 442.

41   Document 46, "Gespräch Gobachev mit dem Staatsvorsitzenden Honecker am 7. Oktober 1989 [Auszug]," in Aleksander Galkin and Anatolij Tschernjajew, Michail *Gorbatschow und die Deutsche Frage: Sowjetische Dokumente, 1986–1991* (Munich: Oldenbourg Verlag), 187–190, quotes at 189.

42   Hans-Hermann Hertle, "The Fall of the Wall," in *The End of the Cold War* [TECW], Cold War International History Project Bulletin, Issue 12/13 (Fall/Winter 2001), 133.

43   Krenz, *Herbst '89*, 120.

44   "Standpunkt zur Sicherung der Zahlungsfähigkeit bis 1995/96," DL/226/1258, BArch Lichterfelde, 153–157.

45   Schürer, Beil, König, Schalck, and Polze, Untitled, September 28, 1989, DE/1/58166, BArch Lichterfelde.

46   Schalck to Krenz, October 13, 1989, DL/226/1195, BArch Lichterfelde, 17–20.

47   Krenz, *Herbst '89*, 146.

48   Quoted in Hertle, *Der Fall der Mauer,* 114.

49   Sarotte, *Collapse,* loc. 1849 of 8079, Kindle.

50   Sarotte, *Collapse,* loc. 2118 of 8079, Kindle.

51   Krenz's *Herbst '89* passim. Schürer, *Gewagt und Verloren,* 164.

52   Mark Kramer, "The Demise of the Soviet Bloc," 842.

53   Sarotte, *Collapse,* loc. 2194 of 8079, Kindle.

54   Hertle, ed., *Das Ende der SED,* 269.

55   Schalck to Krenz, October 13, 1989, DL/226/1195, BArch Lichterfelde, 3–5.

56   Alexander Schalck-Golodkowski, *Deutsch-deutsche Erinnerugen* (Reinbek: Rowohlt, 2001), 322.

57   Schalck, *Erinnerugen,* 323.

58   "Vermerk über ein informelles Gespräch des Genossen Alexander Schalck mit dem Bundesminister und Chef des Bundeskanzleramtes der BRD, Rudolf Seiters, und mit dem Mitglied des Vorstandes der CDU, Wolfgang Schäuble, am 24.10.1989," in Hertle, *Der Fall der Mauer,* 439–443.

59   Krenz, *Herbst '89*, 224.

60   "Ton-Aufzeichnung eines Telefonats zwischen Egon Krenz und Helmut Kohl, 26.10.1989," in Hertle, *Der Fall der Mauer,* 447.

61   Schalck, *Erinnerugen,* 325.

62   Schalck, *Erinnerugen*, 325–326.

63   The Interior Ministry and the Stasi had also received direction from the Politburo on October 24 to begin drafting the new travel law. See Sarotte, *Collapse*.

64   Gerhard Schürer, Gerhard Beil, Alexander Schalck, Ernst Höfner, and Arno Donda, "Analyse der ökonomischen Lage der DDR mit Schlußfolgerungen, Vorlage für das Politbüro des Zentralkomitees der SED, 30.10.1989," in Hertle, *Der Fall der Mauer*, 448–460, here 451.

65   Schürer et al., "Analyse der ökonomischen Lage," 454.

66   Schürer et al., "Analyse der ökonomischen Lage," 455.

67   Schürer et al., "Analyse der ökonomischen Lage," 455, 457.

68   Schürer et al., "Analyse der ökonomischen Lage," 459, 460.

69   Hertle, *Der Fall der Mauer*, 148–149.

70   Krenz, *Herbst '89*, 246, 249.

71   Krenz, *Herbst '89*, 249, 250.

72   Krenz, *Herbst '89*, 266.

73   "Document No. 1: Memorandum of Conversation between Egon Krenz, Secretary General of the Socialist Unity Party (SED), and Mikhail S. Gorbachev, Secretary General of the Communist Party of the Soviet Union (CPSU), 1 November 1989," in TECW, 144.

74   Krenz, *Herbst '89*, 267.

75   "Document 1: Memorandum," TECW, 144.

76   "Document 1: Memorandum," TECW, 144.

77   Krenz, *Herbst '89*, 267.

78   "Document 1: Memorandum," TECW, 144.

79   Krenz, *Herbst '89*, 276.

80   Sarotte, *Collapse*, loc. 2340 and 2377 of 8079, Kindle.

81   Schalck, "Vermerk über ein informelles Gespräch des Genossen Alexander Schalck mit dem Bundesminister und Chef des Bundeskanzleramtes der BRD, Rudolf Seiters, und dem Mitglied des Vorstandes der CDU, Wolfgang Schäuble, am 06.11.1989," in Hertle, *Der Fall der Mauer*, 483–486.

82   Krenz, *Herbst '89*, 302.

83   Schalck, *Erinnerugen,* 327.

84   Sarotte, *Collapse,* loc. 2396 and 2423 of 8079, Kindle.

85   Document 74, "Besprechung der beamteten Staatssekretäre," 6 p.m., November 6, 1989, in *Deutsche Einheit: Sonderedition,* 482.

86   "Document 3: Letter from Alexander Schalck to Egon Krenz, November 7, 1989," in *TECW,* 153.

87   Krenz, *Herbst '89,* 305.

88   Text provided untitled in *Deutsche Einheit: Sonderedition,* 491.

89   Gerhard Lauter interview in Hertle, *Der Fall der Mauer,* 330.

90   "Document 7: Transcript of the Tenth Session of the SED Central Committee," in *TECW,* 156.

91   "Document 8: Günter Schabowski's Press Conference in the GDR International Press Center," in *TECW,* 157–158.

92   Sarotte, *Collapse,* chap. 6.

93   Schalck and König to Schürer, November 14, 1989, DL/226/1206, BArch Lichterfelde, 55–59.

10   Discipline or Retreat

1   Horst Teltschik, *329 Tage: Innenansichten der Einigung* (Berlin: Siedler Verlag, 1991), 52.

2   For arguments characteristic of this viewpoint, see Kristina Spohr, *Post Wall, Post Square: How Bush, Gorbachev, Kohl and Deng Shaped the World after 1989* (New Haven, CT: Yale University Press, 2020); Jeffrey Engel, *When the World Seemed New: George H. W. Bush and the End of the Cold War* (Boston: Houghton Mifflin Harcourt, 2017); Mary Elise Sarotte, *1989: The Struggle to Create Post-Cold War Europe* (Princeton, NJ: Princeton University Press, 2009); and Philip Zelikow and Condoleezza Rice, *To Build a Better World: Choices to End the Cold War and Create a Global Commonwealth* (New York: Twelve, 2019) and their *Germany Unified and Europe Transformed: A Study in Statecraft* (Cambridge, MA: Harvard University Press, 1995). Leading German-language accounts include Andreas Rödder, *Deutschland einig Vaterland: Die Geschichte der Wiedervereinigung* (Bonn: Bpb, 2010); Bernd Florath, "Die SED im Untergang," in *Das Revolutionsjahr 1989: Die demokratische Revolution in Osteuropa als transnationale Zäsur,* ed. Bernd Florath (Göttingen: Vandenhoeck & Ruprecht, 2011); and Klaus-Dietmar Henke, ed., *Revolution und Vereinigung 1989/90: Als in Deutschland die Realität die Phantasie überholte* (Munich: Deutscher Taschenbuch Verlag, 2009). For views on the process from many vantage points, see Frédéric Bozo, Andreas Rödder, and Mary Elise Sarotte, eds., *German Reunification: A Multinational History* (London: Routledge, 2017). These works build on the original conclusions of the first

wave of German historiography anchored by the monumental four-volume *Geschichte der Deutschen Einheit* published in the late 1990s.

3   Vladislav Zubok has charted a course very much in line with the arguments in this chapter in "With His Back against the Wall: Gorbachev, Soviet Demise, and German Reunification," *Cold War History* 14, no. 4 (2014): 619–645 and his chapter in Bozo, Rödder, and Sarotte, eds., *German Reunification.*

4   Zubok, "With His Back," 625.

5   Memorandum of Telephone Conversation, Bush-Kohl, November 29, 1989, George H. W. Bush Presidential Library (GHWBL), College Station, Texas.

6   Memorandum of Conversation, Bush and Kohl, February 24, 1990, GHWBL, accessed January 20, 2020, https://bush41library.tamu.edu/files/memcons-telcons/1990-02 -24--Kohl.pdf.

7   Anatolii Cherniaev, ed., *V Politbiuro TsK KPSS: Po zapisiam Anatoliia Cherniaeva, Vadima Medvedeva, Georgiia Shakhnazarova* (Moscow: Gorbachev-Fond, 2006), 383.

8   William Taubman, *Gorbachev: His Life and Times* (New York: W. W. Norton, 2017), 450.

9   Cherniaev, ed., *V Politbiuro TsK KPSS,* 425.

10   Iu. S. Moskovskii to N. I. Ryzhkov, March 22, 1989, Russian State Archive of the Economy (GARF), f. 5446, o. 150, d. 72, Yegor Gaidar Online Archive (GOA).

11   *A Study of the Soviet Economy,* vol. 1 (Washington, DC: International Monetary Fund, 1991), 59, table II.2.7.

12   L. A. Whittome, "Memorandum for Files: Meeting with Dr. Storf and Colleagues of the Deutsche Bank," August 16, 1990, File 7, Box 2, Office of the Managing Director—Alan Whittome Papers, International Monetary Fund (IMF) Archives.

13   Underlining in the original. Iu. S. Moskovskii to N. I. Ryzhkov, August 12, 1989, GARF, f. 5446, o. 150, d. 73 [numbers difficult to read], GOA.

14   "Na zasedanii Politbiuro TsK KPSS 24 iiulia 1986 goda," July 21, 1986, in Aleksander Galkin and Anatolii Cherniaev, eds., *Mikhail Gorbachev i germanskii vopros* (Moscow: Ves' mir, 2006), 16.

15   Aleksander Galkin and Anatolii Cherniaev, eds., *Michail Gorbatschow und die Deutsche Frage* (Berlin: Oldenbourg, 2012), 84n24.

16   Andrei Grachev, *Gorbachev's Gamble: Soviet Foreign Policy and the End of the Cold War* (Malden, MA: Polity Press, 2008), 135.

17   "Obmen rechami vo vremia torzhestvennogo obeda," June 12, 1989, in Galkin and Cherniaev, eds., *Mikhail Gorbachev i germanskii vopros,* 167.

18   "Beseda M.S. Gorbacheva s Villi Brandtom," October 17, 1989, in Galkin and Cherni-aev, eds., *Mikhail Gorbachev i germanskii vopros*, 227–228.

19   Cherniaev, ed., *V Politbiuro TsK KPSS*, 521–524.

20   Cherniaev, ed., *V Politbiuro TsK KPSS*, 525–529.

21   K. F. Katushev to the Council of Ministers, December 12, 1989, GARF, f. 5446, o. 162, d. 1457, GOA.

22   Sarotte, *1989*, 68.

23   Andreas Rödder, "Transferring a Civil Revolution into High Politics," in Bozo, Röd-der, and Sarotte, *German Reunification*, 44.

24   A point picked up on by British diplomats. See Mr. Broomfield (East Berlin) to Mr. Hurd, November 13, 1989, in *Documents on British Policy Overseas*, ser. 4, vol. 7, *German Unification, 1989–1990 [DBPO]*, 111.

25   Hans Modrow, *Aufbruch und Ende* (Hamburg, Germany: Konkret Literatur Verlag, 1991), 41.

26   "Gespräch des Bundesministers Seiters mit dem Staatsratsvorsitzenden Krenz und Ministerpräsident Modrow," November 20, 1989, in Hanns Jürgen Küsters and Daniel Hof-mann, eds. *Deutsche Einheit: Sonderedition aus den Akten des Bundeskanzleramt 1989/90* (Munich: R. Oldenbourg, 1998), 558.

27   Modrow, *Aufbruch und Ende*, 52.

28   "Helmut Kohl's Ten-Point Plan for German Unity (November 28, 1989)," German History in Documents and Images, accessed February 20, 2020, http://germanhistorydocs .ghidc.org/pdf/eng/Chapter1_Doc10English.pdf.

29   See Sarotte, *1989*, 75.

30   Quoted in Engel, *When the World*, 278–279.

31   Bush and Kohl telcon, November 29, 1989, GHWBL, accessed January 20, 2020, https://bush41library.tamu.edu/files/memcons-telcons/1989-11-29--Kohl.pdf.

32   Letter from Mr. Powell (No. 10) to Mr. Wall, January 20, 1990, in *DBPO*, 215–219.

33   "Iz besedy M.S. Gorbachevas G.D. Gensherom," December 5, 1989, in *Mikhail Gor-bachev i germanskii vopros*, 276–277.

34   "Very critical" from Document 98, "Vorlage des Ministerialdirektors Teltschik an Bundeskanzler Kohl," November 21, 1989, in *Sonderedition*, 563. The other quotes from Document 101, "Schreiben des Bundeskanzlers Kohl an Präsident Bush," November 28, 1989, in *Sonderedition*, 569.

35   Document 105, "Fernschreiben der Ständigen Vertretung bei der DDR an den Chef des Bundeskanzleramtes," December 1, 1989, in *Sonderedition*, 591.

36   Underlining original. Document 116, "Vorlage des Ministerialrats Ludewig an den Chef des Bundeskanzleramtes Seiters," *Sonderedition,* 625–626.

37   For December 1989 and January 1990, the party was actually the SED-PDS, before removing the SED name completely in February 1990. One leader Modrow could not apprehend was Alexander Schlack-Golodkowski, who fled to the West in early December. Schalck-Golodkowski, *Deutsche-Deutsche Errinerungen* (Reinbek bei Hamburg, Germany: Rowohlt, 2001).

38   Mr Bloomfield (East Berlin) to Mr. Hurd, December 6, 1989, in *DBPO,* 151–156.

39   Document 129, "Gespräch des Bundeskanzlers Kohl mit Ministerpräsident Modrow im erweiterten Kreis," December 19, 1989, in *Sonderedition,* 670.

40   Helmut Kohl, *Erinnerungen, 1982–1990* (Munich: Knauer eBook, 2014), loc. 13338 of 14521, Kindle.

41   Quoted in Engel, *When the World,* 321.

42   On the Soviets' commission on the "German-German question," set up in the fall of 1989 under Shevardnadze's direction, see Zubok, "With His Back," 625.

43   Cherniaev, ed., *V Politbiuro TsK KPSS,* 541.

44   "Material k dokladu o sotsial'no-ekonomicheskom polozhenii strany," January 2, 1990, RGAE, f. 2324, o. 33, d. 741, GOA.

45   Subsidy figure from table 1 in Byung-Yeon Kim, "Causes of Repressed Inflation on the Soviet Consumer Market, 1965–1989: Retail Price Subsidies, the Siphoning Effect, and the Budget Deficit," *Economic History Review* 55, no. 1 (February 2002), 109. Budget deficit figure from table J.3 in International Monetary Fund, *A Study of the Soviet Economy* (Washington, DC: International Monetary Fund, 1991), 123.

46   "Material k dokladu o sotsial'no-ekonomicheskom polozhenii strany," January 2, 1990, RGAE, f. 2324, o. 33, d. 741, GOA.

47   Chris Miller, *The Struggle to Save the Soviet Economy: Mikhail Gorbachev and the Collapse of the USSR* (Chapel Hill: University of North Carolina Press, 2016), 152.

48   Quoted in Taubman, *Gorbachev,* 503.

49   Teltschik, *329 Tage,* 101–102.

50   Modrow, *Aufbruch und Ende,* 49, 119.

51   "Iz besedy M.S. Gorbacheva s Kh. Modrovym," January 30, 1990, in *Mikhail Gorbachev i germanskii vopros,* 312–324. The 30 percent drop was calculated using Modrow's number for the shortfall in the first quarter, 1.2 million, multiplied by 4 and subtracted from the annual planned delivery total of 17 million tons.

52   "Obsuzhdenie germanskogo voprosa na uzkom soveshchanii v kabinete General'nogo sekretaria TsK KPSS," January 26, 1990, in *Mikhail Gorbachev i germanskii vopros,* 307–311.

Also, "The Diary of Anatoly Chernyaev, 1990," trans. Anna Melyakova, National Security Archive, accessed February 3, 2020, https://nsarchive2.gwu.edu/NSAEBB/NSAEBB317 /chernyaev_1990.pdf, 11.

53   Document 106, "Minute from Mr. Hurd to Mrs. Thatcher," January 25, 1990, in *DBPO*, 224.

54   Sarotte, *1989*, 134.

55   Sir C. Mallaby (Bonn) to Mr. Hurd, February 5, 1990, in *DBPO*, 252.

56   Document 138, "Gespräch des Bundeskanzlers Kohl mit Ministerpräsident Modrow," February 3, 1990, in *Sonderedition*, 753–756.

57   Document 157B, "Schritte zur deutschen Wirtschaftseinheit," in *Sonderedition*, 752–753.

58   Kohl, *Erinnerungen, 1982–1990*, loc. 13792 of 14521, Kindle.

59   For this political calculus, see Document 157, "Vorlage des Regierungsdirektors Mertes an Bundeskanzler Kohl," February 2, 1990, in *Sonderedition*, 749–750.

60   See Teltschik's notes on the campaign, *329 Tage*, 153–175.

61   For one perspective on this change, see the comments by the former head of the Soviet mission in Berlin, Valentin Koptelsev, in Grachev, *Gorbachev's Gamble*, 156.

62   Brent Scowcroft to the President, January 13, 1990, OA/ID 91117-009, U.S.-Soviet Relations Chronological Files, USSR Collapse Files, Scowcroft Files, GHWBL.

63   Quoted in Engel, *When the World*, 315.

64   "Enhancing the Political Role of NATO," March 14, 1990, 1989–1990 Subject Files, Condoleezza Rice Files, GHWBL.

65   This pledge, and others like it in February 1990, has subsequently become the subject of enormous controversy and debate. Among many, see Joshua R. Itzkowitz Shifrinson, "Deal or No Deal? The End of the Cold War and the U.S. Offer to Limit NATO Expansion," *International Security* 40, no. 4 (Spring 2016): 7–44; Mary Elise Sarotte, "Not One Inch Eastward? Bush, Baker, Kohl, Genscher, Gorbachev, and the Origin of Russian Resentment toward NATO Enlargement in February 1990," *Diplomatic History* 34, no. 1 (January 2010): 119–140, and "A Broken Promise? What the West Really Told Moscow about NATO Expansion," *Foreign Affairs* 93, no. 5 (September/October 2014): 90–97; and Mark Kramer, "The Myth of a No-NATO-Enlargement Pledge to Russia," *Washington Quarterly* 32, no. 2 (April 2009): 39–61.

66   Memorandum of Conversation, Baker, Gorbachev, and Shevardnadze, February 9, 1990, in Thomas Blanton, Svetlana Savranskaya, and Vladislav Zubok, eds., *Masterpieces of History: The Peaceful End of the Cold War in Europe, 1989* (New York: Central European University Press, 2010), 675–684.

67   Memorandum of Conversation, Baker, Gorbachev, and Shevardnadze, in *Masterpieces of History.*

68   "Iz besedy M.S. Gorbacheva s G. Kolem odin na odin," February 10, 1990, in *Mikhail Gorbachev i germanskii vopros,* 345, 333.

69   Document 166, "Vorlage des Ministerialdirektors Teltschik an Bundeskanzler Kohl," no date but placed in the volume in early February before Kohl's visit to Moscow, in *Sonderedition,* 772–773.

70   Memorandum of Conversation, "Meeting with Helmut Kohl, Chancellor of the Federal Republic of Germany," February 24, 1990, GHWBL, accessed February 5, 2020, https://bush41library.tamu.edu/files/memcons-telcons/1990-02-24--Kohl.pdf.

71   Iu. S. Moskovskii to S. A. Sitarian, April 25, 1990, GARF, f. 54456, o. 162, d. 1463, GOA.

72   V. V. Rerashenko to S. A. Sitarian, April 4, 1990, GARF, f. 5446, o. 162, d. 1464, GOA.

73   K. F. Katuchev to S. A. Sitarian, April 13, 1990, GARF, f. 5446, o. 162, d. 1515, GOA; V. A. Bikov to S. A. Sitarian, April 11, 1990, GARF, f. 5446, o. 162, d. 1492, GOA.

74   Document 90, "Zapis' Besedy A.N. Iakovleva s Chlenom Nabliudatel'nogo Soveta 'Doiche Bank AG' F. Kristiansom (FRG)," April 4, 1990, in *Perestroika, 1985–1991: Neizdannoe, Maloizvestnoe, Zabytoe,* ed. Alexander Yakovlev (Moscow: Mezhdunarodnyi fond "Demokratiia," 2008), 443–446.

75   S. A. Sitarian to N. I. Ryzhkov, May 3, 1990, GARF, f. 5446, o. 162, d. 1464, GOA.

76   Quoted in Vladislav Zubok, "Gorbachev, German Reunification, and Soviet Demise," in Bozo, Rödder, and Sarotte, *German Reunification,* 95.

77   "Zapiska V.M. Falina M.S. Gorbachevu," April 18, 1990, in *Mikhail Gorbachev i germanskii vopros,* 398–408.

78   Document 250, "Non-paper der Regierung der UdSSR," April 19, 1990, in *Sonderedition,* 1023–1024.

79   Document 253, "Gespräch des Bundeskanzlers Kohl mit Botschafter Kwizinskij," April 23, 1990, in *Sonderedition,* 1026–1030.

80   Shevardnadze read it and forwarded it to Gorbachev. Document 267, "Gespräch des Bundeskanzlers Kohl mit Außenminister Schewardnadse," May 4, 1990, in *Sonderedition,* 1084–1090.

81   "The Diary of Anatoly Chernyaev," May 5, 1990, 29.

82   Teltschik, *329 Tage,* 220–221.

83   Yuli Kvitsinskii, *Vor dem Sturm: Erinnerungen eines Diplomaten* (Berlin: Siedler, 1993), 25.

84   Teltschik, *329 Tage*, 220–221.

85   Teltschik, *329 Tage*, 226–227.

86   We do not have a transcript of this opening meeting, so the best sources are Teltschik and Kvitsinskii. "Great detail," Teltschik, *329 Tage*, 230.

87   Quotes from Kvitsinskii's recollection of the meeting, Kvitsinskii, *Vor dem Sturm*, 27.

88   Teltschik, *329 Tage*, 232.

89   Kvitsinskii, *Vor dem Sturm*, 27.

90   Document 277, "Gespräch des Ministerialdirektors Teltschik mit Präsident Gorbatschow," May 14, 1990 in *Sonderedition*, 1114–1118.

91   Teltschik, *329 Tage*, 243.

92   Document 284, "Schreiben des Bundeskanzlers Kohl an Präsident Gorbatschow," May 22, 1990, in *Sonderedition*, 1136.

93   Memorandum of Conversation, Secretary Baker and Mikhail Gorbachev, May 18, 1990, OA/ID 91126-004, File: Gorbachev (Dobrynin) Sensitive 1989-June 1990 [4], Scowcroft Files, GHWBL.

94   Memorandum for the Record, "Aid to the Soviet Union," May 29, 1990, OA/ID 91118-003, File: USSR Collapse: US-Soviet Relations Thru 1991 (April-May 1990) [2], Scowcroft Files, GHWBL.

95   "Economic Aid for the USSR—the $20 Billion Question," May 25, 1990, OA/ID CF01309-003, "Chron File: May 1990-June 1990," Nicholas Burns Files, GHWBL.

96   Brent Scowcroft to the President, "A Strategic Choice: Do We Give Aid to the Soviet Union?," May 29, 1990, File "U.S.-USSR Soviet Relations [2]," Condoleezza Rice Files, GHWBL. See also, Zelikow and Rice, *To Build a Better World*, 272.

97   Memorandum for the Record, "Aid to the Soviet Union," GHWBL.

98   Nicholas Brady to the President, May 24, 1990, OA/ID CF01309-002, File "May 1990-June 1990," Burns Chronological Files, GHWBL.

99   Brent Scowcroft to the President, "A Strategic Choice," GHWBL.

100   Anatoly Chernyaev, *My Six Years with Gorbachev* (University Park: Pennsylvania State University Press, 2000), 266. At the Washington summit, Gorbachev momentarily accepted Germany's right to join NATO based on the "Helsinki Principle" that each state had the right to choose its own alliances. However, he and his team retracted the admission, so the question of German membership in NATO remained open until Kohl's summit in the Soviet Union in July.

101   Quoted in Grachev, *Gorbachev's Gamble*, 158.

102   Document 277, "Gespräch des Ministerialdirektors Teltschik mit Präsident Gorbatschow," May 14, 1990, in *Sonderedition,* 1114–1118.

103   Memorandum of Ryzhkov to CC CPSU, June 29, 1990, quoted in Zubok, "With His Back," 640–641.

104   Kohl actually expressed this confidence even before receiving the letter. Quote from Memorandum of Conversation, Bush and Kohl, June 8, 1990, GHWBL. For reaction to the letter, see Teltschik, *329 Tage,* 265.

105   Document 329, "Vorlage des Ministerialdirektors Teltschik an Bundeskanzler Kohl," June 27, 1990, in *Sonderedition,* 1275–1276.

106   Zelikow and Rice, *To Build a Better World,* 476–477n50.

107   Sarotte, *1989,* 171.

108   Zelikow and Rice, *To Build a Better World;* Sarotte, *1989,* 176.

109   Quoted in Zelikow and Rice, *To Build a Better World,* 286.

110   Taubman, *Gorbachev,* 519–521.

111   Helmut Kohl, *Erinnerugen, 1990–1994* (Munich: Knaur, 2014), loc. 2156 of 10167, Kindle. Teltschik, *329 Tage,* 316.

112   Document 350, "Gespräch des Bundeskanzlers Kohl mit Präsident Gorbatschow," July 15, 1990, in *Sonderedition,* 1340–1348.

113   Document 353, "Gespräch des Bundeskanzlers Kohl mit Präsident Gorbatschow im erweiterten Kreis," July 16, 1990, in *Sonderedition,* 1355–1367.

114   Document 353, "Gespräch des Bundeskanzlers Kohl," in *Sonderedition,* 1361–1363. "Profitable for both sides" was actually from the West German foreign minister Hans-Dietrich Genscher.

115   T. G. Stepanov-Mamaladze's diary and notes from July 16, 1990, quoted in Zubok, "With His Back," 642–643.

116   Minutes of Real Sector Meeting R-15, August 17, 1990, File 1, Box 3, Office of Managing Director - Alan Whittome Papers, IMF Archives.

117   Minutes of Real Sector Meeting R-4, August 14, 1990, File 1, Box 3, Office of Managing Director—Alan Whittome Papers, IMF Archives.

118   Document 399, "Vorlage des Vortragenden Legationsrats I Kaestner an Ministerialdirektor Teltschik," August 27, 1990, in *Sonderedition,* 1500–1502.

119   Document 415, "Telefongespräch des Bundeskanzlers Kohl mit Präsident Gorbatschow," September 7, 1990, in *Sonderedition,* 1527–1530.

120   All the preceding quotes from the Soviet memorandum of the conversation. The German transcript has not been released. "Iz telefonnogo razgovora M.S. Gorbacheva s G. Kolem," September 10, 1990, in *Mikhail Gorbachev i germanskii vopros*, 563–566.

121   Philip D. Zelikow and Condoleezza Rice, *Germany Unified and Europe Transformed: A Study in Statecraft* (Cambridge, MA: Harvard University Press, 1995), 363–365.

122   "The Diary of Anatoly Chernyaev," September 15, 1990, 53.

Conclusion

1   Quoted in Charles S. Maier, "The Collapse of Communism: Approaches for a Future History," *History Workshop*, no. 31 (Spring 1991): 34–59, quote at 39.

2   On his economic argument, made to Lithuanians on the street, see William Taubman, *Gorbachev: His Life and Times* (New York: Simon & Schuster, 2017), 503–504. On his confidence they would stay in the union, see Robert Service, *The End of the Cold War: 1985–1991* (London: Macmillan, 2015), loc. 8753 of 14516, Kindle.

3   Hans-Hermann Hertle and Gerd-Rüdiger Stephan, eds., *Das Ende der SED: Die letzten Tage des Zentralkomitees* (Berlin: Links, 2014), 363.

4   "Document No. 19: Notes of CC CPSU Politburo Session," March 10, 1988, in *Masterpieces of History: The Peaceful End of the Cold War in Europe, 1989*, ed. Thomas Blanton, Svetlana Savranskaya, and Vladislav Zubok (New York: Central European University Press, 2010), 265–267.

5   Kvitsinskii quoted in "With His Back against the Wall: Gorbachev, Soviet Demise, and German Reunification," *Cold War History* 14, no. 4 (2014): 643.

6   Mieczysław Rakowski, *Dzienniki polityczne 1987–1990* (Warsaw: Wydawn, "Iskry," 2005), 517, 562.

7   John Hoskyns, "Government Strategy," June 12, 1979, PREM 19/24 f11, Margaret Thatcher Foundation, Thatcher MSS (digital collection), accessed December 14, 2017, https://www.margaretthatcher.org/document/115016.

8   Hoskyns, "Government Strategy."

9   Hoskyns, "Government Strategy."

10   Some of these quotes have been rearranged from their original order to present a coherent summary of Hoskyns's argument. Hoskyns, "Government Strategy."

11   "Our Problems and Possibilities: An Interview with Karoly Grósz," translated and added to Memorandum for Files, "Hungary—Interview with Mr. Karoly Grosz," December 4, 1986, Box 159, File 1, European Department Immediate Files, Country Files (EURAI CF), International Monetary Fund (IMF) Archives.

ACKNOWLEDGMENTS

Over the course of writing this book, I have accrued as many debts as the governments I have studied. Just as they did, I told myself (and those to whom I became indebted) that I was putting the borrowed time, money, or expertise toward enlightened ends. Unlike the subjects of my study, I hope that I have actually done so and that my creditors can see in this book a handsome return on their investment.

When I began this project at Cornell University, I could not have asked for a better group of scholars to provide guidance and support. Fred Logevall is an exemplary scholar and writer, and to have him as my advisor was the height of good fortune. Where others surely would have resisted my attempts to roam expansively (and often confusedly) over diverse subjects, geographies, and time periods in search of a project, he welcomed it. I thank him for his boundless confidence, patience, guidance, and support. Holly Case was always generous with her time, insightful in her commentary, and keen to push the boundaries of my thinking in new and fascinating ways. This book is certainly bigger in scope and more interesting in content because of her many contributions. For much of my time working on this project, I felt (as many other scholars have) that I was merely catching up on things Peter Katzenstein had long since learned. I quickly learned that was a very good spot for a young scholar to be in. Whatever precision and insight the argument of this book holds, it owes a great deal of it to Peter's consistent request (no, demand) that I be clearer about what, exactly, I was trying to say. Finally, Louis Hyman welcomed me into the History of Capitalism community and showed me the ropes with enthusiasm and insight. He connected me early and often with key resources in financial history, and the book is much better for having been subjected to his singular critique.

Robert Bothwell, Margaret MacMillan, and Arne Kislenko first taught me how to think like a historian when I showed up as a wide-eyed undergraduate in their classroom at Trinity College, University of Toronto. I quite simply would not have become a historian without their extraordinary influence, and their expectations for clarity of thought and precision of expression remain, all these years later, the standards to which I aspire. I thank them for their inspiration that will last a lifetime.

Beyond Cornell and Toronto, I was fortunate to learn from a group of brilliant scholars far and wide. At Yale University's International Security Studies, I was lucky to join the long line of scholars who have drawn wisdom and inspiration from Paul Kennedy and John Gaddis. Most of all, I am indebted to the late Nuno Monteiro for believing in me, showing me how to live intellectual life to the fullest, and helping me navigate the road ahead. I miss his passion, intellect, humor, and guidance dearly.

For their words of advice and encouragement, and with apologies to anyone I have forgotten, I also thank Csaba Békés, Duccio Basosi, Daniel Bessner, Gábor Egry, Stefano Bottani, Hal Brands, Lukas Dovern, David Engerman, Zoltán Farkas, Federico Romero, Beverly Gage, Molly Geidel, Max Graf, Dariusz Grala, Hans-Hermann Hertle, Daniel Immerwahr, Doug Irwin, Jonathan Kirshner, Stephan Kieninger, Stephen Kotkin, Matthias Kranke, Pál Germuska, Melvyn Leffler, Stefan Link, Chris Miller, Attila Mong, Emmanuel Mourlon-Druol, Samuel Moyn, Nicholas Mulder, Sándor Horvath, David Painter, Tobias Rupprecht, Oscar Sanchez-Sibony, Daniel Sargent, Mary Sarotte, André Steiner, Péter Mihályi, Arne Westad, William Wohlforth, and Philip Zelikow.

It is a joy to thank a standout group of peers from whom I have learned so much. At Cornell, Brian Rutledge became my sounding board for all things life and scholarship. Alberto Milian, Maté Rigo, Ryan Edwards, Chris Tang, Mattias Fibiger, Brian Cuddy, Tim Sorg, Max McComb, and Mark Deets are all far better historians than they are soccer players, though it was on the pitch that we had the most fun. Thank you all for your friendship. At International Security Studies, I found a community of scholars and friends like no other. Thanks to Jan Stöckmann, Michael De Groot, Ian Johnson, Evan Wilson, Mike Brenes, Emily Whalen, Susie Colbourn, Peter Slezkine, Claire Yorke, Michael Joseph, Michael Franczak, John Maurer, Tim Choi, Jean-François Bélanger, Mariya Grinberg, Veysel Simsek, and Eliza Gheorghe for the thoughts and laughs. I am particularly indebted to Max Krahé and Michael De Groot for the countless conversations we shared about the topics covered in this book.

Opportunities to present portions of this book have been invaluable in helping me develop and refine my ideas. Thank you to the organizers and audiences at forums hosted by Cornell University; the Society for Historians of American Foreign Relations; the University of Toronto; the Graduate Institute Geneva; the London School of Economics; the Research Colloquium for Economic and Social History at Goethe Universität; the American Historical Association; International Security Studies at Yale University; the University of Texas at Austin; the

Miller Center at the University of Virginia; Harvard Business School; the Association for Slavic, East European, and Eurasian Studies; Dartmouth College; the University of Padua; the Business History Conference; the International History Seminar at Georgetown University; the European University Institute; the Yale Moscow Grand Strategy Group; the Albritton Center for Grand Strategy at the Bush School; the Imre Kertész Kolleg at Universität Jena; and Università Ca' Foscari.

I won the academic lottery when the Bush School of Government and Public Service at Texas A&M University invited me to join their faculty ranks. I thank all my colleagues for their welcome and support, particularly the chair of the International Affairs Department, Gregory Gause. John Schuessler and Jasen Castillo, the visionary codirectors of the Albritton Center for Grand Strategy, believed in me and this project from the moment I stepped on campus, and have supported it through to the end. I thank them for their guidance and leadership. Kelley Robbins, Peg Hosea, Julia Lawrence, Caroline Lawrence, and Connie Vitulli provided administrative and logistical support for this project, and I thank them for their efforts.

Numerous organizations provided financial support to make this book possible. The Marion and Frank Long Fellowship from Cornell University's Reppy Institute for Peace and Conflict Studies supported a year of research in Washington, DC that launched this project. The German Academic Exchange Service (DAAD) supported a very pleasant and productive year of research in Germany and across Europe. My host professor at Goethe-Universität Frankfurt am Main, Werner Plumpe, enthusiastically supported this project and introduced me to an important community of German scholars from whom I have learned a great deal. I would like to thank Johanna Rumpeltes and Frederic Steinfeld, in particular, for welcoming Amanda and me to Frankfurt with open arms and remaining such good friends over many years. The National Fellowship at the University of Virginia's Miller Center supported a year of research and writing at a critical phase in this project's development. Thanks to Brian Balogh for his inspired leadership of that wonderful program. Daniel Sargent, my "dream mentor" at the Miller Center, not only inspired the book through his own research on the history of international economics and politics in the 1970s but also provided expert commentary on the entire work.

It has been a great joy to work with Harvard University Press on this project. I thank Kathleen McDermott for her belief in this project from its very early days and her flexibility and guidance as the project continued to evolve. Through Kathleen, I was fortunate to participate in the "Recovering Forgotten History" manuscript workshop in Warsaw and Kraków in the summer of 2017. I thank Professors Wojciech Bieńkowski and Przemysław Gasztold for their expert review on the entire manuscript. Similarly, the two anonymous readers who reviewed the manuscript for the press provided incisive suggestions that improved the final product a great deal. Kathi Drummy has ably assisted with all the editorial details; Jamie Armstrong shepherded the manuscript through the production process; and Cheryl Lenser compiled the index. I thank them all for their work on my behalf.

I have been extremely fortunate to work with a series of bright and dedicated research assistants through this project. For support with translations and research in Polish, I thank Alexander Sikorski and Jakub Bartoszewski. For support with translations and research in Hungarian, I thank Patrice Yaro and Balint Szoke. Anastasiia Posnova checked my Russian translations and tracked down documents for me in archives in Moscow, while True Sweester provided excellent research support at the Hoover Archives after COVID-19 made travel impossible. I thank them all for their hard work, and I look forward to following how they impact the world in the years ahead.

Finally, there has always been my family. My mom and dad, Ellen and Mike Bartel, have supported me through thick and thin, and there was plenty of both on the long road through the writing of this book. My dad deserves special thanks for editing every word of every chapter. Over a lifetime of friendship, my brother, Mitch, has influenced me in ways that go far beyond this book, but he supported and influenced this effort too.

Most important, however, has been my wife, Amanda. If, for some strange reason, a future historian wanted to write a history of this book, he or she would not have to search very hard to find the thesis: Fritz met Amanda, and everything else—from the first vague inklings of what this project could be to the last lines of the book's conclusion—started falling into place. Through her love, commitment, editing, and contributions to endless hours of discussion about every facet of this book, Amanda added more to this project than I can ever know or say. Our daughters, Adeline and Nora, arrived as this book neared completion. Lucky for me, this project has come to an end, but life with them is only just beginning. I have made a life out of studying the past, but these days, it is the future—their future—that's got me thinking.

INDEX